1588: Bad luck for the Spanish King Philip ('the Lip'): His fleet, the 'Armada', gets kicked in the pants by Drake's smaller English fleet. Terrible storms off Scotland finish off his fleet. There is still Spanish gold at the bottom of the sea off Scotland and Ireland.

A WORLD MAP
of a different kind

showing how the English language has travelled the world

1066: William the Conqueror and the Normans conquer 'England'. Bad luck, Will: No fish 'n' chips yet!

1993: Channel Tunnel: The British are afraid the French will come again. They don't: The food is better In France!

"In fourteen hundred and ninety-two Columbus sailed the ocean blue." (Well – *dark green* and *greyish* don't rhyme with 'two', do they?)

D1666689

I'm sure I've forgotten something…

1947: India becomes independent from Britain.

Indian Indians, not American Indians, silly!

Toot-toot! (Horn of Africa)

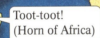

1768: Captain Cook discovers the Aborigines, who had been hiding there for 40,000–60,000 years.

British colonies here and there (the Africans are not happy). The British eventually go home, but leave their language behind.

n't stop here, folks!

South Africa (obviously)

Uh-oh. Discovered!

1787/88: First Fleet voyage to Australia (Capt. Arthur Phillip). Over 500 convicts are happy to be alive when they land at Sydney Cove. The journey took 8 months. All the people in the First Fleet could have fitted into 3 jumbo jets, and been there in about 24 hours.

Marie Mehnert

Learning English

PASSWORD GREEN 5

Unterrichtswerk für Gymnasien

Herausgeber: Werner Beile und Alice Beile-Bowes

von Werner Beile, Alice Beile-Bowes, Marion Horner,
Axel Plitsch und Terry Wynne

sowie Birgit Beile-Meister

S.74

Ernst Klett Verlag
Stuttgart Düsseldorf Leipzig

Learning English – Password Green 5 für Klasse 9 an Gymnasien

Herausgeber:
Prof. Dr. Werner Beile und Alice Beile-Bowes M.A., Wuppertal und Iserlohn

von
Alice Beile-Bowes M.A. und Prof. Dr. Werner Beile, Wuppertal und Iserlohn;
Marion Horner M.A., Cambridge; Axel Plitsch, Velbert; Terry Wynne B.A., Esslingen
sowie
Dr. Birgit Beile-Meister, Münster

Beratende Mitarbeit:
Beate Fähnrich, Langerwehe; Dieter Firmenich, Duisburg; Georg Graef, Wiesbaden;
Hans-Dieter Hase, Witten; Gerhard Hoffmann, Siefersheim; Detlef Kunz, Wuppertal;
Berthold Sturm, Trebel; Thomas Tepe, Münster
sowie
Dr. Herbert Holtwisch, Emsdetten

Visuelle Gestaltung: Christian Dekelver, Weinstadt; Nicholaas Boden, Berlin

Kassetten/CDs zu diesem Band

 Begleitkassette/CD zum Schülerbuch für zu Hause und für den Unterricht mit Texten aus den *Topics* und der *Further Reading*, Liedern und Gedichten (Klettnummer 546358/546391). Lieferung durch jede Buchhandlung oder, wo dies auf Schwierigkeiten stößt, zuzüglich Portokosten per Nachnahme vom Verlag.

 Kassette/CD zum Hörverstehen für den Unterricht mit zusätzlichen Hörverstehenstexten zu den *Topics* im *Schülerbuch* und *Workbook* und zu den *Klassenarbeiten* (Klettnummer 546359/546392).
Lieferung ausschließlich direkt an Lehrerinnen und Lehrer, Schulstempel erforderlich.

Software zu diesem Band
Passend zu diesem Band wird es multimediale Lernprogramme geben. Die Programme werden abwechslungsreiche Übungsformen zu Wortschatz und Grammatik bieten – unterstützt durch Text, Bild und Ton.

1. Auflage   A 1 ¹¹ ¹⁰ 9 8 / 2009 2008 2007

Alle Drucke dieser Auflage können im Unterricht nebeneinander benutzt werden, sie sind untereinander unverändert. Die letzte Zahl bezeichnet das Jahr des Druckes.
© Ernst Klett Verlag GmbH, Stuttgart 1999. Alle Rechte vorbehalten.
Internetadresse: http://www.klett.de

Redaktion: Heinz-Peter Gerlinger, Sheila McBride

Herstellung: Udo Ehrenberg
Layout: Christian Dekelver, Weinstadt
Satz und Reproduktionen: Schwabenverlag AG, Ostfildern
Umschlaggestaltung: Christian Dekelver, Weinstadt
Druck: W. Wirtz, Speyer. Printed in Germany.
ISBN: 3-12-546350-5

ISBN 3-12-546350-5
9 783125 463509

A WORD BEFORE YOU START ...

Der fünfte Band von *Password* sieht anders aus als die Bände 1 bis 4.

Es gibt keine Units mehr, sondern **Topics** (Themeneinheiten). Jede *Topic* besteht aus zwei oder drei **Modules** (Modulen):
1. das **Text module**: Hier sollt ihr euch auf die Arbeit mit weitgehend authentischen Texten konzentrieren.
2. das **Language module**: Hier lernt ihr neue Redemittel und Fertigkeiten und neue Grammatik und wiederholt bekannte Grammatik (**Revision**).
3. das **Word module**: Hier steht die Wortschatzarbeit im Vordergrund.

Eine kleine Überraschung: Dieses Buch könnt ihr **in einer anderen Reihenfolge** durchnehmen, als die *Topics* 1 bis 6 im Buch stehen.
Beispiel: *Topic* 4 vor *Topic* 3 (etwa weil es besser zu aktuellen Begebenheiten oder zum fächerübergreifenden Unterricht passt). Keine Sorge! Durch einen kleinen Kniff haben wir das möglich gemacht: Im **Vocabulary**-Teil wird für die Auflistung der neuen Vokabeln pro *Topic* jeweils das Ende von Band 4 als Grundlage genommen, so dass man nicht unbedingt abhängig von der vorherigen *Topic* ist. So kann man die Reihenfolge – wenn man möchte – individuell und flexibel gestalten. Und wenn bei dieser flexiblen Vorgehensweise eine 'neue' grammatische Struktur in einem authentischen Text vorkommen sollte, müsst ihr sie verstehen, aber nicht gleich produzieren können.

Am Ende des Buches, wenn ihr alle *Topics* durchgearbeitet habt, könnt ihr bestimmt alles!

Es ist auch möglich, den **Verweisen** (z.B.: Lang. module p. 18) im Buch zu folgen und gelegentlich eine andere Seite durchzunehmen, auf die das Buch verweist. Warum auch nicht?
Vielleicht möchtet ihr ab und zu einen der Texte der fakultativen **Further Reading** einschieben, auf die das Buch auch hinweist: ⟨Further reading p. 90⟩ Hier könnt ihr selbst weiterlesen. Viel Spaß dabei!

Ansonsten gibt es in jeder *Topic* 1–2 **Strategy Pages**, die euch eine bestimmte Fertigkeit beibringen oder eine bekannte Fertigkeit vertiefen.

Zu jedem neuen Grammatikpensum und zu den Wiederholpensen findet ihr ab S. 102 Regeln und Erklärungen in der **Grammar.**

Das neue Vokabular ist im **Vocabulary** ab S. 116 in der Reihenfolge angelegt, in der die sechs *Topics* im Buch erscheinen. Bei vielen authentischen Texten werden nur die wichtigsten Wörter zum Lernen im *Vocabulary*-Teil aufgeführt. Den Rest findet ihr im **Dictionary** hinten im Buch mit einem Gesamtverzeichnis aller neuen Wörter von *Password* Band 1 bis 5. Oder es gibt einen Hinweis auf die Benutzung eines englisch-deutschen Wörterbuchs.

INHALTSVERZEICHNIS

TOPIC 3 — THE GENERATION GAME

Zeichenerklärung

▯ Dieses Symbol verweist auf den Gebrauch des *file*.

▯D Dieses Symbol verweist auf den Gebrauch eines Wörterbuchs.

Lang. module p. 18 Dieser Verweis bedeutet: Die entsprechende Seite oder Übung des *Language module* kann bereits jetzt durchgenommen werden.

⟨Further reading p. 80⟩ Dieser Verweis bedeutet: Hier schließt sich der fakultative *Further-Reading*-Text an.

Auf der Begleitkassette/CD zum Schülerbuch (Klettnummer 546358/546391) verfügbar.

Auf der Kassette/CD zum Hörverstehen (Klettnummer 546359/546392) verfügbar. Die Texte sind im Begleitbuch für den Unterricht (Klettnummer 546353) und im Skriptheft (Klettnummer 546351) abgedruckt.

⟨ ⟩ fakultative Teile/Elemente

▷ Der Dreieckspfeil weist auf komplexere Aufgaben /Aufgabenteile hin, die sich auch zur Differenzierung nach oben eignen.

CONTENTS

- Text module:
  Becoming a pop star, TV viewing,
  a radio play
- Strategy page:
  Listening to the radio
- Language module:
  Revision of present tenses
  Participles
- Word module:
  Working with difficult words

1. Look at the pictures. Talk about your impressions in class.
2. What is a star? Gather ideas and then write a short text. (Think of stars from all kinds of fields.)
3. Try to explain the role of the media in making a star – how it is done and why it is done.
Think of examples you know.

⟨Further reading p. 80⟩

SWITCHED ON

1 How to become a pop star

1 **1. Pick a name**

Silver Spoon! That's a good name.
Unfortunately a sugar company picked it
years ago. Still, there are many left. If you've
5 got a pudding-bowl haircut and want to form
a guitar band, pick a short name. If you've got
long hair, scream a lot and if you want to form
a rock band, try something macho and
horrific like Megacorpse.

10 **2. Get a gimmick**

Songs don't have to be that great to be a hit.
An example: You're in a heavy metal band.
No one is interested 'cos your metal is like
everyone else's metal – loud, proud and …
15 erm … heavy. What do you need? You need a
gimmick. What you do therefore is make a
metal version of a song sung by a famous pop
star. This gimmick will get people buying the
record because everybody knows the song
20 and they'll be curious to hear your version.

4. Write some songs

Er, yeah. It does help, I find, to write some   30
songs. And make 'em good ones. If not, get
someone else to do it for you. Most people do
nowadays.

5. Pal up with someone important

There are a few people in the industry who   35
have the power to give a monkey a record
contract if they wish to do so. Find out the
names of these important A&R men (Artist
and Repertoire, the people who look out for
new talent) at the record companies. Don't   40
expect results right away. You may have to
write them hundreds of letters before you get
an answer.

**6. Hang out next to the DJ box at your
    local club**   45

DJs are very important in today's music scene.
If they're not called in to mix songs or remix
them, they often make their own records.
Hang around your trendiest local club's
trendiest local DJ and sing brilliantly, and very   50
loudly.

Snappy name
The Um...
Teddy Bear's Picnic
GOSPEL RAP VERSION
Good gimmick
DEBUT SINGLE

3. Get a manager

'Ey, kid. You've got talent. I'll manage you.
That'll be £50 a month, please.' This person is
not a good manager. A good manager is
25 someone who likes your music, understands
where you're coming from, has lots of record
company contacts and takes only a small part
of your money.

7. Get radio airplay

Every Friday, crowds of record company
people hang around Radio One in London,
waiting for the new airplay list. This piece of   55
paper tells them how often (if at all) the
station will play the songs. If you get a good
listing, the record will be played more often
and you'll sell more singles.

60 **8. Pal up with rock journalists**
Your music can be the worst in the world, but
if the music journalists decide they like it,
then everyone in the music industry – from
your radio stations to your record company
65 bosses – will decide that they like it too.

9. Learn how to cope in interviews
Journalists really haven't got the power to sell
records (it's TV and radio that do that), but
they have the power to make you look stupid
70 – and if they can, they will. So you should
follow these interview guidelines.
  (a) Think carefully before answering
      questions.
  (b) Give long answers.
75 (c) Never walk out of an interview.

10. Change your image every ten months
Some stars are famous for changes to their
images. One day they're blonde, the next
they're brunette. They know that if they keep
80 their fans interested, then even if they don't
buy the record they'll buy their posters and
T-shirts and books. If it's good enough for
them, it's good enough for you.

(from: *Tell Madonna I'm at lunch*, by Vici McCarthy)

1. a) Take five minutes to write down your reaction to the instructions. Be prepared to present
      your ideas to the class.
   b) Pick out a piece of advice i) that you find sensible, ii) that you would hate to follow,
   iii) where you would do the opposite. Give your reasons.

2. 'Stars are made not born.' On the basis of information in the text discuss this statement.

3. Who do you think the text was written for? Do you think the writer is serious? Why or why
   not?

4. Start a file page for pop music. Think of different ways to organize the vocabulary you collect.

▷ 5. **Suggestions for a group project**
   You are a group of young people who dream of becoming pop stars. You must convince an
   A&R man that you are the new supergroup. Make an information pack for the record company, including information on your group and a letter to the A&R man. You can also write a
   song text and plan a video. If you like, you can also record a demo tape or make a video about
   your group and your music.

Lang. module p. 18, 19

Discussing the content and purpose of a text

SWITCHED ON

2 What's on tonight?

1. TV – our most popular sport?

a) Decide on one of the photos and write down what your thoughts are.

b) Talk about your viewing habits with a partner or in a small group:

> I often watch TV with … /
> I always switch on …
> when … / I hate soap
> operas because … / …

2. Viewing with a plan

Check this extract from a British TV guide. (The context may help you to understand words you don't know!)

a) When can you watch the news and the weather? And what about sport?

b) How many films are on tonight? Which films would you (not) like to watch?

c) Say which programme these people might watch: an old lady; a 14-year old boy or girl; your father / mother; … What makes you think so?

3. Pick your programme

a) Scan the TV guide again. Choose three programmes you would like to watch and say why.

b) *Pay TV* and *View on Demand* are getting more popular every year. What programmes would you be willing to pay for?

(from: *The Daily Mail*)

BBC 1

5.35	**NEIGHBOURS**
6.0	**NEWS; WEATHER.**
6.30	**LOOK EAST**
7.0	• **ANIMAL PEOPLE:** Peter Sissons highlights the danger posed by mountain lions.
7.30	**TOMORROW'S WORLD:** Insight into a simple, but remarkably effective, lung cancer detector.
8.0	**CRIMEBEAT:** How banks are fighting back against the increase in credit card fraud by adopting a French 'smart card' system.
8.30	**THE NATIONAL LOTTERY LIVE:** Degrees perform their new single.
8.45	**POINTS OF VIEW:** Viewers air their opinions: followed by The Nation's Favourite Love Poem.
9.0	**NEWS; REGIONAL NEWS; WEATHER;** followed by National Lottery Update.
9.30	• **THE X FILES:** An FBI raid on a religious cult leads Mulder into an encounter with a mysterious woman.
10.15	**CHALK:** The staff welcome a new arrival to Gallast High.
10.45	**FILM: The Cover Girl Murders (1993):** Six models are stalked by a killer during a photo shoot on a remote island. Mystery thriller.
12.10	**FILM:** Delusion (1991).

ITV

5.40	**NEWS; WEATHER**
6.0	**HOME AND AWAY**
6.23	**ANGLIA WEATHER**
6.25	**ANGLIA NEWS**
7.0	**EMMERDALE:** Chris confronts Kelly about her mysterious one-off pay rise, while Pollard gets up to his old tricks.
7.30	**CORONATION STREET:** Sworn enemies Mike and Don face each other once more.
8.0	• **THE NATIONAL TELEVISION AWARDS:** See Pick of the Day.
10.0	**NEWS; LOTTERY RESULT; WEATHER.**
10.29	**ANGLIA AIR WATCH**
10.30	**ANGLIA NEWS; WEATHER**
10.40	**FILM: Basic Instinct (1991):** Thriller, starring Michael Douglas as a hard-drinking cop who investigates a grisly icepick murder.
1.0	**COLLINS AND MACONIE'S MOVIE CLUB.**
1.30	**REAL STORIES OF THE HIGHWAY PATROL**
1.50	**FILM: Lambada: The Forbidden Dance** (1990): Romantic drama.
3.35	**INTERNATIONAL MOTOR RACING .**

GRANADA PLUS

3.30	**SURGICAL SPIRIT** When Sheila becomes director of surgery and she and Jonathan become an item, which announcement will cause the greater stir?
4.00	**MISSION: IMPOSSIBLE**
5.00	**HAWAII FIVE**-O McGarrett uncovers a gold-smuggling racket whilst investigating the murder of a housewife.
6.00	**FAMILIES** Fiona and Simon worry about having to leave the flat. Rebecca makes a revelation to Isabelle.
6.30	**CLASSIC CORONATION STREET** Stan is cleared by the police when questioned about his stolen cart. There is continuing tension between Ray and Deirdre.
7.00	**BLIND DATE**
8.00	**MISSION: IMPOSSIBLE** The IMF team take on the leader of a neo-Nazi group.
9.00	**CLASSIC CORONATION STREET** 9.30 The Comedians 10.00 Hawaii Five-O 11.00 Close
	• recommended

4. Make a survey of the viewing habits of your classmates.

- Decide in groups what you would like to know from your classmates.
  (Think about types of programmes, viewing times, channels etc.)
- Compare your ideas in class.
- Develop a grid and carry out your survey.
- From the results of your survey, write what TV means to you and your class.

pupil	programme	times	channel
A			
B			

5. Just for fun

(from: *Calvin and Hobbes* by B. Watterson)

6. TV and radio in Britain and America

INFO BOX	Public TV	Commercial TV	Public Radio	Commercial Radio
GB	BBC1/BBC2 no advertising people buy a licence for their TV set	ITV / Channel 4 / Channel 5 / satellite & cable channels (sports, music, game shows, cartoons, news, …) with advertising	BBC Radio 1-5 / about 50 local radio stations no advertising	about 200 independent radio stations (Classic FM, Talk Radio,…) with advertising
US	more than 350 public stations (run by universities, cities or local governments) sponsors	more than 1,000 stations (ABC, CBS, NBC, …) / satellite & cable TV with advertising	Community Radio / National Public Radio (more than 600 stations) no advertising	more than 10,000 stations all over the USA with advertising

(source: *CORPORATION OF PUBLIC BROADCASTING, USA; RADIO LICENSING AGENCY, GB*)

a) Read the information about TV and radio in Britain and America.
b) Then, in a group, work out what is the same in your country and what is different. Take notes.
c) Give a short talk to the class.

Lang. module p. 20–22

⟨Further reading p. 81⟩

Comparing TV and radio in different countries

SWITCHED ON

3 The Martians have landed!

1. What does the title of this text make you think of?

Orson Welles' radio play threw America into a panic

1   A few minutes after eight o'clock on the night of Sunday, October 30, 1938, a serious voice interrupted a radio broadcast in America: "Ladies and gentlemen, I have a
5   brief announcement to make … "
The words that followed were broadcast in a programme which covered the United States, and they unleashed horrific scenes of panic. For the announcement was that
10   Martians had landed in North America. There were many severe battles and the USA was being taken over by men from Mars.
The announcement was part of a radio play
15   – but one so realistic that most people took it for fact.
The programme had started quietly enough. At 8 p.m. listeners heard: "The Columbia Broadcasting System presents Orson Welles
20   and his Mercury Theatre Of The Air in *War of the Worlds* by H. G. Wells."
Not that there were many listeners. After sixteen Mercury Theatre shows, CBS bosses knew that their drama series was
25   not a hit. It had only 3 per cent of the listening audience. Most people were listening on Saturday nights to The Charlie McCarthy Show.
That was why Welles was putting every
30   effort into *War of the Worlds*. He knew that CBS would drop his show if it did not find a new sponsor. And it would not get a sponsor if it did not find more listeners.
Welles and his team had been working on
35   the play for five days. They had rehearsed it,

(from: *The World's Greatest Mistakes*, slightly adapted)

ORSON WELLES IN
THE WAR OF THE WORLDS
BY H.G. WELLS

The original 1938 broadcast that panicked America

rewritten the script, and rehearsed again. But when they listened to the tape of their work so far, they were not happy.
Welles said: "Our only chance is to make it as realistic as possible." So the team stayed up all night adding new elements to the script. By Sunday night, the studio was covered with paper cups and food packets after a nervous eight-hour rehearsal. But at 7.59 p.m. everyone agreed that this show had a chance.
What followed over the next 24 hours got the Mercury Theatre talked about. It also won listeners from the McCarthy Show, and sooner than Welles had thought.
By chance, the McCarthy Show had a new singer that Sunday night. He was unknown. He started at ten minutes past eight, and bored listeners began looking for anything better on CBS. When they joined *The War of the Worlds* they had no idea that a play was in progress. All they knew was that strange things were happening along the east coast. The CBS announcer was telling them so …

2. Write down 15 words from the text that you think are important. Compare your list with a partner. Have you missed anything?

3. After you have listened to the extract (see Strategy Page, p. 17) think how **you** would have reacted? Write a letter to CBS either to complain or to praise the programme.

Strategy Page: Listening to the radio

You are going to hear a short extract from Orson Welles' radio play 'The War of the Worlds' based on H. G. Wells' book of the same name.

1. First read this summary of what listeners could hear up to this point.

> Orson Welles, "the director and star of this broadcast", speaks – saying how the earth was watched from space by clever but cold-hearted and envious creatures that "slowly and surely drew their plans against us".
> The actual radio play begins. We hear a weather report, then a normal music programme from a hotel in New York. An announcer interrupts the programme to read "a special announcement from the Intercontinental Radio News", saying that volcanic disturbances had been seen on the surface of Mars. The music starts again.
> Next Carl Phillips, a radio reporter, interviews the astronomer Professor Pearson at Princeton. During the interview the professor gets a message saying that something has hit the earth some- where near Princeton. The interview ends, there is a short piano interlude. The announcer comes on again and reads a report. Something has fallen on a farm near Grover's Mill, New Jersey. Jets of flame are coming from it. Carl Phillips is on his way there. Music. Next the listeners hear the two men at the Wilmott farm. There are unusual noises; a strange object in a pit is described. Carl Phillips moves closer and becomes more and more excited as the top of the object starts moving. People shout; the top falls off, and Phillips describes humped shapes coming out: their eyes, their huge bodies. He ends, "The thing's rising up now and the crowd falls back – it's seen plenty. The most extraordinary experience! I'll pull the microphone with me while I talk. I'll have to stop the description till I can find a new position. Hold on, will you please."

1

5

10

15

2. a) Before you listen: Remember that –
   - this is a historical recording, and parts may be difficult to understand;
   - there are many different accents in the English speaking world, and this is an American recording;
   - it is a radio play, so expect background noises.

   b) While you listen: just try to understand the gist. Note down the different parts of the extract, who is speaking and what they are talking about;

   c) After you have listened once: discuss what you have understood, and listen again. There is a transcript of this extract on p.82 to help you.

   d) Listen again and add the background noises, the way people speak and the atmosphere to your notes.

> ——— **TIP** ———
> If necessary, listen to a part of this extract 2–4 times and read the transcript.

3. The Orson Welles radio play was so realistic that across the whole of America people got into a panic. Families ran out of their homes, furniture was put into trucks and cars. There were soon traffic jams everywhere, and in New York members of the US navy were called to their ships to fight for their country. Sum up the ways in which Orson Welles made the play so realistic.

Useful expressions

an atmosphere of reality is created by ...
(the interview/report) sounds authentic because ...
the listener has the impression that ...
(the speaker) speaks in an excited/calm/normal way, as if ...
the type of music makes the listener feel ...

⟨Further reading p. 82⟩

Listening to a radio play

17

SWITCHED ON

A Revision: Conversations

1 a) Listen to this conversation at a party for media people. It is between a radio reporter with a **G1** regular late-night programme, Sam Spice, and a top model, Kathleen Primrose. They are comparing their very diffcrent working days. Work with a partner. One of you makes notes on the reporter's working day, and the other on the model's day.

b) Sam and Kathleen try to phone each other. But it isn't easy to get the other person on the phone.

Assistant: Radio Nightlife speaking. Can I help you?
Model: Hello. This is Kathleen Primrose speaking. Can I speak to Sam, please?
Assistant: I'm sorry. He's talking on the other phone right now.
Model: OK, I'll try again later. Goodbye.

c) With the information you collected in part a), write a dialogue between Kathleen and Sam's assistant, or Sam and Kathleen's assistant. Be prepared to present your dialogue in class.

G2

2 a) Look at these pairs of sentences closely and describe the differences.
1. He talks on the phone a lot. He's talking on the phone right now.
2. She usually works in a studio. But today she's working outside in a park.

> a) Verbs like *talk* and *work* express an activity, and are called dynamic verbs. You can use them in both the simple and the progressive form.

b)

> People who hate breakfast
> I don't understand
> Breakfast means a lot to me,
> Coffee in my hand,
> It smells good and it tastes good,
> So this is what I say –
> I want breakfast three times a day.

> b) Some verbs express a state. These are called stative verbs. They don't have a dynamic meaning, so they aren't normally used in the -ing form.

c) Here are some more stative verbs:
think, love, sound, like, know, feel, need, wish.
Put them in the correct groups:

hate	understand	smell	want

3 a) Complete the text with the verbs in the correct form – (present simple or present progressive).
It's four o'clock in the morning. Kathleen (to lie) awake in bed. She (to switch) on the radio. It is Sam Spice's programme, and he (to talk). Then he (to begin) to play a CD. She (to pick) up her mobile phone and (to dial) the studio number. She (to know) that he sometimes (to telephone) while the music (to play). "Hi, who (to speak), please?" She (to say), "Hello, this is Kath here. Could you play "When shall I see you again?" for me, please?" "That (to sound) like an interesting song," he (to say) …

▷ b) Continue the story with a partner.

Using dynamic and stative verbs

4 a) Susi is a tennis player but she isn't playing tennis today. Look at these sentences and try to find translations which show the different meanings.

G3

Susi is ill.
She is being sensible.
She has flu.
She is having a day in bed.

b) Talk about the people in these pictures. Simple or progressive?
Example: The man in the first picture is having a haircut.

to have …
a haircut
a lot of money
an argument
a headache
a new car
a bath

5 a) Look at this part of a telephone conversation between a tennis star and her agent.
– "Listen, Susi. Can I meet you on Saturday to discuss your plans for next week?"
– "On Saturday? Well no, Al. I'm too busy. I'm training in the morning. Then I'm having lunch at 12.30 with the club president. In the afternoon I'm going to a meeting, and in the evening I'm driving to Bristol."
What verb form does Susi use to talk about her plans? How can you tell that she isn't describing what she is doing at the moment?

b) Imagine you are a sports star. You haven't got a match or competition for two weeks, so you are trying to keep next week free for private plans. Make a diary for the rest of next week.

c) With a partner, make a dialogue between yourself and your agent, like this.
Agent: Can you give an interview to a newspaper on Sunday?
You: No, I can't do that. I'm meeting my old school class on Sunday.

Here are some ideas.

SUN	Meet my old school class 11a.m.
MON	10.30 Jogging with Sandra 4 p.m. Doctor 7 p.m. Massage
TUES	Buy present for Mum's birthday!!
WED	

Agent:		You:
Someone has asked if you can …	appear on a TV show	I'm sorry. …
Would you like to …	visit a children's hospital	No, certainly not …
Will you be able to …		Yes, I'd like to do that …
Can you …		I won't be able to do that because …

Using the progressive form with stative verbs and for plans

19

SWITCHED ON

 B Watching and being watched

Mel is telling her friend, Scott, that she saw a sports star in a sports shop …

Mel: I saw this guy going through the socks, you see. And he looked familiar, but he had dark
glasses on and I just couldn't think who he was. So I stood watching him for a while and
tried to remember where I had seen him. I kept thinking of a picture. It was an advert with
a man lying on a beach and saying something …   5

Scott: Did he notice you watching him?

Mel: No, I don't think so. Because I was standing near some people trying on anoraks. I
watched him checking labels on the socks and then I saw him coming towards me …

Scott: Wow! What did you do?

Mel: I turned and looked at the anoraks. Then I saw him walking towards an assistant   10
standing by the tennis shirts. So I followed him. When I got near enough to hear him
speaking, I knew it was him.

Scott: Did you ask him for his autograph?

Mel: Of course I did, and he said, 'Yes, sure'. Then he started to ask me about myself but of
course he couldn't hang around chatting all day. He suddenly said he had to go and I   15
last saw him hurrying towards the door …

1 a) Put the right parts together and tell the
story from the assistant's point of view.

— TIP —

Make a list of the verbs that are   **G4**
followed by a noun (or pronoun)
+ -ing for your file.

1. Well, I was watching a guy in dark glasses …
2. But then I also noticed a girl …
3. After a while I saw the guy …
4. And I saw the girl …
5. It seemed as if she wanted to hear him …
6. After he had paid for his socks I noticed
the two of them …
7. When I next looked, I saw the man … and the
girl … I don't know what it was all about!

exchanging a few words.
going through the socks.
going out of the door.
talking to me.
following him.
looking at a piece of paper.
coming towards me.
looking at the guy.

b) If you hadn't used participles, how else could you
have written the sentences in part a?

2 People often tell their friends if by chance they see a famous person doing some everyday
activity. Pretend this has happened to you. Choose a famous person. What did you see / hear /
watch / notice / … this person doing? What did you do? Write a short dialogue with a partner.
Check your list of verbs from exercise 1.

3 Just for fun

1. A celebrity is someone who works all
his life to become well-known. Then,
when he is famous, you see him wearing
dark glasses all the time because he
doesn't want us to recognize him.

2. I heard of a well-known actor who used to
carry a note in his wallet saying, "I am a
famous celebrity. In case of an accident,
please call a reporter."

(from: *The Penguin Dictionary of Jokes*)

Using participles for
observing

20

4 a) These drawings are suggestions for new adverts. What kind of products do you think the people in the pictures are advertising? (Use participles to identify the people.)
Example: I think the man sitting on the beach is advertising sunglasses (… suncream).

▷ b) What scenes would you show to advertise things? Think of people doing different actions.
a car – chocolates – jeans – telephone company – video recorder – sports centre – …
Example: – To advertise a car I would show a driver *looking happy*.

5 The sports star that Mel saw is talking on the radio about what it is like to be famous. Complete the sentences with participles from these verbs. (Sometimes more than one answer is possible. And perhaps you have ideas of your own.)

jump out	run	wait	scream	hide	smile	watch	hurry

1. It isn't easy, you know. Sometimes I just want to sit … behind closed doors at home.
2. I don't really mind the fans who stand … outside my house.
3. But reporters always hang around … in the area, too.
4. And wherever I go, photographers suddenly appear … in front of me.
5. Of course I can't hang around … and do my work.
6. And I try to be friendly to people who come … up to me in the street.
7. I mean, they look so disappointed if I just go … past them.
8. But like I said, at times I could run away from it all …

▷ **6** a) Describe the advantages and disadvantages of being a star or a famous person.
b) What do you think is the most important piece of advice to give someone of your age who wants to become famous?
– Don't allow reporters / photographers … to …
– I would / wouldn't be friendly / let people / …
– You should / shouldn't …

⟨Further reading p. 83⟩

Using participles for shortening

21

SWITCHED ON

Difficult words

1 Many TV programmes are about different groups of people. Adjectives describing people in general can sometimes be used as nouns for groups of people.

<u>the famous</u> (= all famous people)   but: <u>a</u> famous <u>person</u>, <u>some</u> famous <u>people</u>

a) Use the following adjectives to complete these comments from a TV guide:

old	poor	homeless	famous	rich	nervous	young

1. 'Different Worlds': a look at the different lifestyles of the rich and the ...
2. 'Kidshop': Saturday morning entertainment for ...
3. 'Startalk': more interviews with ...
4. 'Down Memory Way': these news reports of the past will be especially interesting for ...
5. 'On the Street': discussion about the problems of ...
6. 'Night of Horror': not a film for ...!

b) Make up similar comments for three or four programmes or films which you know.
c) Which of the following phrases can be replaced by 'the' with an adjective?
a crazy person; the old man; sick people; some rich people; unemployed people; the poor woman; tall people
d) Put the phrases in c) into German. Do you need a noun as often as in English?

2 a) *Hard-working* is a compound adjective.
Example: A person who works hard is a <u>hard-working</u> person. How would you describe: 1. a car that is moving fast? 2. a speech that never ends? 3. a drink that tastes fresh? 4. a boy who looks good? 5. a visitor who can speak English? 6. a plane that is flying low? 7. a girl who loves fun?
b) How many of these compounds can you put into one funny sentence?

D **3** Words like *take*, *make* or *get* can have many meanings, and can be used in many different phrases. Use this extract for *get* from a dictionary to find good translations for what these people said behind the scenes at a film studio.

(from: *Pons Schülerwörterbuch Eng.-Ger., Ger.-Eng.*)

get |get| <got, got, gotten *Am*> I. *tr* 1. be-

geraten III. (*Wendungen*): ~ s.o.'s back up jdn auf die Palme bringen; ~ **the better of s.o.** jdn kleinkriegen; ~ **the boot** (*fam*) entlassen werden; ~ **to the bottom of s.th.** e-r S auf den Grund gehen; ~ **done with** fertig werden mit; ~ **even with s.o.** mit jdm abrechnen; ~ **going** in Gang setzen; ~ **one's hair cut** sich die Haare schneiden lassen; ~ **hold of** zu fassen kriegen; ~ **home** heimkommen, nach Hause kommen; (*fig*) zum springenden Punkt kommen; ~ **married** sich verheiraten; ~ **there** (*fam*) sein Ziel erreichen; ~ **one's own way** seinen Kopf durchsetzen; ~ **the worst of it** am schlechtesten wegkommen; **it's** ~**ting warmer** es wird wärmer; **I** ~ **it** ich begreife schon; **I've got it!** ich hab's!; **I'll** ~ **him for that!** dem werde ich es besorgen!; **get**

I can't go on holiday with Marcia. She really gets my back up.

We need a new idea. – I've got it! This is what we'll do …

He told the director I wasn't good enough for the part. I'll get even with him one day.

I'll try to get hold of him before he flies to L.A.

We had to work late yesterday. I didn't get home till 10 p.m.

You just can't argue with her. You'd always get the worst of it.

It's very difficult to work together with Steven. He always has to get his own way.

Working with difficult words

IMAGES

These two guides contain more or less the same programme information.

1. Use your knowledge about media from Topic 1 to compare their front pages.
2. Decide which of the two in your opinion would be bought by more people, and explain your reasons.

TOPIC 2 THAT'S SCHOOL, TOO!

CONTENTS

- Text module:
  Examinations, activities, problems
- Language module:
  Passive forms, school chat, revision of past tenses
- Word module:
  False friends, paraphrasing, synonyms
- Strategy pages:
  Improving a written text
  Interpreting

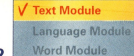
TOPIC 2

1. Which of the pictures do you find most interesting? Try to explain your choice. Would you like to share a school day with these pupils? Why or why not?

2. Compare activities in your school with those you can see here. Do you think activities should be part of a school day? Why or why not?

Discussing, comparing
school activities

THAT'S SCHOOL, TOO!

1 Examinations

Here are a photo, a personal e-mail and a recording of spoken information – all about the exam system in Britain – which a British school has sent to a partner school.

1. Talk about the photo. What is happening? Where are these people? What details do you notice? What is the atmosphere like?

2. Imagine you are one of these students. How might you feel?

3. The e-mail combines facts and feelings.
   a) Pick out any interesting facts about exams in Britain and make a note of them.
   b) What does the writer tell us about his feelings? Do you think you would feel the same?

---

from Patrick Owen, class 11b, Haywood School, Nottingham,
to Jens Schulte, Klasse 10a, June 7th, 3.30 pm.

Here's my latest news. I had my first GCSE (that's short for General Certificate of Secondary Education) on Thursday. We were all really scared. One girl was sick, she was so nervous. It was from 9.15 am to 10.45 am, which was good, because then we didn't have to wait a long time.
First we had to wait outside the Assembly Hall. In alphabetical order!
I was so nervous, I couldn't remember if O came before or after P! The hall looked different, which was a bit of a shock. It was full of special examination tables – all far apart so that no one could cheat (and we weren't allowed to take our bags in either – just our pencil cases, and mascots and sandwiches etc.).
I would be too scared to cheat anyway – they practically put you in the Tower of London if you cheat – anyway you fail the exam!
When everyone was sitting in the right place, a teacher opened the secret envelope with all the exam papers, handed them out and we began. Once you've started, it's not too bad – it's the waiting beforehand that gets to you.
I've got four more exams next week, and three the week after that. Then the holidays start! I'll send you a copy of my results when I get them (if I've passed!).
Write and tell me what the exam system is in your country.

                                                                    Patrick

4. Listen to the recording – two or three times if you need to – and make notes of the facts about the examination system.

5. Discuss what is different from the testing system in your country (what is surprising, what is a good idea, what isn't a good idea, what are the advantages/disadvantages …).

▷ 6. a) Write an account of the examination system in Britain for your file, using the notes you have made from the e-mail and the recording, or write an e-mail to a partner at a British school about the testing system in your country.
b) Compare the testing system in Britain to the system in your country. Say which elements of which system you prefer, and why. You might like to check the strategies on page 36.

⟨Further reading p. 84⟩

2 Activities

Every school in Britain offers activities of some kind. Here is a list of activities available during one year at the Edinburgh Academy, a well-known school in Scotland. In Year 10 and 11 (the 5th forms) the pupils have 'Activities' twice a week, from 3.35 pm to 4.15 pm.

Afternoon Activities

Pupils take an activity on several afternoons until 4.15. Pupils will have to put their name on a list for these in the first week of the Autumn Term, and again at the start of the Summer Term.
*means that this activity is only for Seniors

Aeronautics *	Duke of Edinburgh's Award * (5ths+)	Learning Support
Art	Electronics	Orchestra
Pottery	Environment Club	Philosophy*
Basketball *	Fives	Photography
Chamber Music	Fly-tying	Piping and Drumming
Chemistry for Fun	Greek	Rock Climbing
Chess	Hockey	Scrabble
Computing	Horticulture	Small-bore Rifle Shooting
Concert Band	Judo	Social Service*
Cycling Proficiency & Maintenance	Juggling	Squash
Design technology	Junior Play	Swahili
Drama	Keyboards	Various subject-based activities

D Imagine you are going to go to this school for a year. Look at the list of activities, using a dictionary for words you can't guess. Then choose two activities for the autumn term and the summer term. Write a short letter asking to join in these groups and giving reasons (Keep in mind that if the number of pupils per activity is limited, perhaps only those with the best reasons will get in!).

Lang. module p. 32, 33

Looking at activities in a Scottish school

27

THAT'S SCHOOL, TOO!

3 The School Survival Guide

Problems at school are not just about schoolwork, as this letter to a young people's magazine shows.

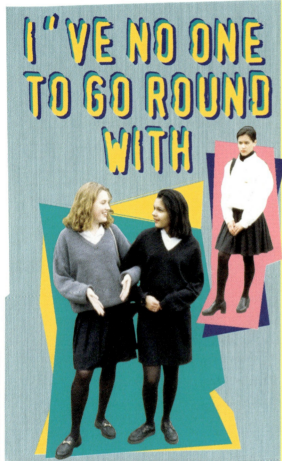

I'm so lonely. My best friend has just moved out of the area and I've no one to go round with. School is horrible now – at break and lunch-time I'm left on my own while everyone else goes off with their friends.

I'm a shy person so please don't tell me to just walk up to someone – I couldn't do that. I want a real friend anyway, not just someone who puts up with me. I hate going to school now – please help.

Of course you shouldn't just walk up to someone! Friendships grow gradually, they don't happen just like that. It's difficult being shy but the best way to make friends is to be friendly. Begin just by smiling and saying hello to people in your class – I'm sure they'll respond. When you hear people talking about the latest soap opera or sports event, or something like that, try to join in a bit, too. It is difficult at first, but it does get easier.

Once you've done this you can see who seems friendliest. Then you'll have to be bold. What about saying something like "I get a bit fed up on my own at lunch-time – would you mind if I came along with you?"

The worst they can say is no – but they'll probably say yes! It'll take a while before you find another 'best friend' but it's a better idea to have a whole circle of friends, anyway – then you won't find yourself alone again.

When you're shy it takes a lot of guts to do all this but once you begin to help yourself, others will be friendly back – you just have to make the first move.

(from: *Shout magazine*)

1. **Reading a letter:**
   Read the *letter* and find out –
   a) why the girl thinks school is horrible now; b) how she describes herself; c) why she needs help.

2. **Reading the answer**
   a) Read through the *answer* quickly to get the general gist.
   b) Find one sentence, or part of a sentence, in each paragraph that more or less sums up the general advice given in the paragraph, and write it down. *Example:* 1st par. "*… the best way to make friends is to be friendly.*"
   c) The writer also gives practical tips. Find a practical tip to go with each of the sentences you have written down. *Example:* 1st par. "*Begin by smiling and saying hello …*"

3. **Giving your opinion**
   Do you think that the answer given is a real help? Why or why not?

Reading about a personal problem

28

4. Looking at phrases

First try to express what the following phrases mean exactly: to be left on your own (l.3), to put up with someone (l.7), it takes a lot of guts (l.25), to make the first move (l.27). Then check in a dictionary, and try to find really good translations for the sentences the phrases are in.

5. Writing a letter

a) Write a letter to the editor of "The School Survival Guide" about any aspect of school life you like or dislike. (It doesn't have to give your true feelings.)

b) One of you collects and re-distributes all the letters. Write an answer to the letter you have received. (Remember to look at the answer to the letter on p. 28 for useful phrases.)

4 A model pupil betrayed

MODEL pupil Emma Doyle thought she was doing the right thing when she reported young people passing drugs around on the school bus.
But all the pupil got for her honesty was a serious
5 assault at the hands of a teenager gang.
For she was tactlessly exposed by the headteacher as his informant.
Emma, 18, said: 'I had always been taught to do the right thing by my teachers and I just didn't
10 think twice about reporting what I saw.
There were lots of young kids on the bus who could see what was going on and, when I thought about my little cousins who go to my school, I didn't want them getting involved.'
15 After reporting the incident to her headteacher,

Emma thought nothing more of it, until she was called to the headteacher's office.
'He asked me to come in and then pointed at the boy who I'd seen passing the drugs. Then he asked me outright: "Is that him?"' 20
It was awful. The boy stared right at me as if to say "you've had it" and I began to feel really nervous about what he'd do.'
Emma's grandfather, Harry Doyle, 64, said: 'When she got off the bus near her home in 25 Troon a gang of 13 and 14-year-old girls jumped on her and started kicking and hitting her. She didn't have a chance.'
Mr Doyle said: 'I'm just amazed that Emma's headteacher could do such a thing.' 30

(from: *The Daily Mail*)

1. Reading newspaper articles

1. As in many newspaper articles of this type, the first few sentences actually give a summary of the article. Can you think why?
2. Look at the first three sentences, and note two or three key words per sentence.
3. Read the rest of the article. Say which paragraphs in the article give you what information about the key words.

▷ 3. Guidelines

When might it be right or wrong to inform a teacher about something? With a partner or in a group, try to work out guidelines.

⟨Further reading p. 85⟩

2. Your opinion

1. *Emma:* Was Emma right to do what she did? What else could she have done?
2. *The headteacher:* What mistake did he make? What else could he have done?
3. *The gang of girls:* Why do you think the gang of girls attacked Emma, when she was trying to protect younger children?

4. Discussion

You have just read about two problem areas at school. But school also has its pleasanter aspects. If you didn't go to school, but had to do your schoolwork on a computer alone at home, what aspects of school would you miss and why?

Lang. module p. 34/35

Reading, discussing and writing about problems

THAT'S SCHOOL, TOO!

5 Adrian Mole is off school

(from: *The Growing Pains of Adrian Mole*, by Sue Townsend, slightly adapted)

Thursday   April 15th
Woke up at 4 a.m. with a toothache. Took six junior aspirins for the pain. At 5 a.m. I woke my mother and father and told them that I was in
5   terrible pain.
My father said, 'It's your own bloody fault for missing your last three dentist's appointments.'
At 5.30 a.m. I asked my father to drive me to the hospital, but he refused and turned over in bed.
10 It's all right for him: he hasn't got any real teeth. I sat up, in agony, and watched the sky get light. The lucky toothless birds started their horrible noise and I swore that from this day forward I would go to the dentist's four times a year,
15 whether I was in pain or not.
At nine o'clock my mother woke me up to tell me that she'd made me an emergency appointment at the dentist's. I told her that the pain had stopped and instructed her to cancel the appointment.

20 **Friday   April 16th**
Woke up at 3 a.m. in agony with toothache. I tried to scream silently but it must have reached my parents' bedroom because my father came into my room and told me to be quiet. He showed no
25 sympathy, just went on about how he had to work tomorrow and he needed his sleep. On his way back to bed he slipped on one of my mother's magazines that she'd left on her side of the bedroom floor. His swearing woke the dog

30 up. Then my mother woke up. Then the birds started. So once again I watched the grey fingers of day make the night light.

Saturday   April 17th
Still in bed with toothache. My parents are
35 showing me no sympathy, they keep saying, 'You should have gone to the dentist's.' I have phoned Pandora: she is coming round tomorrow. She asked me if I needed anything; I said some chocolate would be nice.
She said (quite angrily, I thought), 'Heavens
40 above, Adrian, aren't your teeth rotten enough?'

Monday   April 19th
Dentist's at 2.30, worse luck! 4 p.m.: I am now minus a front tooth! The stupid Australian dentist took it out instead of repairing it. He even had the
45 nerve to wrap it in a bit of paper and give it to me to take home!
I said, 'But I've got a gap!' He said, 'You'll get used to it.' I asked him if another tooth would grow in its place. He said, 'Bloody stupid Poms,'
50 but he didn't answer my question.
As I was stumbling out of his surgery holding my frozen face he said that he had often seen me walking home from school eating chocolate, and it would be entirely my own fault if I was
55 toothless at thirty.
I will walk home another way in future.

exaggeration → Übertreibung

1. Read this extract from Adrian Mole's diary from 15th to 22nd April.
   Write down a few words to give your first impression. (Think about your mood before and after reading it.)

2. Write down in one sentence what happens to Adrian on each day
   (not April 21st, of course!).

3. Describe what you learn about Adrian and his parents?
   In what ways are they typical or not?
   (Think about yourself/your parents/other boys of Adrian's age/other parents).

4. Find funny parts from the diary. Which parts do you think are funniest, and why?

   > The part/extract/episode/paragraph where … makes me laugh/smile.
   > (I find … amusing.)
   > … because the reader expects that … but …
   > Adrian says that … / tries to … /intends to … but …
   > The humour lies in the contrast between …

▷5. Imagine an English-speaking e-mail friend asks you about funny books, magazines, etc. in your country. Write about some that you really find funny, and say why you find them funny.

Tuesday   April 20th
I have now got the kind of face that you see on
60 'Wanted' posters. I look like a mass murderer.
My mother is dead angry with the dentist; she
has written him a letter demanding that he
should make a false tooth free of charge.
School was terrible; Barry Kent started calling me
65 'Gappy Mole' and soon everyone was at it; even
Pandora was a bit cool.
I sent her a note in Physics asking her if she still
loved me. She sent a note back saying,
'I will love you for as long as Britain has
70 Gibraltar.'

Wednesday   April 21st
It has just been on the news that Spain wants
Gibraltar back.

Thursday   April 22nd
75 I couldn't face taking my gap to school this
morning so I stayed in bed until 12.45 p.m.
I asked my mother for an excuse note. I gave
it to Ms Fossington-Gore during afternoon
registration.
80 She read it angrily then said, 'At least your
mother is honest. It makes a change from the
usual lies one has come to expect from most
parents.'
She showed me the letter. It said:

Dear Ms Fossington-Gore,   85
Adrian did not come to school this morning
because he didn't get out of bed until 12.45.
            Yours faithfully,
                Ms Pauline Mole   90
I will ask my father to write my excuse notes in
future; he is a born liar.

Sue Townsend
THE GROWING PAINS OF ADRIAN MOLE

'The funniest, most bitter-sweet book
you're likely to read this year.'*
methuen

▷ **6.** How else can Adrian avoid school?
Write a bit more of his diary.

Wednesday, May 10th
    Woke up at 4 a.m. ...
    My father said, " ...
    At nine o'clock ...
Thursday, May 11th
    Still can't go to school.
    My parents ...
    I have phoned Pandora ...
Friday, May 12th
    I couldn't face school, so ...

6   The Leader

I wanna be the leader
I wanna be the leader
Can I be the leader?
Can I? I can?
Promise? Promise?
Yippee, I'm the leader
I'm the leader

OK what shall we do?

                Roger McGough

What makes this poem funny?

Lang. module p. 36

THAT'S SCHOOL, TOO!

A An unusual school

ITALIA CONTI is a theatre arts school in London which has helped to start the careers of many famous names. Many young would-be stars hope that their lives will be changed by winning a
5 place there. Although the school is sent thousands of applications, after auditions and interviews only twelve people are offered a place each year. Some pupils are given grants, but most fees have to be paid by parents.
10 Italia Conti pupils have classes from 9 am to 5 pm every day. They are taught acting, singing and dancing, but normal subjects like Maths and History can also be found on the timetable. Everyone must take GCSEs so that no one will

be left without qualifications if they don't have any success as actors.

The school is visited regularly by agents looking for new talent. So even while they are still there some lucky pupils may be invited to do TV or film work. For the others there remains the dream that before long they too will be 'discovered'.

---

1 Pick out the elements of Italia Conti that would make it attractive or unattractive to you personally.

2 Look at what some Italia Conti pupils say about their school. Write down the words in the article which report the same information.
   1. 'I hope it will change my life!'
   2. 'Thousands of people send the school applications.'
   3. 'They only offer twelve places.'
   4. 'I'm lucky. I get a grant.'
   5. 'My parents have to pay for me.'
   6. 'They teach us acting.'
   7. 'We do the usual subjects, too.'
   8. 'Maybe someone will 'discover' me soon.'

3 Give examples from the text of the passive a) in the future tense b) after a modal. Describe how these forms are made and make grammar notes for your file.   **G5**

4 Would-be stars often dream about the future. What are their dreams?

Example: 1.

> I will be seen on the big screen.

1. I …
2. My films …
3. Photos of me …
4. Articles …
5. Fan clubs …
6. My life …

interview –
write – recognize –
change – see –
print – show –
start – …

5 Add more 'school' ideas to the wall below. Think of funny sentences, too. Remember: the passive after modals is often used when giving written information or instructions.

| Teachers Pupils Exams School trips Activities … | should may must can have to | (not) be … |

Jokes must be put on every noticeboard.

Homework may not be given to Year 11.

Using passive forms, developing written style

6 a) Here are two statements made by an Italia Conti pupil. G6
   1. They offered my friend a place last June. 2. They gave three pupils a part in a TV advert.

   The verbs <u>offer</u> and <u>give</u> have a direct and an indirect object. Say which is which.

b) You can also say:
   1. My friend was offered a place last June. 2. Three pupils were given a part in a TV advert.
   Try working out, perhaps with a partner, how these passive forms are made.

▷ c) Check your grammar section and find another way to put the sentences in a) into the passive.

7 These statements were made by Italia Conti pupils, who were talking about their school.
   1. 'They send you a date for your audition and interview.'
   2. 'At the audition they give you the chance to show your talent.'
   3. 'During the interview they ask you all kinds of questions.'
   4. 'They don't tell you the result of the audition right away.'
   5. 'They send you a letter – with good or bad news!'
   6. 'It's a great moment when they offer you a place.'
   7. 'Of course they don't promise you a brilliant career.'
   8. 'But they teach you the skills that are important in show business.'
   9. 'At least they give you the chance to make a dream come true.'

> ───── **TIP** ─────
> In written language these expressions can be used in place of 'you':
> – the girls and boys
> – young people
> – everyone
> – the lucky ones
> – …

Put these statements into a form suitable for a written article.
Example: 1. Pupils are sent a date … *or* A date for their audition and interview is sent …

8 Some people broke into the school last night. They have made a terrible mess in the drama room. Imagine you have to write a report. Be prepared to list what has been done and what can/can't/will have to be done now. You can add your own ideas, too.

> The costumes have been pulled out of the cupboards. Most of them can be used again, but they will have to be cleaned.

break – clean – destroy – kick over – pull out – repair – replace – throw around – wash – write – …

9 a) Listen to this interview about another unusual school. Make notes about the school for a magazine article. You will need to know these words:
   F.A. (Football Association) – trials – boarding school – comprehensive school – professional
b) Write a magazine article. Don't forget to organize your information well/write in a suitable style (try to include passive forms)/check your work.

Recognizing and using
personal + modal passives

33

THAT'S SCHOOL, TOO!

B Revision: School chat

A Oh, God! I've just failed another one!

Oh, so it was you who caused all that panic the other day. **C**

It was awful, wasn't it?

Too right. I've never felt so embarrassed in all my life!

You've had it since last Monday. **B**

But I gave it back to you in the maths lesson the next day.

1 Work with the dialogue pairs (A–E).
   a) What do you think the pupils are talking about?
   b) Collect examples of the present perfect and the past simple. What signal words are used? Do you know any other signal words for these tenses? Check your file.

G7

2 a) Say what has happened and what the results are. *Example:* 1. A girl's chair has broken. Now she is lying on the floor.

EXAM RESULTS

   b) What do the people in a) say when they look back later? (Add a few details to make the stories more interesting.) *Example:* 1. Well, I got a shock in the middle of Maths the other day. My chair broke …

IDIOT

3 What are the people below saying? Use sentences with 'for' or 'since'. Add suitable time expressions.
   Example: 1. You've had it for a week now/since last Wednesday.

know each other / not do any homework / have it / be stuck on the first sentence / not see him / not win a game / be the same / not eat anything

--- TIP ---
– FOR a period of time e.g. two hours, a day, many years, …
– SINCE a point in time e.g. 10 o'clock, yesterday, last week, …

G8

1. 'Where's my book? You …'
2. 'I'm so hungry! I …'
3. 'We're best friends. We …'
4. 'Our football team is terrible. They …'
5. 'Is he ill? I …'
6. 'She'll be in trouble. She …'
7. 'Our uniform is old-fashioned. It …'
8. 'I can't do this exercise. I …'

Strange that I didn't see her at school last week.

E

Hasn't anyone told you the news yet?

D

He did it yesterday, he said – but then the dog ran off with it and ate it.

Ha ha – that's one of the best excuses I've ever heard!

TIP
– Use the <u>present perfect</u> when an event in the past is still linked with the present.
– Use the <u>simple past</u> when an event belongs completely in the past.

4 a) In order to find out more, write down two questions about each statement.

1. 'The school hamster ran away the other day.' 2. 'I didn't get to school till ten o'clock this morning.' 3. 'The headteacher wanted to see me yesterday.' 4. 'We had a good time in Science yesterday.' 5. 'We had an important visitor in school last week.'
Example: 1. How did the hamster get out of its cage? – Did you find the hamster again?

▷ b) Work with a partner. Start with the statements in a). Take turns to ask and answer each other's questions.

5 Present perfect or simple past? Write down what these pairs of speakers say to each other.

1. not learn the German words yet/look at them on the bus this morning
2. buy a new CD yesterday/already spend all this month's pocket money
3. do badly in the Maths exam last year/never do very well at Maths
4. be a Newcastle United fan all my life/not have time to watch last Saturday's game
5. just hear the news about the headteacher/find out about an hour ago

Start: 1. 'I haven't learnt the German words yet.' – 'Oh, I looked at them …'

6 Chat to your partner about a situation at school. (It doesn't have to be true.) Look at the ideas for situations on the right. The phrases below will help you to talk about them.

make a funny/silly mistake   get a surprise

lose something   fall asleep in class

…

Useful expressions

– Have you heard what I/… did the other day?
– Well, it happened when …
– It was really strange/great/… because …
– I've never felt so awful/stupid/… in my life!
– Since then I've tried to …

– No, I haven't. Go on – tell me about it.
– Really? I didn't know that.
– Why/Where did you …?
– So how did you/the teacher/… react?
– That's the funniest/strangest thing I've ever heard!

Deciding on the use of present perfect or simple past

35

THAT'S SCHOOL, TOO!

Strategy Page: Improving a written text

1 Look at the piece of work below by a British girl. Say what corrections she has made to her text, and explain how the corrections improve it. (The checklist on the right will help you.) *Example:* She has used the conjunction 'although' to join the first two sentences. The link makes the text more fluent.

Checklist:

- choice of vocabulary
- suitable for written text
- linking words
- starting words/phrases
- avoid repetition

Useful expressions

to replace ... by ...
to link ... by ...
to change/to add/to join ...

to make more interesting by ...
to express ... more clearly.
to give a more exact meaning to ...

Although pupils traditionally
~~People always~~ complain about school lunches/

t food is *Luckily t*
The ~~lunches are~~ not always bad. ~~There~~ is no

school meals
problem with our ~~cafeteria.~~ We have a good

offering *tasty*
cafeteria/ ~~They offer~~ very ~~nice~~ meals and

is a wide choice *from*
snacks. And there ~~are lots of different things. You can have~~ things like

to *Since*
pizza and hamburgers, ~~or~~ soups and salads. ~~And they keep the~~ prices

are kept *As at all schools* *However*
low/ ~~So~~ everyone can eat there. ~~Our cafeteria is open at lunch time.~~ ~~But~~ I

in
read a newspaper article/ ~~It said~~ that there are schools in some parts of

where you *an excellent*
the country/ ~~You~~ can get breakfast ~~there,~~ too. I think that is ~~a very good~~

P *who*
idea. ~~Some~~ pupils come to school without breakfast/ ~~Then they~~ find it

hard to concentrate *In my opinion if* *had* *to eat*
~~hard~~ in lessons. ~~I think~~ they ~~should eat~~ something and drink ~~something~~

t *improve their work* *T*
early in the day/ They might ~~be better~~ in class (then).

2 Copy the paragraph on the right into your exercise book. Use the checklist to improve and correct it. Be prepared to suggest text changes in class.
Decide which corrections work best. (There is no single perfect answer!)

3 Start a file page on 'improving a written text.' Expand the checklist using your own ideas and add more useful expressions.

There is a law in Britain. It says that pupils in Britain must learn certain things like for example English, Maths and Science. The school timetable must have these things. This is OK. Not everyone likes these lessons. But they are necessary if you want to go to university later. You can go on with your education there. Also if you want to leave school and get a job. With PE it is different. Some people are just not good at sports. They feel they are wasting time when they are doing sports. I don't think people should force us to have such things on our timetable. They are not so important later in life.

A Choosing the right word

1 Sometimes English and German words look similar but they have a completely different meaning.

a) Look at the words below. Are they 'true friends' or 'false friends'?
   Example: 'Meaning' is a 'false friend'. It looks like 'Meinung' in German, but it really means 'Bedeutung'.

meaning	computer	note	calendar
poster	uniform		sport
gymnasium	map	floor	art

TIP

Read the words out loud and check your pronunciation. Even 'true friends' usually sound a bit different in English.

2 There are some German words which you can't translate directly into English. (This is often because you don't find these things in Britain or they are different.) How would you explain these words and expressions to a British friend?

1. Klassensprecher   2. Hausmeister   3. Pausenbrot   4. hitzefrei   5. Klassenbuch
6. Arbeitsgemeinschaft

3 a) How would you put the underlined words into German?
   1. I fell over during the lunch <u>break</u>. I was lucky not to <u>break</u> my arm!
   2. There isn't enough <u>room</u> for us all in the music <u>room</u>.
   3. Look in the <u>left</u> side of the cupboard. I think there's some paper <u>left</u> there.
   4. Did you <u>notice</u> anything interesting on the <u>notice</u> board?
   5. What <u>time</u> is it? <u>Time</u> goes so slowly during the last lesson of the day!
   6. I think I'll have a <u>rest</u> before I do the <u>rest</u> of my homework.

b) Think of two different English words you can use for each of the German words below.
   1. Stunde   2. tragen   3. Geschichte   4. leicht   5. Fach   6. schwer
   Write sentences to show them in the correct context.
   Example: 1. a) Our first <u>lesson</u> on Mondays is English.
                    b) I was half an <u>hour</u> late for school yesterday.

▷ c) Sum up in one or two sentences what you have learned in this exercise.

4 In English many words can be used as nouns or verbs, for example:
to <u>talk</u> – to give a <u>talk</u>
to <u>point</u> at – a <u>point</u> on a map
Find more examples for your file and translate them into German.

5 a) Listen to this girl giving a short talk and give your first impressions. Listen again and note down the things the girl describes as 'nice'. What better adjectives could she have used?
   b) Prepare your own short talk about a school trip you have been on. Choose your words carefully. Try to use different adjectives.
   c) Start a 'nice' page for your file. Collect alternative words that you can use in different contexts.

a *nice* journey – an *interesting* journey
nice seats – ...

False friends, paraphrasing, synonyms

THAT'S SCHOOL, TOO!

Strategy Page: Interpreting

1 Sometimes you might have to put German into English, or English into German. For example you might have to explain a German menu to a foreign visitor or interpret for two travellers at a station. With a partner think of possible 'real' situations.

> ─────────── **TIP** ───────────
> - Don't try to translate word for word. Sometimes you need different phrases, or even a different structure.
> - Watch out for 'false friends'.
> - Be careful with the word order.
> - If you don't know the exact word you need, paraphrase it.
> - Remember that there is always more than one possible translation!
> - Countable and non-countable nouns can cause problems. Check G9.

2 To become more aware of some of the problems of interpreting, put these sentences into English. Use the tips above to help you. (Be prepared to say where the problems were and what you did.) *1. Ich gehe gern in die Schule. 2. Ich finde die meisten Lehrer und Lehrerinnen sehr sympathisch. 3. Natürlich macht es keinen Spaß, Klassenarbeiten zu schreiben. 4. Hoffentlich werde ich am Schuljahresende gute Noten bekommen. 5. Ich möchte nicht sitzenbleiben! 6. Unser Klassenlehrer gab uns einen guten Rat.*

3 Interpret for this girl and boy – she doesn't speak English, and he doesn't speak German. Explain to them what the other one wants to ask or say – in the correct language, of course! (Think which words you do not have to translate.)

1. a) She wants to know if it's true that …
   b) Er sagt …

1 | a) *Frage ihn bitte, ob es stimmt, dass es in England viele Internate gibt.*
  | b) *Oh well – there are rather a lot, yes. But most people go to day schools, like comprehensives.*

2 | a) *Ich weiß, die meisten Schüler und Schülerinnen müssen eine Uniform tragen. Aber wie stehen sie dazu? Tragen sie sie gern?*
  | b) *Ha ha! Tell her to imagine herself in a horrible grey skirt and pullover – and then guess the answer to her own question.*

3 | a) *Alles klar! Und muss man das Jahr wiederholen, wenn man in der Schule schlecht abschneidet?*
  | b) *Oh, is that what happens in Germany? You poor things! No, we don't have that system.*

4 | a) *Was passiert, wenn jemand die Schule schwänzt?*
  | b) *Big trouble! Er – you'd better add that I don't have any personal experience!*

4 a) Practise more interpreting in groups of three. One of you only speaks German, one of you only speaks English, and the other person interprets. You can choose what you talk about (music, sport, hobbies, holidays …). Take turns to play the different roles.

▷ b) Look back at the tips at the top of the page. Find an example for each from the conversations which you have just interpreted. Think about how you interpreted and add any further tips or notes on personal problem areas to your page.

IMAGES

1. Speculate about the situation in which this picture has been taken·and the news this girl may have received in this letter from school.

2. Describe what kind of letter could make you feel like this.

Writing about a photo

TOPIC 3 THE GENERATION GAME

Looking at different
family pictures

40

TOPIC 3

1. Write down what the word 'family' makes you think of.
2. Speculate about the families in the pictures. What are the positive aspects of each type of family? What problems might they have?
3. Do you think the people are happy together? Why? Why not?

Talking about family groups

41

THE GENERATION GAME

1 My Sister is a Runaway

A Reader's True Story

Nine months ago my sixteen-year-old sister, Lesley, ran away from home. She told Mum she was going to school, but now we know she came home when the house was empty, packed some clothes, stole Mum's cash card and caught a bus to Glasgow.

When Mum and Dad first realised she'd gone, they thought she'd be back in a couple of hours. She often had arguments with Mum and Dad, but nothing too serious and she hadn't seemed too unhappy.

Lesley still hadn't come home a couple of days later, though, and when Mum and Dad found out that she'd taken the cash card and emptied Mum's bank account from machines round Glasgow, they knew it was serious.

Anyone who's thinking of running away from home should think about what it does to the rest of the family. I'd never seen my dad cry before, but he missed Lesley so much and was scared it was his fault she'd gone. He and Mum keep wondering if they should have been harder on her, or softer on her. They blame themselves for not realising she was unhappy.

Her friends at school acted as if Lesley was some kind of star, as if she'd done something really brave and exciting instead of just selfish and stupid, which is what I think.

Mum and Dad have spent nearly all their money on going to Glasgow looking for Lesley and paying for posters and leaflets to hand out asking if anyone's seen her. Mum's been to every drug and youth advice centre, although she knows they probably aren't allowed to say whether they've seen Lesley.

Every weekend she and Dad still walk round the town centre late at night in case she's sleeping in a doorway, and they even go to concerts, looking for Lesley in the crowd. They come home tired and in tears because they haven't found her. It makes me feel almost guilty for being the one who's still here.

Mum used to look and act really young, but now she's got a lot of grey hairs and takes tablets for depression.

"I'm dreading Christmas day."

"My Sister Is A Runaway"

The only present Anna and her parents want this Christmas is for Anna's sister, Lesley, to come home …

I hate Lesley for doing that to her.

Thanks to her, living with Mum and Dad can be hard. If the TV's on and something comes on about young girls being prostitutes or taking drugs I have to jump up and switch it off quickly, or Mum just starts to cry. Every time the phone rings I see Mum and Dad praying it might be Lesley – it never is, though.

Because of her I can't go out the door without Mum and Dad wanting to know every detail about where I'm going and if I'm ten minutes late from school Mum has almost called the police. Lesley did the stupid thing, but I'm the one who's paying for it.

It's nearly Christmas now – our first Christmas without her. I'm not looking forward to Christmas day because I know how upset Mum and Dad are going to be. Even presents don't interest me. The only present I want is for Lesley to walk through the front door so we can be a proper family again. If you're reading this, Lesley – or if anyone who knows her is, can you tell her – please, please come home.

(from: Shout magazine)

1. What is your first reaction to this true story?
2. To check the facts, choose one aspect of the story and be prepared to report on it to your group or class.
3. What do you think of the parents' reaction?

- What happened?
- What did the parents do?
- How did Anna's life change?
- How does Anna feel about her runaway sister?

Useful expressions

I can understand that they are (upset)/go ... etc.
I think they were right/wrong to (go/look, etc.) ...
They should have (seen ...)/shouldn't have (gone) ...

▷ 4. Lesley's sister thinks Lesley was 'selfish and stupid'. What do you think?

Word module p. 52, ex. 1

2 Runaways & Throwaways: Life on the Streets

Life is hard for the almost 100 million young people on the streets around the world. The United Nations Children's Fund estimated that 90 million young people under 18 are on the streets of the Third World, with 10 million more in industrial nations. Some are there for only a few days, but for many young people around the world, the street is home.

And not all of them are on the streets of their own choice. In the United States while most of the homeless young people have chosen to run away from home, many others have been thrown out, unwanted by their parents. Perhaps 40 percent of U.S. street kids are 'throwaways'. The children on the streets in developing nations – such as the estimated 40 million in Latin America – are mainly there because of poverty.

Runaways in industrial nations usually leave home to escape family problems such as divorce, alcoholism, physical or sexual abuse. But problems on the streets are usually worse. After about six weeks on the streets, most runaway teens (both male and female) have become involved in prostitution, dealing drugs or both.

About 500 shelters in the United States help street kids. The shelters try to help teens get off the streets and back to their families or into foster homes. But the U.S. shelters can only take 10,000 of the nearly 1,5 million young people on the U.S. streets.

(from: *Youth*)

1. How do you feel about the information in this article? Make five statements.

Useful expressions

I didn't know that ...
I wouldn't have thought that ...
I'm (really) surprised that ...

I'm not surprised that ...
The fact that ... doesn't surprise me.
I already knew that ...

▷ 2. Something to think about: Why do you think Lesley ran away?
What problems might she have on the streets?

Lang. module p. 48/49

Expressing personal reactions

THE GENERATION GAME

Strategy Page: Informal Discussion

1. Look at these statistics.

If you think, for example, about the fact that 89 % of young people have a music centre in their bedrooms, you and your friends might want to say things like –

"I've got a music centre in my bedroom, too."
"If you've got your own music centre, there are no family arguments about what to listen to."
"You've got to learn to do things as a family."
"If I had a music centre in my room, I'd never get any work done."

But these are single statements, not a discussion.

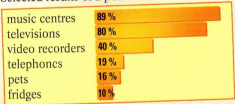

Home comforts

What do teenagers have in their bedrooms?
Selected results of a poll

music centres	89 %
televisions	80 %
video recorders	40 %
telephones	19 %
pets	16 %
fridges	10 %

Source: Interviews with 407 16–19 year-olds in 28 locations across Britain.

(from: *The Glasgow Herald*)

2. Look at this extract from a discussion.

- **I wouldn't have thought that** 89 % of young people had music centres in their bedrooms.
- Well, **I don't find it surprising,** *although* I haven't got one in <u>my</u> bedroom.
- **In my opinion,** it's a good thing to have your own music centre, *then* there are no family arguments about what to listen to.
- **I don't agree with that.** You've got to learn to do things together in a family. *Otherwise* it isn't a family.
- **Sorry, but that's nonsense.** In our family everybody listens to their own music, *but* we're still a family.
- **I'd like to raise another point.** If I had a music centre in my room, I would never get any work done *because* I would always be listening to music. **I do feel that** it distracts you.

In a discussion, all the parts are linked, like a chain.

Which of these phrases can you use for agreeing or disagreeing with someone / giving your reaction to information / putting forward an opinion or an argument of your own / moving the discussion on?

> **TIP**
> The conjunctions are also worth collecting!

3. Start a file page. Collect useful phrases for discussion, sorting the phrases into the four groups above. (You will find phrases for giving your reaction to information on p. 43.)

> **TIP**
> If you have already started a discussion page, check if it needs reorganizing.

"I don't see that as a problem because …"
"The first point I'd like to make is …"
"There's another point we haven't mentioned yet."
"But on the other hand …"

"I agree with what you said."
"One of the main problems/ advantages/disadvantages is …"
"Firstly, secondly, thirdly …"
"I take your point that … but …"

"I would expect …"
"I think you have to look at it from a different point of view."
"I think we ought to consider another point/aspect, namely, that …"

4. Discuss some of the other statistics in the chart at the top of the page, using some of the phrases you have collected from this strategy page.

⟨Further reading p. 86⟩

Linking arguments

3 Forgiving: No Son of Mine

1. Before you listen to the song, read the title and think what the song might be about.
2. The song tells a story. Listen to the song two or three times. Then in class or in a group, try to build up the story.

No Son of Mine

The key to my survival
was never in much doubt
the question was how I could keep sane
trying to find a way out

things were never easy for me
peace of mind was hard to find
and I needed a place where I could hide
somewhere I could call mine

I didn't think much about it
till it started happening all the time
soon I was living with the fear every day
of what might happen at night

I couldn't stand to hear the
crying of my mother
and I remember when
I swore that, that would be the
last they'd see of me
and I never went home again

they say time is a healer
and now my wounds are not the same
I rang the bell with my heart in my mouth
I had to hear what he'd say
He sat me down to talk to me
he looked me straight in the eyes
he said:

You're no son, no son of mine
You're no son, no son of mine
You walked out, you left us behind
and you're no son, no son of mine

oh his words how they hurt me, I'll never forget it
and as the time, it went by, I lived to regret it

You're no son, no son of mine
but where should I go,
and what should I do
you're no son,
no son of mine
but I came here
for help, I came
here for you

Well the years they
passed slowly
I thought about
him every day
what would I do,
if we passed
on the street
would I keep
running away

in and out of hiding places
soon I'd have to face the facts
we'd have to sit down and talk it over
and that would mean going back

they say time is a healer
and now my wounds are not the same
I rang the bell with my heart in my mouth
I had to hear what he'd say

He sat me down to talk to me
he looked me straight in the eyes

he said:

You're no son of mine
...

(Phil Collins and Genesis)

3. Read the lyrics, and fill in the gaps in your understanding of the song.
4. Did the son want to be re-united with his family? What details tell you this?
5. a) Why do you think the father reacted as he did?
   b) What do you think of the father's behaviour?
▷ 6. With a partner or in a group:
   a) Work out how else the story could have ended.
   b) Make four short sentences for a new final verse.

Word module p. 52, ex. 2

Understanding a song

45

THE GENERATION GAME

4 They'll be sorry

They'll be sorry some day.
I'll become a universe-famous actress, win an
Oscar, and tell the world that my parents
deserve absolutely no thanks at all.

5 Then when I have kids, I'll tell the children
that their grandparents were eaten by aliens,
even if my parents are still alive.
I'll fall into a moon crater and die, and everyone will blame my parents.

10 It's no use.
It's just no use.
Sitting on my bed, I look around my room. All
the posters are off the wall, to be stored for the
five years that we will be away. By the time we

15 come back, most of the groups won't even be
popular any more.
I also can't take all my clothes with me. Two
bags each – that's all we can take to the moon.
New moon clothes will be given to us when we

20 get there. I've given most of my clothes to Juna,
who has promised to wear some of my things
each day, so that part of me is at Alan Shepard
High School as long as my class is there.
I've cried so much in the past few days.

25 The tears start again.
There's a knock at the door.
'Aurora, our guests are arriving. I want you to
come downstairs.' It's my father.
'Go away,' I shout. 'I'm not going to a party to

30 celebrate going away from a place that I don't
want to leave.'
He opens the door and comes in.
I pretend that he's not there.

'Aurora.' He moves my hair from in front of my

35 eyes. 'Honey, believe us. We don't want you to
be so unhappy.'
'If you didn't want me to be so unhappy, you
wouldn't move just when I've started a new
school and love it,' I cry.

40 'We've been through this already, so many
times. It's such an honour for Mom and me
to be chosen to go to the moon to do our
research.'
I feel as if my heart is going to break. Maybe
my mother should do a transplant on me and   45
put in a new heart.

'We only want what's best for all of us. Surely
you understand that.'
'Not best for all of us – *you*! Daddy, please let
me stay here.'   50

'No.' He frowns. 'Remember the first time you
stayed overnight at Juna's. You were so homesick that we had to pick you up at three
o'clock in the morning – you, your teddy bear,
and your blanket.'   55
'Daddy, I was six years old,' I remind him. 'I've
stayed over at Juna's house a million times
since then. I don't take my teddy bear with me
any more, and my blanket fell to pieces years
ago. And I promise you, I'm not going to call   60
you to pick me up to take me to the moon.'
He stands up. 'We understand how hard this is
for you. Don't think that we don't. However,
all things considered, we are going to the moon
as a family – because we are a family.'   65

Five years. Even a year seems like an eternity.

'Daddy, please.'
He shakes his head sadly. 'Honey, be sensible.
There are guests downstairs. Take ten minutes,
then join us.'   70

After he leaves, for fifteen minutes I think
about possible disasters that could happen to
him that I couldn't be blamed for.
Even though no life as we know it has been
75 discovered in space, I hope that there is such a
thing as a giant lunar lizard. And I hope that it
eats my father – slowly.
After the monster's done with my father, he
can have my mother and sister for dessert.

80 There's a knock on my door.
This time it's my mother.
She comes in and stands there. 'Everyone
wants to see you. Come downstairs right now
and act like a human being. You don't want to
85 spend the whole evening in this room and miss
saying good-bye to everyone. Juna and Matthew and the rest of your friends are downstairs already.'
I stare at her.
90 She's trying to sound calm, but I can tell that
she's not happy. 'It's up to you. It's your choice.
Come down now or stay up here.'
What a choice, I think. Giving in to them and
joining the party as if everything's okay or not
95 having a chance to see my friends one last
time.
I give in. 'I'll go downstairs.'
She smiles. 'That's my girl. And remember, no
long face. You don't want to turn this party in-
100 to a disaster.'
Since I want to be an actress some day, I'll just
pretend that this is all a play.

SCENE 1: THE PARTY
The heroine enters.
…

(from: *This Place has no Atmosphere* by Paula Danziger)

1   Understanding the story
1. Describe Aurora's reaction to moving.
2. What can you learn from the story about
   her relationship to her parents?
3. What details (words, facts) tell you that
   this story is set in the future?
4. Think what two meanings the title of the
   book could have.

2   Moving
It is not uncommon in countries like Britain,
Ireland, the USA, Canada or Australia for
people to move house, and children to
change schools or go to a new town or city.
Aurora loves her new school but not everybody does in her situation.
Discuss the pros and cons for the whole
family of moving. You could start like this:
"In my opinion moving to a new place
could be quite exciting. For example, you
might meet lots of new people."
(Look again at 'Strategy Page: Informal
discussion' for useful language.)

3   Creative Writing
Imagine you are an author. You have had
this great idea for the beginning of a story,
but now you are stuck.
Either: Develop a story outline for how the
story could continue;
Or: Develop a dialogue between Aurora
and her friends at her farewell party.

The characters:
Aurora: likes Pluto.
Pluto: a computer freak; not interested in
girls, but very interested in the moon.
Juna: Aurora's best friend; likes Pluto too;
is looking forward to wearing Aurora's
clothes while she is away.
Matthew: wants to borrow Aurora's
collection of 'real books' while she is
away, but is afraid to ask directly.

Lang. module p. 50/51

〈Further reading p. 87〉

Reading and continuing
a narrative

47

THE GENERATION GAME

A Paul's 'holiday'

Paul and his friend went to a big open-air pop-concert near London a week ago. They camped in a friend's garden for a couple of nights, and then they moved on. Since then they have 'forgotten' to phone home.

Paul's mother: I do hope Paul is all right. He may be in trouble, or he may need help.

Paul's sister: Come on, Mum. He might arrive home any time and say "What are you worrying about?"

Paul's dad: He has always loved camping. Remember how we all used to go away in the caravan at the weekends.

Mother: And he and his sister sometimes used to sleep in a tent next to the caravan.

Dad: But if there was a funny noise in the night, they would rush into the caravan.

Sister: Dad! That was years ago! We aren't little any more! Parents!

Mother: We could phone that programme on TV where they try to find people that are missing.

Sister: Oh, Mum. You do exaggerate. Paul isn't missing, he's having a holiday!

1 Have you ever experienced or heard about a situation like this? Do you think the parents are right or wrong to worry, and why? What do you think of Paul?

2 a) Use your imagination, and make six suggestions for where the boys may be.　　　　G1
Example: They may be on their way home.
On the other hand, they may not have any money!
b) If the suggestions you made in part a) were true, what problems might the boys have, and what good things might happen to them?
It might rain … / They might … / Someone might … / Their tent might …

3 a) Things, and people, change. Paul used to go on holiday with his parents, but now he　　　G1
sometimes goes away with friends.
Think about your own life, or the life of someone you know.
How has it changed? How have you or has the person changed?
Start like this: I/he/she used to … but now …
b) Imagine how Lesley, the runaway girl, changed.

4 a) Look again at (and listen to) what Paul's mother says in the first line of the dialogue. Try to　　G1
feel what the difference is between 'I hope Paul is all right' and 'I do hope Paul is all right'.
b) What can **you** say in these situations to express strong feelings?
1. You are waiting for a phone call.
2. You have just done a test at school.
3. A friend has just been taken into hospital.
4. A friend has got a new hair style.
5. You want to go to a concert, but you haven't got a ticket.

I do feel sorry for …
I do hope …
I do like …
I do think …

Using 'emphatic do', may, might, used to and could

48

G10

5 Young people have a very good idea of what they need to change in their lives, as these Top Ten New Year's Resolutions from a British newspaper show.

a) Compare the resolutions.

Example: More/fewer girls want to … than boys.

Or: The boys think it's more important to … than the girls.

b) Paul's sister said to their parents, "You know, you got on Paul's nerves with your good advice all the time." What kind of things do you think the parents said to Paul? Use the 'Resolutions' for ideas, and write down eight pieces of 'parents' good advice'.

Example: If you stopped smoking, you might have more money for other things.

Boys	Girls
1 Stop smoking	1 Save money
2 Save money	2 Stop smoking
3 Work harder	3 Stop biting nails
4 Do well in exams	4 Work harder
5 Waste less money	5 Do better at school
6 Do better at school	6 Eat less
7 Respect people more	7 Waste less money
8 Stop biting nails	8 Be more tidy
9 Stop drinking	9 Do well in exams
10 Eat less	10 Get a job

(from: *The Times*)

6 Ask a friend to choose two resolutions. Give him or her six pieces of advice (which needn't be serious!).   G10

For example, your friends would like to get a job at the weekends.

You say: "You could get a job at the zoo – they're looking for someone to play with the monkeys. You'd be great!"

7 a) Try to explain the differences between the two lists of resolutions.
  – What surprises you about the list?
  – Which of these resolutions wouldn't you expect on such a list in your country?
  – What is perhaps missing?

b) Decide on 13 – 15 resolutions for **your** class and make an (anonymous) survey of your class's Top Ten resolutions.

▷ **8** *Either:* Imagine what happens when Paul comes home. Write the dialogue.
  Or: Write the letter that Paul might send to his family. (Try to include examples of 'emphatic *do*', *may, might, used to* and *could*, somewhere in your texts.)

9 Find a good title for the poem.

Some day	Some night	Some night.
I may	I might	Some day.
Pack my bag and run away.	Slip away in the moonlight.	I might.
Some day	I might.	I may.
I may.	Some night.	– But right now I think I'll stay.
– But not today.	– But not tonight.	

John Ciardi

Using auxiliary verbs

49

THE GENERATION GAME

B Revision: Reporting what others have said

It's very useful to be able to report properly what other people have said, as you can see from these situations.

Imagine you are staying with the family of your exchange partner in Wales. (The British school holidays haven't begun yet.)

───── TIP ─────   G1
Before you start, check
that you know the rules
for indirect speech, and
collect verbs like 'to say'.

 1 On the first day some of the neighbours talk to you.

> We had an Austrian girl here last year. She liked it very much.

> We usually go to the seaside on Saturdays. You can come with us if you like.

> It's great to have you here. I'll be able to ask you questions for my German project.

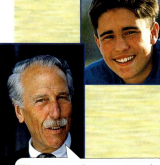

> We can get German TV via satellite. I watched Dortmund versus Hamburg last week.

> You'll find it a bit difficult at first, but you'll soon be able to understand everything.

> You must come down to the Youth Activity Centre. I'm in charge of the computer club.

Tell your exchange partner what they said.
Start like this: "A boy told me that they had had an Austrian girl here last year. He said she had liked it very much. …"

2 a) You go to school with your exchange partner. The class tutor asks you some questions.   G14
  "Did you travel by yourself?"   "Have you done any French?"
  "How long did the journey take?"   "What's your best subject?"
  "When did your school go on holiday?"   "Has Peter organized books for you?"
  "Have you been to Britain before?"   "What teachers have you met?"
  "How long have you been learning   "Will you need a report for your school?"
   English?"   "Do you want to have school dinners?"

  Your exchange partner wants to know what the tutor asked.
  What do you say? Check the rules for indirect questions.
  Start like this: She asked me if I had travelled by myself and she wanted to know how long the journey had taken.

▷ b) Make a role play of the interview with a partner, adding your own answers. Then report the questions and the answers.

3 At the Youth Activity Centre in the evening, some of the youth leaders talk to you.

1. "Your English is very good. How long have you been learning English?"
2. "We're looking for more people for the band. I've heard that you play an instrument. What do you play?"
3. "I've read that many people can only do Maths in their own language. Can you do Maths in English?"
4. "I'm taking one of my groups to the Black Forest. Is that near where you live?"
5. "We're designing a wall picture for the hall. Can you help us?"

Your exchange partner's parents asked you what the different people said.
Start like this: "One of the leaders said that my English was very good.
He wanted to know how long I had been learning English. Another said, …"

4 One day you are home after school, but Alan, your exchange partner, isn't back yet, because **G15**
he's at football practice. The telephone rings. It's your partner's mother, Mrs Griffiths.

a) Listen to the telephone call and make notes on the instructions she gives you. Check with a partner. Have you forgotten anything?

b) Pass the instructions on to Alan, using your notes. Start like this: "Your mum phoned. She's at your grandma's. She told us to take two pizzas …"

> When you report these instructions or imperatives, use:
> She told/asked/wanted us to … She told/asked us not to … She didn't want us to …

5 On another day you have to travel by yourself to Bangor to meet a friend. You are a bit worried that you might get on the wrong bus, and the night before, you have this dream.

You: Does this bus go to Bangor?
Bus driver: No, it has just come from Bangor.
You: Well, how can I get there?
Bus driver: Ask that woman over there. She's the pilot of a hot air balloon.
You: Excuse me, can you fly me to Bangor?
Woman: Climb in and sit down.
You: How much does it cost?
Woman: A song.
You: I don't understand.
Woman: It will cost you a song, a Welsh song.
You: But I don't know any Welsh songs.
    Will a German song do?
Woman: Yes, but don't stop singing, or we'll fall to the ground.

The balloon lifts off and you start to sing, but you can't remember the second verse of the song and the balloon starts to fall, fall, fall …

a) At breakfast the next day, you tell the dream to Mrs Griffiths.
Start like this: "I had a funny dream last night. I asked a bus driver if the bus went to Bangor, but he replied that …

▷ b) Make a funny dream conversation of your own. Then tell it to a partner. ⟨Further reading p. 88⟩

Revising indirect speech

51

THE GENERATION GAME

A Describing people

1 a) Collect the adjectives from 'My sister is a runaway' (p. 42) which describe how people feel.

b) Choose six of them, and say when you might feel that way.
   Example: I would feel unhappy if …

c) Say how you would feel if your brother or sister ran away from home, and why?
   How would you feel when he or she came home? What would you say to him or her?

2 Think back to the song 'No son of mine' (p. 45).
Pick out five adjectives from the list on the right and say why
they are or are not suitable to describe the way the son feels
when he returns home.

> angry – brave – stupid
> afraid – sensible – confident
> selfish – unsure – unhappy
> excited – confused

3 Creative writing: octopoems

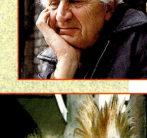

I know someone
who is grey
A lemon that has been
squeezed dry
A cup without a handle
Yesterday's cocoa
The stairs to the cellar
A single sock
at the back of the shelf
A misty day
An old dog

I know someone
who is butter yellow
A lemon
with honey
A china cup
of mint tea
A spiral staircase
A silk scarf
blowing in
a spring breeze
A young cat

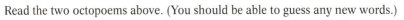

Read the two octopoems above. (You should be able to guess any new words.)

The people in the poems are described/characterized by a word from these **eight categories**:
drinks, weather, fruit, animals, clothing, things in the kitchen, colours, places in the house.

a) Put these categories in the order they
   appear in these octopoems.

b) Look at the ways you can add to the
   words from the categories (e. g. grey/butter
   yellow), or link two categories
   (a china **cup** of mint **tea**).

c) Write your own octopoem.

> Before you start:
> – agree in class on the categories.
> Perhaps you would like to change
> some of them (e. g. months,
> buildings, games …)
> Perhaps make a class octopoem
> collection.

TOPIC 3

B Your potential vocabulary

1 You know more words than you think!
Recognizing prefixes and suffixes is a simple way to
widen your vocabulary, and to understand many more
words. This is called your 'potential vocabulary'.

> – impolite – uninvited
> – discoloured – uncomfortable
> – dissimilar – inexpensive
> – impossible – incomplete

a) These words are all opposites of adjectives you already
know. Look at them, and then make a note of the
prefixes that give a word its opposite meaning.

b) Here are eight example sentences or definitions from an English-English dictionary. Which
word from the list above matches which sentence?
1. People who aren't like each other at all are … .
2. A chair in which you can't sit for long is … .
3. Guests who nobody asked to come are … .
4. A person who often interrupts other people is … .
5. There were two blue socks in the washing machine with the white things, so now the
white things are … .
6. Things which don't cost much are … .
7. A book with some pages missing is … .
8. Something which can't be done is … .

c) Start a file page for prefixes and collect more examples of words with these prefixes and
also new prefixes as you meet them.

2 You should be able to understand these
words. They are all adjectives from words
you know.

> foggy – unpopular – useless – helpful
> – childish – inexcusable – mysterious
> – irreplaceable – imperfect – dishonest
> – unimaginable – monthly – daily
> – changeable

"And tomorrow we can
expect another
sunnycloudyrainyfoggyicysnowy
day."

a) Choose eight adjectives and make example
sentences or definitions as in exercise 1b.
b) Use your sentences to test a partner.

3 Look at the vocabulary section for 'The Generation Game' at the back of the book. Choose
three or four of the words and look them up in a proper dictionary. (Each pupil chooses 3 or 4
different words.) Then make a list of all the words that belong to the word family of these
words. Can you think of ways to connect any of these words, e.g. mind map?

(Further reading p. 89)

Suffixes and prefixes

1 Animal rights and wrongs

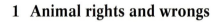

Some people get their kicks from hunting and shooting wild animals. Others like to stare at them imprisoned in zoos and circuses. And amazingly, some people still think that wearing fur is glamorous. Millions of animals are trapped for their fur and millions more are bred on fur farms, like this beautiful wild fox.

Millions of animals are kept behind bars and in dark cramped sheds. They can't feel fresh air, have no freedom to move around and suffer a cruel early death in the slaughterhouse.

Some animals are loved and cared for but many others – like this half-drowned kitten – are cruelly treated and abandoned.

PAUSE FOR
THOUGHT

- If you were writing a list of rights for animals, what would it include?
- In what ways should animal rights differ from human rights?
- From your own experience, what evidence is there that animals have feelings?

TOPIC 4

a) Describe your feelings when you look at the pairs of photos in the Animal Aid leaflet.

> **Useful expressions**
>
> It makes me feel angry/helpless …
> I find … shocking/disgusting/disturbing …

D b) Like the photos, the language shows a contrast. Pick out words or phrases which show this contrast.

c) Write a short text for the pair of photos on the right (from the same leaflet). These words may help you:

experiment – laboratory – research

(If you need to look up more new words in a German-English dictionary, check out the advice on page 64.)

▷ d) Suggestion for an 'afternoon chat show': List the different ways in which people use (and abuse) animals.
Which things on your list do you think are or aren't acceptable? Explain why. What can people do if they want to be 'animal friendly'?

▷ **2 The Battery Hen.**

This poem is written in a country dialect, so you will find unusual verb endings and other strange forms in the poem. Watch out for the word order, too.

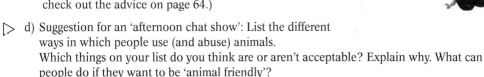

Oh, I am a battery hen,
On me back there's not a germ[1],
I never scratched[2] a farmyard,
And I never pecked[3] a worm[4].
5 I never had the sunshine
To warm me feathers[5] through.
Eggs I lay[6]. Every day,
For the likes of[7] you.
…

10 I might have been a farmyard hen,
Scratchin' in the sun,
There might have been a crowd of chicks[8]
After me to run.
There might have been a cockerel[9] fine
15 To pay us his respects[10],
Instead of sittin' here,
Till someone comes and wrings[11] our necks.

I see the Time and Motion[12] clock
Is sayin' nearly noon[13].
20 I 'spec[14] me squirt[15] of water
Will come flyin' at me soon,
And then me spray[16] of pellets[17]
Will nearly break me leg,
And I'll bite the wire nettin'[18]
25 And lay one more bloody egg.

                  Pam Ayres

1. Use details from the poem to compare the life of a battery hen with the life of a farmyard hen.
2. Discuss whether you think it is good to write a 'humorous' poem about a topic like this.

> 1. Keim, Krankheitserreger 2. scharren
> 3. picken 4. Wurm 5. Feder 6. legen
> 7. so jemand wie 8. Küken 9. junger
> Hahn 10. jmd. seine Aufwartung machen
> 11. (Hals) umdrehen 12. Effizienzprü-
> fung 13. Mittag 14. (ich) erwarte
> 15. Spritzer 16. geworfene Ration
> 17. Kügelchen 18. Maschendraht

Discussing animal abuse/use of humour

THE WORLD AROUND US

Strategy Page: A class debate

In a typical debate
– the chairperson introduces the topic and asks the speakers to give their statements;
– the first speaker gives a prepared statement in favour of the topic;
– the second speaker gives a prepared statement against the topic;
– then members of the audience can put up their hands to speak (the chairperson keeps order);
– the chairperson organizes a vote.

Prepare for a class debate on the topic: **'We should all become vegetarian.'**

1. **Collect useful language.**
   Look at the following expressions. Think what other things different people might want to say, and add more expressions of your own. (The Strategy Page 'Informal discussion' on page 44 might help.)

   Useful expressions

   Chairperson: **Opening**: Our topic for discussion is … This is a very interesting/contro-versial topic which … I would like to call on … to speak in favour of/against the topic.
   Keeping order: *(Your ideas!)*
   Organizing a vote: Would all those in favour of/against the topic please put up their hands? Please write 'for' or 'against' on a piece of paper, and put it …

   Speakers: The first point I would like to make is … Many people are of the opinion that … but …/It is an impossible situation that …

   Members of the audience: I'd like to say that … You must admit that … The point made by the first/second … speaker …

2. **Collect material.**
   a) Sort the statements on the right into those made by vegetarians and those made by meat-eaters.
   b) Try to think of more ideas for or against, and make notes.
   c) Read the Fact Box. Is it the same in your country? Where can you find out more about the topic?

   – 'It's natural to eat meat. Animals kill and eat each other.'
   – 'Eating dead bodies is disgusting!'
   – 'Producing meat wastes crops that could feed a lot of people.'
   – 'Not all farms are factory farms.'
   – 'It's cruel to kill animals.'
   – 'Meat is the best way to get the iron you need in your diet.'
   – 'Some people are too sentimental about animals.'
   – 'Animal farming pollutes the environment.'

   FACT BOX

   • There are over 3 million vegetarians in the UK – about 4.5 % of the population.
   • Around 12 % of young people are vegetarian and 24 % of teenage girls no longer eat red meat.
   • Every week 2,000 more people give up meat.

3. **Prepare your statement.**
   a) Decide if you want to speak for or against the topic, and make notes in support of your opinion.
   b) Prepare a short statement of about two minutes, giving your ideas, reasons and examples.

4. **Hold a class debate.**

Lang. module p. 60

3 Boiling 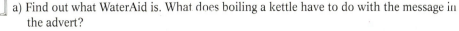 a kettle

a) Find out what WaterAid is. What does boiling a kettle have to do with the message in the advert?

b) Start a 'water' page for your file.

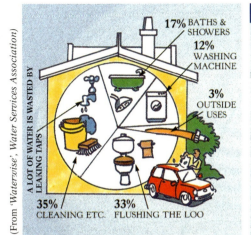

17% BATHS & SHOWERS
12% WASHING MACHINE
3% OUTSIDE USES
35% CLEANING ETC.
33% FLUSHING THE LOO

(From 'Watervise', Water Services Association)
A LOT OF WATER IS WASTED BY LEAKING TAPS

Water Aid

A simple solution for the most basic of needs

In the time it takes to boil a kettle, 30 children will die from unclean water. Here in the UK, putting on the kettle is a routine part of our daily lives. Yet for many people in the Third World, an unclean water supply, nowhere to wash, and no proper toilet frequently brings illness to a family – and can, tragically, cause the death of children.

WaterAid works with local people in Africa and Asia, helping them to dig wells, lay pipe-lines and construct water tanks. Already, WaterAid has helped to bring safe water and sanitation to three million people in the Third World. Any donation you are able to give – no matter how small – will help make a real and lasting difference to the lives of many more.

c) Make a list of all the different things we use water for. Which uses would you describe as a 'basic need'? Explain.

d) Listen to part of a news programme. Note the problems mentioned and compare them with the situation where you live.

e) Make a 'save water' poster. (You can work with a partner.)

f) Look at the pictures below. How many power sources do you recognize? Think about how power is produced in your area/in other parts of your country/in other countries.

– Say what you know about the advantages and disadvantages of different kinds of power. (If you don't know the words in English, look them up.)
– Explain what kind of power you would choose to use in your home, and why.

Useful expressions

hydro-electric power

fossil fuels

wind turbine

nuclear power

solar energy

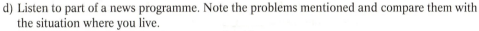

Discussing ecological problems

57

Lang. module p. 61–63

⟨Further reading p. 90⟩

THE WORLD AROUND US

 4 No other choice

This story is based on true events. The names of the people have been changed.

A frightening Moment

It was a clear, icy evening in February when they first saw it.

As usual after school, Ricky Benson had gone out to help his father Bill in the meadows on their
5 Wyoming ranch. Even in winter he loved the feeling of freedom that came from being out in the open air.

Now darkness had fallen. While Ricky and Bill were riding home together in the moonlight a
10 group of cattle on the other side of the meadow suddenly split up and started to run.

'What scared them?' Bill wondered. 'Look! It can't be – it is – it's a wolf!'

They stopped and watched as the animal moved
15 easily across the frozen snow, finally disappearing into the shadows of the Wind River Mountains.

'Awesome,' said Ricky quietly.

'Yes, awesome. And dangerous.' Bill's voice was serious. 'The cattle are right to be afraid.'
20 'But we don't have wolves here. Where has it come from?' Ricky wanted to know.

Bill thought for a minute. 'There's only one possible answer to that question,' he said.

* * * *

The next morning Bill made a telephone call to
25 Yellowstone National Park.

Like most Americans, Bill had heard about the program to bring back wolves into their natural environment in Yellowstone. The project had been welcomed enthusiastically by environmental
30 groups and nature lovers. Already millions of people had traveled to north-western Wyoming in the hope of seeing one of these legendary animals. At this point there were more than forty wolves moving around freely in the park, and plans were
35 being made for more packs in the surrounding area. The Benson ranch was a long way from Yellowstone, but Bill knew that a hungry wolf can travel far. When he told an official he had seen a wolf on his land, however, the official just laughed.
40 'You're 125 miles south of here, you say? Don't worry, there's no wolf down there. We use radio collars to keep a check on where the packs are,

you see. No, it couldn't have been a wolf you saw.' 'I know exactly what I saw,' answered Bill. 'I just hope I don't have to call you again with more 45 serious news.'

* * * *

On Saturday that same week Ricky discovered several dead sheep on one of the higher meadows. The sight was a shock. They had died a 50 terrible and painful death.

'You were right,' Ricky said when he showed the sheep to his father. 'Wolves are real killers.'

'It's the way wolves are, son. It's not the wolf I'm angry with.' 55

Bill was not surprised by this new development, but he was worried. He could not afford to lose his animals. Like most of the other ranchers in that part of Wyoming he was not a rich man. His grandfather had originally settled in the area, and 60 the land had passed from son to son. It had become hard enough for ranchers to survive in the modern world even without new problems. Some of his neighbors had already had to sell their land. Their ranches had been replaced by 65 new homes for 'modern cowboys' – young city people with jobs they could do at the end of a telephone line.

When they got back to the ranchhouse Bill phoned Yellowstone again. 'One of your wolves is 70 killing sheep on my land,' he complained. 'I want to know what you're going to do about it.'

The official still did not believe that a wolf could be so far from Yellowstone. 'I'm sorry about your sheep,' he answered. 'But it has nothing to do 75 with us. Talk to your neighbor – maybe his dog got hungry.'

'My nearest neighbor's dog is a chihuahua!' Bill threw down the telephone angrily.

'There are laws to protect wolves', he told Ricky. 80 'But what about our right to protect our animals? I'm as keen on the environment as anybody, but with this wolf program, the problem is going to get worse, not better.'

'Is there nothing we can do?' asked Ricky.

'There's only one thing we can do. We have no 85 other choice.'

* * * *

At first light the next morning, Bill and Ricky got out the snowmobile. In winter it was the
90 easiest form of transport across the countryside. They had to be prepared to travel fast and far that day. It was a grey morning. The air was cold on their faces as they drove out to the edge of the ranch, near the meadow where the sheep had
95 been killed. They followed the fence round until they found the place where the wolf had broken through the barbed wire.

'There!' Ricky pointed to fresh tracks in the snow. 'It must have come in again last night. Do you think it's still on the ranch?'

'No. Look. Here are some more tracks that lead 100 away again. Come on, Ricky. This might be the best chance we'll have.' Bill stopped for a moment and looked up at the grey sky. 'Unless it snows again,' he added.

They opened up the fence so that they could drive 105 the snowmobile through. Then they moved on as fast as they could, under the snowclouds, following the wolf's tracks away from the meadows towards the mountains. At last they entered a long valley where the snow was deeper 110 on the ground.

'This will slow it down,' said Ricky.

He was right. Long before they could see it the wolf knew they were there. It knew it was in danger and tried to run more quickly. But with 115 each step it sank down into the soft snow and had to pull itself out again. All the time it could hear the snowmobile coming nearer. At the same time the sky was becoming heavier and heavier.

* * * *

At the end of the valley they finally caught up 120 with the wolf. Bill stopped the snowmobile a short way behind. The tired animal turned, but they could see it had no energy left to attack.

'Do it clean, Dad,' Ricky said.

'As clean as I can, son.' 125

Bill picked up the gun and aimed carefully. He shot once, and the wolf was dead.

As they covered it with rocks the snow began to fall.

1. What is your first reaction to the story?

2. The story has five parts. Look at how the first three parts of the story are developed.
   How does the first sentence in each part try to make the reader interested, or carry the story along?
   Comment on the last sentence in the first four parts.

3. Discuss how you think Bill feels when he kills the wolf, and why.

4. Think about the title of the story. Was there really no other choice, or what else could Ricky and Bill have done? Collect ideas.

5. a) Look at how the author chooses to end the story in the fifth part. How do you feel about this ending – does it leave you feeling happy or sad?
   b) Write an alternative ending. Start after the first sentence of the last paragraph.

6. Have a discussion about the wolf project. Divide yourselves into 2 groups – an environmental group and a group of ranchers. Try to find a solution which the two groups can agree on.

Discussing the structure and contents of a story

59

THE WORLD AROUND US

A Revision: Protest action

1 Match the sentences below to the newspaper headlines. Then put the information in the right order, and sum up what happened.

Protesters set up camp in forest

Route of new road changed

Plans for road through forest

A 'If these plans aren't changed, the road will spoil the forest.'

2 'We wouldn't leave this forest even if you paid us a million pounds!'

3 'If we hadn't taken action, they wouldn't have changed the route.'

2 a) What did these people predict when they first heard about the plans for the new road?   **G16**
(Not everybody was against the plans.) Use the ideas from the boxes below.
Start: 1. If some of the trees are cut down, a lot of birds will disappear.
1. Birdwatcher   2. Unemployed man   3. Farmer in the area   4. Woman who works on the other side of the forest.   5. Local garage owner   6. Family with dog

IF		
I/be able to drive through the forest		I/lose some of my land
workers/be needed		a lot of birds/disappear
we/take Prince for a walk in the forest		my journey to work/not take so long
the new road/cut through my farm		my business/grow
some of the trees/be cut down		I/have the chance of a job
more cars/stop at my garage		he/not be able to run around safely

b) Develop the thoughts of these people further and make more possible predictions.
Example: 1. If the birds disappear, this will have an effect on the other wildlife in the area.

3 Think how you can start or end these people's speculations.
1. If we built more and more roads, ...   2. ... there would be a traffic jam all over the country.
3. If nobody had a car, ...   4. If I had to cycle everywhere, ...   5. ... people could drive around in an environmentally friendly way.   6. ... we wouldn't need cars.   7. If someone gave me a sports car for my eighteenth birthday, ...
Example: 1. If we built more and more roads, the countryside would disappear.

4 Would you have done the same as these people? Explain why or why not.
1. 'When I saw a group of protesters outside a fast food restaurant I *joined* them.'
2. 'A friend invited me to the circus, but I *said* no.'
3. 'A woman was collecting money for Greenpeace. I *gave* her everything I had in my purse.'
4. 'When the trucks carrying nuclear waste arrived, I *sat down* in the road to stop them.'
5. 'I needed some suncream. But before I bought it, I *checked* that animals weren't used to test it.'
6. 'I *kicked* a policeman who was trying to push me away during an animals rights demonstration.'
7. 'I saw a woman in a fur coat. I *felt* so angry about it that I *threw* an egg at her.'
Example: 1. "I would have joined the protesters. Fast food helps to destroy the rainforests."
or: "I wouldn't have joined them. I love hamburgers."

B1 Giving additional information

1 a) Read these two sentences. Think of more pressure groups in your country.

> Friends of the Earth is one of the pressure groups which protect the environment.
> Greenpeace, which is a famous pressure group, takes action all over the world.

G17

b) Now read the sentences again, but <u>without</u> the relative clauses. Does each sentence still make sense? Try to explain why or why not.

2 Here is the draft of part of a letter from Sam, a British boy, to his German pen-friend Thomas. Write out the letter, adding the extra information to the right words in the sentences.
Start: 1. In 1995 Shell, which is a big oil company, was at the …

TIP

In non-defining relative clauses you always need a relative pronoun:
– *who* for people
– *which* for things

---

1. In 1995 Shell was at the centre of an environmental argument.
2. It wanted to dump the Brent Spar oil platform in the Atlantic Ocean.
3. Greenpeace members decided to take action.
4. They said that the platform's tanks would pollute the sea.
5. So four activists went on board the Brent Spar.
6. The police could not stop them.
7. In the end public opinion made Shell change its plans.

The police were in boats around the platform.

The platform was no longer needed.

Shell is a big oil company.

Public opinion supported Greenpeace.

The activists were lowered from the air.

The members of Greenpeace were against Shell's plans.

The tanks were possibly full of waste.

3 a) How are the 'which' clauses in the following sentences from Sam's letter different from the other 'which' clauses on this page? Think how you can translate 'which' in these sentences into German.

> I want to try to save the environment for the future, which is why I joined Friends of the Earth. We often raise money, which can be fun.

b) Use 'which' clauses to add suitable comments to these sentences from Sam's letter.
Example: 1. … which makes it more than 30 years old.
or: … which not many people know.

1. Friends of the Earth was formed in the USA in 1969, which …
2. It informs people about environmental problems, …
3. But it always tries to protest peacefully, …
4. All kinds of people belong to Friends of the Earth, …
5. Running a pressure group isn't cheap, …
6. I once cycled 100 miles to raise money, …
7. At least I'm doing something to help, …

Using non-defining relative clauses

61

⟨Further reading p. 91⟩

THE WORLD AROUND US

B2 In the neighbourhood

Sue and John don't worry about the environment, but their neighbour Mike is very 'green' …

Sue: Look at that old truck parked next door. Mike is having horse manure delivered.
John: It's for his vegetable garden. He was telling me the other day that vegetables grown naturally
are good for your health.
Sue: Good for your health? The smell produced by all that manure will make me ill!

1 Think what Mike would say about the effect of different things on the environment. Make
sentences with past participles. Finish the comments yourself.
Example: Energy *produced* by solar power is clean.

G18

magazines – print on recycled paper
lights – leave on in empty rooms
drinks – sell in plastic/glass bottles
cars – use for short journeys
hamburgers – make from rainforest meat
energy – produce by solar/nuclear power

It's often more elegant to shorten relative clauses
with passive verbs. Just use the past participle.
Vegetables (that are) **grown** naturally …

newspapers – throw out with the rubbish
…

2 a)
When you can't do the job
Or the job isn't fun
Just call on us for help –
You can have the job done!

– When do you use 'have + object + past participle'? G19
– What structure do you use in your own language?
– Explain the difference between these two sentences:
I had the job done. – I had done the job.

b) Read the environment ads in the neighbourhood newsletter. Find out what you can have done.
Start: You can have your tap fixed. You can have horse manure …

**Don't waste water.
I can fix your tap.
Call me on 698124.**

Best horse manure
– we'll deliver it to
your door!
Phone 981784.

**The Scouts collect old
newspapers for
recycling. Tel: 226014.**

Did you know that
dumping fridges with
CFCs damages the
ozone layer? We'll take
away your old fridge
instead. Tel: 604310.

**Invite nature into
your garden. I'll make
a pond for you.
Nick: 262901.**

We repair your roof –
you save heat and
money!
Phone 593244.

**(If you would

like us to print

your ad, please

contact Pip on

764313.)**

3 Imagine you have the power – and the money! – to give orders for work to be done in your
school or in your neighbourhood. Describe what you want to have done to make a more
pleasant environment. You can work with a partner or in a group.
You can start: – We/I want to have more trees planted
– We/I would like to see …

clean up the graffiti/rubbish – repair old fences/walls – build a cycle path – plant trees/
flowers – put in bigger windows – make a pond – …

4 Explain who makes these statements – Mike, Sue or John? Guess what or who they are talking about. G20

   1. 'It neither looks nor smells nice!'

   2. 'Either cooked or uncooked – they're very good for you.'

   3. 'He can be a pain in the neck sometimes, but actually both John and I like him a lot.'

   4. 'Neither Sue nor I would like to be without it. I mean, how would we get around?'

   5. 'I would go to the office on it, but it's both hard work and unsuitable for skirts – so I don't.'

   6. 'Their lifestyle is neither healthy nor environmentally friendly – but they're nice people!'

5 a) Which words on the right go together? Make three pairs. (The statements above can help you.) Can you translate them? G20

both	nor	and
or	either	neither

   b) Link the ideas below with the pairs you made in a). Make up your own sentences.

   1. air pollution/noise   2. cycling/walking   3. drive to work/go by bus   4. graffiti/rubbish

   5. use/waste less energy   6. glass/paper   7. fish/meat   8. you/I

   Example: 1. Bicycles cause neither air pollution nor noise.
       or: Both air pollution and noise can be a problem in big cities.

6 a) Listen to the recording. Sue, John and Mike are talking over the garden fence. Note down the words they use when they agree or they want to say that someone is in a similar situation. G20

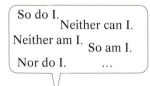

So are we.
Neither…

   b) Listen again. Check if the phrases on your list follow a sentence with a positive verb or a negative verb. Find the rule about when you use 'So …' and when you use 'Neither/Nor …'

7 Work with a partner. Make little dialogues agreeing or disagreeing and adding comments.
   Example: 'I don't like fish.' – 'Neither do I. Just the smell of it makes me feel sick!'
                /'I do. It's good for you, too.'

Start with a statement like this: *If it's the same with you:*   *If it's different with you:*

– I don't like fish.
– I'm a vegetarian.
– I can't cook very well.
– I try to save water.
– I'm not environmentally friendly.
– I never use plastic bags.
– …

So do I.
   Neither can I.
Neither am I.
   So am I.
Nor do I.   …

I don't.   I am.
I can.   I do.
I'm not.   …

8 Can you find the German version of the following and explain what these sayings mean?

| … neither fish nor fowl. | Neither a borrower nor a lender be. | You either sink or swim. |

Using '(n)either/(n)or'

63

〈Further reading p. 92〉

THE WORLD AROUND US

Strategy Page: **Working with a dictionary**

A school in Nottingham has a computer link with a partner school in Karlsruhe …

D 1 Read the message below from an English pupil. These suggestions will help you to look up the new words in an English-German dictionary.
- If you can't find 'independent-minded', look up the two parts of the word separately.
- You probably won't find 'unbothered', so think how the word is formed and look up the main part of the word.
- Your dictionary will explain 'nanny', but you will have to think what it means in the context of 'nanny state' yourself.

> I am interested to hear what you think of public health warnings. In my opinion independent-minded people neither want nor need to be told what they should or should not eat and do. We should be allowed to live our lives unbothered by the nanny state.

D 2 Put into English some notes which the German pupils made before writing their reply.
Use a German-English dictionary to help you.

a) Check the translation of compound words. (Translating the parts of the word doesn't always give you the correct English.)
- Look at the dictionary extract on the right and comment on the English for '*gesunder Menschenverstand*'.
- Use your own dictionary to put the other compounds in the German pupils' notes into English.

b) Check how to use phrases with prepositions correctly. Prepositions are often different in English. If the preposition is part of a phrase, look up the 'headword' of the phrase to find the preposition. How would you translate the prepositions in these phrases?

> … *gesunder Menschenverstand* …
> … *Lebensmittelvergiftung* …
> … *hilfreiche Ratschläge* …
> … *gesundheitsschädlicher Lebensstil* …

> … **men-**
> **schen·ver·ach·tend** *adj* inhuman;
> **Men·schen·ver·stand** *m*: gesunder ~ common sense; **Men·schen·wür·de** *f* human dignity
> **Mensch·heit** *f*: die~~ humanity, mankind
> **mensch·lich** *adj* 1.(nicht tierisch) human

> … *abhängig von* …
> … *auf viele Dinge achten* …
> … *meiner Ansicht nach* …
> … *interessieren sich nicht für* …

D 3 How would <u>you</u> reply to the English pupil? Write down your thoughts about public health warnings. Use a dictionary to help you with the words and phrases you need.

— **TIP** —
Always double-check the translations you find. Some words have more than one meaning.

⟨Further reading p. 93⟩

IMAGES

1. Identify as much of the rubbish in the photos as you can, and discuss how it perhaps got into the sea.
2. More than half the planet is covered by water. What do you think of using the sea to get rid of rubbish?
3. How would you feel about swimming in the sea here in the pictures?

Writing about an environmental problem

TOPIC 5 THE EMERALD ISLE

CONTENTS

- Text module:
  A story from modern-day
  Ireland
  Background information
- Language module:
  Gerund or 'to' with infinitive
  Verbs taking gerund and
  infinitive

ONE ONE
FAITH CROWN

1. What ideas or words come to mind when you hear the name Ireland?

2. What impression do you get of Ireland from these pictures? Would you like to visit it? Why or why not?

3. Start a page on Ireland for your file.

THE EMERALD ISLE

 1 Why don't they just go home?

This story is set in Northern Ireland in the time before the 1998 Peace Treaty. Kathleen, 15, lives out in the country – "just the wrong side of the Border", she says. In the school holidays she is expected to help in the house and on the family's small farm. But at least she has a friend over the fields, Ann O'Connor. Ann is from Belfast, but she spends every summer at her uncle's house in the country.

── **TIP** ──
The history facts on page 69 will help you to understand the background.

I'd just had my dinner and finished up doing the dishes with Teresa when Ann O'Connor came over the field. Her mammy and daddy were down from Belfast, and they were taking her for
5 a run, and would I come?
Would I !
Their car was great. It had big soft seats. I didn't know teachers had big cars. Maybe Ann was right, and I should be a teacher. Some hopes!
10 We went over the Border and ended up at Tara, the Hill of the Kings. I know all about it, for I was there before with Sister Attracta in the school bus. If I was a king I wouldn't live at Tara, for it is near nowhere. We went down to
15 the Great Hall of the Kings, which isn't there. All that is there is a big dip in the ground. You have to imagine the walls and the roof. Ann's daddy got excited about it and so did Ann, but I didn't. I can see a big dip in a field any day. Then Ann
20 and I went to the shop, and Ann bought herself a guide book.
'What do you want that for?' I said.
'It's the Hill of Tara,' she said.
'I know it is the Hill of Tara,' I said.
25 'I'm going to read about it,' she said.
I don't know what there was to read about. If it was Paris or someplace like that I might want to read about it.
We drove back over the Border and along up to
30 O'Connor's, where we had our tea. Afterwards we went down by the lake, where James O'Connor and Ann's daddy went over to the old house to have a look through the holes where the windows used to be.
35 'They'd better keep away from it,' I said. 'The soldiers might be there.'
The soldiers sometimes use it as a hidey-hole, where they can watch the Border road, not that you'd see them. They're very clever at getting
40 about the place when they don't want to be seen. Our Teresa almost stepped on one in the lane, one night, and she didn't know who was

the worst scared, herself or the soldier. Mind you, it was the soldier who had the gun.
'Having the soldiers here is a pest,' I said.
Ann didn't say anything.   45
'If we had our United Ireland, there'd be no soldiers,' I said. 'Why don't they just go home? There's no sense in them running round here waiting to get shot at.'
'Och, I don't know,' Ann said.   50
'*What* don't you know?' I said. 'The Brits caused all the trouble. If they would just get out of Ireland we'd have North and South together in one country and it would be fine.'
Ann made a face.   55
'Everybody knows that!' I said.
'Everybody round here,' Ann said. 'That's not everybody. There's a lot of people where I come from who want to stay British.'
'Then they've no sense,' I said.   60
'How do you know?' she said.
'Sure everybody knows it,' I said. 'You ask anybody round here and you'll get the same answer. If we get the British out and have a United Ireland then we'll all be happy.'   65
'It's not as easy as that, Kathleen,' she said. 'If you took a vote on it, you'd lose.'
'If we can't vote them out, we'll blow them out!' I said. Everybody knows Northern Ireland was set up that way at the beginning, so there   70
would be more Protestants in it than us. That's why their Ulster is just six counties, and not the nine counties it used to be. If it was nine counties we'd outvote them. That's the Brits' democracy for you!   75
'*Would you*?' she said. 'Bomb people, I mean?'
'No,' I said. 'I never bombed anybody. But there's them that would.'
'And then you'll all settle down in a banana republic!' she said. 'No jobs, no hope, no   80
money, no prospect but the pub!'
'The British said that that would happen to the Republic. They thought the Irish couldn't run a

country,' I said. 'But we did it. The Republic is
85 no big deal, but it is still in business … and
some of its business is unfinished.'
'The Northern bit,' said Ann, 'The All Ireland
Catholic Holy State!'
That was a real shaker!
90 'Are you *for* the Protestants, then?' I said.
'No,' Ann said.
'Who are you for then?'
'Ordinary people,' she said. 'Not men with big
drums running Catholics out of the shipyard, and
95 not Irish heroes in behind the hedge with their
bombs, waiting to blow other Irishmen to bits.'
I couldn't figure it out at all. You'd think Ann was
a Brit. I *know* James O'Connor is not a Brit, and
James O'Connor is her uncle and her own
00 daddy is his brother. It must be living in Belfast
with the Protestants that does it.
Ann went off and left me, and that was hard to
take. I was thinking about what she said, coming
back round the low field, on the way home.
05 She lives up in Belfast. She knows what it is
like. How could she not know what it is like?
Anybody round here could tell her, anybody at
all. *And* they could tell her the cause of it.

(from: *Starry Night,* by Catherine Sefton)

1. a) Kathleen thinks she lives 'just the wrong
   side of the border'. Why do you think
   she would prefer to live on the other side
   of the border?
   b) Compare how Kathleen and Ann react to
   Tara. What does this tell us about their
   characters?
   c) Summarize Kathleen's opinions about (a)
   British soldiers in Ireland, and (b) the
   idea of a United Ireland. How does Ann
   react to what Kathleen says? (You may
   need to 'read between the lines'.)

▷ 2. In what ways are Kathleen and Ann's
   backgrounds different? How might this
   influence their opinions?

3. a) Explain what you think Ann means when
   she says she is for the 'ordinary people'.
   b) Imagine Ann writes to Kathleen to
   explain her feelings. What do you think
   she would say?

⟨Further Reading p. 94⟩

2 A look at history

- Ireland has a very long history, and
  many historic and prehistoric sites can
  be visited. The Hill of Tara was the
  coronation site of the High Kings
  of Ireland.
- In the 17th century, the English took
  land away from the Catholic Irish and
  'planted' English and Scottish settlers
  there, who were Protestants. The
  Protestants of today are often, though
  not always, descendants of those first
  Protestants.
- Ireland became part of the United
  Kingdom in 1801. Southern Ireland
  (later known as the Republic of
  Ireland or Eire) became an indepen-
  dent country again in 1921. But the
  six counties of Northern Ireland
  (Ulster), which were mainly
  Protestant, remained part of the
  United Kingdom.
- The population of the Republic of
  Ireland is approximately 95%
  Catholic, while the population of
  Northern Ireland is around 60%
  Protestant. The Protestant majority
  wish to stay British, while the
  Catholics would like to see a United
  Ireland.
- Catholics and Protestants in Ulster
  mainly lead separate lives. They often
  live in separate areas, especially in
  Belfast and Derry, and go to different
  schools, clubs or pubs.
- British soldiers were sent to Ulster in
  1968/9 to keep the peace when
  violence broke out between the two
  groups, especially the Catholic IRA
  and the Protestant UVF.
- The peace treaty of 10th. April 1998
  (Good Friday) gave a new start to the
  people of Northern Ireland after years
  of unrest. But a peace process takes
  time, and there have been people on
  both sides who were still willing to
  shoot others and plant bombs.

Discussing characters,
reading historical facts

THE EMERALD ISLE

A Aspects of Ireland

Ireland is supposed to be the only country in Europe to have fewer inhabitants now than in the 19th century. But for the first time in history, more Irish people are said to be
5 returning to Ireland than leaving it. A lot of young Irish people left to find jobs in Europe for a few years. Many of them enjoy working abroad but they are now looking forward to returning to Ireland as more and more
10 European firms decide to build new factories there and the economy continues to improve. There are estimated to be about 70 million people at least partly of Irish descent in the world, and about 42 million of these in the
15 USA. Many Irish people never stop dreaming of returning to Ireland. And if you want to find out how to celebrate like the Irish, then join them anywhere in the world on

St. Patrick's Day (March 17th). How is this possible? Ireland has a long tradition of 20 emigration. For many people in Ireland in the 18th and 19th centuries life was very hard, and many dreamed of making a new life in America or Australia. For a father or eldest son it often meant leaving the family behind 25 until he had earned enough to send money home for boat tickets for the rest of the family. Potatoes were the main food for the many poor people in the country, who depended on having a good potato crop to 30 live. When, in 1845 and again in 1846, the potato crop was hit by disease, people began to starve. Hundreds of thousands sold everything to pay for tickets to America, Australia or England, but over a million died 35 of hunger or disease.

1. Make five or six comments on the information in this text.

> Useful expressions
>
> I didn't realize that …   I'd like to know more about …   I don't find it surprising that …
> I didn't expect that …   I can't believe that …   I had already heard that …

---

2. Strategy box: Grammar and vocabulary   **G21**

1 This text contains many examples of words which are followed by *to* + the infinitive and others which take the gerund.
   1. Pick out such verbs, verb phrases and adjectives, and note them with a short example.
      Example: the Republic of Ireland <u>is supposed to be</u> the only country …
      the <u>only</u> country <u>to</u> have …
   2. Decide how best to organize your examples, and how to learn them.

2 In German you might need a different structure.
   1. Look again at your examples, and think how to say the same thing in German.
   2. Interpret for a German speaker and an Irish person.

– Ich freue mich darauf, Irland zu besuchen.   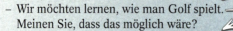   – It's a beautiful country. I'm very proud of being Irish.

– Wir möchten lernen, wie man Golf spielt. Meinen Sie, dass das möglich wäre?   – That's no problem. There are plenty of public golf courses to choose from.

– Wir besuchen sehr gerne alte Burgen.   – Well, if you're interested in visiting ruined castles there's enough to see.

– Wir haben nur ein Problem – in Irland soll es angeblich sehr viel regnen.   – If you mean to come to our green island, you can't expect to have weather like they have in Italy!

B Irish – a living language

G21

- I'm learning Irish from a TV programme. I must remember to watch tonight. I forgot to watch on Monday.
- The government is trying to support the use of the Irish language whenever possible, and certainly more people can speak it now than a few years ago.
- My grandfather remembers speaking Irish all the time with family and neighbours, but now they usually speak English.
- If you want to visit a place where most people still speak Irish, it will mean going to remote places on the south or west coasts.
- I mean to go to Irish classes this winter. I'd like to speak it as well as my children. They all have to learn it at school.
- A family I know tried speaking Irish on Mondays, English on Tuesdays, and so on, but it didn't work because most TV programmes were in English.
- I'll never forget asking the way to Dun Laoghaire, and pronouncing it so badly that nobody understood me.

1. Add examples of verbs followed by both the gerund and the infinitive with 'to' to your list in your file. Try to find good translations to show the different meanings.

2. Think of reasons why more people in Ireland speak English than Irish.

▷ 3. Discuss whether it is important to keep a language like Irish alive.

⟨Further reading p. 95⟩

C Holidaying in Ireland

There are many holidays on horse-back offered in Ireland. You ride for perhaps 4–6 hours a day, and your luggage is taken from hotel to hotel. Both experienced riders and beginners can take part. Read this extract from a brochure, and check on a map where the route is.

Either: Develop a dialogue with a partner, discussing what you would or wouldn't like to do in the programme.

Or: Write a letter to a friend, commenting on the programme. Use the phrases you collected in the strategy box.

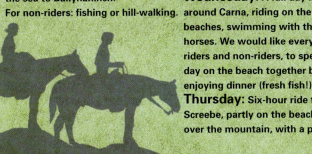

The Connemara Trail

Monday: We meet in Galway and drive to Ballyconneely, where we pick up the horses for a three hours' ride through mountains overlooking the sea to Ballynahinch. For non-riders: fishing or hill-walking.

Tuesday: Four hours' ride across the mountains to Carna. For non-riders: deep-sea fishing, cycling or hill-walking.

Wednesday: A full day in and around Carna, riding on the beaches, swimming with the horses. We would like everybody, riders and non-riders, to spend the day on the beach together before enjoying dinner (fresh fish!)

Thursday: Six-hour ride to Screebe, partly on the beach, partly over the mountain, with a packed lunch on the way. For non-riders: cycling and fishing.

Friday: Before lunch we cross a beautiful high mountain, from the top of which we can see for miles. Packed lunch on the other side, in the forest. Afternoon: riding on soft forest roads. Spend the night in Oughterard. For non-riders: golf or fishing.

Saturday: Ride over mountains overlooking Galway Bay to Barna village on the sea. Then drive to Galway for the last night. For non-riders: sightseeing and shopping.

(from: *The Connemara Trail*, William Leahy, Galway)

Gerund and *to* with infinitive; commenting

71

CONTENTS

- Text module:
  People and places,
  an Australian song,
  background information
  an Australian story
- Language module:
  English in the world
  Creative writing
- Strategy page:
  Cultural awareness

G'day! I'm Tricia, and I come from Sydney. ('Sinny', we Aussies call it!) It's the biggest city in Australia, with a population of about 4 million now. I really love the harbour area with the Opera House.

Australians love surfing! Most of us live in the cities round the coast anyway, so the kids learn to surf quite early. The waves 'surfies' ride on can be ten to twenty feet high!

An American friend said everything here was the wrong way round – or upside down! The further north you go here in Oz, the hotter it gets. And when you go south, it gets colder! If you come here in January, it's summer – and if you're here in July, it's winter. He even said we drove on the wrong side of the road. Well, OK – but we got that idea from the Poms.

Ayers Rock is one of the most famous places in Australia. It is visited every year by thousands of tourists from all over the world. It is an important place to the Aborigines, who have their own name for it – 'Uluru'.

Contrasts in life "down under"

Australia is the hottest and driest continent. Aborigines still live in the so-called 'red heart' of Australia but the only other people who endure the difficulties of life in the 'outback' are the ranchers and their families.

Many of Australia's forests have been cleared by settlers. But some of Queensland is tropical and it still has rainforest where the trees can be thousands of years old.

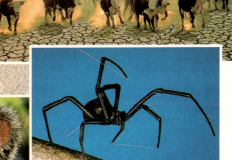

Have you heard these ones?

What do you get if you cross a kangaroo with an elephant?
Big holes all over Australia.

What do you call a kangaroo in Antarctica?
Lost.

We have animals which you don't find anywhere else in the world, except zoos, of course. There are cute koalas, for example, which eat the leaves of gum trees – these would kill most other animals. We get sharks off the coast and there are crocodiles in some lakes and rivers. But even more dangerous are our spiders, like the redback or the funnel web.

1. What contrasts do you notice in this information about Australia? Think about the places where people live and the wildlife. Check the map of Australia at the back of your book.

2. Think about life in your country. What is *different* in Australia? Collect ideas from these pages and add your own ideas.

Discussing life in Australia

73

DOWN UNDER

 1 I am Australian

I came upon the prison ship
Bowed down by iron chains
I fought the land, endured the lash
And waited for the rains
I'm a settler, I'm a farmer's wife
5   On a dry and barren run
A convict then a freeman
I became Australian
I'm the daughter of a digger
Who sought the mother lode
10   The girl became a woman
On the long and dusty road
I'm a child of the Depression
I saw the good times come
I'm a bushie, I'm a battler
15   I am Australian
We are one, but we are many
And from all the lands on earth we come
We'll share a dream and sing with one voice
I am, you are
20   We are Australian
I'm a teller of stories
I'm a singer of songs

I am Albert Namatjira
I paint the ghostly gums
I am Clancy on his horse
I'm Ned Kelly on the run   25
I'm the one who waltzed Matilda
I am Australian
I'm the hot wind from the desert
I'm the black soil of the plains
I'm the mountains and the valleys   30
I'm the drought and flooding rains
I am the rock, I am the sky
The rivers when they run
The spirit of this great land
I am Australian   35
I came from the Dreaming
From the dusty red soil plains
I am the ancient heart
The keeper of the flame
I stood upon the rocky shores   40
I watched the tall ships come
For forty thousand years I'd been
The first Australian

Ghost Gum, Central Australia, Albert Namatjira, Australia Day 1993

45c   Australia

2   A look at history

1 • The first inhabitants, the Aborigines, came from the north by boat. This was 40,000 years ago – or even earlier.

2 • The time of the creation of the world is known to the Aborigines as 'Dreamtime' or the 'Dreaming'. There are many traditional songs and legends that tell of the creation of the land, its plants, animals and people.

3 • The first European settlement was for convicts. The prisons in Britain had become so full that ships full of convicts were sent to start a colony on the 'new' continent. They arrived in 1788.

4 • The convicts' first job after their arrival at Sydney Cove, was to cut down trees and prepare the land for building. When their 'time' as prisoners was over, they were given their freedom. For many, it was a chance to start a completely new life.

5 • Life was hard for the new settlers, but the British colony became richer when gold was discovered in New South Wales and Victoria in 1851.

6 • Many Australian rivers and lakes are usually quite dry. Until 1950 Lake Eyre in South Australia had had no water in it at all for 100 years!

7 • For many years, most immigrants came from Britain. During the 20th century, large numbers came from other European countries, especially Italy and Greece. Now most new-comers are from Asian countries. More than 5 million settlers from nearly 200 different countries have come in the past 50 years.

1. Match up the information points with lines from the song. You can find the places in Australia on the map at the back of your book.

2. Who are the groups who make up the population of Australia today?

3. Which line do you think sums up the message of the song? Why do you think so?

3 Matthew meets No-name

Matthew lives in a small town on the edge of the Australian Bush. He has set off alone to look for some rock paintings he has heard of. He finds them and is very excited but later he realizes he is lost and his mood changes …

PAT LOWE

THE GIRL WITH NO NAME

In the shelter of the rock, where he had found a spot away from the wind, Matthew shivered. He had never before spent a night alone in the bush. He had been
5 camping a few times, with a group of friends, but that had felt quite different. He wished Nick or one of the others was here now. On all those earlier trips with the other boys, their camping places had never been
10 far off the beaten track.
He didn't doubt he would be found sooner or later. He knew that if he wasn't home tomorrow his father would have a search party out first thing the next morning. He'd
15 eaten his apple hours ago, and most of the fruit and nuts. He still had water in his bottle but at the back of his mind he thought: What if they don't find me in time? What if my water runs out?
20 If only it wasn't so cold. All he had on was a T-shirt and shorts. Now and then Matthew got up and walked a few steps back and forward near the rock, moving his arms to warm himself up.
25 It was an endless night – the worst night Matthew could ever remember. With sunrise the wind got up again, and Matthew walked about and did some exercises until his circulation was pumping. His optimism
30 returned: Matthew took a good look at the place where he had spent the night. The rock wasn't bad as a shelter from the wind. But I could build it up at the sides with branches, he thought. He spent some time breaking off
35 branches, and the work warmed him up. Next he tried to find something to lie on. He collected dry leaves, but decided they would be more uncomfortable than the dusty ground, and maybe not much warmer.
40 The optimism Matthew had felt earlier began to leave him. He was beginning to see that there was a world of difference between

reading and thinking about survival, and actually having to do it.
Despondent, Matthew sat down under the 45
overhang of the rock. Suddenly, he thought he heard a sound. He sat very still, listening. Then he heard a voice quite close by, laughing softly. It was a young voice. He stood up quickly, turned, and saw a girl 50
standing there.
'Hello!' said Matthew in surprise.
'Where did you come from? What's your name?'
'I know your name,' said the girl as an 55
answer.
'You're Matthew Scott.'
'How do you know that?', Matthew was astonished.
'Everybody know you, your father work at 60
the prison.'
The girl's voice was soft, and she spoke English with a particular accent, as if she were not speaking her own language.
'Do you know the way back to Goanna 65
Gorge?' Matthew said. 'I got lost yesterday, I've been here all night.'
'I know. I seen your tracks.' She looked

DOWN UNDER

around. 'Why didn't you make a fire?'
70 'No matches.'
'Plenty bush matches,' said the girl, pointing
to a small tree not far from where they were
standing.
'Do you know how to make a fire from
75 sticks?' asked Matthew.
''Course. Blackfeller got to know.'
'Well, I wish you'd show me.'
She went to the tree and picked up a couple
of straight dead branches, then looked
80 around until she found some dry grass. With
the edge of a piece of stone she made a
nick in the side of one of the sticks, and
sharpened one end of the other. Then she
placed the nicked piece flat on the ground,
85 with some of the dry grass just underneath
it. Holding the first stick firmly under the side
of her right foot, she placed the second stick

upright with the sharpened end resting in
the nick she had made in the other. She held
the upright stick between both flat hands   90
and twisted it back and forward.
'Might be I can't light 'im', she remarked.
'We don't do it much.'
'Why's that?'
'Cos we got 'nother kind matches,' she   95
laughed.
Matthew watched as she twisted the stick.
A little bit of smoke rose from the friction
point between the two sticks. She blew, but
the grass didn't catch fire.   100
'No good,' she said.
'Let me have a go,' said Matthew, but he
found it was harder than it looked.
'Never mind,' the girl said cheerfully. 'You
can do it next time.'   105
'You still haven't told me your name,' he
said to the girl.
'I got no name,' she said at last. 'One
woman did pass away. Same name like me.'
'So what do people call you now?'   110
'Kumunyjayi,' said the girl after a pause.
'That mean like, no name.'
'Are we far from Goanna Gorge?' he asked
No-name.
No-name nodded. She stood up straight.   115
Matthew got up, too. The girl threw out her
arm in front of her, pointing. 'That way.' The
words sounded like 'Darray': He wondered
how she knew. She seemed so confident, he
did not for a moment doubt her. He simply   120
followed.

(from: *The girl with no name* by Pat Lowe) (slightly adapted)

1. Where is the turning point in the story? What happens?

2. Describe how Matthew's mood changes throughout the story. Mention the facts, words or
    phrases which show his mood.

3. Compare Matthew's attempt to build a shelter with the girl's fire-making demonstration. What
    does this show about them?

▷ 4. Tell the story from the point of view of No-name.
    Start like this: "In the evening, No-name heard the men talking about the white boy, Matthew
    Scott. He had got lost in the bush, looking for rock-paintings."

5. What do you think happened after line 121.
    Write a suitable ending to the story.

⟨Further reading p. 96⟩

Interpreting feelings
and attitudes in a story

76

ENGLISH IN 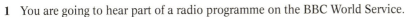 THE WORLD

Did you know that English is ...	... an official language for another 400 million people, most of them in countries that were British colonies?	... a second language for 1 billion other people?	... learnt by four-fifths of Europe's young people?	... learnt by more people all over the world than any other language?
...the first language of more than 400 million people, many of them in North America?		... used by nearly a third of the world's population?	(One fifth learn French.)	... used for 85% of all Internet messages?

1 You are going to hear part of a radio programme on the BBC World Service.

   a) Information on most subjects is easier to understand (and more interesting) if you know something about the subject already. So before you listen: Read the fact box.

   b) Now listen to find out why so many people speak English. Make notes.

   c) Sum up what you already know, and what you have learned, about the position of English in the world today.

2. You will hear a scene at Sydney International Airport. Although they are all speaking English, the speakers are from different countries, so they have different accents.

   a) Listen carefully and guess where the speakers are from: Australia? The United States? India? Britain? France? Japan? How can you tell?

   b) Say what each of the speakers is doing at Sydney Airport.

> **TIP**
> • Don't worry about accents; the words are usually the same. Concentrate on the information.
> • Make logical guesses.

3. One reason why English is a relatively easy language to understand is that many words can be used in two ways – as a noun and as a verb. Think back to the *Matthew meets No-name* story. Re-phrase these sentences, using the matching nouns, and complete the sentences in your own words.

   1. Matthew looked carefully at the place ... (l.30)
   2. She surprised Matthew very much when ... (l.52)
   3. No-name tracked Matthew ... (l.68)
   4. She nicked the side of a stick ... (l.82)
   5. She paused before she ... (l.111)

> **TIP**
> Don't be surprised if you read or hear a noun being used unusually as a verb, or a verb as a noun. This happens a lot, expecially in American and Australian English.

4. Not all verbs and nouns that look the same have similar meanings! (though most of them do.) Using your dictionary where necessary, choose five of these words from *Matthew meets No-name*. Make two sentences to show the two meanings of each word.

   rock – trip – spot – stick – point – back – rest

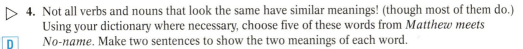

Understanding accents

77

DOWN UNDER

Strategy Page: Cultural awareness

Each country has slightly different patterns of behaviour! So it isn't enough just to be able to speak the language in a foreign country. Here is a humorous look at how to behave in Australia. It is full of exaggerations, of course, but you get the message …!

On arrival at an Australian home it's a good idea to start apologizing the moment you come in through the door. *Being on time* is a good excuse, i.e.: "I'm sorry to be so punctual." On being
5 offered a drink you must excuse yourself for being a bother, or better even, for actually being thirsty. It's advisable to throw in a few apologies to keep the conversation going when sitting down, such as: "I'm sorry, have I sat on the wrong chair?"
10 It's also polite to be sorry for having burped. Even if it's impossible for other people to have heard it, you must bring your hand up to your mouth and stop all conversation with a loud: "I'm terribly sorry, it's awfully rude of me." In France and Ger-
15 many you might be thought gauche if you made such a statement. In Australia a bold apology for even the quietest little burp is considered the quintessence of polite behaviour and your hosts will rush to have you over again.

(from: *How to be normal in Australia* by Robert Treborlang)

1. With a partner, think up some real situations where you might want to apologize. Write mini-dialogues.

You have lent something to somebody, and you'd like it back – you need to ring your parents – you feel sick – you want to disagree – you arrive late for a meal – you want to borrow something – …

> **Useful expressions**
>
> I know it's rude of me but …
> I'm sorry to be … /
>   bother you …
> I'm awfully sorry but …
> I hope you don't mind that …
> I hope it isn't too much
>   trouble but …

2. To become aware of patterns of behaviour, think of a situation in your country like giving or receiving a present, or welcoming guests. Try to look at the situation objectively, and write down for anEnglish-speaking person exactly what happens, what is said, what is expected, etc. (It may help you to think what would be considered rude or unusual behaviour.)

> **TIP**
> When you are in another country, keep your eyes and ears open for patterns of behaviour and polite or friendly things to say and do. Remember: What is polite in your culture may be rude in another culture.

(from: '*How to be normal in Australia*' by Robert Treborlang)

"I'm sorry to bother you and I hope I'm not too much trouble but could you move your foot a little either way because somehow mine seems to have got caught under yours."

IMAGES

1. Look at the picture for a minute and write down your first impressions.

2. Choose a task:
   a) Write the outline for a short story for which this photo could be an illustration.
      Think of a good beginning and ending.
   b) Use this picture as the inspiration for a poem, a song text or an advert.
   c) Write an account of the problems of life in the outback.
      Say why you would or wouldn't enjoy it.

TOPIC 1   **SWITCHED ON**

after p.11

1 Candle in the Wind

Goodbye Norma Jean,
Though I never knew you at all,
You had the grace to hold yourself
While those around you crawled.
They crawled out of the woodwork   5
And they whispered into your brain.
They set you on the treadmill
And they made you change your name.

And it seems to me you lived your life
Like a candle in the wind.   10
Never knowing who to cling to
When the rain set in,
And I would have liked to have known you
But I was just a kid.
Your candle burned out long before   15
Your legend ever did.

Loneliness was tough,
The toughest role you ever played.
Hollywood created a superstar,
20 And pain was the price you paid.
Even when you died
The press still hounded you –
All the papers had to say
Was that Marilyn was found in the nude.

25 Goodbye Norma Jean,
Though I never knew you at all.
You had the grace to hold yourself
While those around you crawled.

Goodbye Norma Jean,
30 From the young man in the 22nd row
Who sees you as something more than sexual.
More than just our Marilyn Monroe.

Elton John and Bernie Taupin

1. What is your first impression of this song?

2. How is the song different from what you usually read about stars?

3. What does the speaker have to say about the role of the media, and about the distinction between 'Norma Jean' and 'Marilyn Monroe'?

4. Pick out two or three lines you find interesting, and talk about them.

Talking about a song

2 A life behind the camera …

(From: *ROCK TALK*, by Julian Colbeck)

Video director

Have you ever dreamed of directing a pop video?
Sara Dunlop, 23, is a pop video and commercials director,
working with successful British bands.

Melissa Turner asked her how she started.

Did you always want to be a director?
Since the age of 12, I've loved films
and videos. At school, I suggested this
to my careers advisor but directing
wasn't in the careers handbook! Being
given a second-hand camera was
important as it allowed me to make my
own short movies.

Did you go to college?
Yes, I did A levels in History, Music
and English and then did a degree at
the University of Westminster in Film,
Video and Photographic Arts. The
course involved making short films
and videos but, unfortunately, we also
had to write essays. I also worked
part-time in a video shop and at a
cinema, which allowed me to watch
films all the time!

Working week?
There are three main stages to making
any film or video, so my weeks can
vary dramatically. If it's before a
shoot, I have meetings with record
companies or advertising agencies.
Everything has to be planned, a script
written and a story board drawn up so
the agency will know what the
finished piece will look like.On a
typical shoot day, it's a very early
start, about 8 a.m., and a late finish.
After the shoot 'post production' is
where all the special effects are put in
and the video is edited.

Best bit? 35
After all the hard work, seeing my
video or advert on TV feels great. And
meeting the bands!

Worst bit?
Worrying that the ad agency or record 40
company won't like it. Also when one
job is over, I have to think about what
I will be doing next.

Holidays?
I work freelance, so it's down to me 45
when I can afford one.

In ten years time?
I want to still be making quality videos
and ads but my main aim is to work
on my feature film … perhaps the next 50
Hollywood blockbuster featuring the
new Johnny Depp!

FACT

A pop video is a commercial for
a group. In the same way that TV
adverts are shown all over the
world to help promote a new
brand of coffee, pop videos are
used to sell records all over the
world.

While you're watching a video
on Top of the Pops, American
viewers can be watching it on
MTV, Dutch audiences can be
watching it on Sky Channel. Add
to that the thousands of clubs
and discos that show them and
you can see why pop videos are
so important. There's no other
way a group can be seen 'live' by
so many people at the same time.

3 The Martians have landed!

(Transcript of an extract from a recording of *War of the Worlds* (H. G. Wells) made by Orson Welles)
The words on the page opposite will help you to understand the text.

(Fade-in:
Carl Phillips: Hold on a minute will you, please? I'll be right back in a minute.)
(MUSIC)
Announcer: We are bringing you an eyewitness account of what's happening on the 10 Wilmott farm, Grover's Mill, New Jersey.
(MUSIC)
We now return you to Carl Phillips at Grover's 15 Mill.
Carl Phillips: Ladies and gentlemen, (may I) ladies and gentlemen, ladies and gentlemen, here I am back of the stone wall that adjoins Mr Wilmott's garden.
20 From here I get a sweep of the whole scene. I'll give you every detail as long as I can talk and as long as I can see. More state police have arrived. They're drawing up a cordon in front of the pit. About thirty of them. No need to push the crowd back now.
25 They're willing to keep their distance. The captain is conferring with someone. I can't quite see who. Oh yes, I believe it's Professor Pearson. Yes it is. Now they've parted, and the professor moves around one side studying the object while the captain and two
30 policemen advance with something in their hands. I can see it now. It's a white handkerchief tied to a pole – a flag of truce. Do those creatures know what that means? What anything means? Wait a minute, something's happening. A humped shape is rising
35 out of the pit. I can make out a small beam of light against a mirror. What's that? – there's a jet of flame springing from the mirror, it leaps right at the advancing men. It strikes them head-on … flames … (screams) … spreading everywhere, coming this way
40 now, about 20 yards to my right …
(Silence for 4/5 seconds)
Announcer: Ladies and gentlemen, due to circumstances beyond our control we are unable to continue the broadcast from Grover's Mill.
45 Evidently there's some difficulty with our field transmissions. However, we will return to that point at the earliest opportunity. In the meantime we have a late bulletin from San Diego, California. Professor Indelkoffer, speaking at a dinner of the
50 California Astronomical Society, expressed the opinion that the explosions on Mars are undoubtedly nothing

more than severe volcanic disturbances on the surface of the planet. We continue now with our piano interlude.
(MUSIC)   5
5 *Announcer:* Ladies and gentlemen, I have just been handed a message that came in from Grover's Mill by telephone.
Just one moment, please.
At least forty people, including six state troopers,   6
10 lie dead, in a field east of the village of Grover's Mill, their bodies burned and distorted beyond all possible recognition. The next voice you hear will be that of Brigadier General Montgomery Smith, commander of the state militia at Trenton, New   6
15 Jersey.
General Montgomery Smith: I have been requested by the governor of New Jersey to place the counties of Mercer and Middlesex as … as far west as Princeton and east to Jamesburg under   7
martial law. No one will be permitted to enter this area except by special pass issued by state or military authorities. Four companies of state militia are proceeding from Trenton to Grover's Mill and will aid in the evacuation of homes   7
within the range of military operations. Thank you.
Announcer: You have just been listening to General Montgomery Smith commanding the state militia at Trenton. In the meantime further   8
details of the catastrophe at Grover's Mill are coming in. The strange creatures, after unleashing their deadly assault, crawled back in their pit and made no attempt to prevent the efforts of the firemen to recover the bodies and extinguish the   8
fire. The combined fire departments of Mercer County are fighting the flames which menace the entire countryside.
We have been unable to establish any contact with our mobile unit at Grover's Mill. But we hope to   9
be able to return you there at the earliest possible moment. In the meantime we take you to … Just one moment please. (2/3 secs. silence) (…)
Ladies and gentlemen, here is a bulletin from Trenton. It is a brief statement informing us that   9
the charred body of Carl Phillips has been identified in the Trenton hospital.
(Fade-out: Now here's another bulletin from Washington, D.C.)

(from: *War of the worlds* by H.G. Wells, adapted by Orson Welles)

4 Death of a Film Star
(For John Owen)

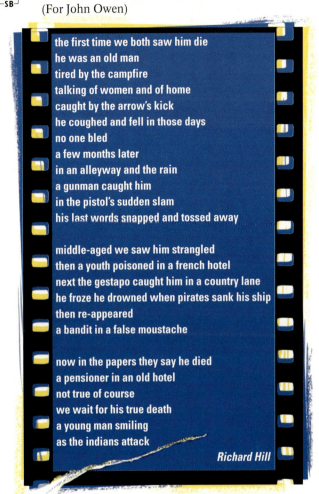

the first time we both saw him die
he was an old man
tired by the campfire
talking of women and of home
caught by the arrow's kick
he coughed and fell in those days
no one bled
a few months later
in an alleyway and the rain
a gunman caught him
in the pistol's sudden slam
his last words snapped and tossed away

middle-aged we saw him strangled
then a youth poisoned in a french hotel
next the gestapo caught him in a country lane
he froze he drowned when pirates sank his ship
then re-appeared
a bandit in a false moustache

now in the papers they say he died
a pensioner in an old hotel
not true of course
we wait for his true death
a young man smiling
as the indians attack

Richard Hill

1. Listen to the poem on the recording. Don't worry if you don't understand all the words yet. Just try to get the main ideas.
   – Say in one or two sentences what the poem is about. The title will help you.
2. Now read the poem.
   – Divide it up into different scenes. (It isn't always easy because there is almost no punctuation. But you can check where the pauses come on the recording.)
   – Which scenes are from films? What kind of films do you think they are?
   – Which scene is real?
3. What do the last three lines tell us about how the speaker sees the film star?
4. What do you think the poem tells us about the speaker?

adjoin -*angrenzen*; advance -*auf etw. zugehen*; aid in the evacuation -*bei der Evakuierung helfen*; eyewitness account -*Augenzeugenbericht*; assault -*Anschlag*; astronomical -*astronomisch*; beam -*Strahl*; beyond ... recognition -*bis zur Unkenntlichkeit*; captain - *Einsatzleiter*; catastrophe - *Katastrophe*; charred -*verkohlt*; circumstances beyond s.o.'s control -*Umstände, die sich der Kontrolle ... entziehen*; command, commander - *befehlen, Befehlshaber*; confer - *sich beraten*; countryside - *Landschaft*; county - *Verwaltungsbezirk(US)*; dinner -*(Abend)essen*; distance - *Abstand*; distorted -*verzerrt*; draw up a cordon -*etw. abriegeln*; due to -*aufgrund*; establish -*herstellen*; evidently - *offensichtlich*; express - *ausdrucken*; extinguish - *löschen*; flag of truce -*Flagge als Friedensangebot*; governor - *Gouverneur*; handkerchief - *Taschentuch*; identify - *identifizieren*; leap -*springen*; made no attempt to prevent - *versuchten nicht zu verhindern*; martial law - *Kriegsrecht*; in the meantime -*in der Zwischenzeit*; menace - *bedrohen*; militia -*Miliz*; mobile unit -*Übertragung vor Ort*; part -*sich trennen*; pass issued by the authorities - *Passierschein(behördlich ausgestellt)*; place -*stellen*; pole -*Stock*; proceed -*sich begeben*; quite -*ganz*; recover -*bergen*; request -*bitten*; spread -*sich ausbreiten*; sweep -*Überblick*; transmission -*Übertragung*; trooper -*Polizist*; undoubtedly - *ohne Zweifel*; within range of operations -*im Aktionskreis*

Understanding a poem

83

TOPIC 2
THAT'S SCHOOL, TOO!

after p.26, 27

1 Dear Examiner

Thank you so much for your questions
I've read them most carefully through
But there isn't a single one of them
That I know the answer to.

I've written my name as instructed
Put the year, the month and the day
But after I'd finished doing that
I had nothing further to say.

So I thought I'd write you a letter
Fairly informally
About what's going on in the classroom
And what it's like to be me.

Mandy has written ten pages
But it's probably frightful guff
And Angela Smythe is copying
The answers off her cuff.

Miss Quinlan is marking our homework
The clock keeps ticking away
For anyone not in this classroom
It's just another day.

Mother's buying groceries
Grandmother's drinking tea
Unemployed men doing crosswords
or watching 'Crown Court' on TV.

The rain has finally stopped here
The sun's just started to shine
And in a back garden in Sefton Drive
A housewife hangs shirts on a line.

A class chatters by to play tennis
The cathedral clock has just pealed
A motor chugs steadily back and forth
Mowing the hockey field.

Miss Quinlan's just seen what I've written
Her face is an absolute mask
Before she collects in the papers
I have one little favour to ask.

I thought your questions were lovely
There's only myself to blame
But couldn't you give me something
For writing the date and my name.

Gareth Owen

1. Who is the speaker and what is the situation?

2. Which verses tell you what is happening around the speaker
   in the poem?

3. What does the speaker describe in these verses? (Is it something he/she sees? or hears?
   or supposes? Is it inside the classroom or outside?)

4. a) Comment on the title of the poem.
   b) Find alternative titles.

5. Pick out humorous elements in the poem and comment on them.

▷ 6. Creative writing: Write about what is happening around you as you sit at your desk. (Question
   three will give you ideas.) If you like, you can also write a poem (of course, the lines don't
   have to be the same length, and it doesn't have to rhyme.).

2 A newspaper article

1. Before you read, look at the picture, the caption and the headline. Try to guess what the article is about.

Classroom cruelty, in black and white

By STEVEN MORRIS

Charlotte, who takes after her white father, and Samantha, who has her mother's darker looks

BOTH are bright girls from a caring home. But while Charlotte Cushen enjoys school, her twin Samantha says life in the same class has become very difficult.

A trick of nature means that Charlotte has inherited her father's fair skin and blue eyes while Samantha has her mother's dark north African looks.

The girls, who like to dress similarly and have the same favourite subjects, say they receive very different treatment from classmates at Holton School in Barry, South Wales.

Samantha said: 'Some children get pictures of gorillas and say I look like them. They also draw pictures of me with big lips and call me names. Sometimes they hit me if I answer back. It makes me feel sad and I want to go home to my mum.'

Charlotte said: 'I don't like it when they call Sam names and I stick up for her. I wish they would stop it. What does it matter that Samantha has darker skin than me? She is just like me. We like the same things. We spend all our time together.'

Mrs. Cushen, 38, who has just finished studying sociology and education at Cardiff University and is working at a hostel for the homeless, said: 'It's heartbreaking to see what Sam has been going through over the last two years. She gets called all sorts of names. The other children tell her she was made in a chocolate machine or say she doesn't wash. Luckily she gets good support from her family. Half her family is black and half white so that helps.'

Mrs Cushen said: 'I haven't been to the school because we deal with it at home.'

Councillor Michael Sharp, chairman of the governors at the school, said: 'This is the first I have heard of it. I have received no complaint from the mother.

The first place you should go to complain is the school. We would be very willing to help. We have an equal opportunities code. If she writes, I will deal with the matter.'

from: *The Daily Mail*

2. Skim through the article quickly. Then sum up the problem in two or three sentences.

3. Imagine Charlotte tells the story to a friend. What does she say?

4. Do you think the parents were right to talk to the newspapers before they talked to the school? Why or why not?

5. How do you think Charlotte and Samantha should behave towards the children who call Samantha names?

▷ 6. Have you ever experienced cruelty – to yourself or to others – in school? Talk or write about it.

Reading and reacting to a newspaper article

1 A mother's love

*Four years ago, the three sons of Carol
Evans learnt that she was very ill and had
been given just six months to live. Their
35-year-old mother underwent*
5 *radiotherapy and chemotherapy and is
now in remission. Then, in July, she won
£50,000 on the pools. The family lives on a
council estate in Sandwell, Walsall.*
Her sons thought they would be going on a
10 shopping spree. Instead, Mrs Evans invested
three parts of the windfall in savings bonds
and put the rest in the bank. She bought a
new bike for Steven, seven, on his birthday,
and gave the same amount to Richard, 15,
15 and to Alan, 16, which they spent on
clothes.
The money, she says, has been invested for
her children's future: "I have no idea how
long I'm going to be here. I nearly died. It's
20 changed my perspective. I'm not rushing out
to spend on some flash holiday."
The win has also led to fierce rows between
her and her two older sons: "They don't
understand that they cannot have all the
25 things they want. They want motorbikes and
go-karts and God knows what. Kids could
get through £50,000 in a few weeks, and
then what's left?"
Richard, her middle son, comes in for his
30 tea. "When Mum won," he complains,
"I thought she'd share the money out more.
She wouldn't even give us the money in one
go in case we wasted it. I thought we should
have got at least twice as much. You can't
35 buy many of the really fashionable
brand-label clothes for that.
Then, when my friends found out we'd won,
they thought I'd have lots of cash on me to
treat them, but my pocket money is the sa-
40 me.
Since we won the money, I get more hassle
from the gangs on the estate – the ones that
are into drugs and carry knives and things.
They keep asking me if I have got any
45 money. So, the money has made a bit of
difference, but it won't change anything –
perhaps it's just made my mum a bit
happier."

What you need to know
– **the pools:** the football pools – if you
  predict the results of football matches
  correctly, you can win a lot of money on
  the pools.
– **an estate:** here: a group of houses or flats
  planned and built at the same time.
– **a council estate:** an estate built by the
  town council for people with low income.
– **the Department of Social Security** pays
  money ('benefits') to people with low or
  no income.

1. **Understanding the gist of the text**
   a) Read the first paragraph. Describe the
      situation. Before you read further, think
      how the story could go on.
   b) Now read the article. Note how these
      people reacted to the money:
      – Mrs Evans – the sons – the sons'
      friends – the gangs.
   c) Say what you think of their reactions
      and why (e.g. right/wrong/typical/
      understandable).

2. **Something to discuss**
   a) Do you think Carol Evans was right not
      to give the boys more money.
   b) Carol Evans says, "It's been nice to win,
      but cruel as well." What does she mean?

(from: *The Independent Magazine*)

2 Don't Forget That

The bed in one house is harder than the other.
When I'm in 63, I always leave my green jumper,
or my pencil case, or something else I need.
It gets quite annoying. One adult saying,
'Remember this,' and the other one saying,
'Don't forget that.'

My room in one house is smaller than the other.
When I'm in 22A I miss Michael Jackson on my wall.
But I suppose I can't have two Michael Jackson posters.
The nights in 63 he talks in his American drawl.
He says 'Carla, how you doing girl?' Or even he says,
'Don't forget that.'

I discuss the houses with the other Carla.
We do the regular polls, decide the pros and cons.
Which house has more ice-cream;
which house gives better dreams;
which house is the most clean, and which says most often,
'Don't forget that.'

Carla and I both agree ice-cream is better in 63.
But then 22A is definitely more tidy.
We get more treats. And more 'quality time'
(I've heard the adults say, 'More like Quality Street!')
And my week wouldn't be the same unless somebody kept saying,
'Don't forget that.'

(from: *Two's Company* by Jackie Kay)

1. What is the situation in the poem?

2. Who is 'the other Carla'?

3. What do you think 'quality time' is? And why do some people say 'more like Quality Street'?

4. Discuss the pros and cons of having two homes, like Carla.

3 A cartoon

WHERE'S MY JACKET?

I'VE LOOKED EVERY-WHERE! UNDER THE BED, OVER MY CHAIR ...

... ON THE STAIRS, ON THE HALL FLOOR, IN THE KITCHEN ... IT'S JUST NOT ANYWHERE!

OH, HERE IT IS! WHO PUT IT IN THE STUPID CLOSET?!?

(from: *Calvin and Hobbes* by B. Watterson)

Do you sympathize more with Calvin or with the person who put his jacket away? Why?

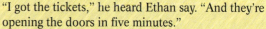
4 The Accidental Tourist

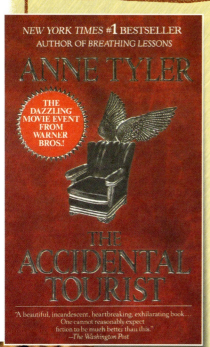

NEW YORK TIMES #1 BESTSELLER
AUTHOR OF BREATHING LESSONS

ANNE TYLER

THE DAZZLING MOVIE EVENT FROM WARNER BROS.!

THE ACCIDENTAL TOURIST

"A beautiful, incandescent, heartbreaking, exhilarating book...
One cannot reasonably expect
fiction to be much better than this."
—The Washington Post

"I got the tickets," he heard Ethan say. "And they're opening the doors in five minutes."

"All right," Macon told him, "let's plan our strategy."

"Strategy?"

"Where we're going to sit." 5

"Why would we need strategy for that?"

"It's you who asked to see this movie, Ethan. I would think you'd take an interest in where you're sitting. Now, here's my plan. You go around to that line on the left. Count the little kids. I'll count the 10 line on the right."

"Aw, Dad –."

"Do you want to sit next to some noisy little kid?"

"Well, no."

"And which do you prefer: an aisle seat?" 15

"I don't care."

"Aisle, Ethan? Or middle of the row? You must have some opinion."

"Not really."

"Middle of the row?" 20

"It doesn't make any difference."

"Ethan. It makes a great deal of difference. Aisle, you can get out quicker. So if you plan to buy a snack or go to the restroom, you'll want to sit on the aisle. On the other hand, everyone'll be 25 squeezing past you there. So if you don't think you'll be leaving your seat, then I suggest –."

"Aw, Dad, for Christ's sake!" Ethan said.

"Well," Macon said. "If that's the tone you're going to take, we'll just sit any damn place we happen to 30 end up."

"Fine," Ethan said.

"Fine," Macon said.

(from: *The Accidental Tourist* by Anne Tyler)

1. What relation is Ethan to Macon?

2. What is the conversation about?

3. Which of these words describe how Macon thinks, and which go together with Ethan's attitude?

   plan – doesn't make any difference – take an interest in – strategy – any damn place – have an opinion – doesn't care

4. What can you tell about Macon's character from what he says. (You can use some of the words from the box for your answer.)

5 The Tombstone

Josh sitting on a tombstone in the Plowman plot of earth. Sitting on Great-grandfather, which seemed a very proper place.

5 *Maximilian Plowman.*
Born 21. 6. 1821.
Died 5. 5. 1910
Founder of Ryan Creek
He always gave his fellow man
10 *the benefit of the doubt*

Gosh, Great-grandfather, I wonder who thought that up? Aunt Clara perhaps? It's nice to have it chipped in the stone they put on top of your
15 head. You're a hundred years older than I am, did you know that? Almost to the day. A hundred years ago and you were fourteen and seven months. What do you know about that? What was it like in
20 1836?
What was it like then, Great-grandfather, a hundred years back?
Were you like me, everybody's football, always getting kicked?
25 Did you know you were going to found a town? Did you know you were going to build a bridge? Did you know you'd start a family that'd end up with Josh sitting on your tombstone paying his respects? Growing up is
30 a funny thing, would you say that? Wondering whether you'll be famous, not dead sure you want to be or not. If you've got to go through life crying for everybody else and laughing at yourself.

Rosemary Caroline Plowman 35
(née Braddock). Born 22. 3. 1831.
Died 14. 7. 1868
In loving memory of an
adored wife
With God who loves her too 40

You had to go on forty-two years without her, Great-grandfather. You didn't have her for very long. Dead in the ground and younger than Mum. Gosh, Great-grandfather, I'm 45 sad about that. Is that why people don't talk about her much?
Dead for so long they can't remember. It's sad to be dead for so long that no one remembers. 50
Rosemary Caroline Plowman (née Braddock).
I want to put a flower here for you.

Jane Braddock Plowman.
Born 14. 7. 1868. 55
Lived three hours With Jesus

Oh, golly, Great-grandfather. No one ever told me that. I'm so sad. I'm so sorry. You lost your little baby and you lost your sweetheart, too.
On the same day. That's not fair. And here am 60 I sweating about a cricket match. Did you cry, Great-grandfather? Were you a big strong man who never got upset?
I'll bet you cried. I'll bet you couldn't see for tears. I do feel close; I'd like you to know 65 that.

(from: *Josh* by Ivan Southall)

1. Talk about your reaction to this extract from a young adult novel.

2. Work out how old Josh's great-grandparents became. (Perhaps find out when your greatgrandparents lived, and how old they became.)

3. Compare what Josh knew about his greatgrandparents with what he find out.

4. Describe how his perception of his great-grandparents changes.

▷ 5. Imagine it's one hundred years into the future, and you are Josh's great-grandson or -daughter. Write a text like „The Tombstone" about Josh's life. (You can use or change bits of the text if you like. What about inventing a tombstone text for Josh?)

1 **Earth and Sun and Moon**

In the morning we will wake up and take to the air
Look back at the planet – I'm glued to my chair
Southern half is burning as we climb through the sky
Sea-birds softly falling, smoke 'way up high

There's the contours of the mountains, the deserts and plains
And a hurricane is blowing, and it turns once again
Now there's oil spills in the water where Columbus once sailed
And there's history and mystery and it's rolling away

I wish you could see this great mystery
Earth and sun and moon, human tribe, thin blue line
Earth and sun and moon will survive.

Sediment is flowing from river to sea
Now where are the mighty nations, no lines to be seen
An axe upon the broken ground, the sigh of the trees
And it's floating in the ether, it brings me to my knees

Too messed up to care, anyone got a wing and a prayer

In the blink of an eye thank you and good night

Earth and sun and moon, human tribe, one thin blue line
Earth and sun and moon will survive, will survive, we will survive

Tim Moginie

1. Sum up the main ideas that 'Earth and Sun and Moon' expresses.

2. Comment on how viewing the earth from the air helps the description.

3 Find words or phrases which you think are especially effective, and explain why you like them. (Interesting image? Good sound? …?)

4. Think up more phrases which could be used in a song like this. Maybe you would like to write your own song or poem about the environment.

2 The Bollin Valley campaign

This text is about events that really happened …

'Arooga! Arooga!' It was 3.45 in the morning when the alarm call woke Jackie in her tent. She was already in her clothes. She and the other protesters always slept like that. They
5   knew that sooner or later the bailiffs would arrive to try and evict them from the six camps they had set up in the Bollin Valley woods. The old woods were where Manchester Airport was planning to build a second runway.
10 'Arooga! They're hitting Ziontree camp! Jimi Hendrix will be next!' Jackie crawled out quickly and ran to a rope ladder hanging from a tree nearby. A minute later she was high above the ground in one of the treehouses in
15 the Jimi Hendrix camp. As soon as Kate and Mick, two other protesters, had climbed up beside her she pulled up the rope behind them all. They could hear noises and shouts coming from Ziontree.
20 'What do you think is going on?' asked Jackie. This was the first time she had ever taken part in anything like this. Kate and Mick had both been in action before, in other environmental campaigns.
25 'Hard to say exactly,' answered Kate. 'I just hope that everyone had time to get into the trees or the tunnels.' Jackie shivered when she thought of the tunnels some protesters had dug in the woods. They had enough food and water
30 for weeks down there, but she would never be able to lock herself away under the ground. However she wanted to help, too. That was why she had decided not to start her nursing course in London and had come north to
35 Manchester. That was why she was now waiting nervously in a tree in woods. She did not have to wait long. 'Here they come!' shouted Mick. His words were lost in the noise of engines as a group of bailiffs came
40 through the trees on four-wheel motorbikes. They jumped off and grabbed a few protesters who were still on the ground. The others shouted and whistled from the trees. In the meantime a second group of men had
45 arrived with climbing equipment. One of them started to climb the tree Jackie and her friends were in. 'Come down!' the man shouted. 'We don't want anyone to get hurt.' 'Quick! Get to another tree!' yelled Kate. She
50 led the way across a rope bridge to the next tree. All the trees were linked in this way so that the protesters could cross from one tree to another and escape. But the bailiffs had planned carefully, too. As
55 soon as they saw that a tree was empty, they switched on their powerful saws. They cut through the main branches, bringing the treehouse and the ropes down. At last the protesters were left isolated in only a few trees.
60 Some were able to climb down on their own. Some, like Jackie, were helped by the bailiffs to get safely down to the ground. It was the end of Jackie's campaign. As she and the other protesters were led away, they were
65 met by television cameras and reporters. Some local people who had already heard what was happening that morning had come to watch, too. 'Well done!' came a voice from the crowd.
70 'Thanks for trying to save our valley.'

1. On the recording you will hear different opinions about the Bollin Valley campaign.
   – Before you listen think about the situation yourself. Make a list of possible arguments for and against what the campaigners did.
   – Now listen and compare your ideas with what you hear. Note down any new arguments.

2. From what you know, would you have taken part in the campaign? Explain why or why not.

Forming an opinion about a controversial issue

91

3 Highly desirable – highly damaging

a) Gold in Britain

People's desire for the exotic or unusual can lead to environmental damage. A first example is the discovery of gold in Britain.

Klondiker: Julia Francis pans for gold in the Forest of Dean

© Simon Barr/The Sunday Times 1996

THE BRITISH KLONDIKES

Gairloch

Loch Carron

Tyndrum

Ochils Hills

Duns

Leadhills

Gold is found across Britain in ancient rocks laid down 350m years ago. In Scotland, Wales and western England gold is common but it took powerful computers to find the most profitable sites.

There are also thought to be large deposits of gold beneath London, the home counties and eastern England but they are too deeply buried under younger rocks to be mined commercially. But it might be profitable in Leicestershire and possibly Norfolk where outcrops of gold-bearing rock have been forced to the surface.

Cockermouth

Prestatyn Hills

Leicester

Nor

Gloucester/
Forest of Dean

Haverfordwest

Exeter

= GOLD MINE

= GOLD

Source: British

Graphic: Simon Barr

In a four-year study, called the Midas Project, geologists have found huge deposits of gold under towns, cities and the countryside throughout Britain. The deposits were discovered using computers into which information was fed about the kind of rock where gold is found throughout the world. This was then compared with the database of the rock structure of Great Britain. Many of the deposits are considered to be large enough for mining. Near Exeter, for example, the gold is believed to be lying quite close to the surface. However, local environmentalists are angry. "It's another example of someone destroying the countryside to get rich. We don't need gold." Some of the richest deposits lie in environmentally sensitive areas such as Scotland and the Lake District. Many landowners, however, would not like to have mines on their lands.

Discuss the pros and cons of mining for gold in Europe.

b) Trekking in the Himalayas

Trekking in the Himalayas sounds like a very unusual holiday. But it is a second example of how people's desire for the unusual can damage the environment. Read the following notes from a trekking permit.

Write down ten ways in which some trekkers have obviously damaged the environment or disturbed the local culture.

Useful expressions

Some trekkers have obviously …
There has been a problem because …
It would seem as if …
… appear …
It can be assumed …

TREKKING PERMIT

HIS MAJESTY'S GOVERNMENT
MINISTRY OF HOME
IMMIGRATION OFFICE
POKHARA
DEPARTMENT OF IMMIGRATION

NOTE:

1. Trekking permit: trekkers should keep this along with them while trekking.
2. Trekking permit: should be shown to immigration authorities or police on demand.
3. Trekkers are not allowed to trek in notified areas previously known as restricted.
4. Please kindly surrender this card at Immigration Department or at any port of exit after the completion of trekking.
5. Deviation from the prescribed routes in the trekking permit will be treated as a violation of law.
6. Let the Himalayas change you – do not change them. So remember, while you are on trekking:
   (a) Protect the natural environment.
   - Leave the campsite cleaner than you found it.
   - Limit deforestation – make no open fires.
   - Burn dry papers and packets in a safe place.
   - Keep local water clean and avoid using pollutants.
   - Plants should be left to flourish in their natural environment.
   - Help your guides and porters to follow conservation measures.
7. Respect local traditions, protect local cultures, maintain local pride.
   - When taking photographs, respect privacy.
   - Respect holy places.
   - Refrain from giving money to children since it will encourage begging.
   - Respect for local etiquette earns you respect.
8. Filming in restricted or notified areas without permission is strictly prohibited.

THANKS!

– Department of Immigration

Reflecting on trekking

93

1 "1999"

1. Oh, I.R.A. and U.V.F. this song is just for you
    As you sit down at the table now to see what you can do
    At last you've come together after all the tears and time
    It's sad you didn't do it back in Nineteen Sixty-Nine
2. History calls you savages but I know that isn't true   5
    For we grew up together and I am part of you
    We all had dreams and hopes and fears and someone else to blame
    It took so long to realise our dreams were all the same.

Chorus: *You know our dreams were all the same but who would dare proclaim*
    in the anger and the pain our dreams were all the same   10

3. We felt the taste of hunger when the factory went away
    And then they closed the hospital they said it didn't pay
    And as the rich got richer and kept promising the sky
    All we got were promises and coloured flags to fly
4. I remember well your little girl she had ribbons in her hair   15
    When she came to play that summer's day with the children in the square
    To think they could be here today still laughing and alive
    If strong men had been wise men in 1979
5. It was always all or nothing there was nothing in between
    Compromise was treachery that's the way it seemed   20
    Well now we're left with nothing but a future we must find
    And count the cost of the chances lost in 1989
6. Oh I.R.A. and U.V.F. this song is just for you
    As you sit down at the table now to see what you can do
    At last you've come together after all the tears and time   25
    It's sad you didn't do it back in Nineteen Ninety-Nine.   Tommy Sands

1. a) The language of songs is often very emotive. This means that the singer tries to involve
       people in the emotions he himself is feeling.
       Look at these words and phrases which Tommy Sands uses:

    > after all the tears and time (l.3) savages (l.5) I am part of you (l.6) our dreams were all the
    > same (l.8) we felt the taste of hunger (l.11) all we got were promises (l.14) if strong men had
    > been wise men (l.18)

    Which emotions is the singer trying to express? (loyalty/pride/sadness/sympathy/anger/...)
    b) Find more emotive words and phrases in the song and try to say what emotions they
       provoke.

2. The phrases used in songs often have a 'hidden' meaning. Look at the phrases in exercise 1
    again. Explain what they mean, using your knowledge of the history of Ireland and the
    political situation today.

3. Now listen to the song.
    a) Try to sum up its message.
    b) How do you feel about using songs and music as a way to put across a message like this?

▷ 4. What do you feel strongly about in your own country? Write down your feelings about it. Be
    prepared to read out your text to the class.

2 Ceantar na nOileán.

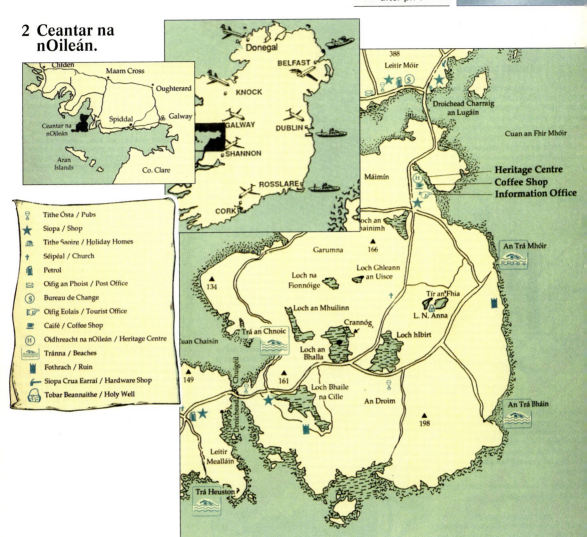

🍺	Tithe Ósta / Pubs
★	Siopa / Shop
🏠	Tithe Saoire / Holiday Homes
✝	Séipéal / Church
⛽	Petrol
✉	Oifig an Phoist / Post Office
Ⓢ	Bureau de Change
☞	Oifig Eolais / Tourist Office
☕	Caifé / Coffee Shop
Ⓗ	Oidhreacht na nOileán / Heritage Centre
〰	Tránna / Beaches
⬛	Fothrach / Ruin
🔧	Siopa Crua Earraí / Hardware Shop
⚱	Tobar Beannaithe / Holy Well

Here is a map of one of the Oileán islands off the west coast of Ireland, where many families still speak Irish. The islands are so small that you will only find them on a large map of Ireland.

1. The chart contains English and Irish words. Why do you think both words are given?
2. Listen to an Irish person saying some of the Irish words.
   a) Write down the English words for what she says.
   b) Why do you think some of the words are only given in English, or have an Irish word which is very similar
3. Look at the map again, and find out
   a) the Irish word for 'beach' (sing. and plur.),
   b) the Irish word for 'lake' (it's the same in Scottish Gaelic);
   c) what sound the letters 'si' stand for in Irish.
▷ 4. Look at maps of Ireland and Northern Europe. How could you travel from your home to this group of small islands?

Understanding a map with Irish words

The Children

He was almost ready to go when I found him. He was, to be exact, tying the final things to his blackened and blistered truck.

5 "Another newspaper man?"

"The Weekly, Mr Allen. We thought there might be something more to it," I said gently. "We know the dailies never tell a straight story."

"They did this time," he replied. "I'm not
10 making excuses. But I'll pay! I'll pay for the rest of my life."

The marks of fire were all over him. Burned boots and clothes, singed eyebrows, blistered face and hands, little marks all over his hat
15 where sparks had fallen. The waves of smoke were still coming up from the valley. Fifty yards away, the dusty track marked the western border of destruction. The ground on this side was the first brown earth I had seen since
20 leaving Burt's Creek; Allen's house the first survivor of the houses I had passed.

"It must have been hell!" I said.

"That?" He made a gesture of indifference. "That's nothing. It'll come good again. It's the
25 children."

"I know."

He was looking away from me now, in the way of a man living something all over again, something he can't leave alone. It was the most
30 unhappy assignment I had ever been given. I couldn't get out of my mind the hatred in the faces of some men down on the main road when I'd asked the way to the Allen home. I took out my cigarettes, and was pleased when
35 he took one. A man won't do that if he has decided not to talk to you.

"How did it come to be you?" I asked.

"Vince chose me because I had the truck with me. I'd been down the valley to bring up more
40 men."

"Then it isn't true …"

"That I wanted the job because of my own kids? No! That's a damned lie. I didn't even have a reason to be worried about my own kids
45 just then. I'm not trying to get out of it, but there's plenty of others to blame. Those children should never have been there to begin

with. They should have been sent down to the valley on Friday or kept in their homes."

He turned, pointing to the top of Wanga Hill. 50 Through the smoke we could make out the little heap of ruins closely surrounded by black and naked spars that had once been trees.

"Just look at it!" he said vehemently. "Trees right up to the fences! A school in a small field 55 – in a country like this!"

His arm fell. "But what's the use of talking? I was told to go and get the kids out, and I didn't do it. I got my own. Nothing else matters now."

"You thought there was time to go and pick up 60 your own children first, and then go on to the school, Mr Allen?"

"That's about it," he assented unhappily.

I'd felt all along that he did want to talk to someone about it. It came now suddenly. 65

"I'll tell you this: there isn't another person in the world who would have done anything else. I should be shot – I wish to God they would shoot me! – but I'm still no worse than anyone else. I was the one it happened to, that's all. 70 Them people who lost kids have a perfect right to hate my guts, but supposing it had been one of them?

Suppose it had been you … what would you have done?" 75

I just looked at him.

"You know, don't you? In your own heart you know?"

"Yes, I know."

"The way it happened, you'd think somebody 80 had laid a trap for me.

Vince had heard that the fire had jumped the main road and was working up the far side of Wanga. And he told me to take the truck and make sure the kids had been got away from the 85 school. All right – now follow me. I get started. I come along the low road there. I get the idea right away that I'll pick up my own wife and kids afterwards. But when I reach that bit of open country, I look up. And, so help me God, 90 there's smoke. Now that can only mean one thing: that part of the fire is heading this way. I can see the roof of my house, and there's smoke showing at the back of it. And I've got a

95 wife and kids there. The other way there's twenty kids, but there's no smoke showing yet. What would you expect me to do?"

He would see the answer in my face.

"When did you first realise you were too late 100 for the school?"

"As soon as I pulled up here. My wife had seen me coming. She ran up to the truck as I stopped, shouting and pointing behind me."

He closed his eyes and shivered. "When I looked back, I couldn't see the school."

105 I waited while he closed his eyes and shook his head slowly from side to side.

"You turned back …"

"Yes, damn my soul! I turned back. There was fire everywhere. Look at the truck. The road was alight both sides all the way back. 110 Just the same, it would have been better if we'd gone on."

A minute or two later I said goodbye. He was reluctant to take my hand.

"I kept telling myself somebody else might have 115 got the kids out," he whispered. "But nobody did. And on top of everything my own place got missed!"

In the afternoon, standing near the ruins of the hotel, I saw him passing … 120

A big, fire-scarred truck rolling slowly down the road … Here and there people searching the ashes of their homes stood upright and watched with hard and bitter faces.

(from: *Stories from the Waterfront* by John Morrison) (slightly adapted)

1. Try to work out what makes this story moving.

2. Discuss the question of blame in this story.

3. Explain what Mr Allen means when he says (l.106) "… it would have been better if we had gone on."

4. Write the newspaperman's report for "The Weekly".

HISTORY KALEIDOSCOPE

after p.79

1. Some historical background is useful if you are visiting Great Britain.
a) What historical facts or figures do you already know? Make a list.
b) Read the information below, and match it up with the photos.
c) Make a time chart in your exercise book, or on paper for your classroom.
   Fill in historical facts and events.
Add your own ideas from part a).

1 The stories behind the stones

1. Stonehenge, near Salisbury, is the finest stone circle in Europe. It was built between 3000 BC and 1500 BC by Celtic peoples, the first known inhabitants of Britain. It is like a huge calendar – on Midsummer's Day the sun rises exactly over the main stone and shines on the middle of the circle.

a)

2. Hadrian's Wall was built by the Romans to keep the Scots in the North. The Romans came in 55 BC and left in about 400 AD, as the Roman Empire collapsed. Then the Angles and Saxons began to move into Britain in the south and east (Angle-land = England), and the Britons were forced into the mountains of the north and west.

The Scottish, Irish and Welsh languages spoken today are a development of those early Celtic languages.
Place names beginning with 'Aber-' or 'Ca(e)r' or ending in 'don' are of Celtic origin, and those ending in 'chester', like Manchester or Winchester show where Roman camps (castra) used to be.

b)

3. Today when we think of the Tower of London we think of the Crown Jewels, but it was originally built by William the Conqueror, a Norman from the north of France, the last foreigner to conquer England (in 1066). He had about 40 castles built throughout England, in important strategic places, e.g. York, Nottingham and Windsor (home of today's Royal Family.) Many of these can still be visited.

c)

d)

4. Fountains Abbey is only one of many ruins of abbeys and monasteries in England. You may have heard of Henry the Eighth (with the six wives – "divorced, beheaded, died; divorced, beheaded, survived"). When Henry wanted to divorce his first wife, as she hadn't had a son, in order to marry Anne Boleyn, the pope refused to give him a divorce. Henry then declared himself head of the Church of England, and so obtained his divorce. When the abbeys and monasteries protested, Henry had them closed. Throughout the centuries, local people have taken stones from the former monasteries to build their own homes.

2 Women who made their mark on history

5. Elizabeth (1558–1603), daughter of Henry VIII and Anne Boleyn, was queen for 45 years. She never married, and she showed that a woman on her own could rule her country as well as any man – and better than most. England was a small country, but under Elizabeth it became wealthy and respected. Schools and hospitals were founded, theatres were opened. England's greatest poet, William Shakespeare, wrote his plays and poems, the English sailor Francis Drake sailed around the world. When King Philip of Spain tried to invade England in 1588, his great 'Armada' of 130 ships with 8000 men was defeated by the small and fast English ships. This was the beginning of England's sea power.

6. With the invention of new machines and the steam engine in the 1760s began the Industrial Revolution. People started to leave the country, hoping for work in the new factories and coalmines, but the pay was so bad that the whole family had to work. Working and living conditions were terrible. When Victoria came to the throne, Britain's cities were dark, dirty places.
During Victoria's reign (1843–1901), Britain became an even more powerful and wealthy country, the "workshop of the world". Britain's many colonies were brought together in the "British Empire". Many reforms of working conditions, especially for women and children, were introduced, and primary schools were built for all children.

7. In the Victorian age, more and more men had won the right to vote. But women – half the population – still did not have the vote in 1900. Emmeline Pankhurst decided as a girl to fight for women's rights. She went to her first political meeting when she was 14. Later, helped by her daughters Christabel and Sylvia, Emmeline organized the women's movement to win the vote.
In 1914, war with Germany came. As men went off to fight, women took their place in the factories. These women helped to win the war. Now the government had to give women the vote. In 1918 the first women voted, and in 1928, all men and women over 21 got the right to vote. In the same year, Emmeline Pankhurst died.

8. Queen Elizabeth II came to the throne in 1953. In the second Elizabethan age, the last of the former colonies became independent. Yet through the Commonwealth and the widespread use of English, Britain remains the focus of the English-speaking world. This second Elizabethan age, too, will go down in history, perhaps as the Technological Revolution or the Communication Revolution.

2. Find out (from parents, grandparents…) how much has changed since 1953, when Elizabeth II came to the throne. (Think of things like TV, telephone, food, travel…)

e)

f)

g)

h)

Reading about famous women

99

3 The road to democracy

Democracy and parliament seem normal to us, but many years ago it was the Monarch who had complete power. Here are some of the milestones on the long road to democracy.

- When King John raised high taxes to pay for his unpopular wars, the barons led their armies against him and made him sign the Magna Carta in 1215. This gave 'free men' certain rights (although most people were not 'free men').

- 50 years later the first parliament met – the 'Lords' in one room, the 'commoners' in another. English was now used as well as Norman French.

- In 1536 Henry VIII took away rights from the church, becoming the Head of the Church of England. British Kings and Queens are still Head of the Church of England, at least in name.

- Although Elizabeth I worked with Parliament, the kings following her didn't. In fact Charles I ruled for 11 years (1629–1640) without a parliament. This led to civil war. In the end the king was

executed and Oliver Cromwell became Lord Protector (1654). So the rights of the kings passed to a commoner. On his death, however, Parliament decided to have a Monarch again, and England has always had a king or queen since, as well as a parliament.

- Only a few years later, however, King James again tried to rule without a parliament. Members of parliament secretly asked James's daughter Mary and her husband Prince William of Orange to come to England as king and queen – not 'by right', but by invitation. It was a revolution without fighting – a Glorious Revolution (1688).
  But first they had to sign the 'Bill of Rights' (1689), which made sure that Britain could never be ruled without or against Parliament. England had become a constitutional monarchy.

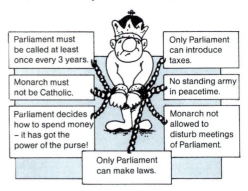

Parliament must be called at least once every 3 years.

Only Parliament can introduce taxes.

Monarch must not be Catholic.

No standing army in peacetime.

Parliament decides how to spend money – it has got the power of the purse!

Monarch not allowed to disturb meetings of Parliament.

Only Parliament can make laws.

- By 1928, all men and women in Britain had the right to vote (universal suffrage). New forms of 'people power' begin to develop, e. g. strikes, referenda.

1. What can you assume from the notes you have read on the Magna Carta and the Bill of Rights about the powers earlier monarchs had, or the way they ruled?
2. Collect other forms of 'people power', and discuss if they are all equally democratic.
3. Which European countries still have a monarchy? Discuss the role of a monarchy in the modern world.

4 Parliament today

The Houses of Parliament (Westminster)

Nr. 10 Downing Street, the home of the Prime Minister

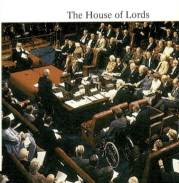

The House of Lords

Parliament today

Parliament consists of two Houses – the **House of Commons** and the **House of Lords**. The House of Commons has 659 elected Members, representing 659 constituencies, or areas of the country. The House of Lords has about 1200 non-elected Members (bishops, archbishops, dukes, earls, and about 350 respected citizens, who have been made Members by the Monarch.

Every **Member of Parliament** (**MP**), even the Prime Minister, has to be elected directly by the voters of a constituency. The person with the largest number of votes at the General Election becomes the Member for that constituency, even if perhaps 70 % of the voters voted for other people. This is known as the 'first-past-the-post'-system.

Scotland and Wales have separate parliaments for internal affairs.

The House of Commons

1. Find out which party is in power in the United Kingdom, and the names of the Prime Minister, the Foreign Secretary and the Leader of the Opposition.
2. Check in the Internet for more up-to-date information. (www.parliament.uk)
3. Compare this voting system with the voting system in your country.

TIP

To learn the facts in the History Kaleidoscope more easily, make a puzzle. Write important names or events on pieces of paper. Then write notes for each on other pieces of paper. Mix them and try to match them. Then exchange with a partner.

Looking at facts about and pictures of parliament

GRAMMAR

Jeder Grammatikabschnitt (G) gehört zu einer bestimmten Seite vorne in den Topics; diesen Seitenverweis **page 17** findet ihr rechts oben vor jedem Abschnitt.

Die Grammatikseiten helfen euch beim Englischlernen.
Ihr könnt sie benutzen,
- wenn ihr Hausaufgaben macht,
- wenn ihr euch auf eine Klassenarbeit vorbereitet,
- wenn ihr nicht sicher seid, wie ein Grammatikphänomen zu erklären ist,
- wenn ihr eine Übersicht braucht, z. B. wie in G1.

Von besonderer Hilfe sind:

Revision: – Hier wird etwas übersichtlich dargeboten, erweitert oder wiederholt.

 – Vorsicht! Hier ist etwas besonders kompliziert.

GRAMMATICAL TERMS

Englisch	Englisches Beispiel	Lateinisch / Deutsch
adjective	Robert is a **good** friend.	Adjektiv / Eigenschaftswort
adverb	He **often** works **quickly**.	Adverb / Umstandswort
of frequency	I **never** get up late.	Häufigkeitsadverb
of manner	They are skating **slowly**.	Adverb der Art und Weise
auxiliaries G5	**mustn't, needn't, can, may, might, have to**	Hilfsverben
clause	**… which they really liked.**	Satzteil
comparative	**bigger, more boring**	Komparativ / 1. Steigerungsform
conditional G6	… we **would** win.	Konditional
conditional perfect G6	… we **would have** won.	Konditional der Vergangenheit
conjunction	**and, or, because, when** etc.	Konjunktion / Bindewort
consonant	**b, f, g, t** etc.	Konsonant / Mitlaut
countable noun G9	**bottle, apple**	zählbares Nomen
direct speech	**"I'm hungry."**	Direkte Rede
dynamic verbs	He**'s getting up**. He **gets up**.	Dynamisches Verb / Tätigkeitsverb
for G8	**for two years**	seit (Zeitdauer)
genitive	Jenny is **David's** cousin. / the photo **of** a dog	Genitiv / Wes-Fall
gerund G21	I like **cooking**. / **Cooking** is fun.	Gerundium
'going to'	**I'm going to** buy a CD.	das 'going to'-Futur

indirect speech G13–15	She said **she was hungry.**	Indirekte Rede
infinitive G21	**to play, to live, to be**	Infinitiv / Grundform
infinitive structures G20	I don't know how **to say** this … /	Infinitivstrukturen
	I heard them **sing.**	
irregular verb	**be, go, come** etc.	unregelmäßiges Verb
noun	**book, girl, cousin**	Nomen (Substantiv)/Hauptwort
object	She must clean **the cage.**	Objekt/Satzergänzung
passive G5–G6	English **is spoken** here.	Passiv / Leideform
past participle	**checked, seen, done** etc.	Partizip Perfekt / Mittelwort
		der Vergangenheit
past perfect	He **had finished**, so he left.	Plusquamperfekt
past progressive G7	he **was eating**, we **were eating**	Verlaufsform der Vergangenheit
past simple G7	We **finished** and **went** home.	Imperfekt / einfache
		Vergangenheit
personal pronoun	**she, he** etc.	Personalpronomen /
		persönliches Fürwort
possessive (adjective)	**my, your, his, her** etc.	Possessivbegleiter /
		besitzanzeigendes Fürwort
predicate	They **are playing a game.**	Prädikat / Satzaussage
present perfect	It **has disappeared.**	Perfekt / vollendete Gegenwart
simple G7		
present perfect	She **has been doing** her home-	Verlaufsform des Perfekt
progressive	work for hours.	
present simple G1	I often **go** to school by bike.	einfaches Präsens /
		einfache Gegenwart
present simple for	The train **leaves** at 9.	einfaches Präsens in
the future		futurischer Bedeutung
present progressive G1	Today **I'm going** by bus.	Verlaufsform der Gegenwart
pronoun	**she, he, it, we, you, they**	Pronomen / Fürwort
quantity	**a box of, two pounds of**	Menge
reciprocal pronoun	**each other**	Reziprokes Pronomen
reflexive pronoun	**myself, yourselves**	Reflexivpronomen
regular verb	**work, look, invite**	regelmäßiges Verb
relative clause G17–18	**… who isn't here.**	Relativsatz
relative pronoun G17–18	**who, which, that**	Relativpronomen
sentence	**Let's go home.**	Satz
sentence with 'if'	**If** it rains tomorrow, …	If-Satz
signal word	**sometimes, usually** etc.	Signalwort
since G8	**since last week**	seit (Zeitpunkt)
stative verb	**be, know, like, want**	statisches Verb / Zustandsverb
subject	**The bike** is in the shop.	Subjekt / Satzgegenstand
substitute verb	**be able to, needn't**	Ersatzverb
superlative	**biggest, most boring**	Superlativ / 2. Steigerungsform
syllable	**'Hap-py'** has two syllables.	Silbe
uncountable noun	**bread, butter** etc.	nicht zählbares Nomen
verb + adjective	It **tastes wonderful.**	Verb + Adjektiv
verb + adverb	Please **write clearly.**	Verb + Adverb
verb of perception	**see, hear, smell**	Verb der Wahrnehmung
vowel	**a, e, i, o, u**	Vokal / Selbstlaut
'will / won't'	He **will** go but she **won't.**	das 'will'-Futur

G1 Revision: Present simple and present progressive

Present simple

The ABI studios **stand** on the corner of Church Road and Mount Street.
Kathleen *never* **arrives** late for work.

She **gets up** *every* morning at 6 o'clock.
She **doesn't** *often* **go out** in the evenings.
At the weekend she *sometimes* **has** breakfast in bed.

She *usually* **cleans** her car on Saturday afternoons.
– And what **do** you *normally* **do** on Sundays, Kathleen?

– *First* I **read** my mail, *then* I **do** some sport and *after that* I **watch** television.

The present simple is used:

– for something which is always true.

Signal words:	always, never

– for something which happens regularly.

Signal words:	every …, often, sometimes

– for things which are normal or usual

Signal words:	usually, normally

– for a series of actions

Signal words:	first, then, after that

Present progressive

Come on Asim. We**'re waiting** for you.
What on earth **are** you **doing**?
I**'m looking** for my ticket.

I**'m meeting** the club president *at 12.30*.
Susi **is going** to a meeting *next week*.

The present progressive is used:

– for actions which are happening at the time of speaking.

– for actions which are planned or arranged for the future, normally with an adverb of future time.

G2 Dynamic and stative verbs

Dynamic verbs describe an activity and can be used in both the simple and the progressive form.

Progressive form	Simple form
– Come on, Asim. It's 7 o'clock. – I**'m getting** up, Mum.	Asim **gets** up at 7 o'clock every morning.
– Where's Dad? – He**'s listening** to the news.	He always **listens** to the news before breakfast.

Stative verbs describe a state. They are only used in the simple form.

Verbs of state:	be, become
Verbs of liking and disliking:	like, dislike, love, hate
Verbs of thinking:	know, understand, think, believe, feel
Verbs of wanting:	want, wish
Verbs of perception:	taste, smell, sound, feel, look
Verbs of possession:	have, own

TIP BOX

If you can watch somebody doing something, then it's an activity, e.g. you can watch somebody playing football or making a pizza, but you can't watch somebody '*knowing*' *something* or '*being*' from America. So *play* and *make* are dynamic verbs, *know* and *be* are stative verbs

G3 Verbs which can be stative or dynamic

page 18/19

Some verbs which are normally stative can sometimes be used to describe an activity. Then they can be used in the progressive form.

	STATIVE	DYNAMIC
be	Miguela **is** a crazy girl, = SEIN	but today she's **being** sensible for a change. = SICH VERHALTEN
have	The Costners **have** a new kitchen. = BESITZEN	At the moment they're **having** breakfast there. = ESSEN
feel	This jacket **feels** very wet. = SICH ANFÜHLEN	I'm **feeling** cold. = SICH FÜHLEN

G4 Using participles

page 20/21

a) for observing actions (especially after verbs of perception like *hear, notice, see, watch*)

	verb of perception	object	present participle
Yesterday we	saw	someone	acting strangely in a shop.
We	watched	him	putting something under his jacket.
Then we	noticed	a woman	walking towards him.
We	heard	her	asking him to come with her.

This structure is used when someone sees or hears part of an action. Sometimes they miss the beginning or the end. Often they miss both.

b) for shortening relative clauses

What we didn't know at the time was:
The man **who was** acting strangely was the store detective.
The man **acting** strangely was the store detective.

He wanted to test assistants **who were** doing a training course.
He wanted to test assistants **doing** a training course.

The woman **who was** speaking to the man was a shop assistant.
The woman **speaking** to the man was a shop assistant.

Sentences which have a relative clause with an *-ing* form can be made shorter by leaving out the **relative pronoun** (*who, which, that*) and the form of **be** (*is, are, was, were*). ⇨ G18

c) for combining two actions which someone does at the same time

The woman stood. **She spoke** to the man for about five minutes.
The woman stood speaking to the man for about five minutes.

The man then went. **He hurried** towards the door.
The man then went hurrying towards the door.

The woman came up to us. **She was smiling.**
The woman came up to us smiling.

We can join two sentences with the same subject by leaving out the subject of the second sentence and using only the *-ing* form of the verb.

G5 Modal auxiliaries and the passive

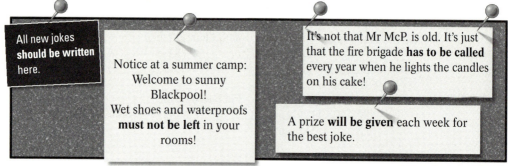

All new jokes **should be written** here.

Notice at a summer camp: Welcome to sunny Blackpool! Wet shoes and waterproofs **must not be left** in your rooms!

It's not that Mr McP. is old. It's just that the fire brigade **has to be called** every year when he lights the candles on his cake!

A prize **will be given** each week for the best joke.

Be + past participle = passive

Subject	(modal)	form of 'be'	past participle	
School rules		are	made	by teachers.
School rules	should	be	made	by the pupils.
Pupils	may	be	asked	to do homework.
Uniforms	must	be	worn	in school.
Drinks	must not	be	taken	into classrooms.
Snacks	can	be	bought	in the cafeteria.
Bicycles	have to	be	locked	by their owners.
Parents	will	be	invited	to parents' evenings.

The passive is used in formal speech, especially in writing.

G6 The passive form of verbs with two objects

page 33

a) Some verbs can have two objects. Look at these two sentences.
1. They gave me **a prize**. 2. They gave a prize **to me**.
Both have the same basic meaning.
In both *prize* is the **direct object** and *me* or *to me* is the **indirect object.**

b) There are also two different possibilities in the passive.

I was given a prize.

They gave *me* **a prize.**

A prize was given to me.

Here we put at the end the object that we want to stress.
In 'I was given **a prize**,' we stress the object.
In 'A prize was given **to me**,' we stress the indirect object.

They teach first-year *pupils* **the basic skills.** ⟹ First-year pupils are taught **the basic skills.**
OR The basic skills are taught to **first-year pupils.**

G7 Revision: Talking about the past

page 34/35

Terrible Tim's story

It was a beautiful day yesterday, so I **walked** to school.

| Past simple to describe a new action |

Suddenly a figure in a mask **jumped** out in front of me: "Hands up or I'll shoot!" The robber was pointing a rather dangerous-looking banana at me, so I **did** as I was told.

"Give me back my Spice Girls CD. You**'ve had** it for weeks." Now I recognized the voice – it was Crazy Daisy. "That's not true, Daisy, you only gave it to me on Saturday…

| Present perfect to show something started in the past and has lasted up till now. |

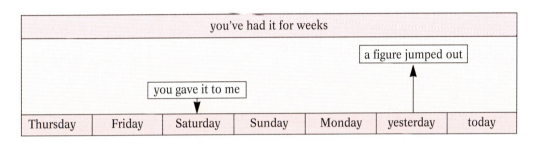

| Thursday | Friday | Saturday | Sunday | Monday | yesterday | today |

you've had it for weeks

you gave it to me

a figure jumped out

• The **past tense** is used for past events that are completely in the past. This is often shown
i) by adverbs like:
ago, yesterday, last …, then, when … at that time
ii) with days – *on Monday*
iii) with months – *in June*
iv) years – *in 1998*

– When **did** you **take** your exams?
– I **took** my GCSEs in June.
  I **got** my results two days ago.

• The **present perfect** is used for past events that are linked to the present in some way.

1. Events which started in the past and have lasted up to the present. This is shown by the adverbs *for, since, how long*.

– How long **have** you **been** at Haywood?
– I**'ve been** here *for* three years.

2. Events which have happened in the recent past. This is often shown by the adverbs *just, only just, recently*.

I**'ve** *just* **taken** my GCSEs.
Have you **seen** Mrs Dale *recently*?

3. Events during a time in the past up to the present, when it is not said exactly when the events happened.
Especially with adverbs like: *ever, never, up to now, already, yet, in my life*

– **Have** you **had** your exam results *yet*?
– No, I think the postman **has lost** the letter.
– I**'ve** *never* **heard** such an excuse in all my life!

G8 Since and for

page 32

– How long have you known Susan?
– I've known her for about seven months, since February to be exact.

Wie lange kennen Sie Susan schon?
Ich kenne sie seit ungefähr sieben Monaten, seit Februar, um genau zu sein.

I have known her

FOR → ← **SINCE**

FOR	**SINCE**
fifteen years, three months, two weeks, six weeks, half an hour, a long time	Tuesday, last month, 1998, January, 3 o'clock, yesterday, lunch
WITH A PERIOD OF TIME	**WITH A DEFINITE POINT OF TIME**

G9 Countable and uncountable nouns   Zählbare und nicht zählbare Nomen

page 36

girl	a girl, one girl, two girls, three girls …
egg	an egg, one egg, two eggs, three eggs …

Countable nouns have a plural form. You can also use *a* or *one* with them.

weather, butter, bread
advice, fun, hair, information

Uncountable nouns have no plural form. You cannot use *a* or *one, two, three* … with them.

Pass me **the butter**, please.
Let me give you **some advice**.
We don't have **any information** on this topic.
No risk, **no fun**.
Can I have **two pieces of bread**?

You can use:
the
some
any
no
a piece of/… pieces of
with uncountable nouns.

Some English uncountable nouns are countable in German:

Can I give you **a piece of advice**?
We have **no information** on this topic.
My **hair** is too long. I need a haircut.

*Darf ich Ihnen **einen Rat** geben?*
*Wir haben **keine Informationen** zu diesem Thema.*
*Meine **Haare** sind zu lang. Ich muss sie schneiden lassen.*

"Have you ever had a nice day?"

G10 The modal auxiliaries *may*, *might* and *could*

May, **might** and **could** express *possibility*.

– Where's Zoe? – I'm not sure – she **may** be in the bathroom. Brad, can you help her with her home-work, she said she **may** need help.

May is used when the speaker is not sure what the situation is, but can make a good guess.

– You should use your notes, Zoe. You **might** find it easier then.
– You **might** get an 'A' this time.
– Yes! And pigs **might** fly.
– If we start now, we **might** have time to watch that film.

Might is used to speculate about something, even if it is not probable.

Might is especially used in conditional sentences.

– I've done ten sentences but I still don't understand it.
– You **could** try going back to the story in your book.

Could is often used to suggest a possibility, especially to give advice.

G11 *used to*   page 48/49

My father **used to** smoke but he's given up now, thank goodness.
We **used to** bake our own bread, but now we buy it from the supermarket.
Our town **used to** be so beautiful – now they've built all those horrible new buildings.

Used to describes what somebody did in earlier times but which they don't do any more. It can also describe a situation which is no longer true.

> **TIP BOX**
> • the best way to translate *used to* into German is to use *früher*
> • *used to* is only used in this form – there is no other tense
> • don't mix up *to use* and *used to*
>   I **used** a hammer – Ich **benutzte** einen Hammer.
>   I **used to** believe in Santa Claus – **Früher** glaubte ich an den Weihnachtsmann
> • the negative form is *didn't use to*

G12 The emphatic *do*   page 48/49

I **do** like your jeans!
I **do** hope you're not going to cry during this film.
Perhaps money **does** talk after all.

Do/does are used in front of an infinitive to express strong feelings.

Ich mag deine Jeans wirklich sehr!
Ich hoffe bloß, dass du bei dem Film nicht anfängst zu weinen.
*Vielleicht ist letztendlich das Geld **doch** das Entscheidende.*

In German there are different ways of expressing the **emphatic 'do'**.

Grammar

G13 Revision: Reporting what people have said

page 50/51

a)

Some verbs for reporting
add that
explain that
inform s. o. that
* say (that)
* think (that)
* tell s. o. (that)

* *that* is optional here

b)

Words which can change in indirect speech	
I ⇨ she/he	this morning ⇨ that morning
my ⇨ her/his	yesterday ⇨ the day before
we ⇨ they	last week ⇨ the week before
our ⇨ their	tonight ⇨ last night
this ⇨ that	tomorrow ⇨ the next day
here ⇨ there	two days ago ⇨ two days before

c)

Tense changes in indirect speech (backshift)	
Direct speech	**Indirect speech**
simple present	simple past
present progressive	past progressive
simple past present perfect	past perfect
past progressive present perfect progressive	past perfect progressive
'will' future	conditional

I arrived here yesterday at 10 o'clock. My exchange partner is very nice. I'm sure we will become good friends. Love, Bronwyn.

Bronwyn told us that she **had arrived there the day before** at 10 o'clock. She said that her exchange partner **was** very nice. She added that she **was** sure **they would** become good friends.

G14 Reporting questions

page 50/51

Question in direct speech	⇨ Indirect speech
Without question word "Are you from Germany?" "Have you been to London?" "Did you see the Tower?"	**ask/want to know + if/whether** ⇨ Mrs Watkins **asked** me if I was from Germany. ⇨ She wanted to know **if/whether** I had been to London. ⇨ She wanted to know **if/whether** I had seen the Tower.
With question word "How long have you been in Wales?" "When did you arrive?"	**ask/want to know + question word** ⇨ She **asked** me how long I had been in Wales. ⇨ She **wanted to know** when I had arrived.

If there is no question word in the direct question then we use *if/whether* in the indirect speech. If there is a question word in the direct question then we must use it in the indirect speech.

15 Reporting instructions or imperatives

page 51

Instructions/imperatives	Reported instructions/imperatives
"If you travel to Wales take our advice – you should pack warm clothes. Don't forget your waterproofs. Please don't complain about the weather."	Our teachers told us **to take** their advice. They advised us **to pack** warm clothes. They warned us not **to forget** our waterproofs. They asked us **not to complain** about the weather.

Instructions and imperatives usually change to infinitives in indirect speech.
The infinitives are used with reporting verbs. (*advise, warn, ask* …).

We can also use *should/should not*.

They said we **should** pack warm clothes.
They told us we **should not** complain about the weather.

"No, he's not ours! We thought you'd brought him."

TOPIC 4   THE WORLD AROUND US

G16 Revision: Conditional sentences

page 60

Conditional sentences are used to speculate about the future or about the past. There are three basic types.

Type 1

If you **use** less water, you **will save** money. If we **don't start** saving energy now, it **will be** too late. IF-CLAUSE + *PRESENT SIMPLE*, MAIN CLAUSE + *WILL*   ⇨

Type 1 is used to **predict** something in the **future**. The speaker believes that this event is probable or logical.

Type 2

If we **built** more wind farms, we **wouldn't need** so much nuclear energy. If we **didn't use** our cars so often, we **would have** a lot less pollution. IF-CLAUSE + *SIMPLE PAST*, MAIN CLAUSE + *WOULD*   ⇨

Type 2 is also used to **speculate** about the **future**. In this case the speaker is often not sure whether this situation will come true.

If I **were** President, I would close down all the nuclear power stations. If it **were** possible, we would do it. If he **were** an animal, he'd be a pig. If I **was** President, I would close down all the nuclear power stations.   ⇨

Type 2 is often used to **speculate** about **events** which are very unlikely or even impossible. In this case we often say "If I/he/she/it *were* …". It is also possible to use the normal form "If I/he/she/it *was* …"

Type 3

If you **had worn** a hat, you **wouldn't have burned** so badly. IF-CLAUSE + *PAST PERFECT*, MAIN CLAUSE + *WOULD HAVE*   ✗⇦

Type 3 is used when the speaker is **speculating** about the **past**. This situation is no longer possible.

G17 Defining and non-defining clauses

page 61

> Have you heard about the people **who went on board the Brent Spar to protest**?
> There are lots of firms **that dump their waste at sea**.

- If you leave out the relative clauses in these sentences, the rest of the sentence doesn't make sense.
- This type of relative clause is called a **defining relative clause** because it answers the question "Which people?" or "What about these firms?". It is **necessary** for the meaning of the whole sentence.
- The relative pronouns *who*, *which* and *that* can be used in defining relative clauses. There are **no commas** round defining relative clauses.

Shell, **which is one of the richest companies in the world**, was forced to change its plans. Prince Charles, **who is very interested in environmental questions**, wrote to Shell and asked them to change their plans.

- If you leave out the relative clause in these sentences, the rest of the sentence makes perfect sense – it is complete in itself.
- This means that the relative clause is simply adding information and is called a **non-defining relative clause**. It is **not necessary** for the meaning of the whole sentence.
- The relative pronoun *that* is not used in this type of relative clause. There are usually commas before and after a non-defining relative clause.

G18 Shortened relative clauses
page 62

Newspapers **which are** printed on recycled paper are better for the environment.
⇨ Newspapers printed on recycled paper are better for the environment.
Energy **that is** produced by nuclear power is expensive.
⇨ Energy produced by nuclear power is expensive.

Defining relative clauses can be shortened in this way if the verb in the relative clause is in the passive form. The relative pronoun and the form of 'be' are left out. ⇨ G4

G19 'have something done'
page 62

I **have** my hair **cut** once a month. = *Ich lasse mir die Haare einmal im Monat schneiden.*

HAVE + OBJECT + PAST PARTICIPLE –> have something done

This structure can be used in all tenses. Here are a few examples:
My grandma **has** her hair **done** every week. ⇨ *Meine Oma lässt sich jede Woche die Haare frisieren.*
We **have had** our house **painted**. ⇨ *Wir haben unser Haus anstreichen lassen.*
My mum **had** her car **repaired** last week.⇨ *Meine Mutter hat letzte Woche ihr Auto reparieren lassen.*
I **will have** the new fridge **delivered**. ⇨ *Ich werde den neuen Kühlschrank liefern lassen.*
You **should have** that tap **fixed**. ⇨ *Du solltest dir den Wasserhahn reparieren lassen!*

 Be careful. Don't confuse: 'I have my car repaired.' = Somebody else does it.
　　　　　　　　　　　　　　　　'I have repaired my car.' = I did it myself.

G20 '(n)either/(n)nor'
page 63

Paul: There's **either** beef **or** ham for tea. Which do you want?
Jan: **Either**. I like **both** beef **and** ham. What about you Jo?
Jo: **Neither**: I eat **neither** beef **nor** ham. I'm a vegetarian.
Sam: **So** am I. I never eat meat.
Jo: **Neither** do I. But I eat fish.

In short answers you use *either* and *neither* without 'or'.

When you agree with a positive statement, use '**So am I/do I/… .**'
When you agree with a negative statement, use '**Neither/Nor do I/am I/ … .**'
Note the word order in these short answers.

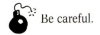 Be careful.

TOPIC 5   IRELAND

G21 Infinitive and gerund

page 66–71

• **verb + infinitive or verb + gerund**

> – I **want to clean** my bike today.
> – Oh, that's a horrible job.
> – Not for me, I **enjoy cleaning**.

The structure you use after a verb depends on which verb you use. Some verbs are followed by an infinitive (*to* …), some are followed by a gerund (*… -ing*).

Examples:

Verb + infinitive
agree, decide
expect, hope
offer, promise
want

Verb + gerund
avoid, enjoy
finish, imagine
mind, risk
suggest

• **verb + infinitive or gerund with almost no difference in meaning**

> I know a lot of people **like to dance**, but I don't **like dancing** much myself.

Some verbs can be followed by an infinitive (to …) or by a gerund (… ing).

verb + to … or … ing
begin, hate, like, prefer, start

 Would you like **to dance**?
Would like is always followed by the infinitve.

• **verb + infinitive or gerund with a difference in meaning**

remember

> – Did you **remember to invite** Kathleen and Ann?
> – Well, I **remember inviting** Ann, but I'm not sure about Kathleen.

⇨ daran denken
⇨ sich erinnern an

forget

> I **forgot to send** my girlfriend a birthday card.
> I'll never **forget meeting** my girlfriend for the first time.

⇨ vergessen, etwas zu tun
⇨ (nie) vergessen, wie man etwas gemacht hat

stop

> Mr O'Connor **stopped smoking** two years ago.
> The soldier **stopped to smoke**.

⇨ etwas aufgeben
⇨ anhalten, um etwas zu tun

try

> We are **trying to help** young people in our town.
> If you have a problem, **try talking** to somebody.

⇨ versuchen, etwas zu tun
⇨ etwas ausprobieren
  "Versuch's mal mit …"

mean

> I **meant to ask** her, but I forgot.
> If you want to help young people, it will **mean giving** up a lot of your free time.

⇨ beabsichtigen
⇨ bedeuten

• other infinitive constructions

The infinitive is used:
– **after** *the first…, the last…, the only…*

Robert was **the first guy** in our class **to have** a motorbike.
Pete was **the only one to notice** my new shoes.

⇨ der Erste, der
⇨ der Einzige, der

– **when** *to* means *in order to*

He sold everything **to pay** for his boat ticket.

⇨ um …, zu

– **after** *be supposed to, be said to, be estimated to*

Irish **is supposed to be** one of the oldest languages in Europe.
Queen Elizabeth **is said to be** the richest woman in the world.
English is **estimated to have** a vocabulary of 1.2 million words.

⇨ ist angeblich/soll

⇨ ist, so sagt man/soll

⇨ man schätzt, dass

• preposition + gerund
Prepositions are always followed by a noun or the noun form of a verb – the gerund.

– adjective + preposition

You shouldn't be **afraid of dogs/making** mistakes.
She's **excited about the trip/going** to Ireland.
We're **interested in art/working** together with you.

Where you can use a noun after 'to' you can use a gerund.

– verb + preposition + gerund

I **look forward to the party/meeting** you.
He **dreamt of the game/being** a football star.

Also: *believe in, depend on, worry about*

TIP BOX

'to' + infinitive or gerund?
Ask the question:
Can 'to' be followed by a noun in my sentence?
1. Example: 'I **hope to** … the football match.'
   The answer is 'no', so we need an infinitive.
   'I **hope to go to** the football match.'
2. Example: I'm **looking forward to** … the football match.'
   The answer is 'yes', so we use a gerund.
   'I'm **looking forward to going to** the football match.'

- Die neuen Wörter stehen in der Reihenfolge, wie sie im Text vorkommen. Einige der Vokabeln können mehrmals vorkommen, damit ihr – wenn erwünscht – flexibel mit den *Topics* im Buch arbeiten könnt. (Das Vokabular aller sechs *Topics* wird auf der Grundlage von Band 4 aufgeführt.)

- Ein Kringel vor dem Wort, z.B. °*to gather,* bedeutet: müsst ihr wiedererkennen, wenn es wieder auftaucht.

- Eine Spitzklammer, z.B. ⟨grace⟩, heißt: nur fakultativ, muss nicht gelernt werden.

- Die Lautschrift, z.B. [staɪl], zeigt euch genau die Aussprache. Habt ihr Probleme mit einem Lautzeichen, so hilft S. 117.

- Die Mittelspalte bietet allerlei Beispielsätze, Erklärungen und Bilder – alles, was euch das Verstehen und Lernen erleichtert. Das neue Wort wird in Beispielsätzen mit einer Tilde (~) ersetzt.

 True friend (im Deutschen (fast) das gleiche Wort)

 False friend (im Deutschen hat es eine andere Bedeutung)

 Hier ist besondere Vorsicht geboten.

Ansonsten gilt:

BE   heißt: *British English*
AE   heißt: *American English*
↔   heißt: das Gegenteil von
ugs.   heißt: umgangssprachlich

Auf den nächsten Seiten findet ihr wieder **Lerntipps** sowie das **Dictionary** zum Nachschlagen, S. 157
Bei manchen Texten werden nur die wichtigsten Wörter zum Lernen aufgeführt. Die übrigen findet ihr im **Dictionary,** oder es gibt einen Hinweis auf die Benutzung eines Wörterbuchs (englisch-deutsch).

Englische Lautzeichen (English sounds)

Selbstlaute (Vowels)

[ɑ:] car, father; ähnlich wie in *Bahn*
[ʌ]   number, bus, mother
[e]   yes, pen, friend; ähnlich wie in *nett*
[ə]   a sticker; ähnlich wie in *bitte*
[ɜ:] girl, her, turn
[æ]   bag, cat, that
[ɪ]   it, a bit, six; ähnlich wie in *Kind*
[i:] she, see, please; ähnlich wie in *tief*
[ɒ]   on, dog, what; ähnlich wie in *Kopf*
[ɔ:] door, four, morning
[ʊ]   put, look; ähnlich wie in *Schutt*
[u:] you, two, blue; ähnlich wie in *du*

Doppellaute (Diphthongs)

[aɪ] nice, five, bye; ähnlich wie in *kein*
[aʊ] now, pound; ähnlich wie in *Frau*
[eə] there, chair, their
[eɪ] name, say, table
[ɪə] here, clear
[ɔɪ] boy; ähnlich wie in *Scheune*
[əʊ] no, go, show
[ʊə] secure

Mitlaute (Consonants)

[j]   yes, you; wie das deutsche *j* in *ja*
[l]   let's, blue, school, twelve
[g]   get, glass; wie in *Gold, gerade*
[ŋ]   morning; wie in *singen*, kein [g] sprechen!
[ŋg] English; wie [ŋ], jedoch mit nachfolgendem [g]
[r]   ruler, radio, red
[s]   see, sister, class; stimmloses *s* wie in *reißen*
[z]   is, dogs, cars; stimmhaftes *s* wie in *brausen*
[ʒ]   television; wie in *Jalousie* und *Gelee*
[dʒ] German, orange; wie in *Dschungel*
[ʃ]   she, fish; wie in *Tisch*
[tʃ] teacher, child; wie in *deutsch*
[ð]   the, this, mother; stimmhafter Laut
[θ]   thank you; stimmloser Laut
[v]   vet, of; wie in *Wasser*
[w]   one, what, sandwich
[x]   och; wie in *ach*
[:]   bedeutet, dass der vorangehende Laut lang ist, z. B. blue [blu:]
[']   bedeutet, dass auf der folgenden Silbe die Hauptbetonung liegt, z. B. hello [hə'ləʊ]
[ˌ]   bedeutet, dass auf der folgenden Silbe die Nebenbetonung liegt, z. B. exercise book ['eksəsaɪz ˌbʊk]
[‿]   zwischen zwei Wörtern bedeutet, dass man den letzten Laut des ersten Wortes zum nächsten Wort hinüberzieht, z. B. come on [kʌm‿ɒn]

Das englische Alphabet (The English alphabet)

a [eɪ]	b [bi:]	c [si:]	d [di:]	e [i:]	f [ef]	g [dʒi:]	h [eɪtʃ]	i [aɪ]
j [dʒeɪ]	k [keɪ]	l [el]	m [em]	n [en]	o [əʊ]	p [pi:]	q [kju:]	r [ɑ:]
s [es]	t [ti:]	u [ju:]	v [vi:]	w ['dʌblju:]	x [eks]	y [waɪ]	z [zed]	

TOPIC 1   SWITCHED ON

topic [ˈtɒpɪk]	= subject s.th. you talk or write about	Thema, Themenbereich

Text module

Photo pages

content [ˈkɒntent]	A book often begins with a table of ~s.	Inhalt
module [ˈmɒdjuːl]	🙂 a complete part that can be added to other parts	Modul, Bauelement; Lerneinheit
to **view** [vjuː]	to ~ a TV programme = to watch it	besichtigen; betrachten; *hier*: fernsehen
revision [rɪˈvɪʒn]		Wiederholung (von Lernstoff)
2 °*to gather* [ˈgæðə]		*sammeln*

1   How to become a pop star

You will find the other new words from
this text in the Dictionary.

to **pick** [pɪk]		aussuchen
unfortunate(ly) [ʌnˈfɔːtʃənət(lɪ)]	We went to a ski resort, but ~ly there wasn't any snow.	leider; unglücklich(er- weise)
haircut [ˈheəkʌt]		Haarschnitt, Frisur
pudding-bowl haircut [ˈpʊdɪŋbəʊl ˈheəkʌt]		„Pilzkopf"-Frisur
to **form** [fɔːm]	50 states ~ the USA.	formen, bilden, gründen
horrific [hɒˈrɪfɪk]	= horrible; ⟷ lovely	entsetzlich, schrecklich
gimmick [ˈgɪmɪk]	🙂 ~s are used to get people's attention, for example, if a new bookshop gives away flowers on Valentine's Day.	Gag, Gimmick
heavy [ˈhevɪ]	Are you sure you can carry that? It's very ~.	schwer
metal [ˈmetəl]	Gold and silver are types of ~.	Metall; *hier:* Rockmusik
heavy metal band [ˌhevɪ ˈmetəl bænd]	A ~ plays a certain type of rock music.	Heavy Metal Band (Hardrock)
version [ˈvɜːʃn]	🙂 Sometimes singers record their ~ of another singer's pop song.	Version
to **get s.o. doing s.th.** [get]		jdn. dazu bringen, etwas zu tun
record [ˈrekɔːd]	🙂 CDs replaced ~s. Today, the word ~ is often used for 'CD'.	Schallplatte; Aufnahme
talent [ˈtælənt]	🙂 If you can do s.th. very well, you have a ~ for it.	Talent
That'll be ... [ˈðætl biː]	~ £ 8.30, please.	Das macht ...
nowadays [ˈnaʊədeɪz]	= the present time	heute, heutzutage
to **pal up with** *(s.o.)* [pæl ˈʌp wɪð]	to get to know s.o. and become friends	sich anfreunden/ zusammentun mit
monkey [ˈmʌŋkɪ]	*here:* a beginner in the music business	Affe; *hier:* Anfänger/in
contract [ˈkɒntrækt]	A German footballer has just signed a ~ with an Italian club.	Vertrag
to **look out** *(for)* [lʊk ˈaʊt]	= to look for	Ausschau halten (nach)
result [rɪˈzʌlt]	The ~ of the game was Nottingham 1: Newcastle 1.	Resultat, Ergebnis

right away [ˌraɪt_əˈweɪ]	⟷ later	sofort
to **call in** [kɔːl_ˈɪn]	to ask s.o. to do s.th. for you – usually for money	beauftragen, hinzuziehen
trendy [ˈtrendɪ]	very modern, belonging to the latest fashion	modern, schick, 'in'
airplay [ˈeəpleɪ]	the time during which a record is played on the radio	*hier:* Sendezeit
if at all [ɪf ət_ˈɔːl]		wenn überhaupt
listing [ˈlɪstɪŋ]	Radio ~s show how often records are played.	*hier:* Position
journalist [ˈdʒɜːnəlɪst]	A ~ writes for a newspaper or a magazine.	Journalist/in, Reporter/in
to **decide** (*on*) [dɪˈsaɪd_ɒn]	I just can't ~: shall I take the green skirt or the red one?	sich entscheiden (für)
to **cope** [kəʊp]	It's not too much work for me. I can ~.	fertig werden mit, zurechtkommen
guideline [ˈgaɪdlaɪn]	= rule	Richtlinie
to **walk out of** [ˌwɔːk_ˈaʊt_əv]	to get up and leave in the middle of s.th.	etwas mitten drin verlassen
brunette [bruːˈnet]	= having brown hair	brünett
1 **reaction** [rɪˈækʃn]		Reaktion
2 °*basis* [ˈbeɪsɪs]		*Basis, Grundlage*
5 °*to convince* [kənˈvɪns]		*überzeugen*
°*demo tape* [ˈdeməʊ teɪp]		*Demo-Aufnahme*

2   What's on tonight?

What's on? [ˌwɒts_ˈɒn]	'What's on tonight?' – 'I don't know. Look in the newspaper.'	was gibt es/was kommt/was läuft?
2 °*extract* [ˈekstrækt]		*Auszug*
TV guide [tiːˈviː ˌgaɪd]		Fernsehzeitschrift, Fernsehprogramm
3 °*Pay TV* [ˈpeɪ tiːˌviː]		*Pay TV*
°*View on Demand* [ˌvjuː_ɒn dɪˈmɑːnd]		*View on Demand*
4 °*to carry out* [ˌkærɪ_ˈaʊt]		*durchführen*
6 **licence** [ˈlaɪsəns]	In Britain, you are only allowed to watch BBC television when you have paid for a TV ~.	Lizenz; *hier:* Fernsehgebühr
TV set [tiːˈviː ˌset]		Fernseher, Fernsehgerät
university [ˌjuːnɪˈvɜːsətɪ]	The ~ of Oxford is very famous.	Universität
government [ˈgʌvənmənt]		Regierung; *hier:* Kommunal-, Stadtverwaltung
sponsor [ˈspɒnsə]	Football teams wear the name of their ~ on their shirts.	Sponsor, Geldgeber
Commercial TV [kəˈmɜːʃl tiːˈviː]	= TV companies that are owned privately	*hier:* Privatsender
cable [ˈkeɪbl]	You can get some TV channels via satellite and some via ~.	Kabel
independent (*of*) [ˌɪndɪˈpendənt_ɒv]	The USA became ~ in 1776.	unabhängig (von)
°*to give a talk* [gɪv_ə ˈtɔːk]		*einen Vortrag/eine Rede halten*

3 The Martians have landed!

You will find all the other new words from this text in the Dictionary.

1	**Mars** [mɑːz]	~ is also called 'the red planet'.	*Name eines Planeten*
	Martians [ˈmɑːʃənz]	people from Mars	Marsmenschen
	to **interrupt** [ˌɪntəˈrʌpt]	Don't ~. John hasn't finished speaking.	unterbrechen, ins Wort fallen
	gentleman/men [ˈdʒentlmən/men]	Ladies and gentlemen! Welcome to tonight's show!	Herr/Herren
	brief [briːf]	⟷ long	kurz
	announcement [əˈnaʊnsmənt]	Quiet, please. I have to make an important ~.	Ankündigung
	to **unleash** [ʌnˈliːʃ]	to set (a dog) free; *here:* to set off s.th. dangerous or bad	frei lassen; *hier:* auslösen
	severe [sɪˈvɪə]	Is the pain very ~? = Does it hurt very much?	ernst; *hier:* schwer, schlimm
	battle [ˈbætl]	there were many ~s = there was a lot of fighting	Kampf, Schlacht
	realistic [rɪəˈlɪstɪk]	If s.th. is ~, it seems like real life.	realistisch
	most [məʊst]	many, more, ~; ~ people have a radio.	die meisten
	effort [ˈefət]	Try harder! Make an ~!	Leistung; *hier:* Anstrengung, Mühe
	to **rehearse** [rɪˈhɜːs]	= to practise (e.g. your role in a play)	proben, einüben
	element [ˈelɪmənt]	= a part	Bestandteil, Element
	rehearsal [rɪˈhɜːsl]	verb of 'to rehearse'	Probe
	by chance [baɪ ˈtʃɑːns]	I didn't plan it that way. It just happened ~.	zufällig
	progress [ˈprəʊgres]	⚠ Always singular!	Fortschritt(e)
	in progress [ɪn ˈprəʊgres]	= happening	im Gange
	announcer [əˈnaʊnsə]	the person who makes an announcement	Ansager/in
3	°*to praise* [preɪz]		*loben*

Strategy Page: Listening to the radio

1	**director** [dɪˈrektə]	the person in charge of a play or film	Regisseur
	creature [ˈkriːtʃə]	= a living thing, an animal	(Lebe-) Wesen, Geschöpf, Kreatur
	volcanic [vɒlˈkænɪk]	⚠ Spelling!	vulkanisch
	disturbance [dɪˈstɜːbəns]		Störung; *hier:* (Vulkan)-Ausbruch
	surface [ˈsɜːfɪs]	Whales have to come to the ~ of the water for air.	Oberfläche
	astronomer [əˈstrɒnəmə]	a person who is very interested in the stars	Astronom/in
	professor [prəˈfesə]	a person who teaches at university	Professor/in
	interlude [ˈɪntəluːd]	the time between two radio programmes, for example	Zwischenspiel, Intermezzo
	jet [dʒet]	The fire brigade put out the fire with a ~ of water.	Strahl

flame [fleɪm]	The ~ of a candle is very hot.	Flamme
pit [pɪt]	= a deep hole in the ground	Grube
humped ['hʌmpt]		bucklig

shape [ʃeɪp]	The ~ of s.th. is its form.	Gestalt
plenty ['plentɪ]	= a lot; *here:* enough	viel; *hier:* genug
	'Would you like some more to eat?' – 'No, thanks. I've had ~.'	
extraordinary [ɪk'strɔ:dənrɪ]	⟷ normal	außergewöhnlich
experience [ɪk'spɪərɪəns]	I got lost in London once. That was a frightening ~.	Erfahrung, Erlebnis
position [pə'zɪʃn]	the place where s.o. or s.th. is	Stellung, Position
to **hold on** [həʊld͜'ɒn]	Just ~ a minute, please. = Wait a minute, please.	*hier:* warten
2 *gist* [dʒɪst]		*das Wesentliche*
transcript ['trænskrɪpt]		*Transkript*
3 *to create* [krɪ'eɪt]		*erzeugen, (er)schaffen*

Language module

A Revision: Conversations

2 *dynamic* [daɪ'næmɪk]		*dynamisch; hier: Tätig-keits-/Handlungs-*
state [steɪt]		*Zustand*
stative ['steɪtɪv]		*hier: Zustands-*
5 **translation** [træns'leɪʃn]	noun of 'to translate'	Übersetzung
6 **agent** ['eɪdʒənt]		Agent/in
°*president* ['prezɪdənt]		*Vorsitzende/r, Präsident/in*
match [mætʃ]		*hier:* (Fußball-/Tennis-) Spiel; Streichholz

B Watching and being watched

anorak ['ænəræk]	a jacket you wear when it rains	Anorak
label ['leɪbl]	When you buy clothes, the ~ tells you the size and price.	Etikett, Preisschild
3 **celebrity** [sɪ'lebrətɪ]	a famous person	berühmte Persönlichkeit
wallet ['wɒlɪt]		Brieftasche, Geldbeutel
case [keɪs]	In ~ of fire, phone 999.	Fall
4 °*product* ['prɒdʌkt]		*Produkt, Erzeugnis*
°*to identify* [aɪ'dentɪfaɪ]		*identifizieren*
5 °*wherever* [weə'revə]		*wo auch immer, egal wo*

Word module

Difficult words

1 °*in general* [ɪn 'dʒenərl]		*im Allgemeinen*
2 **plane** [pleɪn]	~s land at airports.	Flugzeug

Images

You will find all the other new words in
the Dictionary.

image ['ɪmɪdʒ]   Bild; Image
  °*to contain* [kənˈteɪn]   *beinhalten, enthalten*
1 °*front page* [frʌnt ˈpeɪdʒ]   *erste Seite, Titelseite*

Vocabulary Tips

You have been learning English for four years now, so you will already know different ways of
learning vocabulary. But now you are older, and perhaps there are more suitable ways.
Here are some tips:

• **learn words in pairs,** e.g. opposites *(heavy-light)*, synonyms *(horrific - horrible)*, words
that go together (like *pudding* and *bowl*)

• **collect words that are difficult to spell**

• don't just learn 'new' words, **learn words
that you have perhaps forgotten.** Example:
the false friend *curious* is in the text on
p. 12. If you have forgotten it, learn it again!

• **collect new vocabulary in topic groups,** and
add new words as you meet them

• **look at old lists in your file** (you'll be
surprised which words you know very well,
and which you have forgotten completely)

• **from every new text you read,** pick out
three or four phrases that you like, or that
you could use yourself, e.g. *they'll be
curious to hear, how to become, ...*

Verbs which are sometimes followed by a noun or pronoun and ...ing

to see ⎫
to notice ⎬ s.o. ⎫ doing s.th.
to watch ⎭   ⎬ running
                        ⎭ standing

to hear ⎫ s.o. ⎫ shouting
to listen to ⎭   ⎬ talking
                      ⎭ whispering

to smell s.th. ⎫ cooking
                   ⎬ burning

to feel ⎫ the ground moving
           ⎬ your heart beating

*'I'm so sorry. Are you really a TV star? I watch a lot of television
but I never pay any attention to it'.*

topic ['tɒpɪk] | = subject
s.th. you talk or write about | Thema, Themenbereich

Text module

Photo pages

content ['kɒntent] | A book often begins with a table of ~s. | Inhalt
module ['mɒdjuːl] | a complete part that can be added to other parts | Modul, Bauelement; Lerneinheit
exam(ination) [ɪg,zæm(ɪ'neɪʃn)] | to take an ~ = to take a test | Prüfung, Prüfungs-, Klausur
to **paraphrase** ['pærəfreɪz] | to give the same meaning in different words | umschreiben
synonym ['sɪnənɪm] | ~s are words that have the same or a very similar meaning, e.g. fall *(AE)* and autumn *(BE)*. | Synonym
to **interpret** [ɪn'tɜːprɪt] | to translate what s.o. has said or is saying | *hier:* dolmetschen; interpretieren, deuten
1   **choice** [tʃɔɪs] | I had no ~. = I had to do it. | Wahl, Auswahl

1   Examinations

system ['sɪstəm] | The school ~s in Britain and Germany are different. | System
3   to **combine** [kəm'baɪn] | | kombinieren, verbinden
General Certificate of Secondary Education (GCSE) ['dʒenərəl sə'tɪfɪkət_əv 'sekəndərɪ ,edjuː'keɪʃn] | In Britain, you have to take an exam in every subject you want to get a ~ in. | *britisches Äquivalent der Mittleren Reife; hier:* GCSE-Prüfung
alphabet ['ælfəbet] | | Alphabet
alphabetical [,ælfə'betɪkl] | A,B,C ... Please put the words into ~ order. | alphabetisch
apart [ə'pɑːt] | ⟷ together | auseinander
no one ['nəʊ wʌn] | ⟷ everyone | keiner
to **cheat** [tʃiːt] | If you copy an answer from your neighbour during an exam, that's ~*ing*! | mogeln
to **fail** [feɪl] | I got a GCSE in French but I ~*ed* in German. | durchfallen, nicht bestehen
envelope ['envələʊp] | You send a letter in an ~. | Umschlag
exam paper [ɪg'zæm ,peɪpə] | The questions you have to answer in an exam are written on an ~. | Prüfungsaufgaben, Aufgabenstellung
to **hand out** [hænd_'aʊt] | to give s.th. away to a lot of people | austeilen, verteilen
beforehand [bɪ'fɔːhænd] | | vorher, zuvor
result [rɪ'zʌlt] | I hope I get my exam ~s soon. I want to know if I've failed or not. | Resultat, Ergebnis
to **pass** (an exam) [pɑːs] | ⟷ to fail | *hier:* bestehen
6   **account** [ə'kaʊnt] | | *hier:* Bericht; (Bank-)Konto
element ['eləmənt] | = a part | Bestandteil, Element

Examination words

To take a test/examination	Questions	Feelings
to pass	easy	excited
to fail	clear	confident
to cheat	fair	sure
results	hard	unsure
to mark	unclear	nervous
to prepare	difficult	terrified
to get ready	terrible	
to revise		
to understand		**Writing**
to rcmember	**Answers**	
to forget		word
to know	details	phrase
to try	short	paragraph
to worry	long	reason
to care	clever	argument
to check	brilliant	summary
to read through	right	to report
to re-read	correct	to describe
to decide	wrong	to define

Mistakes

stupid
silly
bad

2   Activities

You will find all the new words from this text in the Dictionary.

°*various* ['veərɪəs]   *verschieden*
°*to keep s.th. in mind*   *an etwas denken*
   [ˌkiːpˌɪn 'maɪnd]
°*to limit* ['lɪmɪt]   *begrenzen, beschrän-*
                                          ken, einschränken

3   The School Survival Guide

You will find all the other new words from this text in the Dictionary.

survival [sə'vaɪvl]	managing to stay alive	Überleben, Überlebens-
lonely ['ləʊnlɪ]	If you have to move to a new town where you don't know anyone, you will feel ~ at first.	einsam
on one's own [ɒn wʌnzˌ'əʊn]	I had nobody to talk to. I was *on my own*.	allein
shy [ʃaɪ]	I'm very ~. I'm scared of talking to s.o. I don't know.	schüchtern
could/couldn't [kʊd/'kʊdnt]	~ you turn the radio down, please?	könnte/st/n (... nicht)
to **put up with s.o.** [pʊtˌ'ʌp wɪð]	If you ~, you do not really like them but just tolerate them.	jdn. ertragen, dulden

gradual(ly) ['grædʒʊəl(ɪ)]	to grow ~ly = to grow slowly	allmählich, nach und nach
to **respond** [rɪ'spɒnd]	= to react, to answer	reagieren, antworten
event [ɪ'vent]		Ereignis; Veranstaltung, *hier:* Wettkampf *(Sport)*
to **join in** [dʒɔɪn ˌ'ɪn]		teilnehmen (an)
(it) **does** (get easier) [dʌz]	⚠ do/does + infinitive! it ~ work = it really works!	wirklich, tatsächlich, doch
bold [bəʊld]	to be ~ = to do s.th. you are scared of	mutig
to **come along** *(with s.o.)* [kʌm ˌə'lɒŋ]	= to join s.o., to go together with s.o.	sich (jdm.) anschließen, mitgehen (mit jdm.)
2 °*general* ['dʒenərəl]		*allgemein*
°*gist* [dʒɪst]		*das Wesentliche*
to **sum up** [sʌm ˌ'ʌp]		zusammenfassen
4 to **express** [ɪk'spres]		ausdrücken
5 °*editor* ['edɪtə]		*Redakteur/in*
°*to re-distribute* [ˌriːdɪ'strɪbjuːt]		*neu verteilen*

4 A model pupil betrayed

> You will find all the other new words from this text in the Dictionary.

to **betray** [bɪ'treɪ]	You promised to tell no one where I was, but you did! You ~ed me!	verraten
honesty ['ɒnəstɪ]	⚠ Pronunciation! noun of 'honest'	Ehrlichkeit
assault [ə'sɔːlt]	to be the victim of an ~ = to be attacked	Angriff
tactless(ly) ['tæktləs(lɪ)]	when you say s.th. to a person, without thinking about the negative effect your words could have	taktlos, *hier:* gedanken-los
to **expose** [ɪk'spəʊz]	to make public what s.o. has done	aufdecken, enthüllen
informant [ɪn'fɔːmənt]	= a person who gives information, who informs s.o. of s.th.	Informant/in
s.th. is going on [ɪz ˌgəʊɪŋ ˌ'ɒn]	= is happening	etwas ist los, passiert
involved *(in)* [ɪn'vɒlvd ˌɪn]	= having s.th. to do with s.th./s.o.	engagiert, beteiligt; *hier:* verwickelt, hinein-gezogen
incident ['ɪnsɪdənt]	= event	Ereignis, Vorfall
to **point** *(at)* ['pɔɪnt]	The robber didn't say anything. He just ~ed at my bag.	zeigen (auf)
to **amaze** [ə'meɪz]	= to surprise	erstaunen, verwundern
2 to **protect** [prə'tekt]	= to look after	(be)schützen, aufpassen auf
3 **guideline** ['gaɪdlaɪn]	= rule	Richtlinie

5 Adrian Mole is off school

> You will find the other new words from this text in the Dictionary.

bloody ['blʌdɪ]		blutig; *hier:* verdammt *(ugs.)*
fault [fɔːlt]	It's not my ~ that we're late.	Schuld, Fehler
dentist ['dentɪst]	the doctor who looks after your teeth	Zahnarzt/ärztin

agony [ˈægənɪ]	If you're in ~, s.th. hurts very much.	starke Schmerzen
toothless [ˈtuːθləs]	= without teeth	zahnlos
to **instruct** [ɪnˈstrʌkt]	to give instructions	anweisen, instruieren
to **cancel** [ˈkænsl]	I'm sorry but I'll have to ~ my appointment for tomorrow.	absagen
sympathy [ˈsɪmpəθɪ]	to have ~ for s.o. = to share s.o.'s feelings	Mitleid, Mitgefühl
to **slip** [slɪp]		ausrutschen
rotten [ˈrɒtn]	= bad	schlecht, kaputt, faul
worse luck! [wɜːs ˈlʌk]		(so ein) Pech! (ugs.)
minus [ˈmaɪnəs]	~ a tooth = with a tooth missing	ohne, mit ... weniger
nerve [nɜːv]	He had the ~ to phone me at 2 a.m.	Nerv; hier: Frechheit
to **wrap** [ræp]	I've already ~ped Susan's present.	einpacken
gap [gæp]	= a hole	Lücke, Loch; hier: Zahnlücke
to **get used to** [get ˈjuːst tʊ]	I'll never ~ getting up early in the morning.	sich gewöhnen an
to **stumble** [ˈstʌmbl]	to be unsure on your feet	stolpern
mass (murderer) [mæs (ˈmɜːdərə)]	A ~ murderer is s.o. who has killed a lot of people.	Masse, Menge; hier: Massen(mörder)
dead [ded]	= very. I'm ~ against it.	hier: sehr, absolut (ugs.)
to **demand** [dɪˈmɑːnd]	to ask for s.th. in a very strong way	verlangen
free of charge [ˌfriːˌ əv ˈtʃɑːdʒ]	If s.th. is ~, it doesn't cost anything.	kostenlos
Gappy Mole [ˌgæpɪ ˈməʊl]	Adrian is called '~' because of the gap in his teeth.	Spitzname für Adrian
to **be at it** [biːˌ ˈætˌ ɪt]	= to be doing s.th.	dabei sein, etwas zu tun
Physics [ˈfɪzɪks]	~ is one of the sciences. As a school subject, it is spelled with a capital letter.	Physik
to **face** doing s.th. [feɪs]	= to not be afraid of doing s.th.	es fertigbringen, etwas zu tun
one [wʌn]	like German 'man', except that it always includes the speaker	hier: man
Yours faithfully [jɔːz ˈfeɪθfəlɪ]	At the end of a business letter you can write ~.	Hochachtungsvoll, Mit freundlichen Grüßen
liar [ˈlaɪə]	s.o. who lies	Lügner/in
°*slightly adapted* [ˌslaɪtlɪ əˈdæptɪd]		*leicht geändert*
1 °*extract* [ˈekstrækt]		*Auszug*
4 **episode** [ˈepɪˌsəʊd]	part of a story	Episode; Begebenheit
amusing [əˈmjuːzɪŋ]	S.th. that makes you laugh or smile is ~.	lustig, amüsant
to **intend** [ɪnˈtend]	I have decided to do s.th. = I ~ to do s.th.	vorhaben
contrast [ˈkɒntrɑːst]	= difference	Unterschied, Kontrast

Linking new and old vocabulary

You already know a lot of words. So many of the new words you learn may be in the same word family as words you know already, e.g. *liar* (new) – *to lie* (known). This often makes learning easier.

Tip 1: When you learn a new word like this, revise the ones you already know.

Tip 2: If you notice any other links, use them!

To wrap – you spell it with a 'w', like *to write* and *wrong*.

new		known
toothless	–	tooth, teeth
informant	–	information
to instruct	–	instructions
worse luck	–	you're lucky
nerve	–	nervous

Can you find more examples? Add them to your file cards!

Language module

A An unusual school

theatre [ˈθɪətə] — Theater

would-be [ˈwʊdbiː] — A ~ actress is a girl who wants to become an actress. — Möchtegern-

application [ˌæplɪˈkeɪʃn] — You send an ~ when you want to get a job. — Bewerbung; Antrag
audition [ɔːˈdɪʃn] — To get a place in a theatre school you have to show how well you can act in an ~. — Aufnahmeprüfung (Vorsingen, -spielen)

grant [grɑːnt] — money to help pay for a course — Zuschuss, Studienhilfe
fee [fiː] — s.th. you pay — Gebühr
agent [ˈeɪdʒənt] — 😊 a person who looks for people with talent — Agent/in

talent [ˈtælənt] — 😊 If you are very good at s.th., you have ~. — Talent

to **remain** [rɪˈmeɪn] — I've done questions 1 to 8, so only 9 and 10 ~. — (übrig) bleiben

before long [bɪˌfɔː ˈlɒŋ] — soon, in a short time — bald
1 °**to pick (out)** [pɪk] — aussuchen, heraussuchen

°**attractive** [əˈtræktɪv] — attraktiv, anziehend
2 **article** [ˈɑːtɪkl] — s.th. written in a newspaper or magazine — Artikel
4 **screen** [skriːn] — on the big ~ = in cinema films — Bildschirm; *hier:* Leinwand

6 °**object** [ˈɒbdʒɪkt] — Gegenstand; *hier:* Objekt

7 **right away** [ˌraɪt‿əˈweɪ] — = immediately — sofort
suitable [ˈsjuːtəbl] — right in a certain situation — passend, geeignet
8 to **replace** [rɪˈpleɪs] — My watch doesn't work any more. I'll have to ~ it. — ersetzen

9 **trial** [ˈtraɪəl] — = a kind of audition for football players — Auswahlspiel
boarding school [ˈbɔːdɪŋ ˌskuːl] — a school where pupils live during the term — Internat
comprehensive school [ˌkɒmprɪˈhensɪv ˌskuːl] — Most schools in Britain are ~s. — Gesamtschule
professional [prəˈfeʃənl] — If you earn your money playing basketball, you're a ~ basketball player. — professionell, Berufs-

style [staɪl] — = the way you do s.th. — Stil

B Revision: School chat

6 to **react** [rɪˈækt] — reagieren

Word module

Strategy Page: Improving a written text

1 °**correction** [kəˈrekʃn] — Verbesserung, Korrektur
°**conjunction** [kənˈdʒʌŋkʃn] — Konjunktion
°**repetition** [ˌrepɪˈtɪʃn] — Wiederholung
exact [ɪgˈzækt] — 😊 — genau, exakt
since [sɪns] — *here:* because — *hier:* da
as [æz] — *hier:* wie
however [haʊˈevə] — *here:* but — jedoch, aber
to **concentrate** (*on*) [ˈkɒnsəntreɪt‿ɒn] — ⚠ I'm so tired that I can't ~ on my work. English: non-reflexive German: reflexive — sich konzentrieren (auf)

2	**single** ['sɪŋgl]	on its/one's own, just one		einzige/r/s
	education [ˌedjʊ'keɪʃn]	To get an ~ you have to go to school.		Erziehung; Bildung; *hier:* Ausbildung
3	°*to expand* [ɪk'spænd]			*erweitern*

Choosing the right word

1	**calendar** ['kæləndə]	⚠ Spelling! A ~ shows you every day of the year.	Kalender
5	°*to give a talk* [gɪv‿ə 'tɔːk]		*einen Vortrag/eine Rede halten*
	seat [siːt]	the noun of 'to sit'	Sitz, Autositz

Strategy Page: Interpreting

1	**translation** [træns'leɪʃn]	noun of 'to translate'	Übersetzung
2	°*aware (of)* [ə'weər‿əv]		*bewusst*

Images

image ['ɪmɪdʒ]		Bild; Image

LUANN By Greg Evans

to breathe – atmen
stuff – Zeug, Stoff

TOPIC 3   THE GENERATION GAME

topic ['tɒpɪk]	= subject s.th. you talk or write about	Thema, Themenbereich

Text module

Photo pages

generation [ˌdʒenə'reɪʃn]	😊 ⚠ Pronunciation!	Generation
content ['kɒntent]	A book often begins with a table of ~s.	Inhalt
module ['mɒdjuːl]	😊 a complete part that can be added to other parts	Modul, Bauelement; Lerneinheit
informal [ɪn'fɔːml]	If you don't have to do s.th. in a certain way or form, you can do it ~ly.	ungezwungen; inoffizi- ell; *hier*: nicht formell, nicht förmlich
°*auxiliary* [ɔːg'zɪliəri]		*Hilfs-*
°*suffix* ['sʌfɪks]		*Nachsilbe, Suffix*
°*prefix* ['priːfɪks]		*Vorsilbe, Präfix*

1   My Sister is a Runaway

	You will find the other new words from this text in the Dictionary.	
to **dread** [dred]	⚠ Pronunciation! to *read* [riːd], but to *dread* [dred] = to be scared of; ⟷ to look forward to	befürchten; Angst haben vor
(sixteen-)**year-old** ['jɪəˌəʊld]	My *sixteen*-~ sister is the oldest of my brothers and sisters. *But:* My youngest sister is five years old.	(sechzehn-)jährige/r
to **run away** [rʌn ə'weɪ]	*here:* to leave home without telling your family	weglaufen; *hier*: ausrei- ßen
cash card ['kæʃ ˌkaːd]	You can use your ~ to get money when the banks are shut.	Geldautomatenkarte
to **catch** (a bus) [kætʃ]	= to get (a bus) To get to the railway station, you'll have to ~ the bus at 8.05.	(einen Bus) nehmen, kriegen
account [ə'kaʊnt]	The bank keeps your money in a bank ~.	*hier*: (Bank-) Konto; Bericht
machine [mə'ʃiːn]		*hier*: Automat
to **think of** ['θɪŋk əv]	to be thinking of doing s.th. = to plan to do s.th.	denken an; *hier*: vorha- ben, etwas zu tun
to **be s.o.'s fault** [biː ... 'fɔːlt]	It *isn't my fault* – I wasn't there when it happened.	jdns. Schuld sein
to **keep doing s.th.** [kiːp]	= to do s.th. again and again I *kept asking* her to tell me why she was so unhappy.	etwas wiederholt tun
soft(ly) [sɒft(lɪ)]	⟷ hard	leise; weich; *hier*: nicht streng
to **blame oneself** *(for)* ['bleɪm wʌnˌself fə]	to think that something is your fault	sich Vorwürfe machen
some **kind** of ['sʌm ˌkaɪnd əv]	'What's that?' – 'Some ~ of fruit.'	irgendein, irgendeine Art von
brave [breɪv]	You have to be ~ to do this.	tapfer, mutig

selfish ['selfɪʃ]	A ~ person only thinks about himself/ herself and not about other people.	egoistisch, selbstsüchtig
to **spend** (money) [spend]	I've already *spent* all my pocket money on CDs.	*hier*: ausgeben
to **hand out** [hænd_'aʊt]	to give s.th. away to a lot of people	austeilen, verteilen
youth advice centre [ˌjuːθ_əd'vaɪs ˌsentə]	a place where young people can go when they need help or advice	*Beratungsstelle für Jugendliche*
in case [ɪn 'keɪs]	Take a pullover with you ~ it gets cold.	falls, für den Fall, dass
doorway ['dɔːweɪ]	People without homes sometimes sleep in the ~s of shops.	*hier*: (Haus-) Eingang
to feel **guilty** [fiːl 'gɪltɪ]	If you know you have done s.th. wrong, you feel ~..	sich schuldig fühlen; *hier*: ein schlechtes Gewissen haben
the one who [ðə 'wʌn huː]	'Did Anna run away?' – 'No, Lesley is ~ ran away.'	der/diejenige, der/die
depression [dɪ'preʃn]	~ makes you feel unhappy all the time.	Depression
thanks to ['θæŋks tə]	We'll finish the job on time, ~ your help.	wegen
to **switch off** [swɪtʃ_'ɒf]	←→ to switch on (the light, the TV, the radio etc.)	abstellen, abschalten
to **pray** [preɪ]	to hope very much	beten; *hier*: sehr auf etwas hoffen
upset [ʌp'set]	When my dog died last summer, I was very ~.	bestürzt, betrübt
proper(ly) ['prɒpə(lɪ)]	For some people, a birthday is only a *proper* birthday if they have a cake and a party.	richtig/e/r/s, ordent- lich/e/r/s
1 **reaction** [rɪ'ækʃn]	noun of 'to react'	Reaktion
2 **aspect** ['æspɛkt]		Aspekt, Seite
3 **expression** [ɪk'spreʃn]		Ausdruck

Describing reactions – a list of useful adjectives

To feel ...		To find something...	
angry	miserable	boring	interesting
confused	nervous	disappointing	likeable
disappointed	responsible	embarrassing	nasty
embarrassed	sad	exciting	pleasant
enthusiastic	scared	fantastic	scary
excited	shocked	frightening	sensible
frightened	surprised	funny	silly
helpless	upset	horrible	stupid
interested		important	surprising

---

2 Runaways & Throwaways: Life on the Streets

You will find the other new words from this text in the Dictionary.

| **throwaway** ['θrəʊəweɪ] | ~s is a name for children who have been made to leave their homes by their parents. | *obdachlose Kinder und Jugendliche, deren Eltern sie rausgewor- fen haben* |
| **United Nations Children's Fund** [juːˌnaɪtɪd 'neɪʃnz 'tʃɪldrənz 'fʌnd] | | UN Kinderhilfsorgani- sation |

to **estimate** ['estɪmeɪt]	I ~ that there are 40 million ... = I think there are about 40 million ...	(ein)schätzen
industrial [ɪn'dʌstrɪəl]	Germany, France and Great Britain are ~ nations.	hier: Industrie-
choice [tʃɔɪs]	I had no ~. = I had to do it.	Wahl, Auswahl
of one's own choice [əv wʌnz_'əʊn 'tʃɔɪs]	= not being made to do s.th.	freiwillig, aus eigener Wahl
to **choose**, chose, chosen [tʃuːz, tʃəʊz, 'tʃəʊzn]	It's my turn to ~ what we'll do at the weekend.	wählen, aussuchen
developing [dɪ'veləpɪŋ]	~ countries are not industrial countries yet.	hier: Entwicklungs-
Latin America ['lætɪn_ə'merɪkə]	= the countries south of the USA	Lateinamerika
divorce [dɪ'vɔːs]	When a man and a woman do not want to be married any longer, they can get a ~.	Scheidung
abuse [ə'bjuːs]	Different forms of ~ are the main reason why young people run away.	Missbrauch
worse [wɜːs]	bad, ~, worst	schlimmer
teen [tiːn]	You are called a ~ when you are between thirteen and nineteen years old.	Teenager, Jugendlicher zwischen dreizehn und neunzehn Jahren
involved (in) [ɪn'vɒlvd_ɪn]	If you are on the streets, it's difficult not to become ~ in drug selling.	engagiert, beteiligt; hier: verwickelt, hinein-gezogen
shelter ['ʃeltə]	a place where homeless people can spend the night	Schutz; hier: Obdach-losenunterkunft
1 °article ['ɑːtɪkl]		Artikel
statement ['steɪtmənt]	When you give your opinion you make a ~.	Aussage, Beitrag, Meinungsäußerung

Strategy page: Informal discussion

1 °statistic [stə'tɪstɪk]		Statistik
music centre ['mjuːzɪk ˌsentə]	A CD player or a cassette recorder are parts of a ~.	Stereo-, Hifi-Anlage
to **get s.th. done** [get 'dʌn]	I have managed to ~ all my homework ~. Now I can go to the cinema with my friends.	etw. schaffen/etw. fertig-stellen
single ['sɪŋgl]	on its/one's own, just one	einzelne/r/s
°(home) comforts [həʊm 'kʌmfəts]		Annehmlichkeiten (eines Zuhauses)
°to select [sɪ'lekt]		auswählen
result [rɪ'zʌlt]		Resultat, Ergebnis
poll [pəʊl]	You can find out about people's opinions in a ~.	Meinungsumfrage
(video) **recorder** [rɪ'kɔːdə]	a machine with which you can play video tapes	Videorekorder
source [sɔːs]		Ursache, Ursprung; hier: Quelle
°location [ləʊ'keɪʃn]		Ort
2 °extract ['ekstrækt]		Auszug
nonsense ['nɒnsəns]	When someone first said, 'The earth isn't flat, it's like a ball', everyone else said, 'That's ~!'	Quatsch, Unsinn
to **raise** [reɪz]	here: to introduce a new idea	hier: aufwerfen, vorbringen
(I) **do** (feel) [duː]	I ~ feel ... = I really feel ... do/does + infinitive!	(ich glaube) wirklich
to **distract** [dɪ'strækt]	When my brother has his TV on, I can't do my homework. It ~s me.	ablenken

°*to put forward*
[pʊt ˈfɔːwəd] *hier: vorbringen, vorschlagen*
°*to move s.th. on* *etw. vorantreiben, vor-*
[ˌmuːv … ˈɒn] *an/weiterbringen*
°*conjunction* [kənˈdʒʌŋkʃn] *Konjunktion*
3 °*to reorganize* [riːˈɔːgənaɪz] *neu strukturieren, reorganisieren*

to **mention** [ˈmenʃn]	When you ~ s.th., you say it.	erwähnen
on the other hand	On the one hand, I like listening to music.	andererseits
[ɒn ðɪ ˈʌðə ˌhænd]	But ~ it distracts me.	
firstly [ˈfɜːstlɪ]	I would like to mention three things: ~ …	erstens
to **take s.o.'s point** [teɪk]	= to agree with what s.o. has said	jdm. zustimmen
point [pɔɪnt]	what you want to say	(inhaltlicher) Punkt
point of view [ˌpɔɪnt_ə_ˈvjuː]	a way of looking at s.th.	Standpunkt, Sichtweise
ought to [ˈɔːt tə]	= should	sollen
to **consider** [kənˈsɪdə]	= to think about	bedenken, betrachten
namely [ˈneɪmlɪ]	Great Britain has three large parts, ~ England, Wales and Scotland.	nämlich

3 Forgiving: No Son of Mine

You will find the other new words from this text in the Dictionary.

to **forgive**, forgave, forgiven	I ~ you. I know you're really sorry.	vergeben, verzeihen
[fəˈgɪv, fəˈgeɪv, fəˈgɪvn]		
2 °*to build up* [bɪld_ˈʌp]		*aufbauen; hier: zusammenstellen*
°*lyrics* [ˈlɪrɪks]		*Liedtext*
survival [səˈvaɪvl]	In parts of Alaska, ~ can be very difficult in winter.	Überleben, Überlebens-
doubt [daʊt]	to have ~s = not to be sure of s.th.	Zweifel
to **keep** [kiːp]	*here:* to stay	*hier:* bleiben
fear [fɪə]	to show ~ = to show that you are scared of s.th. or s.o.	Angst, Furcht
to **stand** [stænd]	I can't ~ the heat in here any longer. I'll have to open the window.	*hier:* ertragen, aushalten
healer [ˈhiːlə]	a person with the power to make you better	Heiler/in
wound [wuːnd]	The accident victim was bleeding from a ~ in his head.	Wunde
heart [hɑːt]		Herz
mouth [maʊθ]	Your teeth are in your ~.	Mund
to **regret** [rɪˈgret]	to be sorry about s.th.	etwas bedauern, Leid tun
to **pass** [pɑːs]	When you are bored, time ~es very slowly.	*hier:* vergehen
to **face** [feɪs]	= to look at	ins Auge blicken
to **talk s.th. over**	= to discuss s.th. with s.o.	etwas bereden, besprechen
[ˌtɔːk … ˈəʊvə]		
3 **gap** [gæp]	Fill in the ~s, please.	Lücke, Loch
4 °*re-united* [ˌriːjuːˈnaɪtɪd]		*wieder vereint*
6 °*final* [ˈfaɪnl]		*letzte/r/s*
°*verse* [vɜːs]		*Strophe*

You will find the other new words from
this text in the Dictionary.

an **Oscar** ['ɒskə]		an American prize for films, actors, actresses etc.	amerikanischer Film-preis
to **deserve** [dɪ'zɜ:v]		You really ~ the prize. You worked very hard for it.	verdienen
absolutely [ˌæbsə'lu:tlɪ]		'Don't you want to go to the moon?' '~ not!'	vollkommen, völlig; *hier:* absolut
to **blame** [bleɪm]		It's my own fault. I can't ~ anyone else.	die Schuld geben, beschuldigen
• **it's no use** [ɪts ˌnəʊ 'ju:s]		~ crying now. That won't change anything.	es hat keinen Zweck
guest [gest]		When you go to a party, you're one of the ~s.	Gast
honey ['hʌnɪ]		~, could you pass me the bread, please? *(AE)*	Honig; *hier:* Schatz, Schätzchen *(AE)*
research [rɪ'sɜ:tʃ]		to do ~ = to work on a topic and try to find out s.th. new	Forschung
surely ['ʃʊəlɪ]		'~ you've met her!' = 'You must have met her!'	sicherlich, doch, bestimmt
overnight [ˌəʊvə'naɪt]		I'm going to stay ~ at the Martins' house. See you tomorrow!	über Nacht
to **be homesick** [bi: 'həʊmsɪk]		to miss your home and family	Heimweh haben
blanket ['blæŋkɪt]		If you're cold at night, put another ~ on your bed.	Decke; *hier:* Schmuse-decke
to **fall to pieces** [ˌfɔ:l tə 'pi:sɪz]		My book is so old, it is ~*ing* to pieces.	kaputtgehen, sich in seine Bestandteile auflösen
⌐ **all things considered** [ˌɔ:l θɪŋz kən'sɪdəd]		when you have thought about all aspects	wenn man alles in Betracht zieht
• to **join** [dʒɔɪn]		I won't be able to come to the concert tonight. But I'll ~ you later.	*hier:* hinzukommen, hinzugesellen
human being [ˌhju:mən 'bi:ɪŋ]		Dogs and cats are animals, men and women are ~s.	Mensch, menschliches Wesen
whole [həʊl]		= all of s.th.	ganz/e/r/s
it's up to you [ɪts ˌʌp tə 'ju:]		= you have to decide this	es ist deine/Ihre Ent-scheidung
' to **give in to s.o.** [gɪv 'ɪn tə]		to do s.th. because s.o. has made you do it	nachgeben
◦ to **turn s.th. into s.th.** [ˌtɜ:n … 'ɪntə …]		= to change s.th. into s.th.	etwas in etwas ver-/um-wandeln
1 °*relationship* [rɪ'leɪʃnʃɪp]			*Beziehung*
◦ to **be set** *(in)* [bi: 'set]			spielen *(literarisch)*
2 °*pros and cons* [ˌprəʊz ˌənd 'kɒnz]			*Vorteile und Nachteile*
3 °*creative writing* [krɪ'eɪtɪv ˌraɪtɪŋ]			*kreatives Schreiben*
°*author* ['ɔ:θə]			*Autor/in*
°*to be stuck* [bi: 'stʌk]			*nicht weiter wissen, können*
°*outline* ['aʊtlaɪn]			*Skizze, Entwurf*
to **continue** [kən'tɪnju:]		= to go on	fortfahren, weiter-machen (mit); (an)dauern
°*farewell* [feə'wel]			*Abschieds-*

freak [friːk]	*here:* a person who is very interested in computers	*hier*: Enthusiast, Fan
to **borrow** [ˈbɒrəʊ]	If you haven't got a dictionary, you can perhaps ~ one from a friend.	borgen, sich (aus)leihen
direct(ly) [daɪˈrekt(lɪ)]		direkt, unmittelbar

Language module

A Paul's 'holiday'

open-air [ˌəʊpnˈeə]	An ~ concert takes place outside and not in a hall.	Freiluft-
to **camp** [kæmp]	to stay in a tent or a caravan for your holidays	campen, zelten
he may be [meɪ]	~ in trouble = perhaps he is in trouble	vielleicht ist er
to **rush** [rʌʃ]	= to run very fast	schnell laufen, sich beeilen
to **exaggerate** [ɪgˈzædʒəreɪt]	'We went surfing and one wave was as big as a house!' – 'Stop *exaggerating*.'	übertreiben
4 to **express** [ɪkˈspres]		ausdrücken
hair style [ˈheə ˌstaɪl]	the way you have your hair	Frisur

5 °*resolution* [ˌrezəˈluːʃn]		*Vorsatz, Entschluss*
few(er) [ˈfjuː(ə)]	= not many. You can only use '~' with words for things you can count.	wenig(er)
to **get on s.o.'s nerves** [ˌget ɒn … ˈnɜːvz]	= to make s.o. angry	jdm. auf die Nerven gehen
to **smoke** [sməʊk]		rauchen
to **respect** [rɪˈspekt]		achten, respektieren, anerkennen
nail [neɪl]	You have ~s on the end of your fingers.	(Finger-) Nagel
less [les]	= not much. You can only use '~' with words for things you can't count.	weniger, geringer
6 **monkey** [ˈmʌŋkɪ]		Affe
7 °*anonymous* [əˈnɒnɪməs]		*anonym*
8 °*emphatic* [ɪmˈfætɪk]		*betont, betonend*

B Revision: Reporting what others have said

1 **via** [ˈvaɪə]	I'm flying from Düsseldorf to New York ~ London Heathrow.	über, via
versus [ˈvɜːsəs]	= against	gegen
Youth Activity Centre [juːθ ˌækˈtɪvɪtɪ ˌsentə]	Young people come together to take part in many activities in the ~.	Jugendzentrum
3 to **design** [dɪˈzaɪn]	When I leave school, I would like to learn to ~ clothes.	entwerfen
4 °*imperative* [ɪmˈperətɪv]		*hier: Befehlsform*
5 **Bangor** [ˈbæŋgə]		*Stadt in Wales*

Word module

A Describing people

3 °*octopoem* [ˈɒktəˌpəʊɪm]   *Gedicht mit acht Elementen*

   °*to characterize* [ˈkærɪktəˌraɪz]   *charakterisieren, beschreiben*
   °*category* [ˈkætɪgərɪ]   *Kategorie*
   lemon [ˈlemən]   Zitrone

   handle [ˈhændl]   You pick up a cup by its ~. ⟵   Griff

   cocoa [ˈkəʊkəʊ]   a drink that is also called 'hot chocolate'   Kakao
   cellar [ˈselə]   the part of the house that is under the ground   Keller
   silk [sɪlk]   Wool and ~ are natural materials.   Seide
   scarf [skɑːf]   s.th. you wear around your neck, sometimes made of silk   Schal, Halstuch
   breeze [briːz]   = a wind that isn't strong   Brise

B Your potential vocabulary

   °*potential* [pəˈtenʃl]   *möglich, potentiell*
1 to **interrupt** [ˌɪntəˈrʌpt]   Don't ~. Jane hasn't finished talking yet.   unterbrechen, ins Wort fallen

   washing machine [ˈwɒʃɪŋ məˌʃiːn]   You wash your clothes in a ~.   Waschmaschine

"Young Willy's very much like his father, isn't he?"

TOPIC 4   THE WORLD AROUND US

topic ['tɒpɪk]	= subject s.th. you talk or write about	Thema, Themenbereich

Text module

1   Animal rights and wrongs

You will find the other new words from this text in the Dictionary.

content ['kɒntent]	A book often begins with a table of ~s.	Inhalt
module ['mɒdju:l]	⌣ a complete part that can be added to other parts	Modul, Bauelement; Lerneinheit
source [sɔ:s]	Wind, sun and water are all power ~s.	Ursache, Ursprung; *hier*: Quelle
°*relative clause* ['relətɪv ˌklɔ:z]		*Relativsatz*
°*non-defining relative clause* [ˌnɒndɪ'faɪnɪŋ 'relətɪv ˌklɔ:z]		*nicht-notwendiger Relativsatz*
neither ... nor ['naɪðə ... ˌnɔ:]	Our new garage is ~ too big ~ too small – it's just right.	weder ... noch
debate [dɪ'beɪt]	= a formal discussion	Debatte, Diskussion
animal aid [eɪd]	⚠ animal ~ = help for animals No plural!	Hilfe; *hier*: Hilfe für Tiere, Tierschutz
circus ['sɜ:kəs]	~es travel from town to town with their animals.	Zirkus
to **trap** [træp]	In some countries people still ~ animals for their fur.	(mit einer Falle) fangen
to **suffer** ['sʌfə]	to experience s.th. bad	(er)leiden, ertragen
cruel ['kru:əl]	⟷ kind It is ~ to keep animals in small cages.	grausam
death [deθ]	the noun of 'to die'	Tod
kitten ['kɪtn]	a young cat	Kätzchen
to **treat** [tri:t]	to ~ s.o. well/badly = to behave well/badly towards s.o.	behandeln
pause [pɔ:z]	a break	Pause
to **pause** [pɔ:z]	to take a break	Pause machen
to **include** [ɪn'klu:d]	to put in You should ~ all new words in your word file.	aufnehmen, enthalten, einschließen
experience [ɪk'spɪərɪəns]		Erfahrung, Erlebnis
evidence ['evɪdəns]	⚠ No plural! There isn't any ~ that he is the murderer.	Beweis(e)
disgusting [dɪs'gʌstɪŋ]	= horrible This food tastes ~. I don't like it at all.	widerlich, ekelhaft
disturbing [dɪ'stɜ:bɪŋ]	If you find s.th. ~, it makes you feel worried.	beunruhigend
contrast ['kɒntrɑ:st]	⌣ = difference	Unterschied, Kontrast
°*to pick (out)* [pɪk]		*aussuchen, heraussuchen*
experiment [ɪk'sperɪmənt]	Scientists do ~s to see if s.th. will work.	Experiment, Versuch
laboratory [lə'bɒrətrɪ]	'Lab' is short for ~.	Labor

research [rɪ'sɜːtʃ]	You do ~ when you want to find out more about a subject.	Forschung
to **abuse** [ə'bjuːz]	to use s.th. in the wrong way or to treat s.o. cruelly	missbrauchen
acceptable [ək'septəbl]	If s.th. is ~, it is OK and not wrong.	akzeptabel, in Ordnung

2 The Battery Hen

You will find the new words from this text in the Dictionary.

battery hen ['bætərɪ ˌhen]	A ~ is kept in a cage and cannot run around outside.	Batteriehenne
dialect ['daɪəlekt]	☺	Dialekt, Mundart
to **lay**, laid, laid [leɪ, leɪd, leɪd]	Hens ~ eggs.	legen
bloody ['blʌdɪ]		blutig; *hier*: verdammt (*ugs.*)
2 to **discuss** [dɪs'kʌs]	= to talk about s.th.	diskutieren, besprechen
humorous ['hjuːmərəs]	= funny	humorvoll, lustig, komisch

Strategy Page: A class debate

°*chairperson* ['tʃeəpɜːsn]		*Vorsitzende/r, Diskussionsleiter/in*
statement ['steɪtmənt]	When you give your opinion you make a ~.	Aussage, Beitrag, Meinungsäußerung
favour ['feɪvə]		Gefallen; Wohlwollen
in favour of ['feɪvə]	To speak ~ a topic means to speak for it, and not against it.	für (etwas)
audience ['ɔːdɪəns]	the people listening to a radio programme or watching a film in a cinema, for example	Publikum, Zuschauer/innen, Zuhörer/innen
vote [vəʊt]	After the debate we had a ~.	Abstimmung, Wahl
1 **expression** [ɪk'spreʃn]	= a phrase	Ausdruck
controversial [ˌkɒntrə'vɜːʃl]	Hunting foxes is a ~ topic in Britain.	kontrovers, umstritten
point [pɔɪnt]	what you want to say	(inhaltlicher) Punkt
impossible [ɪm'pɒsɪbl]	←→ possible	unmöglich
to **admit** [əd'mɪt]	It was me. I ~ it.	zugeben
2 **fact** [fækt]	s.th. that is true It is a ~ that the earth is round.	Tatsache, Faktum
to **produce** [prə'djuːs]		produzieren, erzeugen, herstellen, hervorbringen
iron ['aɪən]	Steel is made out of ~.	Eisen
sentimental [ˌsentɪ'mentl]	☺ *here:* when you think of animals as if they were human	sentimental, gefühlsbetont
3 **support** [sə'pɔːt]		Unterstützung
in support of [sə'pɔːt]	If you want to speak ~ your opinion, you collect arguments and ideas that will support it.	zur Unterstützung, als Unterstützung von/für

3 Boiling a kettle

You will find the other new words from this text in the Dictionary.

to **boil** [bɔɪl]	Water ~s at 100° Celsius.	kochen
solution [sə'luːʃn]	= answer What is the ~ to the third Maths question?	Lösung, Ergebnis
basic ['beɪsɪk]	= elementary	grundlegend

routine [ruːˈtiːn]	= normal	Routine-, routinemäßig; *hier:* normal
supply [səˈplaɪ]	We get our water from our own spring. That's our water ~.	Versorgung; Vorrat
nowhere [ˈnəʊweə]	←→ anywhere	nirgendwo, nirgends
proper(ly) [ˈprɒpə(lɪ)]	I haven't got a *proper* desk – I do my homework at an old kitchen table.	richtig/e/r/s, ordentlich/e/r/s
frequent(ly) [ˈfriːkwənt(lɪ)]	= often	häufig
illness [ˈɪlnəs]	the noun of 'ill'	Krankheit
to **construct** [kənˈstrʌkt]	= to build	bauen
difference [ˈdɪfrəns]	the noun of 'different'	Unterschied
shower [ˈʃaʊə]	Usually, having a bath uses more water than having a ~.	*hier:* Dusche; Regenschauer
washing machine [ˈwɒʃɪŋ məˌʃiːn]	You wash your clothes in a ~.	Waschmaschine
tap [tæp]	In your house, water comes out of a ~.	Wasserhahn
to **choose**, chose, chosen (to do s.th.) [tʃuːz, tʃəʊz, tʃəʊzn]	*here:* to decide (to do s.th.)	aussuchen, auswählen; *hier:* sich für etwas entscheiden
hydro-electric [ˈhaɪdrəʊ]	~ comes from a Greek word meaning water, so ~-*electric* power is electricity made using the energy of running water.	wasser-, hydro-
fossil [ˈfɒsl]	Oil and coal are ~ fuels. They were formed a very long time ago.	versteinert; *hier:* fossile/r/s
turbine [ˈtɜːbaɪn]	A wind ~ produces power.	Turbine
nuclear [ˈnjuːklɪə]	~ power is very controversial.	Nuklear-, Atom-

4   No other choice

You will find the other new words from this text in the Dictionary.

choice [tʃɔɪs]	the noun of 'to choose'	Wahl, Auswahl
event [ɪˈvent]	= s.th. that happens	Ereignis
meadow [ˈmedəʊ]	a large area of grass for cows or horses to eat	Weide, Wiese
ranch [rɑːnʃ]	= a large farm	Ranch, Viehfarm *(AE)*
cattle [ˈkætl]	A plural word! The ~ are in the meadow.	Vieh
to **split**, split, split *(up)* [splɪtˈʌp]	to move away from each other	aufteilen; *hier:* sich aufteilen
wolf, wolves [wʊlf, wʊlvz]	*Wolves* often hunt in groups.	Wolf, Wölfe
shadow [ˈʃædəʊ]	If the moon shines very brightly, ~s can appear at night, too.	Schatten
awesome [ˈɔːsəm]	Have you ever been to the Rocky Mountains? They're ~.	beeindruckend, ehrfurchtgebietend
pack [pæk]	a ~ of wolves = a group of wolves	*hier:* Rudel, Meute
official [əˈfɪʃl]	*here:* a person who works for the Yellowstone National Park	Angestellte/r in einer öffentlichen Institution, Beamter/in
however [haʊˈevə]	It should be a routine job. ~, accidents can always happen.	jedoch, aber

(radio) **collar** [ˈkɒlə]	When you take your dog for a walk, it has to wear a ~.	Kragen; *hier*: Halsband (mit Peilsender)
sheep [ʃiːp]	⚠ Singular = plural! If you can't sleep, you can always count ~.	Schaf, Schafe
sight [saɪt]	the noun of 'to see'	Anblick; Sehenswürdigkeit
painful [ˈpeɪnfəl]	I broke my arm last year. It was very ~.	schmerzhaft, qualvoll
development [dɪˈveləpmənt]	the noun of 'to develop'	Entwicklung
to **afford** [əˈfɔːd]	I can't ~ the new computer game. It's too expensive.	sich leisten (können)
original(ly) [əˈrɪdʒənəl(ɪ)]	~*ly*, I come from a small village in Wales, but I moved to London ten years ago.	ursprünglich
to **survive** [səˈvaɪv]	A survivor is s.o. who has ~ed.	überleben
to **replace** [rɪˈpleɪs]	If a window is broken, you have to ~ it.	ersetzen
to **protect** [prəˈtekt]	= to look after	(be)schützen, aufpassen auf
snowmobile [ˈsnəʊməbiːl]	You can travel over snow in a ~.	Schneemobil *(AE)*
countryside [ˈkʌntrɪsaɪd]	The ~ in Scotland is very beautiful.	Landschaft
fence [fens]	You need a ~ around a meadow to keep the cattle in.	Zaun
to **point** *(to)* [ˈpɔɪnt tʊ]	He ~ed with his finger *to* the other side of the meadow. – 'Look! A wolf!'	zeigen, deuten (auf); hinweisen
valley [ˈvælɪ]	the low area between two hills	Tal
to **slow s.th. down** [sləʊ ... ˈdaʊn]	to make s.th. go more slowly	verlangsamen
danger [ˈdeɪndʒə]	the noun of 'dangerous'	Gefahr
to **sink**, sank, sunk *(down)* [sɪŋk, sæŋk, sʌŋk ˈdaʊn]	to move or fall lower down	(hinab)sinken
soft(ly) [sɒft(lɪ)]	⟷ hard	leise; *hier*: weich
to **catch up** *(with)* [ˌkætʃ ˈʌp wɪð]	to reach s.o. or s.th. that is in front of you, by walking or running faster	einholen
gun [gʌn]	With a ~ you can shoot a dangerous animal.	Gewehr, Pistole
to **aim** [eɪm]	to point a gun at s.th.	zielen auf
1 **reaction** [rɪˈækʃn]	noun of 'to react'	Reaktion

A checklist of plural forms

• pack, pack**s**; animal, animal**s**
    ranch, ranch**es**; circus, circus**es**
        supp**ly**, supp**lies**; laborato**ry**, laborato**ries**; BUT: vall**ey**, vall**eys**!

• man, m**e**n; woman, wom**e**n; child, child**ren**
        wo**lf**, wo**lves**; li**fe**, li**ves**

• one co**w**	several co**ws**	• City **people are** moving to the country.
one shee**p**	several shee**p**	The **cattle are** scared by the wolf.

• the **evidence is** clear	–	die **Beweise sind** eindeutig
(a piece of evidence)		(ein Beweis)

More **information is** needed.	–	Mehr **Informationen sind** notwendig.
(an interesting piece of information)		(eine interessante Information)
His **advice is** always good.	–	Seine **Ratschläge sind** immer gut.
(a useful piece of advice)		(ein nützlicher Ratschlag)

• The **news is** on in 10 minutes.	–	Die **Nachrichten kommen** in zehn Minuten.
I've just received **an** important **piece** of	–	Ich habe gerade **eine** wichtige **Nachricht**
news.		erhalten.
BUT: The **police have** been informed.	–	Die **Polizei ist** informiert worden.

Language module

A   Revision: Protest action

1	to **take action** [teɪk ˈækʃn]	to do s.th. about s.th.	etwas/Schritte unternehmen
2	to **predict** [prɪˈdɪkt]	to say what is going to happen	vorher-/voraussagen
	garage [ˈgærɑːʒ]		hier: Tankstelle, Autowerkstatt
	effect [ɪˈfekt]	What ~s will global warming have on the weather?	Effekt, Auswirkung
3	°*speculation* [ˌspekjəˈleɪʃn]		*Spekulation, Vermutung*
4	**demonstration** [ˌdemənˈstreɪʃn]	30,000 people took part in the human rights ~.	*hier*: „Demo", Demonstration

B1   Giving additional information

	additional [əˈdɪʃənl]	= more	zusätzlich
1	**pressure** [ˈpreʃə]		Druck
	pressure group [ˈpreʃə ˌgruːp]	Greenpeace is a ~.	*Interessenverband, der z.B. auf die Regierung Druck auszuüben sucht*
2	**platform** [ˈplætfɔːm]	The Brent Spar was an oil ~.	Plattform; *hier*: Bohrinsel
	activist [ˈæktɪvɪst]	s.o. who works publicly for a pressure group, for example	Aktivist/in
3	to **translate** [trænsˈleɪt]	When you don't know how to ~ an English word, you can use an English-German dictionary.	übersetzen

suitable ['suːtəbl/'sjuːtəbl]	If you want to go climbing, you should wear ~ shoes.		passend, geeignet
peaceful(ly) ['piːsfəl(ɪ)]	←→ violent		friedlich

B2 In the neighbourhood

	manure [mə'njʊə]	Horse ~ is very good for your garden.	Mist
	the other day [ðɪ ˌʌðə 'deɪ]	a day or two ago	neulich
	health [helθ]	~ is more important than money.	Gesundheit
1	°*elegant* ['eləgənt]		*elegant*
2	to **have s.th. done** [ˌhæv … 'dʌn]	'Did you repair your bike yourself?' – 'No, I had it repaired.'	etwas machen lassen
6	**similar** ['sɪmɪlə]		ähnlich
8	°*saying* ['seɪɪŋ]		*Redensart, Sprichwort Redewendung*
	to **borrow** ['bɒrəʊ]	'Could I ~ this CD, Lisa?' …	borgen, sich (aus)leihen
	to **lend**, lent, lent [lend, lent, lent]	… 'Yes, you can. But first I'd like the other CD back I *lent* you last week.'	leihen, verleihen

Strategy Page: Working with a dictionary

1	**separate(ly)** ['seprət(lɪ)]	←→ together, joined	separat, getrennt
2	°*extract* ['ekstrækt]		*Auszug*
	°*preposition* [ˌprepə'zɪʃn]		*Präposition*
3	°*to double-check* [ˌdʌbl'tʃek]		*(noch einmal) überprüfen*

Images

	image ['ɪmɪdʒ]	Bild; Image
1	°*to identify* [aɪ'dentɪfaɪ]	*identifizieren*
2	°*to get rid of s.o./s.th.* [get 'rɪd ˌəv]	*jdn./etwas loswerden*

'It's a new idea to stop the British being filthy.'

---

litter – Abfälle
filthy – sehr schmutzig

TOPIC 5   THE EMERALD ISLE

topic ['tɒpɪk]	= subject s.th. you talk or write about	Thema, Themenbereich

Text module

Photo pages

emerald ['emərəld]		Smaragd
isle [aɪl]		Insel
The Emerald Isle [ðiː‿emərəld‿'aɪl]	= the green island	*Name für Irland*
content ['kɒntent]	A book often begins with a table of ~s.	Inhalt
module ['mɒdjuːl]	☺ a complete part that can be added to other parts	Modul, Bauelement; Lerneinheit
background ['bækgraʊnd]	~ information helps you to understand s.th. better.	Hintergrund(-)
°**gerund** ['dʒerənd]		*Gerundium*
1 **mind** ['maɪnd]	If s.th. comes to ~, you think of it.	Kopf, Sinn

1   Why don't they just go home?

	You will find the other new words from this text in the Dictionary.	
to **be set** *(in)* [biː 'set]	The Sherlock Holmes stories are ~ in London.	spielen (in)*(literarisch)*
the **Border** [ðə 'bɔːdə]	~ divides Ireland into two parts.	*die Grenze zwischen Nordirland und der Republik Irland*
soft(ly) [sɒft(lɪ)]	⟷ hard	leise; *hier*: weich
seat [siːt]	the noun of 'to sit'	Sitz; *hier*: Autositz
nowhere ['nəʊweə]	⟷ everywhere	nirgendwo, nirgends
so did ... ['səʊ dɪd]	~ Ann = Ann did, too	(das) tat auch
to **have a look** [ˌhæv‿ə 'lʊk]	'My tooth hurts!' – 'Well, open your mouth and I'll ~.'	sich etwas anschauen
mind you [ˌmaɪnd 'jʊ]		allerdings
gun [gʌn]	~s are very dangerous. You are not allowed to own a ~ unless you have a permit for it.	Gewehr, Pistole
pest [pest]	My little brother is a ~. He's a real pain in the neck.	Plage; *hier*: Nervensäge
to **unite** [juː'naɪt]	The two German states were ~d again in 1990.	vereinen
Och! [ɒx]	People from Scotland and Ireland often say ~ instead of 'Oh!'.	Ach!
to **vote** [vəʊt]	Let's ~! Who is for the plan and who is against it?	wählen, abstimmen
to **set up** [set‿'ʌp]	= to organize	einrichten, arrangieren
beginning [bɪ'gɪnɪŋ]	⟷ end	Anfang, Beginn
county ['kaʊntɪ]	Northern Ireland is divided into different *counties*.	Grafschaft, Verwaltungs- bezirk
to **outvote** [ˌaʊt'vəʊt]	41 people voted against your plan and only 5 were for it, so you were ~d.	überstimmen
democracy [dɪ'mɒkrəsɪ]		Demokratie
to **bomb** [bɒm]	to use bombs against persons or objects	Bomben legen/werfen

prospect ['prɒspekt]	= what might happen in the future The career ~s for engineers are good at the moment.	Aussicht(en), Zukunft
but [bʌt]	= except for	*hier:* außer
The Republic [ðə rɪ'pʌblɪk]	Dublin is in ~ of Ireland.	*hier:* die Republik Irland
holy ['həʊlɪ]	~ is a word connected to religion, e.g., in India, there are ~ cows.	heilig
ordinary ['ɔːdɪnərɪ]	= normal	normal, gewöhnlich
drum [drʌm]	Phil Collins is a singer and also plays the ~s.	Trommel; *(als Plural)* Schlagzeug
hedge [hedʒ]	In the country, you often have ~s next to the road.	Hecke
to react [rɪ'ækt]	How did she ~ when she heard that she had won the prize?	reagieren
°*to summarize* ['sʌməraɪz]		*zusammenfassen*

1

2 A look at history

site [saɪt]	= place; the ~ of a building, the ~ where s.th. important happened	Ort, Platz, Stätte
independent (*of*) [ˌɪndɪ'pendənt_ɒv]	adjective of 'independence'	unabhängig (von)
to remain [rɪ'meɪn]	= stay	(übrig)bleiben
majority [mə'dʒɒrətɪ]	= more than half	Mehrheit
separate ['seprət]	⟷ together, joined	separat, getrennt
violence ['vaɪələns]	the noun of 'violent'	Gewalt
treaty ['triːtɪ]	When different countries or groups of people agree on important issues, they sign a ~.	Vertrag *(zwischen Ländern)*
Good Friday [ˌgʊd 'fraɪdeɪ]	~ is a religious holiday in Germany.	Karfreitag
unrest [ʌn'rest]	⟷ peace	Unruhen

Language module

A Aspects of Ireland

aspect ['æspekt]		Aspekt, Seite
few(er) ['fjuː(ə)]	= not many. You can only use '~' with words for things you can count.	wenig(er)
inhabitant [ɪn'hæbɪtənt]	a person who lives in a certain place	Einwohner/in
is said to be ['sed tə biː]		soll angeblich/ist, so sagt man
economy [ɪ'kɒnəmɪ]	Fewer people are unemployed; the ~ is better than it was.	Wirtschaft, Konjunktur
to continue [kən'tɪnjuː]	= to go on	fortfahren, weiter- machen mit; (an)dauern
to improve [ɪm'pruːv]	= to get better	verbessern, besser machen; besser werden
to estimate ['estɪmeɪt]	I don't know exactly. I would ~ about 10 million.	(ein)schätzen
of (Irish) **descent** [ɒv … dɪ'sent]	If you are ~ *Irish* ~, then at least one member of your family originally came from Ireland.	(irischer) Abstammung

	eldest ['eldɪst]	Susan is the ~ of five children.	älteste/r *(in einer Familie)*
	to **depend** *(on)* [dɪ'pend ɒn]	If you ~ on s.o., you are not independent.	abhängig sein von; sich verlassen auf
1	**expression** [ɪk'spreʃn]	= a phrase	Ausdruck
2	°to **pick** *(out)* [pɪk]		*aussuchen, heraussuchen*
	°to **contain** [kən'teɪn]		*beinhalten, enthalten*
	structure ['strʌktʃə]		Struktur, Konstruktion
	to **interpret** [ɪn'tɜːprɪt]		*hier:* dolmetschen; interpretieren, deuten
	plenty ['plentɪ]	= a lot	viel/e/es, eine Menge
	golf [gɒlf]		Golf
	golf course ['gɒlf ˌkɔːs]	where you play golf	Golfplatz
	to **choose**, chose, chosen [tʃuːz, tʃəʊz, tʃəʊzn]		aussuchen, auswählen

B   Irish – a living language

	to **support** [sə'pɔːt]		stützen, unterstützen
	remote [rɪ'məʊt]	far away from other places, hard to get to	entlegen, abgelegen
	to **pronounce** [prə'naʊns]	Some words, like 'fifth', are hard to ~.	aussprechen
1	**translation** [træns'leɪʃn]	noun of 'to translate'	Übersetzung

What you can say when you don't know an exact number

<u>One</u> brother emigrated to America.	ein ...
His <u>other</u> brothers emigrated two years later.	die anderen ...
The <u>rest of</u> the family went two years after that.	die übrigen ...
<u>They all</u> settled in America.	sie alle ...
<u>Hundreds of thousands of</u> people emigrated.	hunderttausende ...
<u>Over a million</u> died.	über eine Million ...
Ireland has <u>fewer</u> inhabitants now <u>than</u> in the 19th century.	weniger als ...
But <u>more</u> people are going back to Ireland <u>than</u> a few years ago.	mehr als ...
<u>All the</u> children have to learn Irish in school.	alle ...
<u>Most</u> (of their) parents understand a bit of Irish.	die meisten ...
<u>Many of them</u> would like to understand more.	viele von ihnen ...
The population of Northern Ireland is <u>about</u> <u>around</u> 65% Protestant.	ungefähr/zirka
There are about 70 million people <u>completely</u>, <u>mainly</u> or <u>partly</u> of Irish descent.	gänzlich, hauptsächlich, teilweise

C   Holidaying in Ireland

luggage ['lʌgɪdʒ]	When you go on holiday, only take as much ~ as you can carry.	Gepäck
to **take part** [teɪk 'pɑːt]	Are you still looking for actors? I'd love to ~ in your new play.	teilnehmen
°*extract* ['ekstrækt]		*Auszug*
to **comment** ['kɒment]		kommentieren
trail [treɪl]	= path	Weg, Pfad
to **overlook** [ˌəʊvə'lʊk]	'Having a super holiday. Our hotel room ~s the sea!'	überblicken, einen Blick haben auf

Whilst doing a long-overdue clearout at the offices of Ireland's oldest and most respected school of dance, Mrs O' Hara made a terrible discovery ...

---

long-overdue – längst überfällig
to incorporate – einbringen

TOPIC 6   DOWN UNDER

topic ['tɒpɪk]	= subject s.th. you talk or write about	Thema, Themenbereich

Text module

Photo pages

down under [ˌdaʊn‿ˈʌndə]	~ is an informal name for Australia.	(in) Australien, Neusee-land *(ugs.)*
content ['kɒntent]	A book often begins with a table of ~s.	Inhalt
module ['mɒdjuːl]	☺ a complete part that can be added to other parts	Modul, Bauelement; Lerneinheit
Australian [ɒs'treɪlɪən]	the adjective of 'Australia'	australisch, Australier/in
background ['bækgraʊnd]	~ information helps you to understand s.th. better.	Hintergrund(-)
°*creative* [krɪ'eɪtɪv]		*kreativ*
°*awareness* [ə'weənəs]		*Bewusstsein, Gespür*
quite [kwaɪt]	= rather	ziemlich, ganz
Aborigine [ˌæbə'rɪdʒɪnɪ]	The ~s were the first people to live in Australia.	*Name der Ureinwohner Australiens*
continent ['kɒntɪnənt]	Australia and Europe are both ~s.	Kontinent
heart [hɑːt]	Your ~ works like a pump to keep the blood in your body moving.	Herz
to **endure** [ɪn'djʊə]	If you come from a North European country, the heat in African countries can be hard to ~.	aushalten, ertragen
the 'outback' [ðiː‿'aʊtbæk]	In the Australian ~, your nearest neighbour will probably live several miles away.	das australische Hinter-land
rancher ['rɑːntʃə]	☺ Australian word for 'farmer'	Rancher, Viehzüchter/in
to **clear** [klɪə]	*here:* to take the trees away and turn forest into grassland	*hier:* roden, abholzen
tropical ['trɒpɪkl]	The weather can get very hot in ~ countries.	tropisch
cute [kjuːt]	= sweet (of people or animals)	niedlich, süß
koala [kəʊ'ɑːlə]	~s live in trees and eat leaves all day long.	Koalabär
gum tree ['gʌm triː]	The leaves of the ~ are a koala's only food.	Eukalyptusbaum *(ugs.)*
shark [ʃɑːk]	It is dangerous to go swimming where there are ~s.	Haifisch
crocodile ['krɒkədaɪl]		Krokodil
kangaroo [ˌkæŋgə'ruː]	⚠ Spelling! A ~ does not walk or run – it jumps.	Känguru
1 **contrast** ['kɒntrɑːst]	☺ = difference	Unterschied, Kontrast

1   I am Australian

You will find the other new words from this text in the Dictionary.

iron ['aɪən]	When the British prisoners first arrived in Australia, they had ~ chains around their feet.	Eisen
convict ['kɒnvɪkt]	s.o. who is in prison	Sträfling
to **seek**, sought, sought [siːk, sɔːt, sɔːt]	= to look for	suchen

dusty ['dʌstɪ]	When the weather is very dry, the ground becomes very ~.	staubig
the Depression [ðə dɪ'preʃn]	a time when very many people were unemployed	Weltwirtschaftskrise
to **paint** [peɪnt]	You draw with a pencil, you ~ with a brush.	malen
soil [sɔɪl]	Plants grow in ~.	Erde, Boden
plain [pleɪn]	= a very large, flat piece of ground	Ebene
valley ['vælɪ]	the low place ⎯ between two hills	Tal
drought [draʊt]	when it doesn't rain for a very long time	Dürre
flooding ['flʌdɪŋ]	If it rains very much in a short time that can cause ~.	Überflutung
Dreaming = Dreamtime ['driːmɪŋ/'driːmtaɪm]	The Aborigines call their earliest history ~.	„Zeit der Träume" *(die mythische Urzeit der australischen Urein-wohner)*
flame [fleɪm]	The ~ of a candle is very hot.	Flamme
shore [ʃɔː]	where the sea meets the land	Küste, Strand

Use these words to start a memory map for Australia

bush	gum tree	outback	rocky
coast	hot	plain	shark
crocodile	kangaroo	rain	shore
drought	koala	rainforest	sky
dry	lake	red	soil
dusty	land	river	valley
flooding	mountain	rock	water

---

2   A look at history

inhabitant [ɪn'hæbɪtənt]	a person who lives in a certain place	Einwohner/in
creation [krɪ'eɪʃn]	= the making of s.th.	(Er-)Schaffung
settlement ['setlmənt]	a place where people settle	Siedlung
colony ['kɒlənɪ]	⚠ Pronunciation! = settlement	Kolonie, Ansiedlung
arrival [ə'raɪvl]	noun of 'to arrive'	Ankunft
1 °*to match up* [mætʃ'ʌp]		*das Passende zu etw. finden*
point [pɔɪnt]		(inhaltlicher) Punkt
2 °*to make up* [meɪk'ʌp]		*hier: bilden, ausmachen*
3 to **sum up** [sʌm'ʌp]	Please ~ the main parts of the text.	zusammenfassen

3   Matthew meets No-name

You will find the other new words from this text in the Dictionary.

the Bush [ðə 'bʊʃ]	a part of Australia where only very few people live	der australische Busch
spot [spɒt]		Ort, Stelle; Fleck

to **doubt** [daʊt]	⟷ to be sure	bezweifeln
to **search** [ˈsɜ:tʃ]	= to look for	suchen
search party [ˈsɜ:tʃ ˌpɑ:tɪ]	A ~ searches for s.o. who is lost.	Suchtrupp, -mannschaft
to **run out** [rʌn ˈaʊt]	'Can I have a coke, please?' – 'I'm sorry, I've none left. I've ~.'	ausgehen, zu Ende gehen
shorts [ʃɔ:ts]	⚠ Always plural! = short trousers	Shorts
back and forward [ˌbæk ənd ˈfɔ:wəd]	Some people can't sit still when they are nervous, but walk ~.	vor und zurück, hin und her

Watch out for phrases made of pairs of opposites

back and forward   up and down
here and there   right and left
in and out   upstairs and downstairs
inside and outside   near and far
there and back   now and then

endless [ˈendləs]	= without an end	endlos
sunrise [ˈsʌnraɪz]	~ is when the sun appears in the morning.	Sonnenaufgang
optimism [ˈɒptɪmɪzm]	If you have a lot of ~, you believe everything will be all right in the future.	Optimismus
branch [brɑ:ntʃ]	a piece of a tree	Ast, Zweig
difference [ˈdɪfɪəns]	the noun of 'different'	Unterschied
survival [səˈvaɪvl]		Überleben, Überlebens-
soft(ly) [sɒft(lɪ)]	⟷ loud(ly)	weich; *hier*: leise
particular [pəˈtɪkjʊlə]	= special	besondere/r/s, bestimmt/e/r/s
match [mætʃ]	To light a fire you normally need ~*es*.	*hier*: Streichholz
plenty [ˈplentɪ]	= a lot	viel/e/es, eine Menge
to **point** to [ˈpɔɪnt tə]	'Could I have a piece of that cake, please?' he said, and ~*ed to* the chocolate cake.	zeigen, deuten auf; hinweisen
nick [nɪk]		Kerbe, Ritze
to **sharpen** [ˈʃɑ:pn]	When your pencil no longer writes well, you have to ~ it.	(an)spitzen; wetzen, schärfen

Many adjectives are made into verbs by adding –en

sharp	scharf	weak	schwach	flat	flach
to sharpen	schärfen	to weaken	schwächen	to flatten	flach/platt machen
soft	weich	straight	gerade	short	kurz
to soften	weich machen	to straighten	gerade machen	to shorten	kürzen

firm(ly) [ˈfɜ:m(lɪ)]	Don't drop that! Hold it ~*ly*!	fest
upright [ˈʌpraɪt]	⟷ lying down	aufrecht, vertikal
to **twist** [twɪst]	= to turn s.th. round quite fast	drehen

friction ['frɪkʃn]	The result of ~ is heat.	Reibung	
cheerful(ly) ['tʃɪəfəl(ɪ)]	= happy	fröhlich, gut gelaunt	
pause [pɔːz]	⚠ Pronunciation!	Pause	
	⚒ = a break		
to **nod** [nɒd]	In many cultures, to ~ your head means 'yes'.	nicken	
simply ['sɪmplɪ]	= just	einfach	
1 °*turning point* ['tɜːnɪŋ pɔɪnt]		*Wendepunkt*	
2 °*throughout* [θruːˈaʊt]		*überall (in), ... hindurch; hier: im Laufe von*	
to **mention** ['menʃn]	to talk about s.th. for only a short time	erwähnen	
3 °*attempt* [əˈtempt]		*Versuch*	
demonstration [ˌdemənˈstreɪʃn]	*here:* to show s.th.	*hier:* Vorführung, Demonstration; „Demo"	
4 **point of view** [ˌpɔɪnt_ə_ˈvjuː]	a way of looking at s.th.	Standpunkt, Sichtweise	
5 **suitable** ['suːtəbl/'sjuːtəbl]	If you want to go climbing, you should wear ~ shoes.	passend, geeignet	

Language module

English in the world

1 **fact** [fækt]	⟷ fantasy	Tatsache, Faktum	
official [əˈfɪʃl]	Some countries have more than one ~ language.	offiziell; *hier:* Amts-	
billion ['bɪljən]	one thousand million	Milliarde	
position [pəˈzɪʃn]	the place where s.o. or s.th. is	Stellung, Position	
2 to **concentrate** (*on*) ['kɒnsəntreɪt(_ɒn)]		sich konzentrieren (auf)	
°*logical* ['lɒdʒɪkl]		*logisch*	
3 °*relative(ly)* ['relətɪv(lɪ)]		*relativ*	
°*to re-phrase* [riːˈfreɪz]		*umformulieren*	

Strategy Page: Cultural awareness

°*exaggeration* [ɪgˌzædʒəˈreɪʃn]		*Übertreibung*	
to **apologize** [əˈpɒlədʒaɪz]	I'm very sorry. I shouldn't have said that – I ~!	sich entschuldigen	
punctual ['pʌŋktʃʊəl]	= on time. He's never late, he's always ~.	pünktlich	
bother ['bɒðə]	It's no ~. = It's no trouble./I don't mind doing it.	Aufwand, Ärger	
apology [əˈpɒlədʒɪ]	the noun of 'to apologize'	Entschuldigung	
conversation [ˌkɒnvəˈseɪʃn]	to have a ~ with s.o. = to talk to s.o.	Unterhaltung	
polite [pəˈlaɪt]	It's not ~ to be late for an appointment.	höflich	
to **burp** [bɜːp]	Babies have to ~ after they have had their milk.	aufstoßen	
statement ['steɪtmənt]	to make a ~ = to say s.th.	Aussage, Beitrag, Meinungsäußerung	

	host [həʊst]	The person giving a party is the ~.	Gastgeber/in
	to **rush** [rʌʃ]		schnell laufen, sich beeilen
1	to **lend**, lent, lent [lend, lent, lent]		leihen, verleihen
	to **borrow** ['bɒrəʊ]	'Can I ~ your bike, Peter?' – 'No, I'm sorry. I lent it to Michael yesterday.'	borgen, sich (aus)leihen
2	°*to become aware (of)* [bɪ,kʌm_ə'weər_əv]		*sich bewusst werden, erkennen*
	°*patterns of behaviour* ['pætənz ɒv bɪ'heɪvjə]		*Verhaltensmuster*
	°*objective(ly)* [əb'dʒektɪv(lɪ)]		*objektiv*
	to **consider** [kən'sɪdə]	*here:* to think	bctrachteu, bedenken

Images

	image ['ɪmɪdʒ]		Bild; Image
2	to **choose**, chose, chosen [tʃuːz, tʃəʊz, tʃəʊzn]	In a restaurant you can ~ what you want to eat.	aussuchen, auswählen
	°*task* [tɑːsk]		*Aufgabe*
	°*outline* ['aʊtlaɪn]		*Skizze, Entwurf*
	°*illustration* [,ɪlə'streɪʃn]		*Abbildung, Illustration*
	beginning [bɪ'gɪnɪŋ]	⟷ end	Beginn, Anfang
	°*inspiration* [,ɪnspə'reɪʃn]		*Anregung, Inspiration*
	account [ə'kaʊnt]		*hier:* Bericht; (Bank-) Konto

"I wasn't born here but I've adapted to the life in Australia quite well!"

⟨ Topic 1 ⟩

⟨1   Candle in the Wind⟩

You will find the other new words from this
text in the Dictionary.

Norma Jean [ˌnɔːmə ˈdʒiːn]	eigentliche Vornamen von Marilyn Monroe
never … at all [ˈnevə … ətˈɔːl]	gar nicht
grace [greɪs]	Würde
to hold oneself [həʊld]	hier: sich würdevoll verhalten
treadmill [ˈtredmɪl]	Tretmühle
to cling to [ˈklɪŋ tʊ]	(sich) festhalten an
loneliness [ˈləʊnlɪnəs]	Einsamkeit
tough [tʌf]	hart
to create [krɪˈeɪt]	erzeugen, (er)schaffen
the press [ðə ˈpres]	die Presse
to hound [haʊnd]	verfolgen, Jagd machen auf
in the nude [ɪn ðə ˈnjuːd]	nackt
row [rəʊ]	Reihe
Marilyn Monroe [ˌmærɪlɪn mənˈrəʊ]	amerik. Filmschauspielerin
⟨3⟩ distinction [dɪˈstɪŋkʃn]	Unterschied

⟨2   A life behind the camera …⟩

You will find the other new words from this
text in the Dictionary.

to direct [daɪˈrekt]	Regie führen
commercial [kəˈmɜːʃl]	Werbespot
successful [səkˈsesfəl]	erfolgreich
advisor [ədˈvaɪzə]	Berater/in
college [ˈkɒlɪdʒ]	Universität, Hochschule
A-levels [ˈeɪˌlevlz]	das britische Äquivalent des Abiturs
degree [dɪˈgriː]	Hochschulabschluss
to do a degree [ˌduˈə dɪˈgriː]	studieren
to involve [ɪnˈvɒlv]	beinhalten, umfassen
essay [ˈeseɪ]	Aufsatz, Essay
stage [steɪdʒ]	Stadium, Phase
to vary [ˈveərɪ]	sich unterscheiden

dramatically [drəˈmætɪkəlɪ]	sehr, dramatisch
shoot [ʃuːt]	Drehen, Drehtag
to draw up [drɔːˈʌp]	entwerfen
post production [ˌpəʊst prəˈdʌkʃn]	Nachproduktion
special effects [ˌspeʃl ɪˈfekts]	Spezialeffekte
to edit [ˈedɪt]	redigieren
freelance [ˈfriːlɑːns]	freiberuflich
to afford [əˈfɔːd]	sich leisten können
aim [eɪm]	Ziel
feature film [ˈfiːtʃə ˌfɪlm]	Spielfilm
to feature [ˈfiːtʃə]	eine Hauptrolle haben
Johnny Depp [ˌdʒɒnɪ ˈdep]	amerik. Filmschauspieler
to promote [prəˈməʊt]	werben für, Werbung machen für
brand [brænd]	Marke

⟨3   The Martians have landed!⟩

You will find the other new words from this
text in the Dictionary.

fade-in [ˈfeɪdˌɪn]	Einblendung (Radio, Film)
an eyewitness account [ənˈaɪˌwɪtnəsˌəˈkaʊnt]	ein Augenzeugenbericht
to strike [straɪk]	treffen
yard [jɑːd]	Maßeinheit: 1 Yard = 0,91m
bulletin [ˈbʊlətɪn]	Bulletin
Brigadier General [ˈbrɪɡəˌdɪə ˈdʒenərəl]	Brigadegeneral
fade-out [ˈfeɪdˌaʊt]	Ausblendung (Radio, Film)

⟨4   Death of a Film Star⟩

You will find the other new words from this
text in the Dictionary.

death [deθ]	Tod
to cough [kɒf]	husten
alleyway [ˈælɪweɪ]	Gasse, Durchgang
gunman [ˈɡʌnmən]	Pistolenschütze
pistol [ˈpɪstl]	Pistole
slam [slæm]	Knall, Stoß
to snap [snæp]	brechen
to toss away [tɒsˌəˈweɪ]	wegwerfen
to strangle [ˈstræŋɡl]	erwürgen
moustache [məˈstɑːʃ]	Schnurrbart
pensioner [ˈpenʃənə]	Rentner, Pensionär
to divide up [dɪˌvaɪdˈʌp]	aufteilen
punctuation [ˌpʌŋktʃʊˈeɪʃn]	Zeichensetzung

Vocabulary

Vocabulary

152

〈**Topic 2**〉

〈**1   Dear Examiner**〉

You will find the other new words from this text in the Dictionary.

examiner [ɪgˈzæmɪnə]	Prüfer/in
to instruct [ɪnˈstrʌkt]	anweisen, instruieren
fairly [ˈfeəlɪ]	ziemlich
informally [ɪnˈfɔːməlɪ]	informell, nicht förmlich
frightful guff [ˌfraɪtfəl ˈgʌf]	ziemlicher Quark (ugs.)
cuff [kʌf]	Ärmelaufschlag
to tick away [tɪk‿əˈweɪ]	weiterticken
groceries [ˈgrəʊsərɪz]	Lebensmittel
crossword [ˈkrɒswɜːd]	Kreuzworträtsel
to chatter by [ˌtʃætə ˈbaɪ]	plappernd vorbeigehen
to peal [piːl]	schlagen
to chug [tʃʌg]	tuckern
steadily [ˈstedɪlɪ]	ständig
back and forth [ˌbæk‿ənd ˈfɔːθ]	hin und her
to mow [məʊ]	mähen
favour [ˈfeɪvə]	Gefallen, Wohlwollen
to blame [bleɪm]	die Schuld geben, beschuldigen
to comment [ˈkɒment]	kommentieren, sich äußern zu
creative writing [krɪˌeɪtɪv ˈraɪtɪŋ]	kreatives Schreiben

〈**2   A newspaper article**〉

You will find the other new words from this text in the Dictionary.

to take after [teɪk‿ˈɑːftə]	ähneln, ähnlich sein
looks [lʊks]	Ausschen
cruelty [ˈkrʊəltɪ]	Grausamkeit
twin [twɪn]	Zwilling(sschwester/-bruder)
to inherit [ɪnˈherɪt]	erben
to dress [dres]	sich anziehen
treatment [ˈtriːtmənt]	Behandlung
to answer back [ˌɑːnsə ˈbæk]	widersprechen
to stick up for s.o. [stɪk‿ˈʌp]	für jdn. eintreten
to study [ˈstʌdɪ]	studieren
education [ˌedjʊˈkeɪʃn]	hier: Erziehungs- wissenschaft
hostel [ˈhɒstl]	Wohnheim, Unterkunft
to go through s.th. [gəʊ ˈθruː]	etwas durchmachen

support [səˈpɔːt]	Unterstützung
to deal (with) [diːl]	sich befassen mit, sich kümmern um
councillor [ˈkaʊnsɪlə]	Ratsherr
chairman [ˈtʃeəmən]	Vorsitzender
(school) governor [(ˌskuːl) ˈgʌvənə]	Mitglied des Schulbeirats
complaint [kəmˈpleɪnt]	Beschwerde
equal [ˈiːkwəl]	gleich
〈2〉 to skim [skɪm]	überfliegen, schnell lesen

〈**Topic 3**〉

〈**1   A mother's love**〉

You will find the other new words from this text in the Dictionary.

to undergo [ˌʌndəˈgəʊ]	sich unterziehen, durchmachen
in remission [ɪn rɪˈmɪʃn]	Remission, (vorübergehen- der Krankheits- stillstand)
the pools [ðə ˈpuːlz]	(Fußball-) Toto (GB)
council estate [ˈkaʊnsl ɪˌsteɪt]	Siedlung des öffentlichen Wohnungsbaus
shopping spree [ˈʃɒpɪŋ ˌspriː]	hier: Großeinkauf
to invest [ɪnˈvest]	investieren
windfall [ˈwɪndfɔːl]	unverhoffter Glücksfall/ Geldsegen
savings bond [ˈseɪvɪŋz ˌbɒnd]	Schatzbrief
amount [əˈmaʊnt]	Summe
to rush out [rʌʃ‿ˈaʊt]	hinaus-, losstürzen
flash [flæʃ]	protzig
fierce [fɪəs]	heftig
row [raʊ]	Streit
to get through [get ˈθruː]	hier: ausgeben, durchbringen
in one go [ɪn ˌwʌn ˈgəʊ]	auf einmal
brand-label [ˈbrændˌleɪbl]	Marken-
cash [kæʃ]	Bargeld
to treat s.o. [triːt]	jdn. einladen, jdm. etw. spendieren
hassle [ˈhæsl]	Ärger, Theater
to predict [prɪˈdɪkt]	vorher-/ voraussagen
town council [ˌtaʊn ˈkaʊnsl]	Stadtrat
〈1〉 gist [dʒɪst]	das Wesentliche
〈2〉 cruel [ˈkrʊəl]	hier: hart

〈 **2 Don't Forget That** 〉

You will find the other new words from this text in the Dictionary.

jumper ['dʒʌmpə]	Pullover
annoying [ə'nɔɪɪŋ]	lästig, nervig
drawl [drɔːl]	langgezogene Sprechweise (z.B. in den amerik. Südstaaten)
How you doing? [ˌhaʊ ju: 'du:ɪŋ]	Wie geht's dir? (ugs.) (AE)
treat [triːt]	Geschenk, Überraschung

〈 **3 A cartoon** 〉

You will find the other new words from this text in the Dictionary.

closet ['klɒzɪt]	(Kleider-) Schrank (AE)
to sympathize ['sɪmpəθaɪz]	Mitleid/ Verständnis haben für

〈 **4 The Accidental Tourist** 〉

You will find the other new words from this text in the Dictionary.

accidental [ˌæksɪ'dentl]	zufällig
to take an interest in [ˌteɪk ən 'ɪntrəst ɪn]	sich für etw. interessieren
aisle seat ['aɪl ˌsiːt]	Sitzplatz am Gang
row [rəʊ]	Reihe
a great deal of difference [ə ˌgreɪt ˌdiːl əv 'dɪfrəns]	ein großer Unterschied
restroom ['restˌrʊm]	(öffentliche) Toilette (AE)
to squeeze past [ˌskwiːz 'pɑːst]	vorbeizwängen, -quetschen
For Christ's sake! [fə ˌkraɪsts 'seɪk]	Um Himmels Willen! (ugs.)
damn [dæm]	verdammte(r/s)
novelist ['nɒvəlɪst]	Romanschriftsteller/in
to publish ['pʌblɪʃ]	veröffentlichen
gift [gɪft]	Gabe, Geschenk
relation [rɪ'leɪʃn]	Verwandte/r
attitude ['ætɪtjuːd]	Einstellung

〈 **5 The Tombstone** 〉

You will find the other new words from this text in the Dictionary.

tombstone ['tuːmstəʊn]	Grabstein
plot of earth [ˌplɒt əv 'ɜːθ]	hier: Grabstätte
founder ['faʊndə]	Gründer/in
fellow man [ˌfeləʊ 'mæn]	Mitmensch
to give s.o. the benefit of the doubt [...ðə 'benɪfɪt əv ðə 'daʊt]	im Zweifelsfall zu jdns. Gunsten entscheiden
Gosh! [gɒʃ]	Mensch! (ugs.)
to chip [tʃɪp]	einmeißeln
to pay one's respects [ˌpeɪ wʌnz rɪ'spekts]	jdm. seine Aufwartung machen
memory ['memrɪ]	Gedenken, Erinnerung
adored [ə'dɔːd]	geliebt
Golly! ['gɒlɪ]	Menschenskind! (ugs.)
sweetheart ['swiːthɑːt]	Schatz, Liebste(r)
to sweat [swet]	schwitzen; hier: sich Sorgen machen über
match [mætʃ]	Spiel
to get upset [get ʌp'set]	die Fassung verlieren, bestürzt sein über
I'll bet [aɪl 'bet]	ich wette (ugs.)
perception [pə'sepʃn]	Bild, Wahrnehmung, Auffassung von

〈 **Topic 4** 〉

〈 **1 Earth and Sun and Moon** 〉

You will find the other new words from this text in the Dictionary.

to take to ['teɪk tʊ]	hier: sich erheben
to glue [gluː]	kleben, festkleben
to burn [bɜːn]	brennen
softly ['sɒftlɪ]	sanft, leicht
smoke [sməʊk]	Rauch
contour ['kɒntʊə]	Umriss, Kontur
plain [pleɪn]	Ebene
oil spill ['ɔɪl spɪl]	Ölteppich
tribe [traɪb]	Stamm
to survive [sə'vaɪv]	überleben
sediment ['sedɪmənt]	Sediment, Ablagerung
mighty ['maɪtɪ]	mächtig, gewaltig
axe [æks]	Axt
sigh [saɪ]	Seufzer, Seufzen
ether ['iːθə]	Äther
wing [wɪŋ]	Flügel
image ['ɪmɪdʒ]	Bild

⟨2   The Bollin Valley campaign⟩

You will find the other new words from this text in the Dictionary.

bailiff ['beɪlɪf]	Gerichtsvoll-zieher/in
to evict [ɪ'vɪkt]	hinauswerfen, zur Räumung zwingen
woods [wʊdz]	Wald
runway ['rʌnweɪ]	Start- und Landebahn, Runway
rope ladder ['rəʊp ˌlædə]	Strickleiter
beside [bɪ'saɪd]	neben
rope [rəʊp]	Seil, Strick
to shiver ['ʃɪvə]	zittern
to lock oneself away [ˌlɒk … ə'weɪ]	sich selbst einsperren
nursing ['nɜːsɪŋ]	Krankenpflege
engine ['endʒɪn]	Motor
saw [sɔː]	Säge
branch [brɑːnʃ]	Ast
⟨1⟩ campaigner [kæm'peɪnə]	Person, die sich an einer Kampagne beteiligt

⟨3   Highly desirable – highly damaging⟩

You will find the other new words from this text in the Dictionary.

desirable [dɪ'zaɪərəbl]	begehrenswert
desire [dɪ'zaɪə]	Wunsch, Sehnsucht, Verlangen
deposit [dɪ'pɒzɪt]	Vorkommen
database ['deɪtəbeɪs]	Datenbank
to consider [kən'sɪdə]	betrachten als, halten für
surface ['sɜːfɪs]	Oberfläche
sensitive ['sensɪtɪv]	empfindlich, sensitiv
landowner ['lændˌəʊnə]	Landbesitzer/in, -eigentümer/in
Klondiker ['klɒndaɪkə]	*Goldsucher aus dem Nordwesten Kanadas*
Himalayas [ˌhɪmə'leɪəz]	Himalaya
to disturb [dɪ'stɜːb]	stören
to assume [ə'sjuːm]	annehmen, voraussetzen

⟨Topic 5⟩

⟨1   "1999"⟩

You will find the other new words from this text in the Dictionary.

I.R.A. [ˌaɪɑːr'eɪ]	(= *Irish Republican Army*) Irisch-Republikani-sche Armee
U.V.F. [ˌjuː viː'ef]	(= *Ulster Volunteer Force*) Ulster-Freiwilligen-truppe
savage ['sævɪdʒ]	Wilde(r)
fear [fɪə]	Angst, Furcht
to blame [bleɪm]	die Schuld geben, beschuldigen
to dare [deə]	wagen
to proclaim [prə'kleɪm]	verkünden
anger ['æŋgə]	Wut, Zorn
flag [flæg]	Fahne, Flagge
ribbon ['rɪbən]	Band
wise [waɪz]	klug, vernünftig
compromise ['kɒmprəmaɪz]	Kompromiss
treachery ['tretʃərɪ]	Verrat
emotive [ɪ'məʊtɪv]	emotional, gefühlsbetont
to involve [ɪn'vɒlv]	beteiligen an
emotion [ɪ'məʊʃn]	Emotion, Gefühl
loyalty ['lɔɪəltɪ]	Loyalität, Treue
sympathy ['sɪmpəθɪ]	Mitgefühl, Mitleid
to provoke [prə'vəʊk]	hervorrufen, provozieren

⟨2   Ceantar na nOileán⟩

You will find the other new words from this text in the Dictionary.

petrol ['petrl]	Benzin
tourist office ['tʊərɪstˌɒfɪs]	Fremdenver-kehrsamt
heritage centre ['herɪtɪdʒ ˌsentə]	(*volkskundli-ches*) Besucher-zentrum/ Museum
ruin ['rʊɪn]	Ruine
⟨3⟩ Scottish Gaelic [ˌskɒtɪʃ 'geɪlɪk]	*die schottische Form des Gälisch*

〈Topic 6〉

〈The Children〉

You will find the other new words from this text in the Dictionary.

final ['faɪnl]	letzte/r/s
blistered ['blɪstəd]	voller Blasen
gently ['dʒentlɪ]	sanft, behutsam
daily ['deɪlɪ]	Tageszeitung
mark [mɑːk]	Zeichen
singed ['sɪndʒd]	versengt, angesengt
eyebrow ['aɪbraʊ]	Augenbraue
spark [spɑːk]	Funke
smoke [sməʊk]	Rauch
border ['bɔːdə]	Grenze
destruction [dɪ'strʌkʃn]	Zerstörung
survivor [sə'vaɪvə]	Überlebende/r
hell [hel]	Hölle
gesture ['dʒestʃə]	Geste
indifference [ɪn'dɪfrəns]	Gleichgültigkeit
hatred ['heɪtrɪd]	Hass
to be pleased [biː 'pliːzd]	sich freuen
naked ['neɪkɪd]	nackt, bloß
spar [spɑː]	Holzpfosten
fence [fens]	Zaun
to assent [ə'sent]	zustimmen
to head [hed]	gehen, fahren
to shiver ['ʃɪvə]	zittern
to be alight [ə'laɪt]	brennen, in Flammen stehen
reluctant [rɪ'lʌktənt]	unwillig, widerwillig
ruin ['rʊɪn]	Ruine
to search [sɜːtʃ]	suchen, durchsuchen
moving ['muːvɪŋ]	bewegend, ergreifend
blame [bleɪm]	Schuld

〈A HISTORY KALEIDOSCOPE〉

〈1 The stories behind the stones〉

You will find the other new words from these texts in the Dictionary.

stone [stəʊn]	Stein
Stonehenge [stəʊn'hendʒ]	prähistorischer Ort in GB
BC [ˌbiː'siː]	vor Christi Geburt
Celtic ['keltɪk]	keltisch
Midsummer's Day [ˌmɪdsʌməz 'deɪ]	Sommersonnenwende

Hadrian's Wall [ˌheɪdrɪənz 'wɔːl]	Hadrianswall
Scot [skɒt]	Schotte, Schottin
AD [ˌeɪ'diː]	im Jahre des Herrn/nach Christi Geburt
empire ['empaɪə]	Weltreich, Imperium
to collapse [kə'læps]	zusammenbrechen, zugrunde gehen
Angles ['æŋglz]	die Angeln (hist.) Mitglieder eines alten germanischen Völkerstammes
Saxons ['sæksnz]	Sachsen (hist.)
Britons ['brɪtnz]	Mitglieder eines alten britischen Volksstammes
Scottish ['skɒtɪʃ]	schottisch
of ... origin [ɒv ... 'ɒrɪdʒɪn]	... Ursprungs
Norman ['nɔːmən]	normannisch; Normanne, Normannin
foreigner ['fɒrənə]	Ausländer/in
to conquer ['kɒŋkə]	erobern, besiegen
to have s.th. built [hæv 'bɪlt]	etwas bauen/ errichten lassen
throughout [θruː'aʊt]	überall (in)
strategic [strə'tiːdʒɪk]	strategisch
royal ['rɔɪəl]	königlich
ruin ['ruːɪn]	Ruine
abbey ['æbɪ]	Abtei
monastery ['mɒnəstərɪ]	Kloster
to behead [bɪ'hed]	enthaupten, köpfen
to marry ['mærɪ]	heiraten
pope [pəʊp]	Papst
divorce [dɪ'vɔːs]	Scheidung
to declare oneself [dɪ'kleə]	sich erklären/ ernennen zu
to obtain [əb'teɪn]	erlangen
former ['fɔːmə]	ehemalige/r/s
edifice ['edɪfɪs]	Bauwerk, Gebäude

〈2 Women who made their mark on history〉

You will find the other new words from these texts in the Dictionary.

to rule [ruːl]	regieren
wealthy ['welθɪ]	wohlhabend
to found [faʊnd]	gründen
poet ['pəʊɪt]	Dichter/in
sailor ['seɪlə]	hier: Seefahrer
to invade [ɪn'veɪd]	hier: angreifen

The Armada [ɑːˈmɑːdə]   span. Flotte
to defeat [dɪˈfiːt]   besiegen
steam engine   Dampfmaschine
   [ˈstiːm‿endʒɪn]
pay [peɪ]   Lohn, Gehalt,
                             Bezahlung
condition [kənˈdɪʃn]   Bedingung
throne [θrəʊn]   Thron
reign [reɪn]   Regierungszeit,
                             Herrschaft
powerful [ˈpaʊəfəl]   mächtig
workshop [ˈwɜːkʃɒp]   Werkstatt
reform [rɪˈfɔːm]   Reform, (Ver-)
                             Besserung
primary school   Grundschule
   [ˈpraɪmərɪ ˌskuːl]
Victorian [vɪkˈtɔːrɪən]   viktorianisch
more and more   immer mehr
   [ˈmɔːr‿ənd ˈmɔː]
vote [vəʊt]   Wahlrecht
movement [ˈmuːvmənt]   Bewegung
Elizabethan [ɪˌlɪzəˈbiːθn] elisabethanisch
widespread [ˈwaɪdspred] weit verbreitet
focus [ˈfəʊkəs]   Brennpunkt;
                             Mittelpunkt
to go down in history   in die Geschichte
   [gəʊ ˌdaʊn ɪn ˈhɪstərɪ] eingehen

⟨3 The road to democracy⟩

You will find the other new words from these
texts in the Dictionary.

parliament [ˈpɑːləmənt] Parlament
monarch [ˈmɒnək]   Herrscher/in,
                             König/in
tax [tæks]   Steuer
army [ˈɑːmɪ]   Heer, Armee
the 'commoners'   die 'Bürgerlichen'
   [ðə ˈkɒmənəz]
civil [ˈsɪvɪl]   bürgerlich,
                             Bürger-
to execute [ˈeksɪkjuːt] hinrichten
Oliver Cromwell   englischer
   [ˌɒlɪvə ˈkrɒmwəl]   Staatsmann
Lord Protector   Cromwells Titel
   [ˌlɔːd prəˈtektə]
The Bill of Rights   Bürgerrechte
   [bɪl‿əv ˈraɪts]   (hist.)
constitutional   Verfassungs-
   [ˌkɒnstɪˈtjuːʃənl]
to disturb [dɪˈstɜːb]   stören
universal suffrage   allgemeines
   [ˌjuːnɪˈvɜːsl ˈsʌfrɪdʒ]   Wahlrecht
strike [straɪk]   Streik
⟨1⟩ to assume [əˈsjuːm] annehmen
   to rule [ruːl]   regieren

⟨4 Parliament today⟩

You will find the other new words from these
texts in the Dictionary.

The Houses of   das Parlament
   Parliament   (-sgebäude)
   [ˌhaʊzɪz‿əv ˈpɑːləmənt] (GB)
The House of Commons   Unterhaus (GB)
   [ˌhaʊs‿əv ˈkɒmənz]
The House of Lords   Oberhaus (GB)
   [ˌhaʊs‿əv ˈlɔːdz]
to elect [ɪˈlekt]   wählen
constituency   Wahlkreis
   [kənˈstɪtjʊənsɪ]
non-elected [ˌnɒnɪˈlektɪd] nicht-gewählte/r/s
bishop [ˈbɪʃəp]   Bischof
archbishop [ˈɑːtʃˌbɪʃəp] Erzbischof
duke [djuːk]   Herzog
earl [ɜːl]   Graf
citizen [ˈsɪtɪzən]   Bürger/in
Member of Parliament   Mitglied des
   (MP) [ˌmembər‿əv   britischen
   ˈpɑːləmənt (ˌem ˈpiː)]   Unterhauses
The General Election   Parlaments-
   [ˌdʒenərəl‿ɪˈlekʃn]   wahlen
'first-past-the-post'-   Name für das
   system [ˌfɜːst pɑːst ðə   britische
   ˈpəʊst ˌsɪstəm]   Mehrheits-
                             wahlrecht
                             (wörtlich:
                             erster, der (in
                             einem Rennen)
                             am (Ziel-)
                             Pfosten
                             vorbeizieht)
internal affairs [ɪnˌtɜːnl‿ interne
   əˈfeəz]   Angelegen-
                             heiten; Innen-
⟨1⟩ Foreign Secretary [ˌfɒrən Außenminister/in
   ˈsekrətrɪ]
Leader of the   Oppositionsfüh-
   Opposition [ˌliːdər‿əv   rer/in
   ðiː‿ˌɒpəˈzɪʃn]
⟨2⟩ up-to-date [ˌʌp tə ˈdeɪt] auf dem neuesten
                             Stand, aktuell

⟨A World Map⟩

You will find the other new words from these
texts in the Dictionary.

⟨Map of Australia⟩

You will find the other new words from these
texts in the Dictionary.

DICTIONARY

In dieser alphabetischen Wortliste ist das gesamte Vokabular von *Password Green 1, 2 , 3 ,4* und 5 enthalten. Namen werden in einer gesonderten Liste nach dem Vokabular aufgeführt.
– Das Zeichen ° vor einer Angabe bedeutet, dass das Wort zum rezeptiven Wortschatz zählt.
– Das Zeichen ⟨ ⟩ bei einer Angabe weist darauf hin, dass das Wort fakultativ ist. Dazu gehört auch der individuelle Wortschatz und Wörter aus authentischen Texten, die nicht gelernt werden brauchen.
– Das Zeichen * bedeutet, dass der Eintrag ein unregelmäßiges Verb ist und in der Liste der unregelmäßigen Verben auf S. 199/200 nachgeschlagen werden kann.
– Um einen möglichst umfassenden Wortschatzüberblick zu gewährleisten, sind Wendungen, die sich aus verschiedenen Komponenten zusammensetzen, unter mehreren Stichwörtern aufgeführt. So ist z. B. *at home* unter *home* und *at* zu finden.

A

a [ə] ein/eine
   a head [ə'hed] pro Kopf
⟨**A-levels**⟩ ['eɪˌlevlz] *das britische Äquivalent des Abiturs*
⟨to **abandon**⟩ [ə'bændən] aussetzen, verlassen
⟨**abbey**⟩ ['æbɪ] Abtei
⟨**'Aber-'**⟩ ['ɑːbə] Mündung *(kelt.)*
to be **able to** [bɪ_'eɪbl tə] etwas können, die Möglichkeit haben
Aborigine [ˌæbə'rɪdʒɪnɪ] *Name der Ureinwohner Australiens*
about [ə'baʊt] über; wegen; ungefähr
   to ask about ['ɑːsk ˌə baʊt] fragen nach
   to care *(about)* [keə] sich kümmern, sich sorgen
   to complain *(about)* [kəm'pleɪn ə'baʊt] sich beklagen
   to get about [get_ə'baʊt] herumkommen; umherstreifen
   °to talk about ['tɔːk_ə baʊt] sprechen über
   to think about ['θɪŋk_ə baʊt] nachdenken über
   °to write about ['raɪt ə baʊt] schreiben über
   What about …? ['wɒt_ə baʊt] Was hältst du von …?, Was ist mit …?
above [ə'bʌv] über, oben
to go **abroad** [gəʊ_ə'brɔːd] ins Ausland fahren
abseiling ['æpseɪlɪŋ] Abseilen
⟨to be an **absolute** mask⟩ [ˌbɪ ən_ˌæbsəluːt 'mɑːsk] absolut ausdruckslos, wie eine Maske sein
absolutely [ˌæbsə'luːtlɪ] vollkommen, völlig; absolut
abuse [ə'bjuːs] Missbrauch
to **abuse** [ə'bjuːz] missbrauchen
Edinburgh **Academy** [ˌedɪnbʌrə ə'kædəmɪ] *Name einer Schule in Edinburgh*
accent ['æksənt] Akzent
acceptable [ək'septəbl] akzeptabel, in Ordnung
accident ['æksɪdənt] Unfall
⟨**accidental**⟩ [ˌæksɪ'dentl] zufällig
account [ə'kaʊnt] Bericht; (Bank-)

Konto
   ⟨an eyewitness account⟩ [ən_ˌaɪwɪtnəs_ə'kaʊnt] ein Augenzeugenbericht
to **achieve** [ə'tʃiːv] erreichen, schaffen, leisten
across [ə'krɒs] hinüber, (quer)durch
to **act** [ækt] schauspielen, darstellen
   ⟨to act as if⟩ ['ækt_əz_ɪf] sich benehmen/verhalten als ob
action ['ækʃn] "Action"; Aktion, Initiative; °Tätigkeit, Bewegung
   action film ['ækʃn fɪlm] Actionfilm
   to take action [teɪk_'ækʃn] etwas/Schritte unternehmen
activist ['æktɪvɪst] Aktivist/in
activity [æk'tɪvətɪ] Tätigkeit, Aktivität
   Youth Activity Centre [juːθ_ æk'tɪvɪtɪ ˌsentə] Jugendzentrum
actor ['æktə] Schauspieler
actress ['æktrɪs] Schauspielerin
actually ['æktʃʊəlɪ] eigentlich; übrigens; tatsächlich
⟨**AD**⟩ ['eɪ'diː] im Jahre des Herrn/ nach Christi Geburt
°slightly **adapted** [ˌslaɪtlɪ ə'dæptɪd] leicht geändert
to **add** [æd] hinzufügen
additional [ə'dɪʃənl] zusätzlich
address [ə'dres] Adresse
to **address** [ə'dres] adressieren
adjective ['ædʒɪktɪv] Adjektiv
⟨to **adjoin**⟩ [ə'dʒɔɪn] angrenzen
to **admire** [əd'maɪə] bewundern
to **admit** [əd'mɪt] zugeben
⟨**adored**⟩ [ə'dɔːd] geliebt
adult ['ædʌlt] Erwachsener
⟨to **advance**⟩ [əd'vɑːns] auf etw. zugehen, voranschreiten
advantage [əd'vɑːntɪdʒ] Vorteil
adventure [əd'ventʃə] Abenteuer
°**adverb** ['ædvɜːb] Adverb
advert ['ædvɜːt] (Werbe-)Anzeige
to **advertise** ['ædvətaɪz] inserieren, annoncieren, werben
advice [əd'vaɪs] Rat, Ratschlag
   Take my advice. [teɪk maɪ əd'vaɪs] Höre auf mich.
   youth advice centre [ˌjuːθ_əd'vaɪs ˌsentə] *Beratungsstelle für Jugendliche*

advisable [əd'vaɪzəbl] empfehlenswert
⟨**advisor**⟩ [əd'vaɪzə] Berater/in
Aeronautics [ˌeərə'nɔːtɪks] Luftfahrtwesen
⟨internal **affairs**⟩ [ɪnˌtɜːnl ə'feəz] interne Angelegenheiten; Innen-
to **afford** [ə'fɔːd] sich leisten (können)
to be **afraid** [bɪ_ə'freɪd] Angst haben
   I'm **afraid** [ˌaɪm ə'freɪd] leider, tut mir Leid
African ['æfrɪkən] afrikanisch, Afrikaner/in
after ['ɑːftə] nach
   after that [ˌɑːftə 'ðæt] danach
   to be after s.th. ['ɑːftə ˌsʌmθɪŋ] hinter etwas her sein *(ugs.)*
   to go after s.o. [gəʊ_'ɑːftə] jdm. folgen, jdn. verfolgen
   to look after [lʊk_'ɑːftə] aufpassen auf
afternoon [ˌɑːftə'nuːn] Nachmittag
⟨**afterwards**⟩ ['ɑːftəwədz] danach
again [ə'gen] wieder, noch einmal
against [ə'genst] gegen
age [eɪdʒ] Alter
aged [eɪdʒd] im Alter von, … Jahre alt
⟨**agency**⟩ ['eɪdʒənsɪ] Agentur
agent ['eɪdʒənt] Agent/in
ago [ə'gəʊ] vor
agony ['ægənɪ] starke Schmerzen
   agony aunt ['ægənɪ ˌɑːnt] Kummerkastentante
to **agree** *(with)* [ə'griː wɪð] übereinstimmen
animal **aid** [eɪd] Hilfe; Hilfe für Tiere, Tierschutz
⟨to **aid** in the evacuation⟩ ['eɪd_ɪn ðiː_ɪˌvækju'eɪʃn] bei der Evakuierung helfen
⟨**aim**⟩ [eɪm] Ziel
to **aim** [eɪm] zielen auf
air [eə] Luft
   hot air balloon [hɒt_eə bə'luːn] Heißluftballon
   ⟨on the air⟩ [eə] auf Sendung
airplay ['eəpleɪ] Sendezeit
airport ['eəpɔːt] Flughafen
⟨**aisle** seat⟩ ['aɪl ˌsiːt] Sitzplatz am Gang

⟨**alarm**⟩ [ə'lɑ:m] Alarm
⟨**alcoholism**⟩ ['ælkəhɒlɪzm]
Alkoholismus
⟨**alias**⟩ ['eɪlɪəs] alias, unter dem
Namen ... bekannt
⟨**alien**⟩ ['eɪlɪən] Ausländer/in;
Außerirdische/r
⟨to be **alight**⟩ [ə'laɪt] brennen, in
Flammen stehen
all [ɔ:l] alle, ganz
all kinds of [ɔ:l 'kaɪndz‿əv] alle
möglichen Arten
all things considered [‚ɔ:l θɪŋz
kən'sɪdəd] wenn man alles in
Betracht zieht
all-girl ['ɔ:l gɜ:l] ausschließlich/
nur-Mädchen
to be all right [bɪ‿ɔ:l'raɪt] gesund
sein, gut gehen, in Ordnung sein
⟨**alleyway**⟩ ['ælɪweɪ] Gasse,
Durchgang
alligator ['ælɪgeɪtə] Alligator
⟨to **allow** s.o. to do s.th.⟩ [ə'laʊ]
jdm. erlauben/gestatten, etwas zu
tun
to be **allowed to** [bɪ‿ə'laʊd tə] etwas
dürfen, erlaubt sein
almost ['ɔ:lməʊst] fast, beinahe
alone [ə'ləʊn] allein
Leave me alone! [‚li:v mɪ‿ə'ləʊn]
Lass mich in Ruhe!
along [ə'lɒŋ] entlang
to carry along [‚kærɪ‿ə'lɒŋ]
weiterbringen, weitertragen
to come along (with s.o.) [kʌm‿
ə'lɒŋ] sich (jdm.) anschließen,
mitgehen (mit jdm.)
alphabet ['ælfəbet] Alphabet
alphabetical [‚ælfə'betɪkl]
alphabetisch
already [ɔ:l'redɪ] schon
also ['ɔ:lsəʊ] auch
alternative [ɔ:l'tɜ:nətɪv]
alternativ/e/r/s, Alternativ-,
Ausweich-
although [ɔ:l'ðəʊ] obwohl, obgleich
always ['ɔ:lweɪz] immer
a.m. (= **am**) [‚eɪ‿'em] 0.00 – 12.00
Uhr
to **amaze** [ə'meɪz] erstaunen,
verwundern
⟨**amazing**(ly)⟩ [ə'meɪzɪŋ(lɪ)]
erstaunlich(erweise)
ambulance ['æmbjʊləns]
Krankenwagen
American [ə'merɪkən] Amerikaner/
in; amerikanisch
the **Amish** [ðɪ‿'ɑ:mɪʃ] die Amischen
among [ə'mʌŋ] zwischen, bei, unter
⟨**amount**⟩ [ə'maʊnt] Summe
amusement park [ə'mju:zmənt
‚pɑ:k] Vergnügungspark
amusing [ə'mju:zɪŋ] lustig, amüsant
an [ən] ein/eine
⟨**ancient**⟩ ['eɪnʃənt] (ur)alt,
historisch
and [ænd] und
⟨**anger**⟩ ['æŋgə] Wut, Zorn

⟨**Angles**⟩ ['æŋglz] die Angeln (hist.)
Mitglieder eines alten
germanischen Völkerstammes
angry ['æŋgrɪ] böse, zornig
animal ['ænɪml] Tier
animal aid [eɪd] Hilfe für Tiere,
Tierschutz
animal home ['ænɪml ‚həʊm]
Tierheim
announcement [ə'naʊnsmənt]
Ankündigung
announcer [ə'naʊnsə] Ansager/in
⟨**annoying**⟩ [ə'nɔɪɪŋ] lästig, nervig
°**anonymous** [ə'nɒnɪməs] anonym
anorak ['ænəræk] Anorak
another [ə'nʌðə] noch ein/eine
answer ['ɑ:nsə] Antwort
to **answer** ['ɑ:nsə] antworten
⟨to **answer back**⟩ [‚ɑ:nsə 'bæk]
widersprechen
answering machine [‚ɑ:nsrɪŋ
mə'ʃi:n] Anrufbeantworter
anti- ['æntɪ] gegen, Anti-, in
Opposition
any ['enɪ] etwas, einige, irgend-
not ... any ['enɪ] kein/keine
anybody ['enɪ‚bɒdɪ] irgendjemand
not ... anybody ['enɪ‚bɒdɪ]
niemand
anyone ['enɪwʌn] irgendjemand
anything ['enɪθɪŋ] irgendetwas
anyway ['enɪweɪ] jedenfalls,
sowieso; trotzdem
anywhere ['enɪweə] irgendwo
not ... anywhere ['enɪweə]
nirgendwo
AP [‚eɪ 'pi:] Abkürzung für
Advanced Placement: Zusatztest
apart [ə'pɑ:t] auseinander
to **apologize** [ə'pɒlədʒaɪz] sich
entschuldigen
apology [ə'pɒlədʒɪ] Entschuldigung
to **appear** [ə'pɪə] erscheinen,
auftauchen
appetite ['æpɪtaɪt] Appetit
apple pie [‚æpl 'paɪ] englischer
Apfelkuchen
application [‚æplɪ'keɪʃn]
Bewerbung; Antrag
appointment [ə'pɔɪntmənt] Termin
⟨**approximately**⟩ [ə'prɒksɪmətlɪ]
ungefähr
April ['eɪprɪl] April
April Fool's Day [‚eɪprɪl 'fu:lz ‚deɪ]
1. April, Aprilscherz
apron ['eɪprən] Schürze
archaeologist [‚ɑ:kɪ'ɒlədʒɪst]
Archäologe/Archäologin
archaeology [‚ɑ:kɪ'ɒlədʒɪ]
Archäologie
⟨**archbishop**⟩ ['ɑ:tʃ‚bɪʃəp]
Erzbischof
architecture ['ɑ:kɪtektʃə]
Architektur, Baustil
are [ɑ:] bist, sind, seid
area ['eərɪə] Gegend, Gebiet
to **argue** ['ɑ:gju:] streiten, sich
streiten

argument ['ɑ:gjʊmənt] Argument;
Streit
to have an argument [‚hæv‿
ən‿'ɑ:gjʊmənt] sich streiten
to start an argument [stɑ:t‿
ən‿'ɑ:gjʊmənt] einen Streit
anfangen
arm [ɑ:m] Arm
⟨The **Armada**⟩ [ɑ:'mɑ:də] span.
Flotte
armchair ['ɑ:mtʃeə] Sessel
⟨**army**⟩ ['ɑ:mɪ] Heer, Armee
around [ə'raʊnd] zirka
around [ə'raʊnd] um, gegen
to get around [get‿ə'raʊnd]
herumkommen
to hang around [hæŋ‿ə'raʊnd]
herumhängen, -lungern
to move around [‚mu:v‿ə'raʊnd]
sich (umher)bewegen
to run around [rʌn‿ə'raʊnd]
herumlaufen
°to **arrange** [ə'reɪndʒ] arrangieren,
verabreden, ausmachen
to **arrest** [ə'rest] verhaften, gefangen
nehmen
arrival [ə'raɪvl] Ankunft
to **arrive** (at) [ə'raɪv‿ət] ankommen
(an)
arrogant ['ærəgənt] arrogant,
eingebildet
arrow ['ærəʊ] Pfeil
Art [ɑ:t] Kunst
artwork ['ɑ:twɜ:k] Kunstarbeiten
article ['ɑ:tɪkl] Artikel
as [æz] als, während; wie; weil, da
as old as [əz‿'əʊld‿əz] so alt wie
as soon as [æz 'su:n‿æz] sobald, als
as well [əs‿'wel] auch, ebenfalls
⟨**ashes**⟩ ['æʃɪz] Asche
Asian ['eɪʃn] asiatisch, Asiat/in
to **ask** [ɑ:sk] fragen
to ask a question [ɑ:sk‿ə
'kwestʃən] eine Frage stellen
to ask about ['ɑ:sk‿ə‚baʊt] fragen
nach
to ask for ['ɑ:sk fə] fragen nach,
bitten um
⟨**asleep**⟩ [ə'sli:p] schlafend
aspect ['æspekt] Aspekt, Seite
⟨junior **asprin**⟩ [‚dʒu:nɪə‿'æsprɪn]
Schmerzmittel für Kinder
assault [ə'sɔ:lt] Angriff; ⟨Anschlag⟩
assembly [ə'semblɪ] Versammlung
assembly hall [ə'semblɪ ‚hɔ:l] Aula
⟨to **assent**⟩ [ə'sent] zustimmen
assignment [ə'saɪnmənt] Aufgabe,
Hausarbeit (AE)
assistant [ə'sɪstənt] Assistent/in
shop assistant [ə'sɪstənt]
Verkäufer/in
⟨to **assume**⟩ [ə'sju:m] annehmen,
voraussetzen
⟨**astonished**⟩ [ə'stɒnɪʃt] erstaunt
astronaut ['æstrənɔ:t] Astronaut/in
astronomer [ə'strɒnəmə] Astronom/in
⟨**astronomical**⟩ [‚æstrə'nɒmɪkl]
astronomisch, Astronomie-

at [æt] auf, bei, in; um (*Uhrzeit*)
 at first [ət 'fɜ:st] zuerst, zunächst
 at half past nine [ət hɑ:f pɑ:st 'naɪn] um halb zehn
 at home [ət 'həʊm] zu Hause
 at last [ət 'lɑ:st] endlich
 at least [ət 'li:st] zumindest, wenigstens
 at night [ət 'naɪt] nachts, abends
 at school [ət 'sku:l] in/an der Schule
 at that moment [ət ðæt 'məʊmənt] in diesem Moment
 at the back [ət ðə 'bæk] hinten
 at the cinema [ət ðə 'sɪnəmə] im Kino
 °at the front [ət ðə 'frʌnt] vorne
 ⟨at the hands of⟩ [æt ðə 'hændz əv] durch
 at the seaside [ət ðə 'si:saɪd] am Meer
 at the time [ət ðə 'taɪm] damals, zu der Zeit
 at the weekend [ət ðə 'wi·k,end] am Wochenende
 at times [ət 'taɪmz] manchmal, beizeiten
 at work [ət 'wɜ:k] bei der Arbeit
 if at all [ɪf ət 'ɔ:l] wenn überhaupt
 to arrive (*at*) [ə'raɪv] ankommen (an)
 to laugh at ['lɑ:f ət] lachen über
 to look at ['lʊk ət] anschauen, ansehen
 to point (*at*) ['pɔɪnt] zeigen (auf)
 to stare (*at*) [steə] (an)starren
atmosphere ['ætməˌsfɪə] Atmosphäre, Stimmung
heart **attack** ['hɑ:t əˌtæk] Herzanfall, -infarkt
to **attack** [ə'tæk] angreifen
°**attempt** [ə'tempt] Versuch
 ⟨they made no attempt to prevent⟩ [ˌmeɪd 'nəʊ ə'tempt tə prɪ'vent] sie versuchten nicht zu verhindern
attention [ə'tenʃn] Achtung, Aufmerksamkeit
attic ['ætɪk] Speicher, Dachboden
⟨**attitude**⟩ ['ætɪtju:d] Einstellung, Haltung
attraction [ə'trækʃn] Attraktion
°**attractive** [ə'træktɪv] attraktiv, anziehend
audience ['ɔ:dɪəns] Publikum, Zuschauer/innen, Zuhörer/innen
audition [ɔ:'dɪʃn] Aufnahmeprüfung (Vorsingen, -spielen)
August ['ɔ:gəst] August
aunt [ɑ:nt] Tante
 agony aunt ['ægənɪ ˌɑ:nt] Kummerkastentante
Aussie ['ɒzɪ] Australier/in (*ugs.*)
Australian [ɒs'treɪlɪən] australisch, Australier/in
Austrian ['ɒstrɪən] Österreicher/in
authentic [ɔ:'θentɪk] echt, original
°**author** ['ɔ:θə] Autor/in
⟨**authorities**⟩ [ɔ:'θɒrɪtɪz] Behörde(n), Amt

⟨a pass issued by the authorities⟩ [ə 'pɑ:s ˌɪʃu:d baɪ ðiː ɔ:'θɒrɪtɪz] ein behördlich ausgestellter Passierschein
autograph ['ɔ:təgrɑ:f] Autogramm
autumn ['ɔ:təm] Herbst
°**auxiliary** [ɔ:g'zɪlɪərɪ] Hilfs-
available [ə'veɪləbl] erhältlich
⟨**average**⟩ ['ævrɪdʒ] Durchschnitt
to **avoid** [ə'vɔɪd] vermeiden
awake [ə'weɪk] wach, aufmerksam
Duke of Edinburgh's **Award** [ˌdju:k əv ˈedɪnbʌrəz əˌwɔ:d] Auszeichnung des Herzogs von Edinburgh
°**aware** (*of*) [ə'weər əv] bewusst
°to **become aware** (*of*) [bɪˌkʌm ə'weər əv] sich bewusst werden, erkennen
°**awareness** [ə'weənəs] Bewusstsein, Gespür
away [ə'weɪ] weg
 to clear away [ˌklɪər ə'weɪ] wegräumen, abräumen
 to run away [rʌn ə'weɪ] weglaufen; ausreißen
awesome ['ɔ:səm] beeindruckend, ehrfurchtgebietend
awful ['ɔ:fʊl] schrecklich, furchtbar, scheußlich
⟨**axe**⟩ [æks] Axt

B

to do a **baby-sitting** job ['beɪbɪ ˌsɪtɪŋ] als Babysitter jobben
back [bæk] Rücken
to **back** [bæk] (mit dem Auto) zurücksetzen; unterstützen
back [bæk] zurück
 at the back [ət ðə 'bæk] hinten
 ⟨back and forth⟩ [ˌbæk ənd 'fɔ:θ] hin und her
 back and forward [ˌbæk ənd 'fɔ:wəd] vor und zurück, hin und her
 back door [bæk 'dɔ:] Hintertür
 back garden [bæk 'gɑ:dn] Garten hinter dem Haus
 back street ['bækˌstri:t] Seitenstraße
 ⟨to answer back⟩ [ˌɑ:nsə 'bæk] widersprechen
 to go back [gəʊ 'bæk] zurückgehen
 °to go back in time [gəʊ ˌbæk ɪn 'taɪm] in der Zeit zurückgehen
 to talk back [tɔ:k 'bæk] frech antworten
background ['bækgraʊnd] Hintergrund(-)
backyard [ˌbæk'jɑ:d] Hinterhof, (Hinter-)Garten (*AE*)
bacon ['beɪkən] Speck
bad [bæd] schlecht, schlimm
badly ['bædlɪ] schlecht
bag [bæg] Tasche

plastic bag [ˌplæstɪk 'bæg] Plastiktüte
⟨**baggage**⟩ ['bægɪdʒ] Gepäck
⟨**bailiff**⟩ ['beɪlɪf] Gerichtsvollzieher/in
ball [bɔ:l] Ball
balloon [bə'lu:n] Ballon
 hot air balloon [hɒtˌeə bə'lu:n] Heißluftballon
⟨a **banana** republic⟩ [bə'nɑ:nə rɪ'pʌblɪk] eine Bananenrepublik
band [bænd] Popgruppe, Band
 heavy metal band [ˌhevɪ 'metəl bænd] Heavy Metal Band (Hardrock)
⟨**bandit**⟩ ['bændɪt] Bandit, Räuber
Bangor ['bæŋgə] *Stadt in Wales*
bank [bæŋk] Bank
 Bank Holiday [ˌbæŋk 'hɒlədɪ] öffentlicher Feiertag
 food bank ['fu:d bæŋk] *Sammelstelle für Essenspenden (AE)*
bar [bɑ:] Kneipe, Lokal; Stück
 ⟨behind bars⟩ [bɪˌhaɪnd 'bɑ:z] hinter Gitter
 snack bar ['snæk bɑ:] Imbissstube
Bar-B-Q ['bɑ:bɪkju:] Grillparty, Barbecue
⟨**barbed** wire⟩ [ˌbɑ:bd 'waɪ] Stacheldraht
bark [bɑ:k] Borke, Rinde
to **bark** [bɑ:k] bellen
⟨**baron**⟩ ['bærən] Baron
⟨**barren**⟩ ['bærən] unfruchtbar
baseball ['beɪsbɔ:l] Baseball
to be **based on** [ˌbeɪst ɒn] basieren/ beruhen auf
basic ['beɪsɪk] grundlegend
°**basis** ['beɪsɪs] Basis, Grundlage
basketball ['bɑ:skɪtbɔ:l] Basketball
bath [bɑ:θ] Badewanne; Bad
 to have a bath [hæv ə 'bɑ:θ] ein Bad nehmen, baden
bathroom ['bɑ:θru:m] Badezimmer
battery hen ['bætərɪ ˌhen] Batteriehenne
battle ['bætl] Kampf, Schlacht
⟨**battler**⟩ ['bætlə] Kämpfer
bay [beɪ] Bucht, Bai
⟨**BC**⟩ [ˌbi:'si:] vor Christi Geburt
to **be*** [bi:] sein
 he may be [meɪ] vielleicht ist er
 to be at it [bi: 'æt ɪt] dabei sein, etwas zu tun
 to be set (*in*) [bi: 'set] spielen (*literarisch*)
beach [bi:tʃ] Strand
⟨**beam**⟩ [bi:m] Strahl
bear [beə] Bär
 ⟨teddy bear⟩ ['tedɪ beə] Teddybär
to **bear*** [beə] gebären
to **beat*** [bi:t] schlagen
 to beat s.o. at [bi:t] jdn. in/bei etwas schlagen
beautiful ['bju:təfʊl] schön
beaver ['bi:və] Biber
because [bɪ'kɒz] weil

because of [bɪ'kɒz_əv] wegen
to **become*** [bɪ'kʌm] werden
bed [bed] Bett
  bed and breakfast [ˌbedn 'brekfəst] Übernachtung mit Frühstück
  to take to bed [teɪk tə' bed] ins Bett bringen
bedroom ['bedru:m] Schlafzimmer
beefeater ['bi:fˌi:tə] Beefeater
before [bɪ'fɔ:] bevor, vorher; vor
  before long [bɪˌfɔ: 'lɒŋ] bald
  ever before [ˌevə bɪ'fɔ:] jemals zuvor
  just before [dʒʌst bɪ'fɔ:] kurz vor
beforehand [bɪ'fɔ:hænd] vorher, zuvor
to **beg** [beg] betteln
beginner [bə'gɪnə] Anfänger
beginning [bɪ'gɪnɪŋ] Anfang, Beginn
to **behave** [bɪ'heɪv] sich verhalten, sich benehmen
behaviour [bɪ'heɪvjə] Verhalten; Benehmen
⟨to **behead**⟩ [bɪ'hed] enthaupten, köpfen
behind [bɪ'haɪnd] hinter
  ⟨behind bars⟩ [bɪˌhaɪnd 'ba:z] hinter Gitter
human **being** [ˌhju:mən 'bi:ɪŋ] Mensch, menschliches Wesen
to **believe** [bɪ'li:v] glauben
bell [bel] Klingel
to **belong** (to) [bɪ'lɒŋ] gehören
°**below** [bɪ'ləʊ] unten, unter
⟨**beneath**⟩ [bɪ'ni:θ] unter
⟨to give s.o. the **benefit** of the doubt⟩ [...ðə 'benɪfɪt_əv ðə 'daʊt] im Zweifelsfall zu jdns. Gunsten entscheiden
berry ['berɪ] Beere
⟨**beside**⟩ [bɪ'saɪd] neben
best [best] beste/r/s
  best buy [best 'baɪ] Sonderangebot
  best wishes [best 'wɪʃɪz] alles Gute
  ⟨I'll **bet***⟩ [aɪl 'bet] ich wette (ugs.)
to **betray** [bɪ'treɪ] verraten
better ['betə] besser
  had better [ˌhæd 'betə] sollte besser (etwas tun)
between [bɪ'twi:n] zwischen
⟨**beyond** ... recognition⟩ [bɪˌɒnd ...ˌrekəg'nɪʃn] bis zur ... Unkenntlichkeit
  ⟨circumstances beyond s.o.'s control⟩ ['sɜ:kəmstænsɪz bɪˌɒnd ... kən'trəʊl] Umstände, die sich der Kontrolle ... entziehen
bicycle ['baɪsɪkl] Fahrrad
big [bɪg] groß
  big dipper [bɪg 'dɪpə] Achterbahn
biggest ['bɪgɪst] größte/r/s
bike [baɪk] Fahrrad
  by bike [baɪ 'baɪk] mit dem Fahrrad
bikini [bɪ'ki:nɪ] Bikini
⟨The **Bill** of Rights⟩ [bɪl_əv 'raɪts] Bürgerrechte (hist.)
billion ['bɪljən] Milliarde

biodegradable [ˌbaɪəʊdɪ'greɪdəbl] biologisch abbaubar
Biology [baɪ'ɒlədʒɪ] Biologie
bird [bɜ:d] Vogel
  bird of prey [ˌbɜ:d_əv 'preɪ] Raubvogel
birdwatcher ['bɜ:dwɒtʃə] Vogelbeobachter/in
birthday ['bɜ:θdeɪ] Geburtstag
biscuit ['bɪskɪt] Keks
⟨**bishop**⟩ ['bɪʃəp] Bischof
bit [bɪt] Stück(chen); Teil
  a bit [ə'bɪt] ein wenig, ein bisschen
to **bite*** [baɪt] beißen
  to bite off [baɪt_'ɒf] abbeißen
to blow to **bits** [bləʊ tə 'bɪts] in die Luft sprengen/jagen, zerfetzen
⟨**bitter**⟩ ['bɪtə] bitter, verbittert
black [blæk] schwarz
  Black Forest [ˌblæk 'fɒrɪst] Schwarzwald
⟨**blackened**⟩ ['blækənd] schwarz, schwarz gemacht
⟨**blackfeller**⟩ ['blækfelə] Schwarze/r, Ureinwohner Australiens (ugs.)
blacksmith ['blæksmɪθ] Schmied
⟨**blame**⟩ [bleɪm] Schuld
to **blame** [bleɪm] die Schuld geben, beschuldigen
  to blame oneself (for) ['bleɪm wʌnˌself ə] sich Vorwürfe machen
blank [blæŋk] leer
blanket ['blæŋkɪt] Decke; Schmusedecke
to **bleed*** [bli:d] bluten
to **blink** [blɪŋk] (mit den Augen) zwinkern
⟨**blistered**⟩ ['blɪstəd] voller Blasen
block [blɒk] (Wohn-) Block
  a few blocks away [əˌfju: blɒks_ə'weɪ] ein paar Straßen entfernt
⟨**blockbuster**⟩ ['blɒkˌbʌstə] Knüller, Kassenschlager
blond [blɒnd] blond
bloody ['blʌdɪ] blutig; verdammt (ugs.)
blouse [blaʊz] Bluse
to **blow*** [bləʊ] blasen
  to blow over [bləʊ 'əʊvə] umwerfen
  to blow to bits [bləʊ tə 'bɪts] in die Luft sprengen/jagen, zerfetzen
blue [blu:] blau
board [bɔ:d] Tafel
  notice board ['nəʊtɪs ˌbɔ:d] Anschlagbrett, Schwarzes Brett
  on board [ɒn 'bɔ:d] an Bord
boarding school ['bɔ:dɪŋ ˌsku:l] Internat
boardwalk ['bɔ:dwɔ:k] Holzsteg, hölzerne Uferpromenade (AE)
boat [bəʊt] Boot
body ['bɒdɪ] Körper
to **boil** [bɔɪl] kochen
⟨**boiling** point⟩ ['bɔɪlɪŋ pɔɪnt] Siedepunkt
bold [bəʊld] ⟨kühn, nicht zurückhaltend⟩; mutig

to plant **bombs** [pla:nt 'bɒmz] Bomben legen
to **bomb** [bɒm] Bomben legen/ werfen
⟨savings **bond**⟩ ['seɪvɪŋz ˌbɒnd] Schatzbrief
bone [bəʊn] Knochen
book [bʊk] Buch, Heft
  guide book ['gaɪd bʊk] Reiseführer, Stadtführer
⟨to **book**⟩ [bʊk] buchen
bookshop ['bʊkʃɒp] Buchhandlung
bookstore ['bʊkstɔ:] Buchladen, -handlung (AE)
bookworm ['bʊkwɜ:m] Bücherwurm
boot [bu:t] Kofferraum
border ['bɔ:də] Grenze
  ⟨state border⟩ [steɪt 'bɔ:də] Staatsgrenze
bored [bɔ:d] gelangweilt
boring ['bɔ:rɪŋ] langweilig
to be **born** [bɪ 'bɔ:n] geboren werden
to **borrow** ['bɒrəʊ] borgen, sich (aus)leihen
⟨**borrower**⟩ ['bɒrəʊə] Entleiher/in
boss [bɒs] Boss, Chef/-in
both [bəʊθ] beide(s); sowohl als auch
  both ... and ... [bəʊθ] sowohl ... als auch ...
bother ['bɒðə] Aufwand, Ärger
to **bother** ['bɒðə] ärgern, stören, belästigen
bottle ['bɒtl] Flasche
bottom ['bɒtəm] Boden, Grund
bow [bəʊ] Bogen
⟨**bowed down**⟩ [ˌbaʊd 'daʊn] niedergebeugt (unter)
Boxing Day ['bɒksɪŋ ˌdeɪ] 2. Weihnachtstag
boy [bɔɪ] Junge
boyfriend ['bɔɪfrend] Freund
°**bracket** ['brækɪt] Klammer
brain [breɪn] Gehirn
  brain waves ['breɪn ˌweɪvz] Gehirnwellen, -ströme
°**brainstorming** ['breɪnstɔ:mɪŋ] Spontane Ideensammlung
  brainstorming session ['breɪnstɔ:mɪŋ ˌseʃn] Phase der Ideensammlung
branch [bra:ntʃ] Ast, Zweig
⟨**brand**⟩ [brænd] Marke
  ⟨brand-label⟩ ['brændˌleɪbl] Marken-
brandy ['brændɪ] Weinbrand
brave [breɪv] tapfer, mutig
Brazilian [brə'zɪljən] brasilianisch; Brasilianer/in
bread [bred] Brot
break [breɪk] Pause
to **break*** [breɪk] brechen
  to break down [breɪk 'daʊn] zusammenbrechen
  to break out [breɪk_'aʊt] ausbrechen
breakfast ['brekfəst] Frühstück
  bed and breakfast [ˌbedn 'brekfəst] Übernachtung mit Frühstück

⟨**bred**⟩ [bred] gezüchtet
breeze [bri:z] Brise
bridge [brɪdʒ] Brücke
brief [bri:f] kurz
briefcase ['bri:fkeɪs] Aktentasche
⟨**Brigadier** General⟩ ['brɪgə,dɪə 'dʒenərəl] Brigadegeneral
bright [braɪt] hell
brilliant ['brɪljənt] großartig; hervorragend, glänzend, brillant
to **bring*** [brɪŋ] (mit)bringen
  bring-and-buy sale ['brɪŋ_ən 'baɪ seɪl] Basar, Flohmarkt
British ['brɪtɪʃ] britisch
⟨**Britons**⟩ ['brɪtnz] *Mitglieder eines alten britischen Volksstammes*
⟨the **Brits**⟩ [ðə 'brɪts] die Briten, die Engländer (*ugs.*)
broadcast ['brɔ:dkɑ:st] Sendung, Programm
to **broadcast*** ['brɔ:dkɑ:st] senden, übertragen, ausstrahlen
brochure ['brəʊʃə] Broschüre, Prospekt
brother ['brʌðə] Bruder
brown [braʊn] braun
brunette [bru:'net] brünett
brush [brʌʃ] Pinsel
to **brush your teeth** [,brʌʃ wʌnz 'ti:θ] sich die Zähne putzen
°speech **bubble** ['spi:tʃ ,bʌbl] Sprechblase
Buddhist ['bʊdɪst] Buddhist/in
budgie ['bʌdʒɪ] Wellensittich
to **build*** [bɪld] (er-)bauen
  °to build up [bɪld_'ʌp] aufbauen; zusammenstellen
building ['bɪldɪŋ] Gebäude
bulldog ['bʊldɒg] Bulldogge
⟨**bulletin**⟩ ['bʊlətɪn] Bulletin
bully ['bʊlɪ] Schläger, Mobber
to **bully** ['bʊlɪ] schikanieren, tyrannisieren, mobben
⟨to **burn**⟩ [bɜ:n] brennen
  to burn down [bɜ:n 'daʊn] abbrennen
  ⟨to burn out⟩ [bɜ:n_'aʊt] ausbrennen, ausgehen
burp [bɜ:p] Rülpser
to **burp** [bɜ:p] aufstoßen
bus [bʌs] Bus
  bus driver ['bʌs ,draɪvə] Busfahrer/in
  bus stop ['bʌs stɒp] Bushaltestelle
  by bus [baɪ 'bʌs] mit dem Bus
  on the bus [ɒn ðə 'bʌs] im Bus
  to catch (a bus) [kætʃ] (einen Bus) nehmen, kriegen
the **Bush** [ðə 'bʊʃ] der australische Busch
⟨**bushie**⟩ ['bʊʃɪ] Buschbewohner (*australisch*)
business ['bɪznɪs] Geschäft
  (to be) in business [ɪn 'bɪznɪs] laufen, funktionieren
  to do business [,du 'bɪznɪs] Geschäfte machen
busy ['bɪzɪ] beschäftigt; verkehrsreich

but [bʌt] aber; außer
butter ['bʌtə] Butter
to **buy*** [baɪ] kaufen
  bring-and-buy sale ['brɪŋ_ən 'baɪ seɪl] Basar, Flohmarkt
by [baɪ] von
  by 5 p.m. [baɪ 'faɪv ,pi:_'em] bis (spätestens) um 17 Uhr
  by bike [baɪ 'baɪk] mit dem Fahrrad
  by bus [baɪ 'bʌs] mit dem Bus
  by chance [baɪ 'tʃɑ:ns] zufällig
  by the door [,baɪ_ðə 'dɔ:] neben/ bei der Tür
  by the pond [,baɪ ðə 'pɒnd] am Teich
  ⟨by the time⟩ [baɪ ðə 'taɪm] bis
  by the way [,baɪ ðə 'weɪ] übrigens
  to pass by [pɑ:s 'baɪ] vorbeigehen
Bye! [baɪ] Tschüs!

C

cable ['keɪbl] Kabel
  °cable car ['keɪbl kɑ:] *Bezeichnung für die Straßenbahn in San Francisco*
⟨'**Ca(e)r-**'⟩ [keə/kɜ:/kɑ:] Burg (*kelt.*)
café ['kæfeɪ] Café, kleines Restaurant
cafeteria [,kæfɪ'tɪərɪə] Cafeteria
cage [keɪdʒ] Käfig
cake [keɪk] Kuchen
calendar ['kælɪndə] Kalender
call [kɔ:l] Anruf
  emergency call [ɪ'mɜ:dʒənsɪ 'kɔ:l] Notruf
  °telephone call ['telɪfəʊn kɔ:l] Telefongespräch
to **call** [kɔ:l] anrufen; nennen; heißen; rufen
  to call in [kɔ:l_'ɪn] beauftragen, hinzuziehen
  to call on ['kɔ:l ɒn] aufrufen
  to call sb. names [kɔ:l ,sʌmbədɪ 'neɪmz] jmd. beschimpfen
callbox ['kɔ:lbɒks] Telefonzelle
caller ['kɔ:lə] Anrufer/in
calm [kɑ:m] ruhig
camera ['kæmrə] (Film) Kamera
camp [kæmp] Lager
  summer camp ['sʌmə ,kæmp] (Sommer-) Ferienlager
  to set up camp [set_ʌp 'kæmp] zelten, kampieren
to **camp** [kæmp] campen, zelten
⟨**campaigner**⟩ [kæm'peɪnə] Person, die sich an einer Kampagne beteiligt
camper ['kæmpə] Camper/in
camping ['kæmpɪŋ] Campen, Zelten
⟨**campsite**⟩ ['kæmpsaɪt] Zeltplatz, Lager
can [kæn] können
canal [kə'næl] (künstlicher Wasser-) Kanal

to **cancel** ['kænsl] absagen
candle ['kændl] Kerze
canoe [kə'nu:] Kanu
to **canoe** [kə'nu:] Kanu fahren
canoeing [kə'nu:ɪŋ] Kanufahren
canyon ['kænjən] Cañon/Canyon (*Flusstal*)
cap [kæp] Mütze
⟨**captain**⟩ ['kæptɪn] Einsatzleiter
caption ['kæpʃn] Bildunterschrift
car [kɑ:] Auto
  °cable car ['keɪbl kɑ:] *Bezeichnung für die Straßenbahn in San Francisco*
  car boot sale ['kɑ: bu:t ,seɪl] *eine Art Flohmarkt*
  car park ['kɑ: pɑ:k] Parkplatz, Parkhaus
  car-rental [kɑ: 'rentl] Autoverleih
caravan ['kærəvæn] Wohnwagen, Caravan
card [kɑ:d] Karte
  cash card ['kæʃ ,kɑ:d] Geldautomatenkarte
  °name card ['neɪm kɑ:d] Namensschild
to **care** (*about*) [keə] sich kümmern, sich sorgen
  I don't care [dəʊnt 'keə] es ist mir egal
  to care for ['keə fə] sich kümmern um
career [kə'rɪə] Karriere, Laufbahn
Careful! ['keəfʊl] Vorsicht!
careful(*ly*) ['keəfʊl(ɪ)] vorsichtig; sorgfältig
Caribbean [,kærɪ'bi:ən] karibisch, Person aus der Karibik
carnival ['kɑ:nɪvl] Karneval, (Volks-), (Straßen-)Fest
carpet ['kɑ:pɪt] Teppich (boden)
carriage ['kærɪdʒ] Wagen, Kutsche
to **carry** ['kærɪ] tragen
  to carry along [,kærɪ_ə'lɒŋ] weiterbringen, weitertragen
  °to carry out [,kærɪ_'aʊt] durchführen
carsick ['kɑ:sɪk] reisekrank
cartoon [kɑ:'tu:n] °Karikatur; Zeichentrickfilm
case [keɪs] Fall
  in case [ɪn 'keɪs] falls, für den Fall, dass
  pencil case ['pensl,keɪs] Federmäppchen
⟨**cash**⟩ [kæʃ] Bargeld
cassette [kə'set] Kassette
  cassette-recorder [kə'set rɪ,kɔ:də] Kassettenrekorder
  °cassette-surfing [kə'set ,sɜ:fɪŋ] Kassettensurfen, Zapping
castle ['kɑ:sl] Schloss, Burg
cat [kæt] Katze
  cat flap ['kætflæp] Katzentür
catalogue ['kætəlɒg] Katalog
⟨**catastrophe**⟩ [kə'tæstrəfi] Katastrophe
to **catch*** [kætʃ] fangen

to catch (a bus) [kætʃ] (einen Bus) nehmen, kriegen

to catch fire [kætʃ 'faɪə] Feuer fangen

to catch up (with) [ˌkætʃ_'ʌp wɪð] einholen

°category ['kætɪgəri] Kategorie

⟨cathedral⟩ [kə'θiːdrl] Kathedrale, Dom

Catholic ['kæθəlɪk] Katholik/in, katholisch

cattle ['kætl] Vieh

cause [kɔːz] Zweck, Sache

to cause [kɔːz] verursachen

'cause [kɔːz] weil (umgangsspr., kurz für because)

cave [keɪv] Höhle

CD [siː'diː] CD
CD player [siː diː ˌpleɪə] CD-Spieler
CD-ROM [ˌsiː diː 'rɒm] CD-ROM

to celebrate ['selɪbreɪt] feiern

celebration [ˌselɪ'breɪʃn] Feier, Fest

celebrity [sɪ'lebrəti] berühmte Persönlichkeit

cellar ['selə] Keller

⟨Celtic⟩ ['keltɪk] keltisch

centigrade ['sentɪgreɪd] Celsius

centimetre (= cm) ['sentɪˌmiːtə] Zentimeter

⟨central(ly)⟩ ['sentrl] zentral

centre ['sentə] Mitte
city centre [ˌsɪti 'sentə] Stadtmitte
Community Centre [kə'mjuːnəti ˌsentə] Gemeindezentrum
⟨heritage centre⟩ ['herɪtɪdʒ ˌsentə] (volkskundliches) Besucherzentrum/Museum
music centre ['mjuːzɪk ˌsentə] Stereo-, Hifi-Anlage
recycling centre [ˌriː'saɪklɪŋ ˌsentə] Wertstoffsammelstelle
shopping centre ['ʃɒpɪŋ ˌsentə] Einkaufszentrum
sports centre ['spɔːts ˌsentə] Sportzentrum
Youth Activity Centre [juːθ_ æk'tɪvɪti ˌsentə] Jugendzentrum
youth advice centre [ˌjuːθ_əd'vaɪs ˌsentə] Beratungsstelle für Jugendliche

century ['sentʃʊri] Jahrhundert

°certain ['sɜːtn] bestimmte/r/s, gewiße/r/s

certainly ['sɜːtnli] sicher; gern

General Certificate of Secondary Education (GCSE) ['dʒenərəl sə'tɪfɪkət_əv ˌsekəndəri ˌedjuː'keɪʃn] britisches Äquivalent der Mittleren Reife; GCSE-Prüfung

°chain ['tʃeɪn] Kette

to chain ['tʃeɪn] anketten, festketten

chair [tʃeə] Stuhl

⟨chairman⟩ ['tʃeəmən] Vorsitzender

°chairperson ['tʃeəpɜːsn] Vorsitzende/r, Diskussionsleiter/in

chalk [tʃɔːk] Kreide

like chalk and cheese [ˌtʃɔːk_ən 'tʃiːz] wie Tag und Nacht

challenger ['tʃælɪndʒə] Herausforderer

Chamber Music ['tʃeɪmbə ˌmjuːzɪk] Kammermusik

chance [tʃɑːns] Chance, Möglichkeit, Gelegenheit
by chance [baɪ 'tʃɑːns] zufällig

change [tʃeɪndʒ] Wechselgeld
it makes a change from … [tʃeɪndʒ] das ist mal was anderes als …

to change [tʃeɪndʒ] (sich) ändern, verändern; sich umziehen; wechseln
to change s.th. around [tʃeɪndʒ_ ə'raʊnd] umstellen, etwas umändern

changeable ['tʃeɪndʒəbl] wechselhaft

channel ['tʃænl] Kanal, Programm

chapatti [tʃə'pɑːti] pakistan. Brot

character ['kærəktə] Person, Charakter

°to characterize ['kærɪktəˌraɪz] charakterisieren, beschreiben

free of charge [ˌfriː_əv 'tʃɑːdʒ] kostenlos
to be in charge of [bɪ_ɪn 'tʃɑːdʒ_ əv] verantwortlich sein für

charisma [kə'rɪzmə] Charisma, Ausstrahlung

°charity ['tʃærɪti] Wohlfahrt; Wohltätigkeitsverein

⟨charred⟩ ['tʃɑːd] verkohlt

chart [tʃɑːt] Tabelle

to chase [tʃeɪs] jagen, verfolgen

chat line ['tʃæt laɪn] Unterhaltungsleitung

to chat [tʃæt] plaudern, quatschen

⟨to chatter by⟩ [ˌtʃætə 'baɪ] plappernd vorbeigehen

cheap [tʃiːp] billig

to cheat [tʃiːt] mogeln

to keep a check on [ˌkiːp_ə 'tʃek_ɒn] Kontrolle behalten über

to check [tʃek] überprüfen, kontrollieren
to check out [tʃek_'aʊt] überprüfen

°checklist ['tʃeklɪst] Checkliste, Prüfliste

to cheer s.o. [tʃɪə] jdn. anfeuern

cheerful(ly) ['tʃɪəfəl(ɪ)] fröhlich, gut gelaunt

cheerleader ['tʃɪəˌliːdə] Cheerleader (Mädchen, die die Mannschaft anfeuern)

cheese [tʃiːz] Käse
like chalk and cheese [ˌtʃɔːk_ən 'tʃiːz] wie Tag und Nacht

Chemistry for Fun ['kemɪstri fə 'fʌn] Spaß mit Chemie

⟨chemotherapy⟩ [ˌkiːməʊ'θerəpi] Chemotherapie

chess [tʃes] Schach(-spiel)

⟨'-chester'⟩ ['tʃestə] Lager (lat.)

⟨chick⟩ [tʃɪk] Küken

chicken ['tʃɪkɪn] Huhn, Hähnchen
Chicken Massala ['tʃɪkɪn mə'sɑːlə] pakistan. Gericht (aus Huhn)
tandoori chicken 'tʃɪkɪn] indisches Gericht

Chief of Police [ˌtʃiːf_əv pə'liːs] Polizeichef

⟨chihuahua⟩ [tʃɪ'waːwə] Chihuahua

child [tʃaɪld] Kind

°childhood ['tʃaɪldhʊd] Kindheit

childish ['tʃaɪldɪʃ] kindisch

children (pl) ['tʃɪldrən] Kinder
United Nations Children's Fund [juːˌnaɪtɪd 'neɪʃnz 'tʃɪldrənz 'fʌnd] UN Kinderhilfsorganisation
children's home [ˌtʃɪldrənz 'həʊm] Kinderheim

⟨china⟩ ['tʃaɪnə] Porzellan

Chinese [tʃaɪ'niːz] Chinesisch, chinesisch, Chinese/in

⟨to chip⟩ [tʃɪp] einmeißeln

chips (pl) [tʃɪps] Pommes frites

chocolate ['tʃɒklət] Schokolade

choice [tʃɔɪs] Wahl, Auswahl
of one's own choice [əv wʌnz_'əʊn 'tʃɔɪs] freiwillig, aus eigener Wahl

to choose* [tʃuːz] aussuchen, auswählen
to choose* to do s.th. [tʃuːz, tʃəʊz, tʃəʊzn] sich für etwas entscheiden

chopsticks ['tʃɒpstɪks] Stäbchen

chore [tʃɔː] Pflicht, (Haus-)Arbeit

chorus ['kɔːrəs] Refrain

⟨For Christ's sake!⟩ [fə ˌkraɪsts 'seɪk] Um Himmels Willen! (ugs.)

Christmas ['krɪsməs] Weihnachten
Christmas Day [ˌkrɪsməs 'deɪ] 1. Weihnachtstag
Christmas Eve [ˌkrɪsməs 'iːv] Heiligabend
Christmas pudding [ˌkrɪsməs 'pʊdɪŋ] schwerer dunkler Kuchen mit viel Trockenobst

⟨to chug⟩ [tʃʌg] tuckern

church ['tʃɜːtʃ] Kirche

⟨cigarette⟩ ['sɪgəret] Zigarette

cinema ['sɪnəmə] Kino
at the cinema [ət ðə 'sɪnəmə] im Kino

°circle ['sɜːkl] Kreis

indoor circuit [ˌɪndɔː 'sɜːkɪt] Hallenrennbahn

⟨circulation⟩ [ˌsɜːkjə'leɪʃn] Zirkulation, Kreislauf

⟨circumstances beyond s.o.'s control⟩ ['sɜːkəmstænsɪz bɪˌɒnd … kən'trəʊl] Umstände, die sich der Kontrolle … entziehen

circus ['sɜːkəs] Zirkus

⟨citizen⟩ ['sɪtɪzən] Bürger/in

city ['sɪti] Stadt
city centre [ˌsɪti 'sentə] Stadtmitte

⟨civil⟩ ['sɪvɪl] bürgerlich, Bürger-

⟨to claim⟩ [kleɪm] behaupten

to clap [klæp] (Beifall) klatschen

class [klɑːs] Schulklasse; Stunde, Unterricht

classical ['klæsɪkl] klassisch

classmate ['klɑːsmeɪt] Klassenkamerad/in

classroom ['klɑːsrʊm] Klassenzimmer

°if-clause ['ɪf klɔːz] (Teil-) Satz mit "if"

°non-defining relative clause [ˌnɒndɪ'faɪnɪŋ 'relətɪv ˌklɔːz] nicht-notwendiger Relativsatz

°relative clause ['relətɪv ˌklɔːz] Relativsatz

to clean [kliːn] putzen, sauber machen, reinigen

to clean up [kliːn_'ʌp] sauber machen; aufräumen

clean [kliːn] sauber

Clean and Decent Dance [kliːn_ænd 'diːsnt dɑːns] "Sauber-und-anständig"-Tanzveranstaltung

cleaner ['kliːnə] Putzfrau/mann

to clear (away) [ˌklɪər_ə'weɪ] wegräumen, abräumen; roden, abholzen

clear [klɪə] deutlich; klar

clear glass [klɪə 'glɑːs] Weißglas

clearly ['klɪəli] offensichtlich

clever ['klevə] klug, schlau

to climb [klaɪm] besteigen; klettern

climber ['klaɪmə] Bergsteiger/in, Kletterer/in

climbing ['klaɪmɪŋ] Klettern, Bergsteigen

⟨to cling to⟩ ['klɪŋ tʊ] (sich) festhalten an

clock [klɒk] Uhr

⟨time and motion clock⟩ [ˌtaɪm_ənd 'məʊʃn ˌklɒk] Uhr zur Effizienzprüfung

to close [kləʊz] schließen, zumachen

close [kləʊs] knapp; °nah; genau, eingehend

⟨close by⟩ [ˌkləʊs 'baɪ] nahe bei, in der Nähe von

⟨closet⟩ ['klɒzɪt] (Kleider-) Schrank (AE)

clothes [kləʊðz] Kleidung, Kleidungsstücke

clothing ['kləʊðɪŋ] Kleidung

cloud [klaʊd] Wolke

cloudy ['klaʊdɪ] bewölkt

clown [klaʊn] Clown

club [klʌb] Club, Verein

clue [kluː] Hinweis

°cluster ['klʌstə] Gruppe

⟨coach⟩ [kəʊtʃ] (Reise-) Bus

coal [kəʊl] Kohle

coast [kəʊst] Küste

off the coast [ˌɒf ðə 'kəʊst] vor der Küste

coastguard ['kəʊstgɑːd] Küstenwache

⟨cockerel⟩ ['kɒkərəl] junger Hahn

cocoa ['kəʊkəʊ] Kakao

code [kəʊd] Code, Geheimschrift

coffee ['kɒfɪ] Kaffee

coffee house ['kɒfɪ ˌhaʊs] Café

coffee shop ['kɒfɪ ˌʃɒp] Café

coin [kɔɪn] Münze

cola ['kəʊlə] Cola

cold [kəʊld] kalt

°collage [kɒ'lɑːʒ] Collage

⟨to collapse⟩ [kə'læps] zusammenbrechen, zugrunde gehen

(radio) collar ['kɒlə] Kragen; Halsband (mit Peilsender)

to collect [kə'lekt] sammeln; abholen

collection [kə'lekʃn] Sammlung; Leerung, Abholung

⟨college⟩ ['kɒlɪdʒ] Universität, Hochschule

colony ['kɒlənɪ] Kolonie, Ansiedlung

color ['kʌlə] Farbe (AE)

colour ['kʌlə] Farbe

to colour ['kʌlə] färben; anmalen; kolorieren

column ['kɒləm] Spalte; Kolumne

to combine [kəm'baɪn] kombinieren, verbinden

Combined Humanities [kəmˌbaɪnd hjuː'mænətɪz] Gesellschaftswissenschaften, Humanwissenschaften

to come* [kʌm] kommen

to come along (with s.o.) [kʌm_ə'lɒŋ] sich (jdm.) anschließen, mitgehen (mit jdm.)

to come home [kʌm 'həʊm] nach Hause kommen

to come round [kʌm 'raʊnd] vorbeikommen, besuchen

to come to mind [kʌm tə 'maɪnd] in den Sinn kommen

to come top of the class [kʌm ˌtɒp əv ðə 'klɑːs] Klassenbeste/r sein

to come up to s.o. [ˌkʌm_'ʌp tə] auf jdn. zukommen/zugehen

Come on! [kʌm_'ɒn] Los, komm! Gehen wir!

comedy ['kɒmədɪ] Komödie

°(home) comforts [həʊm 'kʌmfəts] Annehmlichkeiten (eines Zuhauses)

comfortable ['kʌmfətəbl] komfortabel, bequem

comic ['kɒmɪk] Comic

⟨to command⟩ [kə'mɑːnd] befehlen

⟨commander⟩ [kə'mɑːndə] Befehlshaber

comment ['kɒment] Kommentar, Bemerkung

to comment ['kɒment] kommentieren

⟨commercial⟩ [kə'mɜːʃl] Werbespot

Commercial TV [kə'mɜːʃl tiː'viː] Privatsender

⟨commercially⟩ [kə'mɜːʃəlɪ] kommerziell

committed [kə'mɪtɪd] engagiert

common ['kɒmən] häufig, (weit) verbreitet

⟨the 'commoners'⟩ [ðə 'kɒmənəz] die 'Bürgerlichen'

⟨The House of Commons⟩ [ˌhaʊs_əv 'kɒmənz] Unterhaus (GB)

to communicate [kə'mjuːnɪkeɪt] kommunizieren, sich verständigen

communication [kəˌmjuːnɪ'keɪʃn] Kommunikation, Verständigung

communist ['kɒmjʊnɪst] kommunistisch, Kommunist/in

Community Centre [kə'mjuːnətɪ ˌsentə] Gemeindezentrum

company ['kʌmpənɪ] Gesellschaft, Firma, Unternehmen

comparative [kəm'pærətɪv] Komparativ

to compare [kəm'peə] vergleichen

to compete with s.o. (for) [kəm'piːt wɪð ˌsʌmwʌn fə] mit jdm. (um etwas) konkurrieren/kämpfen

competition [ˌkɒmpɪ'tɪʃn] Wettbewerb

to complain (about) [kəm'pleɪn ə'baʊt] sich beklagen

⟨complaint⟩ [kəm'pleɪnt] Beschwerde

to complete [kəm'pliːt] beenden, abschließen; °vervollständigen

°complete [kəm'pliːt] komplett/e/r/s, ganz/e/r/s, vollständig/e/r/s

completely [kəm'pliːtlɪ] völlig, ganz, vollkommen

⟨completion⟩ [kəm'pliːʃn] Fertigstellung, Beendigung

°compound [kɒm'paʊnd] Kompositum, zusammengesetztes Wort

comprehensive school [ˌkɒmprɪ'hensɪv ˌskuːl] Gesamtschule

⟨compromise⟩ ['kɒmprəmaɪz] Kompromiss

computer [kəm'pjuːtə] Computer

computer glitch [kəm'pjuːtə ˌglɪtʃ] Computer-Funktionsstörung

computer programmer [kəm'pjuːtə ˌprəʊgræmə] Programmierer/in

Computing [kəm'pjuːtɪŋ] Computerclub

to concentrate (on) ['kɒnsəntreɪt_ˌɒn] sich konzentrieren (auf)

concert ['kɒnsət] Konzert

⟨condition⟩ [kən'dɪʃn] Bedingung

°the conditional [ðə kən'dɪʃənəl] die Konditionalform

°conditional perfect [kən'dɪʃnl 'pɜːfɪkt] Konditional der Vergangenheit

⟨to confer⟩ [kən'fɜː] sich beraten, sich besprechen

confident ['kɒnfɪdnt] selbstsicher/-bewusst, zuversichtlich

to confuse [kən'fjuːz] verwirren

congratulations (pl.) [kənˌgrætjʊ'leɪʃnz] Glückwunsch/-wünsche

°conjunction [kən'dʒʌŋkʃn] Konjunktion

°to connect [kə'nekt] verbinden

connective [kə'nektɪv] Konjunktion, Bindewort

⟨to **conquer**⟩ [ˈkɒŋkə] erobern, besiegen

°**pros and cons** [ˌprəʊz_ənd ˈkɒnz] Vorteile und Nachteile

conservation [ˌkɒnsə'veɪʃn] Erhaltung, Bewahrung; Umweltschutz

to **consider** [kən'sɪdə] betrachten, bedenken

all things **considered** [ˌɔːl θɪŋz kən'sɪdəd] wenn man alles in Betracht zieht

⟨**constituency**⟩ [kən'stɪtjʊənsɪ] Wahlkreis

⟨**constitutional**⟩ [ˌkɒnstɪ'tjuːʃənl] Verfassungs-

to **construct** [kən'strʌkt] bauen

consultant [kən'sʌltənt] Berater/in

contact [ˈkɒntækt] Kontakt, Verbindung

°**contact clause** [ˈkɒntækt ˈklɔːz] Relativsatz ohne Relativpronomen

to **contact** [ˈkɒntækt] kontaktieren, sich wenden an

°to **contain** [kən'teɪn] beinhalten, enthalten

content [ˈkɒntent] Inhalt

°**context** [ˈkɒntekst] Kontext, Zusammenhang

continent [ˈkɒntɪnənt] Kontinent

to **continue** [kən'tɪnjuː] fortfahren, weitermachen mit; (an)dauern

⟨**contour**⟩ [ˈkɒntʊə] Umriss, Kontur

contract [ˈkɒntrækt] Vertrag

contrast [ˈkɒntrɑːst] Unterschied, Kontrast

to **contribute** (to) [kən'trɪbjuːt] beitragen (zu)

⟨circumstances beyond s.o.'s **control**⟩ [ˈsɜːkəmstænsɪz bɪˌɒnd ... kən'trəʊl] Umstände, die sich der Kontrolle ... entziehen

to **control** [kən'trəʊl] kontrollieren, regeln

controversial [ˌkɒntrə'vɜːʃl] kontrovers, umstritten

conversation [ˌkɒnvə'seɪʃn] Unterhaltung

convict [ˈkɒnvɪkt] Sträfling

°to **convince** [kən'vɪns] überzeugen

to **cook** [kʊk] kochen

cooker [ˈkʊkə] Herd

cooking [ˈkʊkɪŋ] Kochen

cool [kuːl] cool; kühl

to **cope** [kəʊp] fertig werden mit, zurechtkommen

copy [ˈkɒpɪ] Kopie; Exemplar

to **copy** [ˈkɒpɪ] abschreiben, kopieren

°to **copy out** [ˌkɒpɪ 'aʊt] abschreiben, herausschreiben

⟨to **draw up a cordon**⟩ [drɔː_ˈʌp_ə 'kɔːdn] etw. abriegeln, einen Kordon (um etw.) ziehen

corner [ˈkɔːnə] Ecke

⟨**coronation**⟩ [ˌkɒrə'neɪʃn] Krönung

to **correct** [kə'rekt] korrigieren, berichtigen

correct [kə'rekt] richtig, korrekt

°**correction** [kə'rekʃn] Verbesserung, Korrektur

corridor [ˈkɒrɪdɔː] Flur

cost [kɒst] Kosten

to **cost*** [kɒst] kosten

costume [ˈkɒstjuːm] Kostüm

⟨**cotton**⟩ [ˈkɒtn] Baumwolle

⟨to **cough**⟩ [kɒf] husten

could [kʊd] konnte; könnte

⟨**council** estate⟩ [ˈkaʊnsl ɪˌsteɪt] *Siedlung des öffentlichen Wohnungsbaus*

⟨town **council**⟩ [ˌtaʊn 'kaʊnsl] Stadtrat

⟨**councillor**⟩ [ˈkaʊnsɪlə] Ratsherr

to **count** [kaʊnt] zählen

countable [ˈkaʊntbl] zählbar

country [ˈkʌntrɪ] Land

in the **country** [ɪn ðə 'kʌntrɪ] auf dem Lande

countryside [ˈkʌntrɪsaɪd] Landschaft

county [ˈkaʊntɪ] Grafschaft, Verwaltungsbezirk

a **couple of** [ə 'kʌpl_ɒv] ein paar, einige

course [kɔːs] Kurs, Lehrgang

golf course [ˈgɒlf ˌkɔːs] Golfplatz

of **course** [əv 'kɔːs] natürlich, selbstverständlich

cousin [ˈkʌzn] Cousin/e

⟨front **cover**⟩ [frʌnt 'kʌvə] Titelseite *(Zeitschrift)*

to **cover** [ˈkʌvə] abdecken; bedecken, zudecken

cow [kaʊ] Kuh

cowboy [ˈkaʊbɔɪ] Cowboy

cracker [ˈkrækə] Knallbonbon

to **cram** [kræm] hineinzwängen, vollstopfen

⟨**cramped**⟩ [ˈkræmpt] beengt, eng

Crash! [kræʃ] *Krach!*

⟨**crater**⟩ [ˈkreɪtə] Krater

to **crawl** [krɔːl] kriechen

⟨to **crawl out of the woodwork**⟩ [ˈwʊdwɜːk] von allen Seiten angekrochen kommen

crazy [ˈkreɪzɪ] verrückt

to go **crazy** [gəʊ 'kreɪzɪ] verrückt werden

cream [kriːm] Sahne; Salbe, Creme

ice cream [ˌaɪs 'kriːm] (Speise-) Eis

°to **create** [krɪ'eɪt] erzeugen, (er)schaffen

creation [krɪ'eɪʃn] (Er-)Schaffung

°**creative** [krɪ'əɪtɪv] kreativ

°**creative writing** [krɪ'eɪtɪv ˌraɪtɪŋ] kreatives Schreiben

creature [ˈkriːtʃə] (Lebe-) Wesen, Geschöpf, Kreatur

cricket [ˈkrɪkɪt] Kricket

crime [kraɪm] Straftat, Verbrechen

crisis [ˈkraɪsɪs] Krise

crisps (pl) [krɪsps] Kartoffelchips

critical [ˈkrɪtɪkl] kritisch, entscheidend

Croatian [ˌkrəʊ'eɪʃn] Kroate, Kroatin, kroatisch

crocodile [ˈkrɒkədaɪl] Krokodil

crop [krɒp] Ernte

to **cross** [krɒs] kreuzen; überqueren

°to **cross out** [krɒs_ˈaʊt] durchstreichen

°**crossword** [ˈkrɒswɜːd] Kreuzworträtsel

crowd [kraʊd] (Menschen-) Menge

⟨**crown**⟩ [kraʊn] Krone

⟨The **Crown** Jewels⟩ [ˌkraʊn 'dʒuːəlz] Kronjuwelen

cruel [ˈkruːəl] grausam; ⟨hart⟩

⟨**cruelty**⟩ [ˈkrʊəltɪ] Grausamkeit

to **cry** [kraɪ] weinen

Cuban [ˈkjuːbən] kubanisch, Kubaner/in

⟨**cuff**⟩ [kʌf] Ärmelaufschlag

cultural [ˈkʌltʃrl] kulturell

culture [ˈkʌltʃə] Kultur

cup [kʌp] Tasse

cupboard [ˈkʌbəd] Schrank

curious [ˈkjʊərɪəs] neugierig

curry [ˈkʌrɪ] Curry

curtain [ˈkɜːtn] Vorhang, Gardine

°**custom** [ˈkʌstəm] Sitte, Brauch

customer [ˈkʌstəmə] Kunde/Kundin

to **cut*** [kʌt] schneiden, sich schneiden

to **cut down** [kʌt 'daʊn] einschränken, kleiner machen; fällen

to **cut through** [kʌt 'θruː] durchkommen, fahren; führen

cute [kjuːt] niedlich, süß

cycle route [ˈsaɪkl ruːt] Fahrradweg

to **cycle** [ˈsaɪkl] mit dem Fahrrad fahren

cycling [ˈsaɪklɪŋ] Fahrradfahren

Cycling Proficiency & Maintenance [ˌsaɪklɪŋ prə'fɪʃənsɪ ənd 'meɪntənəns] Radfahren und Fahrradreparatur

D

dad [dæd] Papa, Vater

⟨**daddy**⟩ [ˈdædɪ] Papa, Papi

⟨**daily**⟩ [ˈdeɪlɪ] Tageszeitung

daily [ˈdeɪlɪ] täglich

to **damage** [ˈdæmɪdʒ] schaden, beschädigen

⟨**damn**⟩ [dæm] verdammte(r/s)

⟨**damned**⟩ [ˈdæmd] verdammt *(ugs.)*

to **dance** [dɑːns] tanzen

dancer [ˈdɑːnsə] Tänzer/in

danger [ˈdeɪndʒə] Gefahr

dangerous [ˈdeɪndʒrəs] gefährlich

⟨to **dare**⟩ [deə] wagen

dark [dɑːk] dunkel

darkness [ˈdɑːknɪs] Dunkelheit, Finsternis

⟨**database**⟩ [ˈdeɪtəbeɪs] Datenbank

date [deɪt] Datum

°to **make a date** [ˌmeɪk_ə 'deɪt] einen Termin setzen

daughter [ˈdɔːtə] Tochter

day [deɪ] Tag

day out [deɪ 'aʊt] Tagesausflug
⟨Midsummer's Day⟩ [ˌmɪdsʌməz 'deɪ] Sommersonnenwende
some day ['sʌm deɪ] eines Tages
St. Patrick's Day [snt 'pætrɪks ˌdeɪ] Tag des Schutzheiligen Irlands
the other day [ðɪ ˌʌðə 'deɪ] neulich
dead [ded] sehr, absolut *(ugs.)*
dead [ded] tot
⟨no big **deal**⟩ [ˌnəʊ bɪg 'di:l] nichts Besonderes *(ugs.)*
⟨a great **deal** of difference⟩ [ə ˌgreɪt ˌdi:l əv 'dɪfrəns] ein großer Unterschied
⟨to **deal** (with)⟩ [di:l] sich befassen mit, sich kümmern um
⟨**dealing**⟩ ['di:lɪŋ] Handel (mit Drogen)
dear [dɪə] Liebes, Schatz *(Anrede)*
Dear ... [dɪə] Liebe/Lieber ... *(als Briefanfang)*
Oh dear! [əʊ 'dɪə] Oje!
death [deθ] Tod
debate [dɪ'beɪt] Debatte, Diskussion
to hold (a debate) [həʊld] diskutieren, debattieren
⟨**début**⟩ ['deɪbju:] Erstlings-
December [dɪ'sembə] Dezember
decent ['di:snt] anständig
to **decide** (on) [dɪ'saɪd] sich entscheiden (für)
⟨to **declare oneself**⟩ [dɪ'kleə] sich erklären/ernennen zu
to **decorate** ['dekəreɪt] verschönern
decoration [ˌdekə'reɪʃn] Dekoration, Ausschmückung
⟨**deep-freeze**⟩ [ˌdi:p'fri:z] Tiefkühltruhe
deep [di:p] tief
deer [dɪə] Hirsch, Reh
⟨to **defeat**⟩ [dɪ'fi:t] besiegen
°to **define** [dɪ'faɪn] definieren, bestimmen
definitely ['defɪnɪtlɪ] bestimmt, ganz sicherlich
°**definition** [ˌdefɪ'nɪʃn] Definition
⟨**deforestation**⟩ [di:ˌfɒrɪ'steɪʃn] Abholzung
degree [dɪ'gri:] Grad;
⟨Hochschulabschluss⟩
⟨to do a degree⟩ [ˌdʊ ə dɪ'gri:] studieren
to **delete** [dɪ'li:t] (aus)löschen, streichen
delicious [dɪ'lɪʃəs] köstlich, lecker
to **deliver** [dɪ'lɪvə] zustellen, liefern
⟨on **demand**⟩ [ɒn dɪ'ma:nd] auf Verlangen
°View on Demand [ˌvju:ˌ ɒn dɪ'ma:nd] *View on Demand*
to **demand** [dɪ'ma:nd] verlangen
democracy [dɪ'mɒkrəsɪ] Demokratie
demonstration [ˌdemən'streɪʃn] "Demo", Demonstration; Vorführung, Demonstration
dentist ['dentɪst] Zahnarzt/ärztin
fire **department** ['faɪə dɪˌpa:tmənt] Feuerwehr *(AE)*

°**department store** [dɪ'pa:tmənt ˌstɔ:] großes Geschäft, Kaufhaus, Warenhaus
to **depend** (on) [dɪ'pend ɒn] abhängig sein von; sich verlassen auf
⟨it depends⟩ [dɪ'pendz] es hängt davon ab, es kommt darauf an
⟨**deposit**⟩ [dɪ'pɒzɪt] Vorkommen
depression [dɪ'preʃn] Depression
the Depression [ðə dɪ'preʃn] Weltwirtschaftskrise
⟨**descendant**⟩ [dɪ'sendənt] Nachkomme
of (Irish) **descent** [ɒv ... dɪ'sent] (irischer) Abstammung
to **describe** [dɪ'skraɪb] beschreiben
description [dɪ'skrɪpʃn] Beschreibung, Schilderung
desert ['dezət] Wüste
°**desert island** [ˌdezət 'aɪlənd] verlassene Insel
to **deserve** [dɪ'zɜ:v] verdienen
to **design** [dɪ'zaɪn] entwerfen
Design technology [dɪ'zaɪn tek'nɒlədʒɪ] Designtechnologie
°to **design** [dɪ'zaɪn] entwerfen
⟨**desirable**⟩ [dɪ'zaɪərəbl] begehrenswert
⟨**desire**⟩ [dɪ'zaɪə] Wunsch, Sehnsucht, Verlangen
desk [desk] Schreibtisch
⟨**despondent**⟩ [dɪ'spɒndənt] deprimiert, mutlos, niedergeschlagen
dessert [dɪ'zɜ:t] Dessert, Nachtisch
destination [ˌdestɪ'neɪʃn] (Reise)Ziel, Bestimmungsort
to **destroy** [dɪ'strɔɪ] zerstören, verwüsten
⟨**destruction**⟩ [dɪ'strʌkʃn] Zerstörung
detail ['di:teɪl] Detail, Einzelheit
detective [dɪ'tektɪv] Detektiv
°**detective** [dɪ'tektɪv] detektivisch
to **develop** [dɪ'veləp] (sich) entwickeln
developing [dɪ'veləpɪŋ] Entwicklungs-
development [dɪ'veləpmənt] Entwicklung
⟨**deviation**⟩ [ˌdi:vɪ'eɪʃn] Abweichung
to **dial** ['daɪəl] wählen
dialect ['daɪəlekt] Dialekt, Mundart
dialogue ['daɪəlɒg] Dialog
diary ['daɪərɪ] Tagebuch
to keep a diary [ki:p ə 'daɪərɪ] ein Tagebuch führen
°to **dictate** [dɪk'teɪt] diktieren
dictionary ['dɪkʃənrɪ] Wörterbuch
so **did** ... ['səʊ dɪd] (das) tat auch
to **die** [daɪ] sterben
diet ['daɪət] Diät
difference ['dɪfrəns] Unterschied
⟨a great deal of difference⟩ [ə ˌgreɪt ˌdi:l əv 'dɪfrəns] ein großer Unterschied
different ['dɪfrənt] verschieden, anders

difficult ['dɪfɪkəlt] schwierig, schwer
difficulty ['dɪfɪkəltɪ] Schwierigkeit
dig [dɪg] Ausgrabung
to **dig*** [dɪg] graben
digger ['dɪgə] Goldgräber, Bergmann
diner ['daɪnə] *amerikan. Schnellgaststätte (AE)*
⟨**dinner**⟩ ['dɪnə] (Abend-) Essen
⟨**dip**⟩ [dɪp] Bodensenke
⟨to **direct**⟩ [daɪ'rekt] Regie führen
direct(*ly*) [daɪ'rekt(lɪ)] direkt, unmittelbar
director [dɪ'rektə] Regisseur
dirty ['dɜ:tɪ] schmutzig, dreckig
disabled [dɪs'eɪbld] behindert
disadvantage [ˌdɪsəd'va:ntɪdʒ] Nachteil
to **disagree** [ˌdɪsə'gri:] nicht übereinstimmen
to **disappear** [ˌdɪsə'pɪə] verschwinden
to **disappoint** [ˌdɪsə'pɔɪnt] enttäuschen
disaster [dɪ'za:stə] Desaster, Unglück, Katastrophe
disc [dɪsk] Diskette
disc jockey ['dɪsk ˌdʒɒkɪ] Diskjockey
discman ['dɪskmən] Discman
disco ['dɪskəʊ] Disko, Disco
discoloured [dɪs'kʌləd] verfärbt
to **discover** [dɪs'kʌvə] entdecken
⟨**discovery**⟩ [dɪs'kʌvərɪ] Entdeckung
to **discuss** [dɪs'kʌs] diskutieren, besprechen
discussion [dɪs'kʌʃn] Diskussion
disease [dɪ'zi:z] Krankheit
disgusting [dɪs'gʌstɪŋ] widerlich, ekelhaft
dish ['dɪʃ] Schale, Schüssel (*pl. auch:* Geschirr)
to do the **dishes** [ˌdu: ðə 'dɪʃɪz] das Geschirr spülen
dishonest [dɪs'ɒnɪst] unehrlich
in **dismay** [ɪn dɪs'meɪ] bestürzt
to **display** [dɪ'spleɪ] zeigen, ausstellen
dissimilar [dɪs'sɪmɪlə] unähnlich
⟨**distance**⟩ ['dɪstəns] Abstand
⟨**distinction**⟩ [dɪ'stɪŋktʃn] Unterschied
⟨**distorted**⟩ [dɪ'stɔ:tɪd] verzerrt, verformt
to **distract** [dɪ'strækt] ablenken
⟨to **disturb**⟩ [dɪ'stɜ:b] stören
disturbance [dɪ'stɜ:bəns] Störung; (Vulkan-) Ausbruch
disturbing [dɪ'stɜ:bɪŋ] beunruhigend
°to **divide** [dɪ'vaɪd] teilen, unterteilen
⟨to **divide up**⟩ [dɪˌvaɪd_'ʌp] aufteilen
divorce [dɪ'vɔ:s] Scheidung
divorced [dɪ'vɔ:st] geschieden
Diwali [dɪ'wa:lɪ] Divali (*hinduist. Fest*)
to **do*** [du:] machen, tun
(I) do (feel) [du:] (ich glaube) wirklich

to do a baby-sitting job ['beɪbɪ ˌsɪtɪŋ] als Babysitter jobben
⟨to do a degree⟩ [ˌduˑ_ə dɪˈgriː] studieren
to do a paper round ['peɪpə raʊnd] Zeitungen austragen
to do business [ˌduˑ 'bɪznɪs] Geschäfte machen
to do homework [du: 'həʊmwɜːk] Hausaufgaben machen
to do the dishes [ˌduː ðə 'dɪʃɪz] das Geschirr spülen
to do the shopping [du: ðə 'ʃɒpɪŋ] einkaufen gehen, die Einkäufe erledigen
to do well [du: 'wel] gut abschneiden, gut machen
⟨to have done with⟩ [hæv 'dʌn wɪð] mit etwas fertig sein
to have s.th. done [ˌhæv ... 'dʌn] etwas machen lassen
dock [dɒk] Dock, Pier, Kai
doctor ['dɒktə] Arzt/Ärztin
(it) does (get easier) [dʌz] wirklich, tatsächlich, doch
dog [dɒg] Hund
⟨dole money⟩ ['dəʊl ˌmʌnɪ] Arbeitslosengeld (ugs.)
dollar ['dɒlə] Dollar
⟨'-don'⟩ [dən] befestigter Ort (kelt.)
°dos and don'ts [ˌduːz_ən_'dəʊnts] was man tun soll(te), und was man nicht tun soll(te)
⟨donation⟩ [dəʊ'neɪʃn] Spende
door [dɔː] Tür
   back door [bæk 'dɔː] Hintertür
   front door [frʌnt 'dɔː] Haustür
   next door [nekst 'dɔː] nebenan
   to go out of the door [gəʊ 'aʊt_əv ðə 'dɔː] das Haus verlassen
°doorbell ['dɔːbel] Türklingel
doorway ['dɔːweɪ] (Haus-) Eingang
°dos and don'ts [ˌduːz_ən_'dəʊnts] was man tun soll(te), und was man nicht tun soll(te)
°to double-check [ˌdʌbl'tʃek] (noch einmal) überprüfen
doubt [daʊt] Zweifel
   ⟨to give s.o. the benefit of the doubt⟩ [...ðə 'benɪfɪt_əv ðə 'daʊt] im Zweifelsfall zu jdns. Gunsten entscheiden
to doubt [daʊt] bezweifeln
down
   down the street [ˌdaʊn ðə 'striːt] die Straße entlang
   down under [ˌdaʊn_'ʌndə] (in) Australien, Neuseeland (ugs.)
   to break down [breɪk 'daʊn] zusammenbrechen
   to burn down [bɜːn 'daʊn] abbrennen
   to cut down [kʌt 'daʊn] einschränken, kleiner machen; fällen
   to note down [nəʊt 'daʊn] notieren, aufschreiben
   to pull down [pʊl 'daʊn] abreißen

to settle down [ˌsetl 'daʊn] zur Ruhe kommen, ein geregeltes Leben führen
to sit down [sɪt 'daʊn] sich (hin)setzen
to slow s.th. down [sləʊ ... 'daʊn] verlangsamen
to wear s.th. down [ˌweə ˌsʌmθɪŋ 'daʊn] abnutzen, abtragen
°to write down [raɪt 'daʊn] aufschreiben
downstairs [daʊn'steəz] unten (im Haus)
   to go downstairs [gəʊ daʊn'steəz] die Treppe heruntergehen
downtown ['daʊntaʊn] Innenstadt, Stadtzentrum, Geschäftsviertel (AE)
dozen ['dʌzn] Dutzend
draft [drɑːft] Entwurf
to drain [dreɪn] entwässern
drainpipe ['dreɪnpaɪp] Abflussrohr
drama hall ['drɑːmə hɔːl] Bühnensaal
   drama group ['drɑːmə gruːp] Theatergruppe
⟨dramatically⟩ [drə'mætɪkəlɪ] sehr, dramatisch
to draw* [drɔː] zeichnen
   to draw (plans) [drɔː] (Pläne) schmieden, aushecken
   ⟨to draw up⟩ [drɔː_'ʌp] entwerfen
   ⟨to draw up a cordon⟩ [ˌdrɔː_ʌp_ə 'kɔːdn] etw. abriegeln, einen Kordon (um etw.) ziehen
drawing ['drɔːɪŋ] Zeichnung, Bild
⟨drawl⟩ [drɔːl] langgezogene Sprechweise (z.B. in den amerik. Südstaaten)
to dread [dred] befürchten; Angst haben vor
dream [driːm] Traum
to dream* [driːm] träumen
   to dream of ['driːm_əv] träumen von
Dreaming = Dreamtime ['driːmɪŋ/'driːmtaɪm] "Zeit der Träume"(die mythische Urzeit der australischen Ureinwohner)
dress [dres] Kleid
⟨to dress⟩ [dres] sich anziehen
   to get dressed [get 'drest] sich anziehen
drink [drɪŋk] Getränk
to drink* [drɪŋk] trinken
drive [draɪv] (Auto-) Fahrt, Strecke
to drive* (on) [draɪv_'ɒn] (weiter)fahren
bus driver ['bʌs ˌdraɪvə] Busfahrer/in
   taxi driver ['tæksɪ ˌdraɪvə] Taxifahrer/in
to drop out [drɒp_'aʊt] (die Schule) abbrechen; aussteigen
   to drop s.th. [drɒp] etwas fallen lassen
   ⟨to drop to⟩ [drɒp] sinken auf
dropout ['drɒpaʊt] Schulabbrecher/in (ohne Abschluss); Aussteiger/in

drought [draʊt] Dürre
to drown [draʊn] ertrinken
drug [drʌg] Droge
drum [drʌm] Trommel; (als Plural) Schlagzeug
Piping and Drumming [ˌpaɪpɪŋ_ənd 'drʌmɪŋ] Dudelsackspielen und Trommeln
dry [draɪ] trocken
duck [dʌk] Ente
⟨due to⟩ [ˈdjuː tʊ] aufgrund
to be due [djuː] fällig sein, soll kommen/da sein
⟨duke⟩ [djuːk] Herzog
   Duke of Edinburgh's Award [ˌdjuːk_əv_'edɪnbərəz_ə_ˌwɔːd] Auszeichnung des Herzogs von Edinburgh
dump [dʌmp] Müllkippe
to dump [dʌmp] (Müll) abladen
dungeon ['dʌndʒən] Verlies, Kerker
during ['djʊrɪŋ] während
dusty ['dʌstɪ] staubig
°dynamic [daɪ'næmɪk] dynamisch; Tätigkeits-/Handlungs-

E

°e-mail ['iːmeɪl] E-Mail
°each [iːtʃ] jede/r/s
   they don't like each other [iːtʃ_'ʌðə] sie mögen sich nicht
eagle ['iːgl] Adler
°ear [ɪə] Ohr
⟨earl⟩ [ɜːl] Graf
early ['ɜːlɪ] früh
to earn [ɜːn] verdienen
earnings (pl.) ['ɜːnɪŋz] Verdienst
earth [ɜːθ] Erde
   ⟨plot of earth⟩ [ˌplɒt_əv_'ɜːθ] Grabstätte
earthquake ['ɜːθkweɪk] Erdbeben
easily ['iːzɪlɪ] leicht
east [iːst] Osten, östlich
easy ['iːzɪ] leicht, einfach
to eat* [iːt] essen
   to eat out [iːt_'aʊt] aus(wärts) essen gehen, zum Essen ausgehen
   to eat up [iːt_'ʌp] aufessen
economy [ɪ'kɒnəmɪ] Wirtschaft, Konjunktur
edge [edʒ] Rand, Kante
⟨edifice⟩ ['edɪfɪs] Bauwerk, Gebäude
Edinburgh Academy [ˌedɪnbʌrə ə'kædəmɪ] Name einer Schule in Edinburgh
⟨to edit⟩ ['edɪt] redigieren
°editor ['edɪtə] Redakteur/in
education [ˌedjʊ'keɪʃn] Erziehung; Bildung; Ausbildung
   ⟨Erziehungswissenschaft⟩ General Certificate of Secondary Education (GCSE) ['dʒenərəl sə'tɪfɪkət_əv 'sekəndərɪ ˌedjuː'keɪʃn] britisches Äquivalent der Mittleren Reife; GCSE-Prüfung

effect [ɪ'fekt] Effekt, Auswirkung
⟨special effects⟩ [ˌspeʃl̩ɪ'fekts] Spezialeffekte
⟨**effective**⟩ [ɪ'fektɪv] wirksam, wirkungsvoll
°**efficient** [ɪ'fɪʃnt] effizient, gut
effort ['efət] Leistung; Anstrengung, Mühe
egg [eg] Ei
Eid [aɪd] *muslimisches Fest*
eight [eɪt] acht
eighteen [ˌeɪ'tiːn] achtzehn
eighty ['eɪtɪ] achtzig
either ['aɪðə] auch nicht
either ... or ['aɪðə ... ɔː] entweder ... oder
elbow ['elbəʊ] Ellbogen
elderly ['eldəlɪ] ältere Leute/ Menschen
eldest ['eldɪst] älteste/r *(in einer Familie)*
⟨**to elect**⟩ [ɪ'lekt] wählen
⟨**The General Election**⟩ [ˌdʒenərəl ɪ'lekʃn] Parlamentswahlen
electric [ɪ'lektrɪk] elektrisch
electricity [ˌɪlek'trɪsɪtɪ] Strom, Elektrizität
electronic [ɪlek'trɒnɪk] elektronisch
°**elegant** ['elɪgənt] elegant
element ['elɪmənt] Bestandteil, Element
elementary [ˌelɪ'mentərɪ] einfach, grundlegend
elephant ['elɪfənt] Elefant
eleven [ɪ'levn] elf
⟨**Elizabethan**⟩ [ˌɪlɪzə'biːθn] elisabethanisch
else [els] sonst
°**What else?** [wɒt 'els] Was sonst?
to be embarrassed [bɪ ɪm'bærəst] verlegen, peinlich berührt sein
embarrassing [ɪm'bærəsɪŋ] peinlich
emerald ['emərəld] Smaragd
The Emerald Isle [ðɪ ˌemərəld 'aɪl] *Name für Irland*
emergency [ɪˌmɜːdʒənsɪ] Notfall, Notlage
emergency call [ɪ'mɜːdʒənsɪ 'kɔːl] Notruf
to emigrate ['emɪgreɪt] auswandern, emigrieren
emigration [emɪ'greɪʃn] Emigration, Auswanderung
⟨**emotion**⟩ [ɪ'məʊʃn] Emotion, Gefühl
⟨**emotive**⟩ [ɪ'məʊtɪv] emotional, gefühlsbetont
°**emphatic** [ɪm'fætɪk] betont, betonend
⟨**empire**⟩ ['empaɪə] Weltreich, Imperium
to employ [ɪm'plɔɪ] beschäftigen
employment [ɪm'plɔɪmənt] Beschäftigung, Arbeit
to empty ['emptɪ] leeren; ein Konto plündern
empty ['emptɪ] leer
⟨**to encourage**⟩ [ɪn'kʌrɪdʒ] fördern, ermutigen

end [end] Ende
to end [end] aufhören, beenden
to end up [end 'ʌp] enden, landen *(ugs.)*
ending ['endɪŋ] Ende, Ausgang, Schluss
endless ['endləs] endlos
endterm ['endtɜːm] Ende des Trimesters (Halbjahres)
to endure [ɪn'djʊə] aushalten, ertragen
enemy ['enəmɪ] Feind/in
energy ['enədʒɪ] Energie
⟨**engine**⟩ ['endʒɪn] Motor
⟨steam engine⟩ ['stiːm ˌendʒɪn] Dampfmaschine
English ['ɪŋglɪʃ] Engländer/in; englisch; Englisch
to enjoy [ɪn'dʒɔɪ] genießen
to enjoy oneself [ɪn'dʒɔɪ] sich amüsieren
enough [ɪ'nʌf] genug
funnily enough ['fʌnɪlɪ ɪ'nʌf] komischerweise
to enter ['entə] ankommen in, einfahren in; einreisen; °eintreten
entertainment [ˌentə'teɪnmənt] Entertainment, Unterhaltung
enthusiastic [ɪnˌθjuːzɪ'æstɪk] enthusiastisch, begeistert
entire [ɪn'taɪə] ganz, vollständig
entrance ['entrəns] Eingang
envelope ['envələʊp] Umschlag
envious ['envɪəs] neidisch
environment [ɪn'vaɪrənmənt] Umwelt, Umgebung
environmental [ɪnˌvaɪərən'mentl] Umwelt-
environmentally friendly [ɪnˌvaɪərn'mentəlɪ 'frendlɪ] umweltfreundlich
episode ['epɪsəʊd] Episode; Begebenheit
⟨**equal**⟩ ['iːkwəl] gleich
⟨**equator**⟩ [ɪ'kweɪtə] Äquator
equipment [ɪ'kwɪpmənt] Ausrüstung
to erase [ɪ'reɪz] löschen, streichen
to escape [ɪ'skeɪp] entfliehen
especially [ɪ'speʃəlɪ] besonders, insbesondere
⟨**essay**⟩ ['eseɪ] Aufsatz, Essay
⟨**to establish**⟩ [ɪ'stæblɪʃ] herstellen, schaffen
⟨council **estate**⟩ ['kaʊnsl ɪˌsteɪt] *Siedlung des öffentlichen Wohnungsbaus*
to estimate ['estɪmeɪt] (ein)schätzen
etc. [ɪt'setərə] usw.
⟨**eternity**⟩ [ɪ'tɜːnɪtɪ] Ewigkeit
⟨**ether**⟩ ['iːθə] Äther
ethnic ['eθnɪk] ethnisch, Volks-
⟨**etiquette**⟩ ['etɪket] Etikette, Umgangsformen
European [ˌjʊərə'piːən] Europäer/in, europäisch
⟨to aid in the **evacuation**⟩ ['eɪd ɪn ðiː ɪˌvækjʊ'eɪʃn] bei der Evakuierung helfen

even ['iːvn] sogar
even if ['iːvn ɪf] auch wenn
⟨even though⟩ [ɪvn 'ðəʊ] obwohl
evening ['iːvnɪŋ] Abend
event [ɪ'vent] Ereignis; Veranstaltung, Wettkampf *(Sport)*
ever ['evə] jemals
ever before [ˌevə bɪ'fɔː] jemals zuvor
every ['evrɪ] jede/jeder/jedes
every time [ˌevrɪ 'taɪm] jedes Mal
everybody ['evrɪˌbɒdɪ] jede/jeder, alle
°**everyone** ['evrɪwʌn] jede/jeder, alle
everything ['evrɪθɪŋ] alles
everywhere ['evrɪweə] überall
⟨**to evict**⟩ [ɪ'vɪkt] hinauswerfen, zur Räumung zwingen
evidence ['evɪdəns] Beweis(e)
⟨**evidently**⟩ ['evɪdəntlɪ] offensichtlich
exact [ɪg'zækt] genau, exakt
°**exactly** [ɪg'zæktlɪ] genau
to exaggerate [ɪg'zædʒəreɪt] übertreiben
°**exaggeration** [ɪgˌzædʒə'reɪʃn] Übertreibung
exam(ination) [ɪgˌzæm(ɪ'neɪʃn)] Prüfung, Prüfungs-, Klausur
exam paper [ɪg'zæm ˌpeɪpə] Prüfungsaufgaben, Aufgabenstellung
to pass (an exam) [pɑːs] bestehen
⟨to set (an exam)⟩ [set] (eine Prüfung, Prüfungsaufgaben) stellen
⟨**examiner**⟩ [ɪg'zæmɪnə] Prüfer/in
example [ɪg'zɑːmpl] Beispiel
to follow someone's example [ˌfɒləʊ ˌsʌmwʌnz ɪg'zɑːmpl] dem Beispiel von jdm. folgen
excellent ['eksələnt] ausgezeichnet, hervorragend
except *(for)* [ɪk'sept fə] außer, bis auf
exchange [ɪks'tʃeɪndʒ] Austausch
to exchange [ɪks'tʃeɪndʒ] austauschen
excited [ɪk'saɪtɪd] aufgeregt
exciting [ɪk'saɪtɪŋ] aufregend, spannend
excuse [ɪks'kjuːs] Entschuldigung, Ausrede
Excuse me. [ɪk'skjuːz miː] Entschuldige, bitte.
⟨**to execute**⟩ ['eksɪkjuːt] hinrichten
execution [ˌeksɪ'kjuːʃn] Hinrichtung
°**exercise** ['eksəsaɪz] Übung
exercise book ['eksəsaɪz bʊk] Schulheft, Übungsheft
⟨port of **exit**⟩ [ˌpɔːt əv 'eksɪt] Ort der Ausreise
⟨**exotic**⟩ [ɪg'zɒtɪk] exotisch
°**to expand** [ɪk'spænd] erweitern
to expect [ɪks'pekt] rechnen mit, annehmen, erwarten
°**expectation** [ˌekspek'teɪʃn] Erwartung
expensive [ɪk'spensɪv] teuer

experience [ɪk'spɪərɪəns] Erfahrung,
Erlebnis
to **experience** [ɪk'spɪərɪəns] erleben;
erfahren
experiment [ɪk'sperɪmənt]
Experiment, Versuch
to **explain** [ɪk'spleɪn] erklären
°**explanation** [ˌeksplə'neɪʃn]
Erklärung
to **explode** [ɪk'spləʊd] explodieren
to **expose** [ɪk'spəʊz] aufdecken,
enthüllen
to **express** [ɪk'spres] ausdrücken
expression [ɪk'spreʃn] Ausdruck
extension [ɪks'tenʃn] Anbau
⟨to **extinguish**⟩ [ɪk'stɪŋgwɪʃ]
löschen, auslöschen
extra ['ekstrə] zusätzlich, extra
°**extract** ['ekstrækt] Auszug
extraordinary [ɪk'strɔːdənrɪ]
außergewöhnlich
eye [aɪ] Auge
⟨**eyebrow**⟩ ['aɪbraʊ] Augenbraue
⟨an **eyewitness** account⟩
[ən ˌaɪˌwɪtnəs ə'kaʊnt] ein
Augenzeugenbericht

F

face [feɪs] Gesicht
to make a face [meɪk ə 'feɪs] das
Gesicht verziehen
to **face** [feɪs] ins Auge blicken
to face doing s.th. [feɪs] es
fertigbringen, etwas zu tun
fact [fækt] Tatsache, Faktum
in fact [ɪn 'fækt] eigentlich,
tatsächlich
factory ['fæktərɪ] Fabrik
⟨**fade**-in⟩ ['feɪd ˌɪn] Einblendung
(Radio, Film)
⟨fade-out⟩ ['feɪd ˌaʊt]
Ausblendung (Radio, Film)
to **fail** [feɪl] durchfallen, nicht
bestehen
to **faint** [feɪnt] ohnmächtig werden,
in Ohnmacht fallen
fair [feə] gerecht, fair; ⟨hell⟩
⟨**fairly**⟩ ['feəlɪ] ziemlich
⟨**faith**⟩ [feɪθ] Glaube
Yours **faithfully** [jɔːz 'feɪθfəlɪ]
Hochachtungsvoll, Mit
freundlichen Grüßen
fall [fɔːl] Herbst (AE)
to **fall*** [fɔːl] fallen, stürzen
to fall asleep [ˌfɔːl ə'sliːp]
einschlafen
to fall off [fɔːl 'ɒf] herunter-,
hinunterfallen
to fall open [ˌfɔːl 'əʊpn] plötzlich
aufgehen, offen stehen
to fall over [fɔːl 'əʊvə] hinfallen
to fall to pieces [ˌfɔːl tə 'piːsɪz]
kaputtgehen, sich in seine
Bestandteile auflösen
to fall to the ground [ˌfɔːl tə
ðə'graʊnd] hinfallen

°**false** [fɔːls] falsch
familiar [fə'mɪljə] vertraut, bekannt
family ['fæməlɪ] Familie
family drama [ˌfæmɪlɪ 'drɑːmə]
Familiendrama
°family tree [ˌfæməlɪ 'triː]
Stammbaum
famine ['fæmɪn] Hungersnot
famous ['feɪməs] berühmt
fan [fæn] Fan
fantastic [fæn'tæstɪk] phantastisch,
toll
fantasy ['fæntəsɪ] Phantasie
far [fɑː] weit
⟨far-out⟩ [ˌfɑːr'aʊt] "super-cool",
einsame Klasse
°**farewell** [feə'wel] Abschieds-
farm [fɑːm] Bauernhof
farmer ['fɑːmə] Bauer, Farmer
⟨**farming**⟩ ['fɑːmɪŋ] Landwirtschaft,
Viehzucht
farmland ['fɑːmlənd] Ackerland
fashion ['fæʃn] Mode
⟨**fashionable**⟩ ['fæʃnəbl] modisch,
schick
fast [fɑːst] schnell
fast food ['fɑːst fuːd]
Schnellgericht
fat [fæt] dick
father ['fɑːðə] Vater
fault [fɔːlt] Schuld, Fehler
to be s.o.'s fault [biː … 'fɔːlt] jdns.
Schuld sein
favour ['feɪvə] Gefallen; Wohlwollen
in favour of ['feɪvə] für (etwas)
favourite ['feɪvərɪt] Lieblings-
to **fax** [fæks] faxen
fear [fɪə] Angst, Furcht
⟨**feather**⟩ ['feðə] Feder
⟨**feature** film⟩ ['fiːtʃə ˌfɪlm] Spielfilm
⟨to **feature**⟩ ['fiːtʃə] eine Hauptrolle
haben
February ['februərɪ] Februar
to get **fed** up with [get ˌfed 'ʌp wɪð]
leid werden, zu viel werden, die
Nase voll haben von (ugs.)
fee [fiː] Gebühr
to **feed*** [fiːd] füttern
to **feel*** [fiːl] (sich) fühlen; glauben
(I) do (feel) [duː] (ich glaube)
wirklich
they feel sorry [ðeɪ fiːl 'sɒrɪ] es tut
ihnen Leid
to feel guilty [fiːl 'gɪltɪ] sich
schuldig fühlen; ein schlechtes
Gewissen haben
to feel sick [fiːl 'sɪk] sich krank/
schlecht fühlen, übel sein
feeling ['fiːlɪŋ] Gefühl
feet (pl) [fiːt] Füße; Fuß
(Maßeinheit)
⟨**fellow** man⟩ [ˌfeləʊ 'mæn]
Mitmensch
⟨**female**⟩ ['fiːmeɪl] weiblich
fence [fens] Zaun
⟨**ferry**⟩ ['ferɪ] Fähre
festival ['festɪvl] Fest, Feiertag,
Festival

a **few** [ə 'fjuː] ein paar, einige
few(er) ['fjuː(ə)] wenig(er)
°**science fiction** [ˌsaɪəns 'fɪkʃn]
Sciencefiction
field [fiːld] Bereich, Feld
⟨**fierce**⟩ [fɪəs] heftig
fifteen [ˌfɪf'tiːn] fünfzehn
fifty ['fɪftɪ] fünfzig
to **fight*** [faɪt] (be-)kämpfen
figure ['fɪgə] Figur
⟨to **figure** s.th. out⟩ [ˌfɪgə … 'aʊt]
begreifen, schlau werden aus
file [faɪl] Ordner; Karteikasten
Filipino [ˌfɪlɪ'piːnəʊ] philippinisch,
Filipino (weibl. Filipina)
to **fill** [fɪl] füllen
°to fill in [fɪl ˌɪn] ausfüllen
film [fɪlm] Film
⟨feature film⟩ ['fiːtʃə ˌfɪlm]
Spielfilm
science fiction film [ˌsaɪəns 'fɪkʃn
fɪlm] Sciencefictionfilm
to **film** [fɪlm] filmen, aufnehmen
⟨**filthy**⟩ ['fɪlθɪ] (sehr) schmutzig,
verdreckt
°**final** ['faɪnl] letzte/r/s
finally ['faɪnəlɪ] zum Schluss,
schließlich
find [faɪnd] Fund
to **find*** [faɪnd] finden, suchen
to find out [faɪnd 'aʊt] erfahren,
feststellen; herausfinden
fine [faɪn] fein, dünn; in Ordnung
finger ['fɪŋgə] Finger
to **finish** ['fɪnɪʃ] beenden, aufhören
⟨to finish off⟩ [ˌfɪnɪʃ 'ɒf] erledigen
to finish up doing s.th. [ˌfɪnɪʃ 'ʌp]
mit etwas fertig werden/etwas
beenden
fire ['faɪə] Feuer; Kamin
fire brigade ['faɪə brɪˌgeɪd]
Feuerwehr
fire department ['faɪə dɪˌpɑːtmənt]
Feuerwehr (AE)
to catch fire [kætʃ 'faɪə] Feuer
fangen
⟨**fire-scarred**⟩ ['faɪəˌskɑːd] vom
Feuer gezeichnet, verbrannt
firework ['faɪəwɜːk] Feuerwerk
firm [fɜːm] Firma
firm(ly) ['fɜːm(lɪ)] fest
first [fɜːst] erste/r/s; zuerst
at first [ət 'fɜːst] zuerst, zunächst
first light ['fɜːst 'laɪt]
Morgengrauen, Tagesanbruch
the first one [ðə 'fɜːst wʌn] der/
die/das Erste
⟨'first-past-the-post'-system⟩
[ˌfɜːst pɑːst ðə 'pəʊst ˌsɪstəm]
Name für das britische
Mehrheitswahlrecht (wörtlich:
erster, der (in einem Rennen) am
(Ziel-) Pfosten vorbeizieht)
firstly ['fɜːstlɪ] erstens
fish [fɪʃ] Fisch
fish and chip shop [fɪʃn 'tʃɪp ˌʃɒp]
Imbissstube (hauptsächlich für
Fisch und Pommes frites)

to **fish** [fɪʃ] angeln, fischen
fishing lake ['fɪʃɪŋ ˌleɪk] Angelsee,
Fischteich
fist [fɪst] Faust
⟨to **fit**⟩ [fɪt] (hinein) passen
fit [fɪt] fit, in Form, gesund
to stay fit [steɪ 'fɪt] fit/in Form/
gesund bleiben
fitness ['fɪtnɪs] Fitness
five [faɪv] fünf
Fives [faɪvz] *traditionelles*
britisches Ballspiel (vergleichbar
mit Squash) in Ordnung bringen
⟨to **fix**⟩ [fɪks] Fahne, Flagge
⟨**flag**⟩ [flæg] Fahne, Flagge
⟨flag of truce⟩ [ˌflæg_əv 'truːs]
(weiße) Flagge als Friedensangebot
flame [fleɪm] Flamme
⟨**flash**⟩ [flæʃ] protzig
flat [flæt] Wohnung
flat [flæt] flach
⟨flat tyre⟩ [flæt 'taɪə] platter
Reifen, Platten
to **flee*** [fliː] fliehen
⟨**fleet**⟩ [fliːt] Flotte
flight [flaɪt] Flug, Ballonfahrt
to **float** [fləʊt] schweben; treiben
flood [flʌd] Flut, Überschwemmung
flooding ['flʌdɪŋ] Überflutung
floor [flɔː] Fußboden
flop [flɒp] Flop, Reinfall, Misserfolg
⟨to **flourish**⟩ ['flʌrɪʃ] gedeihen,
blühen
flower ['flaʊə] Blume
flu [fluː] Grippe
⟨**fluent**⟩ ['fluːənt] flüssig
⟨to **flush** the loo⟩ [ˌflʌʃ ðə 'luː] das
Klo spülen
flute [fluːt] Querflöte
Fly-tying ['flaɪˌtaɪɪŋ]
Kunstfliegenbinden
(Fliegenfischerei)
to **fly*** [flaɪ] fliegen
to fly around [flaɪˌə'raʊnd]
herumfliegen
⟨**focus**⟩ ['fəʊkəs] Brennpunkt;
Mittelpunkt
fog [fɒg] Nebel
foggy ['fɒgɪ] neb(e)lig
⟨**folks**⟩ [fəʊks] Leute *(ugs.) (pl.)*
to **follow** ['fɒləʊ] folgen
to follow someone's example
[ˌfɒləʊ ˌsʌmwʌnz ɪg'zɑːmpl] dem
Beispiel von jdm. folgen
°**following** order ['fɒləʊɪŋ ˌɔːdə]
folgende Anordnung
food [fuːd] Essen
fast food ['fɑːst fuːd]
Schnellgericht
food bank [fuːd bæŋk]
Sammelstelle für Essensspenden
(AE)
foot [fʊt] Fuß
on foot [ɒn 'fʊt] zu Fuß
football ['fʊtbɔːl] Fußball,
Fußballspiel
footballer ['fʊtbɔːlə] Fußballer/in
⟨**footstep**⟩ ['fʊtstep] Schritt

for [fɔː] für; denn; seit *(einer*
Zeitdauer)
for a while [fər_ə 'waɪl] für eine
Weile, eine Zeit lang
⟨For Christ's sake!⟩ [fə ˌkraɪsts
'seɪk] Um Himmels Willen! *(ugs.)*
for instance [fər_'ɪnstəns] zum
Beispiel
for sale [fə 'seɪl] zu verkaufen
to care for ['keə fə] sich kümmern
um
to look for ['lʊk fə] suchen
to pay for ['peɪ fə] (be-) zahlen
to **force** [fɔːs] zwingen; vertreiben
⟨**forecast**⟩ ['fɔːkɑːst] (Wetter-)
Vorhersage
foreign ['fɒrən] fremd, ausländisch
⟨Foreign Secretary⟩ [ˌfɒrən
'sekrətrɪ] Außenminister/in
⟨**foreigner**⟩ ['fɒrɪnə] Ausländer/in
forest ['fɒrɪst] Wald
Black Forest [ˌblæk 'fɒrɪst]
Schwarzwald
to**revermore** [fəˌrevəmɔː] für immer,
für alle Zeiten
back and **forward** [ˌbæk_ənd 'fɔːwəd]
vor und zurück, hin und her
to **forget*** [fə'get] vergessen
to **forgive*** [fə'gɪv, fə'geɪv, fə'gɪvn]
vergeben, verzeihen
form [fɔːm] Form
to **form** [fɔːm] formen, bilden,
gründen
⟨**former**⟩ ['fɔːmə] ehemalige/r/s
⟨back and **forth**⟩ [ˌbæk_ənd 'fɔːθ]
hin und her
forty ['fɔːtɪ] vierzig
°to put **forward** [pʊt 'fɔːwəd]
vorbringen, vorschlagen
⟨from (this day) forward⟩
['fɔːwəd] von (nun) an
to look forward to [lʊk 'fɔːwəd tə]
sich freuen auf
fossil ['fɒsl] versteinert; fossile/r/s
⟨**foster** (home)⟩ ['fɒstə] Pflege-
⟨to **found**⟩ [faʊnd] gründen
⟨**founder**⟩ ['faʊndə] Gründer/in
four [fɔː] vier
fourteen [ˌfɔː'tiːn] vierzehn
⟨**fowl**⟩ [faʊl] Huhn, Geflügel
fox [fɒks] Fuchs
freak [friːk] Enthusiast, Fan
to **free** [friː] befreien
free [friː] frei
free of charge [ˌfriː_əv 'tʃɑːdʒ]
kostenlos
free time [friː 'taɪm] Freizeit
freedom ['friːdəm] Freiheit
⟨**freelance**⟩ ['friːlɑːns] freiberuflich
freeman ['friːmən] freier Mensch
freeway ['friːweɪ] Autobahn *(AE)*
to **freeze*** [friːz] (ge)frieren;
erstarren
freezer ['friːzə] Tiefkühltruhe
French [frentʃ] Französisch,
französisch
french fries *(AE)* ['frentʃ fraɪz]
Pommes frites

frequent(*ly*) ['friːkwənt(lɪ)] häufig
fresh [freʃ] frisch
friction ['frɪkʃn] Reibung
Friday ['fraɪdɪ] Freitag
Good Friday [ˌgʊd 'fraɪdeɪ]
Karfreitag
fridge [frɪdʒ] Kühlschrank
friend [frend] Freund/in
friendly ['frendlɪ] freundlich
environmentally friendly
[ɪnˌvaɪərn'mentəlɪ 'frendlɪ]
umweltfreundlich
friendship ['frendʃɪp] Freundschaft
to **frighten** ['fraɪtn] erschrecken,
Angst einjagen
frightening ['fraɪtnɪŋ]
furchterregend
⟨**frightful** guff⟩ [ˌfraɪtfəl 'gʌf]
ziemlicher Quark *(ugs.)*
from [frɒm] aus, von; vor
⟨from (this day) forward⟩
['fɔːwəd] von (nun) an
it makes a change from …
[tʃeɪndʒ] das ist mal was anderes
als …
°**front page** [frʌnt 'peɪdʒ] erste Seite,
Titelseite
°**at the front** [ət ðə 'frʌnt] vorne
⟨front cover⟩ [frʌnt 'kʌvə]
Titelseite *(Zeitschrift)*
front
front door [frʌnt 'dɔː] Haustür
front garden [frʌnt 'gɑːdn] Garten
vor dem Haus
in front of [ɪn 'frʌnt_əv] vor
⟨to **frown**⟩ [fraʊn] die Stirn runzeln,
sorgenvoll gucken
fruit [fruːt] Obst
fuel [fjʊəl] Treib-, Brenn-, Kraftstoff
full [fʊl] voll
full sentence [fʊl 'sentəns] ganzer
Satz
fun [fʌn] Spaß, Freude
Chemistry for Fun ['kemɪstrɪ fə
'fʌn] Spaß mit Chemie
Have fun! [hæv 'fʌn] Viel Spaß!
it's fun [ɪts 'fʌn] es macht Spaß
°**function** ['fʌŋkʃn] Funktion
United Nations Children's **Fund**
[juːˌnaɪtɪd 'neɪʃnz tʃɪldrənz 'fʌnd]
UN Kinderhilfsorganisation
⟨**funnel** web (spider)⟩ ['fʌnl web
(ˌspaɪdə)] *australische Spinnenart*
funnily enough ['fʌnɪlɪ ɪ'nʌf]
komischerweise
funny ['fʌnɪ] lustig, komisch
fur [fɜː] Fell
furniture ['fɜːnɪtʃə] Möbel
further ['fɜːðə] weiter(e)
future ['fjuːtʃə] Zukunft

G

⟨Scottish **Gaelic**⟩ [ˌskɒtɪʃ 'geɪlɪk]
die schottische Form des Gälisch
game [geɪm] Spiel
game show ['geɪm ʃəʊ] Spielshow

gang [gæŋ] Gang, Bande

gap [gæp] Lücke, Loch; Zahnlücke

Gappy Mole [ˌgæpɪ ˈməʊl] *Spitzname für Adrian Mole*

garage [ˈgærɑːdʒ] Garage; Tankstelle, Autowerkstatt

garbage [ˈgɑːbɪdʒ] Müll, Abfall *(AE)* garbage can [ˈgɑːbɪdʒ ˌkæn] Müll-, Abfalleimer *(AE)*

garden [ˈgɑːdn] Garten back garden [ˈbæk ˌgɑːdn] Garten hinter dem Haus front garden [ˈfrʌnt ˌgɑːdn] Garten vor dem Haus

gardener [ˈgɑːdnə] Gärtner/in

gas [gæs] Gas CFC gases *(chlorofluorocarbons)* [siː ˌef ˈsiː ˈgæsɪz, ˌklɒrəʊfluərəˈkɑːbənz] FCKW-Gase (Fluorchlorkohlenwasser-stoff-Gase) natural gas [ˌnætʃrəl ˈgæs] Erdgas

°to **gather** [ˈgæðə] sammeln

⟨**gauche**⟩ [gəʊʃ] linkisch

G'day! [gəˈdaɪ] Hallo, Tag! *(austral.)*

gear [gɪə] Zeug(s), Sachen *(ugs.)*

⟨Brigadier **General**⟩ [ˈbrɪgəˌdɪə ˈdʒenərəl] Brigadegeneral

°**general** [ˈdʒenərəl] allgemein °in general [ɪn ˈdʒenrl] im Allgemeinen General Certificate of Secondary Education *(GCSE)* [ˈdʒenərəl səˈtɪfɪkət əv ˈsekəndəri ˌedjuːˈkeɪʃn] *britisches Äquivalent der Mittleren Reife*; GCSE-Prüfung ⟨The General Election⟩ [ˌdʒenərəl ɪˈlekʃn] Parlamentswahlen

generation [ˌdʒenəˈreɪʃn] Generation

°**genre** [ˈʒɑ̃ːŋrə] Gattung, Genre

gentleman/men [ˈdʒentlmən/men] Herr/Herren

⟨**gently**⟩ [ˈdʒentli] sanft, behutsam

Geography [dʒɪˈɒgrəfi] Geografie, Erdkunde

⟨**geologist**⟩ [dʒɪˈɒlədʒɪst] Geologe, Geologin

⟨**germ**⟩ [dʒɜːm] Keim, Krankheitserreger

German [ˈdʒɜːmən] Deutsche/r; deutsch; Deutsch

°**gerund** [ˈdʒerənd] Gerundium

⟨**gesture**⟩ [ˈdʒestʃə] Geste

to **get*** [get] bekommen, holen; werden (to get) light [laɪt] hell (werden) to get *(from ... to)* [get] von ... nach ... gehen, kommen to get about [get əˈbaʊt] herumkommen; umherstreifen to get along with s.o. [get əˈlɒŋ wɪð] mit jdm. auskommen/ zurechtkommen to get around [get əˈraʊnd] herumkommen to get dressed [get ˈdrest] sich anziehen

to get fed up with [get ˌfed ˈʌp wɪð] leid werden, zu viel werden, die Nase voll haben von to get home [get ˈhəʊm] nach Hause kommen ⟨to get kicked in the pants⟩ [get ˈkɪkt ɪn ðə ˈpænts] einen Tritt in den Hintern bekommen *(ugs.)* to get lost [get ˈlɒst] sich verlaufen to get married [get ˈmærɪd] heiraten to get mugged [get ˈmʌgd] *auf offener Straße überfallen und ausgeraubt werden* to get off the bus [get ˈɒf] aussteigen to get on s.o.'s nerves [get ˈɒn ... ˈnɜːvz] jdm. auf die Nerven gehen to get on the bus [get ˈɒn] einsteigen ⟨to get one's kicks from⟩ [ˈget wʌnz ˈkɪks frɒm] seinen Spaß haben an to get oneself into [ˌget wʌnˌself ˈɪntə] selbst in etwas geraten/bringen to get out (of a car) [get ˈaʊt] aussteigen to get ready [get ˈredɪ] sich bereitmachen, sich vorbereiten °to get rid of s.o./s.th. [get ˈrɪd ɒv] jdn./etwas loswerden to get s.o. doing s.th. [get] jdn. dazu bringen, etwas zu tun to get s.th. done [get ˈdʌn] etw. schaffen/etw. fertigstellen to get shot at [get ˈʃɒt æt] beschossen werden to get stuck [get ˈstʌk] stecken bleiben ⟨to get through⟩ [get ˈθruː] ausgeben, durchbringen to get to [ˈget tə] erreichen, gelangen zu °to get together [get təˈgeðə] zusammenkommen to get up [get ˈʌp] aufstehen; stärker werden ⟨to get upset⟩ [get ʌpˈset] die Fassung verlieren, bestürzt sein über to get used to [get ˈjuːst tʊ] sich gewöhnen an

ghost [gəʊst] Geist, Gespenst

⟨**ghostly gum = Ghost gum**⟩ [ˌgəʊstli ˈgʌm] *Eukalyptusbaumart*

giant [ˈdʒaɪənt] Gigant, Riese

giant [ˈdʒaɪənt] gigantisch, riesengroß, riesig, Riesen-

⟨**gift**⟩ [gɪft] Gabe, Geschenk

gimmick [ˈgɪmɪk] Gag, Gimmick

girl [gɜːl] Mädchen

girlfriend [ˈgɜːlfrend] Freundin

°**gist** [dʒɪst] das Wesentliche

to **give*** [gɪv] geben to give orders [gɪv ˈɔːdəz] Befehle erteilen, Anweisungen geben

°to give a talk [gɪv ə ˈtɔːk] einen Vortrag/eine Rede halten to give away [ˌgɪv əˈweɪ] weggeben, verschenken to give in to s.o. [gɪv ˈɪn tə] nachgeben ⟨to give s.o. the benefit of the doubt⟩ [...ðə ˈbenɪfɪt əv ðə ˈdaʊt] im Zweifelsfall zu jdns. Gunsten entscheiden to give up [ˌgɪv ˈʌp] aufgeben

glad [glæd] froh

⟨**glamorous**⟩ [ˈglæmərəs] glamourös

glass [glɑːs] Glas clear glass [klɪə ˈglɑːs] Weißglas

glasses *(pl.)* [ˈglɑːsɪz] (eine) Brille

computer **glitch** [kəmˈpjuːtə ˈglɪtʃ] Computer-Funktionsstörung

global warming [ˌgləʊbl ˈwɔːmɪŋ] globale (Erd-) Erwärmung, Erwärmung der Erdatmosphäre

⟨**glorious**⟩ [ˈglɔːrɪəs] herrlich, fantastisch ⟨The Glorious Revolution⟩ [ˌglɔːrɪəs ˌrevəˈluːʃn] Die Glorreiche Revolution

⟨to **glue**⟩ [gluː] kleben, festkleben

⟨**go-kart**⟩ [ˈgəʊkɑːt] Gokart Go Kart Rally Cross [ˈgəʊ kɑːt ˌrælɪ ˈkrɒs] "Gokart Rally Cross" ⟨in one go⟩ [ɪn ˌwʌn ˈgəʊ] auf einmal

to **go*** [gəʊ] gehen, fahren s.th. is going on [ɪz ˌgəʊɪŋ ˈɒn] etwas ist los, passiert to go abroad [gəʊ əˈbrɔːd] ins Ausland fahren to go after s.o. [gəʊ ˈɑːftə] jdm. folgen, jdn. verfolgen °to go back in time [gəʊ ˌbæk ɪn ˈtaɪm] in der Zeit zurückgehen to go camping [ˌgəʊ ˈkæmpɪŋ] zum Camping/Zelten fahren to go crazy [gəʊ ˈkreɪzɪ] verrückt werden ⟨to go down in history⟩ [gəʊ ˌdaʊn ɪn ˈhɪstərɪ] in die Geschichte eingehen to go down the street [gəʊ ˈdaʊn] die Straße entlang gehen to go downstairs [gəʊ daʊnˈsteəz] die Treppe heruntergehen to go in [gəʊ ˈɪn] hineingehen to go off with [gəʊ ˈɒf wɪð] weggehen mit to go on [gəʊ ˈɒn] weitermachen, weiterreden to go on-line [gəʊ ˈɒnlaɪn] online gehen, sich ins Computernetz einschalten to go out of the door [gəʊ ˈaʊt əv ðə ˈdɔː] das Haus verlassen to go shopping [gəʊ ˈʃɒpɪŋ] einkaufen gehen to go straight to [gəʊ ˈstreɪt] direkt gehen zu/in to go swimming [gəʊ ˈswɪmɪŋ] schwimmen gehen

⟨to go through s.th.⟩ [gəʊ 'θruː]
etwas durchmachen
to go to ['gəʊ tə] gehen zu, gehen
nach
°to go to sleep [ˌgəʊ tə 'sliːp]
einschlafen
to go upstairs [gəʊ ʌp'steəz] die
Treppe hinaufgehen
to go with ['gəʊ wɪð]
zusammenpassen
to go wrong [gəʊ 'rɒŋ] schief
gehen
goal [gəʊl] Tor
God [gɒd] Gott
gold [gəʊld] Gold
gold rush ['gəʊld rʌʃ] Goldrausch
⟨**gold-bearing**⟩ ['gəʊld beərɪŋ]
goldhaltig
golf [gɒlf] Golf
golf course ['gɒlf ˌkɔːs] Golfplatz
⟨**Golly!**⟩ ['gɒlɪ] Menschenskind!
(ugs.)
Good Friday [ˌgʊd 'fraɪdeɪ]
Karfreitag
good [gʊd] gut
Good lord [gʊd 'lɔːd] Großer Gott
Good morning [ˌgʊd 'mɔːnɪŋ]
Guten Morgen
good-looking [gʊd 'lʊkɪŋ] gut
aussehend
to be good at s.th. [bɪ 'gʊd ət]
etwas gut können
Goodbye [gʊd'baɪ] Auf Wiedersehen
goody-goody ['gʊdɪ ˌgʊdɪ]
"Tugendlamm", Musterkind (ugs.)
⟨**gorilla**⟩ [gə'rɪlə] Gorilla
⟨**Gosh!**⟩ [gɒʃ] Mensch! (ugs.)
⟨**gospel**⟩ ['gɒspl] Gospel
have **got** [gɒt] haben
government ['gʌvənmənt]
Regierung; Kommunal-,
Stadtverwaltung
⟨**governor**⟩ ['gʌvənə] Gouverneur
⟨(school) governor⟩ [(ˌskuːl)
'gʌvənə] Mitglied des Schulbeirats
to **grab** [græb] (er)greifen, packen,
schnappen
⟨**grace**⟩ [greɪs] Würde
grade [greɪd] (Schul-) Note (AE)
gradual(ly) ['grædʒʊəl(ɪ)]
allmählich, nach und nach
graffiti [grə'fiːtɪ] Graffiti
grammar ['græmə] Grammatik
gran [græn] Oma, Omi
grandfather ['grænˌfɑːðə] Großvater
grandma ['grænmɑː] Großmutter
grandmother ['grænˌmʌðə]
Großmutter
Grandpa ['grænpɑː] Großvater
grandparents ['grænˌpeərənts]
Großeltern
Granny ['grænɪ] Oma
grant [grɑːnt] Zuschuss,
Studienhilfe
grass [grɑːs] Gras
⟨**grassland**⟩ ['grɑːslænd] Grasland
grave [greɪv] Grab
great [greɪt] groß; toll, prima

⟨a great deal of difference⟩
[ə ˌgreɪt ˌdiːl əv 'dɪfrens] ein großer
Unterschied
great-great-great- grandfather
['greɪt 'greɪt 'greɪt 'grændˌfɑːðə]
Ur-Ur-Ur-Großvater
Greek [griːk] Grieche/Griechin,
griechisch, Griechisch
green [griːn] grün
grey [greɪ] grau
⟨**greyish**⟩ ['greɪɪʃ] gräulich
grid [grɪd] Raster
grill [grɪl] Grill
grin [grɪn] Grinsen
to **grin** [grɪn] grinsen
grizzly ['grɪzlɪ] Grizzly
⟨**groceries**⟩ ['grəʊsərɪz]
Lebensmittel
gross [grəʊs] widerlich (AE)
ground [graʊnd] Boden
sports ground ['spɔːts graʊnd]
Sportplatz/-gelände
to fall to the ground [ˌfɔːl tə
ðə 'graʊnd] hinfallen
group [gruːp] Gruppe
drama group ['drɑːmə gruːp]
Theatergruppe
pressure group ['preʃə ˌgruːp]
Interessenverband, der z.B. auf
die Regierung Druck auszuüben
sucht
to **grow*** [grəʊ] anbauen; wachsen
to grow up [grəʊ 'ʌp] aufwachsen;
erwachsen werden
to have a **guess** [hæv ə 'ges] raten
I **guess** [ges] wohl (AE)
to guess [ges] raten
guest [gest] Gast
⟨frightful **guff**⟩ [ˌfraɪtfəl 'gʌf]
ziemlicher Quark (ugs.)
guide [gaɪd] Führer/in
guide book ['gaɪd bʊk]
Reiseführer, Stadtführer
TV guide [tiː'viː ˌgaɪd]
Fernsehzeitschrift,
Fernsehprogramm
guided tour [ˌgaɪdɪd 'tʊə] Führung
guideline ['gaɪdlaɪn] Richtlinie
Guides [gaɪdz] Pfadfinderorganisation für Mädchen
to feel **guilty** [fiːl 'gɪltɪ] sich schuldig
fühlen; ein schlechtes Gewissen
haben
guitar [gɪ'tɑː] Gitarre
gum tree ['gʌm triː]
Eukalyptusbaum (ugs.)
⟨ghostly gum = Ghost gum⟩
[ˌgəʊstlɪ 'gʌm]
Eukalyptusbaumart
gun [gʌn] Gewehr, Pistole
⟨**gunman**⟩ ['gʌnmən]
Pistolenschütze
⟨to hate s.o.'s **guts**⟩ [heɪt …'gʌts]
jdn. sehr hassen (ugs.)
⟨a lot of guts⟩ [ə ˌlɒt əv 'gʌts]
Mumm, Mut (ugs.)
guy [gaɪ] Typ (ugs.); Mann,
männliche Person (ugs.)

Guy Fawkes' Night [ˌgaɪ 'fɔːks
naɪt] Guy Fawkes' Nacht
guys [gaɪz] Leute (ugs.)
gym [dʒɪm] Abk. für Turnhalle
gymnasium [dʒɪm'neɪzjəm]
Turnhalle

H

°viewing **habits** ['vjuːɪŋ ˌhæbɪts]
Sehgewohnheiten
hacker ['hækə] Hacker/in
had better [ˌhæd 'betə] sollte besser
(etwas tun)
⟨you've had it⟩ [juːv 'hæd ɪt] du
bist erledigt (ugs.)
hair [heə] Haar
hair style ['heə ˌstaɪl] Frisur
haircut ['heəkʌt] Haarschnitt, Frisur
pudding-bowl haircut ['pʊdɪŋbəʊl
'heəkʌt] "Pilzkopf"-Frisur
half [hɑːf] halb
at half past nine [ət hɑːf pɑːst
'naɪn] um halb zehn
hall [hɔːl] Flur, Diele; Saal, Aula
assembly hall [ə'semblɪ ˌhɔːl] Aula
drama hall ['drɑːmə hɔːl]
Bühnensaal
Hallowe'en [ˌhæləʊ'iːn] Tag vor
Allerheiligen
ham [hæm] Schinken
hamburger ['hæmbɜːgə] Hamburger
to **hammer** ['hæmə] hämmern
hamster ['hæmstə] Hamster
hand [hænd] Hand
⟨Hands off!⟩ [ˌhændz 'ɒf] Finger
weg!
⟨at the hands of⟩ [ət ðə 'hændz
əv] durch
on the other hand [ɒn ði 'ʌðə
ˌhænd] andererseits
to hold hands ['həʊld 'hændz] sich
an der Hand halten
to put up one's hand [ˌpʊt ʌp wʌnz
'hænd] die Hand heben
to **hand** out [hænd 'aʊt] austeilen,
verteilen
⟨**handkerchief**⟩ ['hæŋkətʃɪf]
Taschentuch
handle ['hændl] Griff
handsome ['hænsəm] gut aussehend,
hübsch
°**handwriting** ['hændˌraɪtɪŋ]
Handschrift
hang* [hæŋ] hängen
to hang around [hæŋ ə'raʊnd]
herumhängen, -lungern
to hang out [hæŋ 'aʊt] sich
aufhalten/herumtreiben
Hannukah [hæ'nuːkə] Chanukka
(jüd. Fest im Dez.) (hebr.:
hanukka = Einweihung)
to **happen** ['hæpn] passieren,
geschehen
happiness ['hæpɪnɪs] Glück,
Zufriedenheit, Fröhlichkeit
happy ['hæpɪ] glücklich

harbor ['hɑːbə] Hafen *(AE)*
harbour ['hɑːbə] Hafen
hard [hɑːd] angestrengt, intensiv;
hart; schwer
hard rock [hɑːd 'rɒk] Rockmusik
⟨to be hard on⟩ [biː 'hɑːd ɒn]
streng sein mit
has got [hæz 'gɒt] hat
⟨**hassle**⟩ ['hæsl] Ärger, Theater
hat [hæt] Hut
to **hate** [heɪt] hassen, nicht mögen
⟨to hate s.o.'s guts⟩ [heɪt …'gʌts]
jdn. sehr hassen *(ugs.)*
⟨**hatred**⟩ ['heɪtrɪd] Hass
haunted walk [ˌhɔːntɪd 'wɔːk] *ein
Rundgang, bei dem es spukt*
to **have*** [hæv] haben
Have fun! [hæv 'fʌn] Viel Spaß!
have got [hæv 'gɒt] haben
to have a bath [hæv ə 'bɑːθ] ein
Bad nehmen, baden
to have a guess [ˌhæv ə 'ges] raten
to have a look [ˌhæv ə 'lʊk] sich
etwas anschauen
to have a sense of humour [sens əv
'hjuːmə] (einen Sinn für) Humor
besitzen
to have an argument [ˌhæv
ən ˈɑːgjʊmənt] sich streiten
to have an influence on [ˌhæv
ən ˈɪnflʊəns ɒn] beeinflussen
⟨to have done with⟩ [hæv 'dʌn
wɪð] mit etwas fertig sein
to have lunch [hæv 'lʌntʃ] zu
Mittag essen
to have room for [hæv 'ruːm fɔː]
Platz haben für
to have s.th. done [ˌhæv … 'dʌn]
etwas machen lassen
⟨to have s.th. built⟩ [hæv 'bɪlt]
etwas bauen/errichten lassen
to have to [ˈhæv tə] müssen
he [hiː] er
he may be [meɪ] vielleicht ist er
head [hed] Kopf
⟨to **head**⟩ [hed] gehen, fahren
headache ['hedeɪk] Kopfschmerzen
heading ['hedɪŋ] Überschrift
headline ['hedlaɪn] Schlagzeile
headteacher [ˌhed'tiːtʃə]
Schulleiter/in
°**headword** ['hedwɜːd] Stichwort
healer ['hiːlə] Heiler/in
health [helθ] Gesundheit
healthy ['helθɪ] gesund
⟨**heap** of ruins⟩ [ˌhiːp əv 'ruːɪnz] ein
Haufen Trümmer/Überreste
to **hear*** [hɪə] hören
heart [hɑːt] Herz
heart attack ['hɑːt ə ˌtæk]
Herzanfall, -infarkt
⟨my heart was in my mouth⟩ [maɪ
'hɑːt wəz ɪn maɪ 'maʊθ] mir
schlug das Herz bis zum Hals
°to learn s.th. by heart [ˌlɜːn baɪ
'hɑːt] etwas auswendig lernen
heat [hiːt] Hitze, Wärme
heaven ['hevn] Himmel

⟨**heavens** above⟩ [ˌhevənz ə'bʌv]
Meine Güte!, Du lieber Himmel!
(ugs.)
heavy ['hevɪ] schwer
heavy metal band [ˌhevɪ 'metəl
bænd] Heavy Metal Band
(Hardrock)
hedge [hedʒ] Hecke
⟨**hell**⟩ [hel] Hölle
Hello [hə'ləʊ] Hallo, Guten Tag
helmet ['helmɪt] Helm
°**help** [help] Hilfe
to **help** [help] helfen
It might help if … [ɪt ˌmaɪt 'help ɪf]
Es könnte helfen, wenn …
helpful ['helpfəl] hilfreich
helpless ['helplɪs] hilflos
battery **hen** ['bætərɪ ˌhen]
Batteriehenne
her [hɜː] ihr/ihre; ihr/sie
here [hɪə] hier
Here it is. ['hɪər ɪt ˌɪz]
Bitte schön.
Here you are. ['hɪə juˌ ɑː]
Bitte sehr.
⟨**heritage** centre⟩ ['herɪtɪdʒ ˌsentə]
*(volkskundliches)
Besucherzentrum/Museum*
hero ['hɪərəʊ] Held
heroine ['herəʊɪn] °Heldin;
⟨Hauptfigur⟩
herself [hɜː'self] (sie) sich (selbst);
selbst
Hi! [haɪ] Hallo! *(zu Freunden)*
to **hide*** [haɪd] verstecken
⟨**hidey-hole**⟩ ['haɪdɪhəʊl] Versteck,
Schlupfloch
⟨**hiding** place⟩ ['haɪdɪŋ ˌpleɪs]
Versteck
high [haɪ] hoch
highway ['haɪweɪ] Landstraße *(AE)*
hill [hɪl] Hügel, Berg
him [hɪm] ihm/ihn
himself [hɪm'self] (er) sich (selbst);
selbst
Hindu ['hɪnduː] Hindu, hinduistisch
to **hire** ['haɪə] leihen, mieten
skate hire ['skeɪt ˌhaɪə]
Schlittschuhverleih
his [hɪz] sein/seine
Hispanic [hɪ'spænɪk] hispanisch,
Person aus einem
spanischsprachigen Land (z. B.
Mexiko)
to **hiss** [hɪs] zischen
historic [hɪ'stɒrɪk] historisch
°**historical** [hɪ'stɒrɪkl] historisch,
geschichts-
History ['hɪstərɪ] Geschichte
⟨to go down in history⟩ [gəʊ ˌdaʊn
ɪn 'hɪstərɪ] in die Geschichte
eingehen
hit [hɪt] Hit, Erfolg
to **hit*** [hɪt] (eine Taste) drücken;
schlagen; treffen
to hit the roof [hɪt ðə 'ruːf] an die
Decke gehen
hobby ['hɒbɪ] Hobby

hold* [həʊld] halten
to hold (*a debate*) [həʊld]
diskutieren, debattieren
to hold hands [həʊld 'hændz] sich
an der Hand halten
to hold on [həʊld ˌɒn] warten
⟨to hold oneself⟩ [həʊld] sich
würdevoll verhalten
°to hold up [həʊld ˌʌp]
hochhalten
hole [həʊl] Loch
holiday ['hɒlɪdeɪ] Urlaub
Bank Holiday [ˌbæŋk 'hɒlɪdeɪ]
öffentlicher Feiertag
holiday maker ['hɒlədɪ ˌmeɪkə]
Urlauber/in
on holiday [ɒn 'hɒlɪdeɪ] im Urlaub
to **holiday** ['hɒlədeɪ] Urlaub/Ferien
machen
holidays ['hɒlɪdeɪz] Ferien
holy ['həʊlɪ] heilig
home [həʊm] Zuhause, Heim
°(home) comforts [həʊm 'kʌmfəts]
Annehmlichkeiten (eines
Zuhauses)
at home [ət 'həʊm] zu Hause
children's home [ˌtʃɪldrənz 'həʊm]
Kinderheim
Home Sweet Home ['həʊm ˌswiːt
'həʊm] "Trautes Heim, Glück
allein" *(Sprichwort)*
home-made [ˌhəʊm 'meɪd] selbst
hergestellt
°home town ['həʊm taʊn]
Heimatstadt
to come home [kʌm 'həʊm] nach
Hause kommen
to get home [get 'həʊm] nach
Hause kommen
homeland ['həʊmlənd]
Heimat(land)
homeless ['həʊmlɪs] obdachlos
the **homeless** ['həʊmlɪs] Heimat-/
Obdachlose
homeroom ['həʊmruːm] Zimmer
des Klassenlehrers/-lehrerin
to be **homesick** [biː 'həʊmsɪk]
Heimweh haben
homework ['həʊmwɜːk]
Hausaufgaben
to do homework [du 'həʊmwɜːk]
Hausaufgaben machen
honest ['ɒnɪst] ehrlich, aufrichtig
honesty ['ɒnəstɪ] Ehrlichkeit
honey ['hʌnɪ] Honig; Schatz,
Schätzchen *(AE)*
honor ['ɒnə] Ehre *(AE)*
hope [həʊp] Hoffnung
in hope of [ɪn 'həʊp əv] in der
Hoffnung auf
⟨Some hopes!⟩ ['sʌm 'həʊps] Schön
wär's! *(ugs.)*
to **hope** [həʊp] hoffen
horrible ['hɒrɪbl] schrecklich,
fürchterlich
horrific [hɒ'rɪfɪk] entsetzlich,
schrecklich
horror ['hɒrə] Horror

horse [hɔ:s] Pferd
  on horse-back [ɒn 'hɔ:sbæk] zu
  Pferd
Horticulture ['hɔ:tɪ,kʌltʃə]
  Gartenbau
hospital ['hɒspɪtl] Krankenhaus
host [həʊst] Gastgeber/in
⟨**hostel**⟩ ['hɒstl] Wohnheim,
  Unterkunft
hot ['hɒt] heiß
  hot air balloon [hɒt‿eə bə'lu:n]
  Heißluftballon
hotel [həʊ'tel] Hotel
⟨**to hound**⟩ [haʊnd] verfolgen, Jagd
  machen auf
hour ['aʊə] Stunde
house [haʊs] Haus
  coffee house ['kɒfɪ ,haʊs] Café
  ⟨The House of Commons⟩ [,haʊs‿
  əv 'kɒmənz] Unterhaus (GB)
  ⟨The House of Lords⟩ [,haʊs‿əv
  'lɔ:dz] Oberhaus (GB)
houschusband ['haʊs,hʌzbənd]
  Hausmann
  ⟨The **Houses** of Parliament⟩
  [,haʊzɪz‿əv 'pɑ:ləmənt] das
  Parlament(-sgebäude) (GB)
housewife ['haʊswaɪf] Hausfrau
housework ['haʊsw3:k] Hausarbeit
how [haʊ] wie
  how many [haʊ 'menɪ] wie viele
  how much [haʊ 'mʌtʃ] wie viel
  ⟨How you doing?⟩ [,haʊ ju:
  'du:ɪŋ] Wie geht's dir? (ugs.) (AE)
  no matter how [nəʊ ,mætə 'haʊ]
  egal wie
however [haʊ'evə] jedoch, aber
huge [hju:dʒ] riesig, gewaltig
human ['hju:mən] menschlich
  human being [,hju:mən 'bi:ɪŋ]
  Mensch, menschliches Wesen
  human rights organization
  [,hju:mən 'raɪts ,ɔ:gənaɪ'zeɪʃn]
  Organisation für Menschenrechte
humming ['hʌmɪŋ] summend,
  brausend, surrend
humorous ['hju:mərəs] humorvoll,
  lustig, komisch
to have a sense of **humour** [sens‿əv
  'hjʊmə] (einen Sinn für) Humor
  besitzen
humped ['hʌmpt] bucklig
hundred ['hʌndrəd] Hundert
hunger ['hʌŋgə] Hunger
hungry ['hʌŋgrɪ] hungrig
to **hunt** [hʌnt] jagen
Hurray! [hʊ'reɪ] Hurra!
⟨**hurricane**⟩ ['hʌrɪkən] Hurrikan,
  Sturm
in a **hurry** [,ɪn‿ə 'hʌrɪ] in Eile
to **hurry** ['hʌrɪ] sich beeilen
  to hurry (up) [hʌrɪ 'ʌp] sich
  beeilen
to **hurt*** [h3:t] schmerzen, weh tun
husband ['hʌzbənd] Ehemann
hydro-electric ['haɪdrəʊ] wasser-,
  hydro-

I

I [aɪ] ich
  I'd like [aɪd 'laɪk] Ich möchte.../
  hätte gern...
ice [aɪs] Eis
  ice cream [,aɪs 'kri:m] (Speise-) Eis
  ice cream van ['aɪskri:m ,væn]
  Eiswagen
  ice-skating ['aɪs ,skeɪtɪŋ]
  Schlittschuhlaufen
  ice-stadium ['aɪs ,steɪdjəm]
  Eisstadion
  to ice-skate ['aɪsskeɪt]
  Schlittschuh laufen
iced tea [aɪs 'ti:] Eistee
icy ['aɪsɪ] eisig; vereist; gefroren
idea [aɪ'dɪə] Idee; Vorstellung
  no idea [,nəʊ‿aɪ'dɪə] keine
  Ahnung
°to **identify** [aɪ'dentɪfaɪ]
  identifizieren
idiot ['ɪdɪət] Idiot
if [ɪf] wenn; falls, ob
  even if ['i:vn‿,ɪf] auch wenn
  if at all [ɪf ət‿'ɔ:l] wenn überhaupt
  If I were you ... [ɪf‿,aɪ wə 'ju:] An
  deiner Stelle ...
  °if-clause ['ɪf klɔ:z] (Teil-) Satz mit
  "if"
  It might help if ... [ɪt ,maɪt 'help ɪf]
  Es könnte helfen, wenn ...
to **ignore** [ɪg'nɔ:] ignorieren
ill [ɪl] krank
illness ['ɪlnəs] Krankheit
°**illustration** [,ɪlə'streɪʃn] Abbildung,
  Illustration
image ['ɪmɪdʒ] Bild; Image
°**imaginary** [ɪ'mædʒɪnərɪ] imaginär,
  erfunden, vorgestellt
imagination [ɪ,mædʒɪ'neɪʃn]
  Vorstellungskraft, Fantasie
to **imagine** [ɪ'mædʒɪn] sich
  vorstellen (in der Fantasie)
immediately [ɪ'mi:djətlɪ] sofort,
  gleich
immigrant ['ɪmɪgrənt] Immigrant/
  in, Einwanderer/Einwanderin
to **immigrate** ['ɪmɪgreɪt]
  immigrieren, einwandern
immigration [,ɪmɪ'greɪʃn]
  Immigration, Einwanderung
°**imperative** [ɪm'perətɪv]
  Befehlsform
imperfect [ɪm'pɜ:fɪkt]
  unvollkommen
impolite ['ɪmpə,laɪt] unhöflich
⟨**importance**⟩ [ɪm'pɔ:tns]
  Bedeutung
important [ɪm'pɔ:tnt] wichtig
impossible [ɪm'pɒsəble] unmöglich
impression [ɪm'preʃn] Eindruck,
  Gefühl
⟨**imprisoned**⟩ [ɪm'prɪznd] gefangen
  gehalten, eingesperrt
to **improve** [ɪm'pru:v] verbessern,
  besser machen; besser werden
in [ɪn] in, auf

(to be) in business [ɪn 'bɪznɪs]
  laufen, funktionieren
in a hurry [,ɪn‿ə 'hʌrɪ] in Eile
in case [ɪn 'keɪs] falls, für den Fall,
  dass
in fact [ɪn 'fækt] eigentlich,
  tatsächlich
in favour of ['feɪvə] für (etwas)
in front of [ɪn 'frʌnt‿əv] vor
°in general [ɪn 'dʒenərl] im
  Allgemeinen
in hope of [ɪn 'həʊp‿əv] in der
  Hoffnung auf
in love with [ɪn 'lʌv wɪð] verliebt
  (sein)
in my opinion [ɪn 'maɪ ə,pɪnjən]
  meiner Meinung nach
⟨in one go⟩ [ɪn ,wʌn 'gəʊ] auf
  einmal
in order to [ɪn‿'ɔ:də tə] um ... zu
in progress [ɪn 'prəʊgres] im Gange
⟨in remission⟩ [ɪn rɪ'mɪʃn]
  Remission, (vorübergehender
  Krankheitsstillstand)
in support of [sə'pɔ:t] zur/als
  Unterstützung
in the country [ɪn ðə 'kʌntrɪ] auf
  dem Lande
⟨in the meantime⟩ [ɪn ðə
  'mi:ntaɪm] in der Zwischenzeit
in the morning [ɪn ðə 'mɔ:nɪŋ] am
  Morgen, vormittags
⟨in the nude⟩ [ɪn ðə 'nju:d] nackt
in the playground [ɪn ðə
  'pleɪgraʊnd] auf dem Schulhof
°in turn [ɪn 'tɜ:n] der Reihe nach
°in turns [ɪn 'tɜ:nz] abwechselnd
involved (in) [ɪn'vɒlvd] engagiert,
  beteiligt; verwickelt,
  hineingezogen
to call in [kɔ:l‿'ɪn] beauftragen,
  hinzuziehen
°to fill in [fɪl‿'ɪn] ausfüllen
to give in to s.o. [gɪv‿'ɪn tə]
  nachgeben
to go in [gəʊ‿'ɪn] hineingehen
to join in [,dʒɔɪn‿'ɪn] sich
  beteiligen, mitmachen; teilnehmen
  (an)
to let s.o. in [let ,sʌmwʌn‿'ɪn] jdn.
  hereinlassen
incident ['ɪnsɪdənt] Ereignis, Vorfall
to **include** [ɪn'klu:d] aufnehmen,
  enthalten, einschließen
including (=**inc.**) [ɪŋ'klu:dɪŋ]
  einschließlich, auch
income ['ɪŋkʌm] Einkommen
incomplete [,ɪnkəm'pli:t]
  unvollständig
Independence Day [,ɪndɪ'pendəns
  ,deɪ] Unabhängigkeitstag (amerik.
  Nationalfeiertag)
independent (of) [,ɪndɪ'pendənt
  (ɒv)] unabhängig (von)
  ⟨independent (-minded)⟩
  [,ɪndɪ'pendənt(,maɪndɪd)]
  selbständig (denkend),
  unabhängig

Indian ['ɪndɪən] indisch, Inder/in
⟨**indifference**⟩ [ɪn'dɪfrəns] Gleichgültigkeit
°**indirect** speech [ˌɪndɪrekt 'spiːtʃ] indirekte Rede
indoor ['ɪndɔː] Innen-, Hallen-
indoor circuit [ˌɪndɔː 'sɜːkɪt] Hallenrennbahn
industrial [ɪn'dʌstrɪəl] Industrie-
industry ['ɪndəstrɪ] Industrie
inexcusable [ˌɪnɪk'skjuːzəbl] unverzeihlich
inexpensive [ˌɪnɪk'spensɪv] billig, preisgünstig
infinitive [ɪn'fɪnɪtɪv] Infinitiv, Grundform
to have an **influence on** [ˌhæv‿ən‿'ɪnfluəns‿ɒn] beeinflussen
to **influence** ['ɪnfluəns] beeinflussen
to **inform** [ɪn'fɔːm] informieren, benachrichtigen
informal [ɪn'fɔːml] ungezwungen; inoffiziell; nicht formell, nicht förmlich
⟨**informally**⟩ [ɪn'fɔːməlɪ] informell, nicht förmlich
informant [ɪn'fɔːmənt] Informant/in
information [ˌɪnfə'meɪʃn] Information, Auskunft
inhabitant [ɪn'hæbɪtənt] Einwohner/in
⟨to **inherit**⟩ [ɪn'herɪt] erben
insect ['ɪnsekt] Insekt
to **insert** [ɪn'sɜːt] einwerfen, hineinstecken
inside [ˌɪn'saɪd] innerhalb; in
°**inspiration** [ˌɪnspə'reɪʃn] Anregung, Inspiration
for **instance** [fər‿'ɪnstəns] zum Beispiel
⟨**instant**⟩ ['ɪnstənt] sofort
instead of [ɪns'ted‿əv] statt, anstatt, an Stelle von
to **instruct** [ɪn'strʌkt] anweisen, instruieren
instruction [ɪn'strʌkʃn] Anweisung
instrument ['ɪnstrʊmənt] Instrument
to **intend** [ɪn'tend] vorhaben
interactive [ˌɪntər'æktɪv] interaktiv
⟨to take an **interest** in⟩ [ˌteɪk‿ən 'ɪntrəst‿ɪn] sich für etw. interessieren
to **interest** ['ɪntrəst] interessieren
interested ['ɪntrəstɪd] interessiert
to keep s.o. interested [ˌkiːp ˌsʌmwʌn 'ɪntrəstɪd] dafür sorgen, dass jd. interessiert bleibt
interesting ['ɪntrəstɪŋ] interessant
interlude ['ɪntəluːd] Zwischenspiel, Intermezzo
⟨**internal** affairs⟩ [ɪn'tɜːnl‿ə'feəz] interne Angelegenheiten; Innen-
°**international** [ˌɪntə'næʃnəl] international
internet ['ɪntənet] Internet
to **interpret** [ɪn'tɜːprɪt] interpretieren, deuten; dolmetschen

to **interrupt** [ˌɪntə'rʌpt] unterbrechen, ins Wort fallen
interview ['ɪntəvjuː] Interview, Gespräch
to **interview** ['ɪntəvjuː] befragen, interviewen
interviewer ['ɪntəvjuːə] Interviewer/in
into ['ɪntʊ] in … (hinein)
to run into [rʌn‿'ɪntə] zusammenstoßen mit
to turn s.th. into s.th. [ˌtɜːn … 'ɪntə …] etwas in etwas ver-/umwandeln
°**intonation** [ɪntə'neɪʃn] Intonation, Satzmelodie
to **introduce** (oneself) [ˌɪntrə'djuːs] einführen, einleiten; (sich) vorstellen/bekannt machen
⟨to **invade**⟩ [ɪn'veɪd] angreifen
to **invent** [ɪn'vent] erfinden
invention [ɪn'venʃn] Erfindung
⟨to **invest**⟩ [ɪn'vest] investieren
°**invitation** [ˌɪnvɪ'teɪʃn] Einladung
to **invite** [ɪn'vaɪt] einladen
to **involve** [ɪn'vɒlv] ⟨beinhalten, umfassen⟩; ⟨beteiligen an⟩
involved (in) [ɪn'vɒlvd(‿ɪn)] engagiert, beteiligt; verwickelt, hineingezogen
Irish ['aɪrɪʃ] irisch
Irishman ['aɪrɪʃmən] Ire
iron ['aɪən] Eisen
irregular [ɪ'regjʊlə] unregelmäßig
irreplaceable [ɪrɪ'pleɪsəbl] unersetzlich
is [ɪz] ist
is said to be ['sed tə biː] soll angeblich/ist, so sagt man
is supposed to be [ɪz sə'pəʊzd tə biː] ist angeblich/soll
°**island** ['aɪlənd] Insel
°desert island [ˌdesət 'aɪlənd] verlassene Insel
isle [aɪl] Insel
The Emerald Isle [ðiː‿ˌemərəld‿'aɪl] Name für Irland
⟨**isolated**⟩ ['aɪsəleɪtɪd] abgeschnitten, isoliert
⟨a pass **issued** by the authorities⟩ [ə 'paːs ˌɪʃuːd baɪ ðiː‿ɔː'θɒrɪtɪz] ein behördlich ausgestellter Passierschein
it [ɪt] es/ihm
(it) does (get easier) [dʌz] wirklich, tatsächlich, doch
it makes a change from … [tʃeɪndʒ] das ist mal was anderes als …
It might help if … [ɪt ˌmaɪt 'help ɪf] Es könnte helfen, wenn …
it's no use [ɪts ˌnəʊ 'juːs] es hat keinen Zweck
it's up to you [ɪts‿ˌʌp tə 'juː] es ist deine/Ihre Entscheidung
its [ɪts] sein/seine

J

jacket ['dʒækɪt] Jacke
jam [dʒæm] Marmelade
traffic jam ['træfɪk ˌdʒæm] Verkehrsstau
January ['dʒænjʊərɪ] Januar
⟨**jealousy**⟩ ['dʒeləsɪ] Eifersucht
jeans [dʒiːnz] Jeans
jelly ['dʒelɪ] Wackelpudding
jet [dʒet] Strahl
⟨jumbo jet⟩ ['dʒʌmbəʊ dʒet] Jumbojet
Jew [dʒuː] Jude, Jüdin
jewel ['dʒuːəl] Juwel, Edelstein
⟨The Crown **Jewels**⟩ [ˌkraʊn 'dʒuːəlz] Kronjuwelen
Jewish ['dʒuːɪʃ] jüdisch
job [dʒɒb] Arbeit; Aufgabe
to do a baby-sitting job ['beɪbɪ ˌsɪtɪŋ] als Babysitter jobben
jogging ['dʒɒgɪŋ] Joggen
to **join** [dʒɔɪn] hinzukommen, hinzugesellen; verbinden; beitreten, sich anschließen
to join in [dʒɔɪn‿'ɪn] teilnehmen (an)
°to join together [dʒɔɪn tə'geðə] verbinden
joke [dʒəʊk] Witz
to play a joke [ˌpleɪ‿ə 'dʒəʊk] einen Streich spielen
journalist ['dʒɜːnəlɪst] Journalist/in, Reporter/in
journey ['dʒɜːnɪ] Reise
joy [dʒɔɪ] Freude, Vergnügen
juggling ['dʒʌglɪŋ] Jonglieren
juice [dʒuːs] Saft
July [dʒʊ'laɪ] Juli
⟨**jumbo** jet⟩ ['dʒʌmbəʊ dʒet] Jumbojet
to **jump** [dʒʌmp] springen
to jump up [dʒʌmp‿'ʌp] aufspringen
⟨**jumper**⟩ ['dʒʌmpə] Pullover
June [dʒuːn] Juni
Junior Play ['dʒuːnɪə ˌpleɪ] (Unterstufen-) Theatergruppe
⟨junior asprin⟩ [ˌdʒuːnɪər‿'æsprɪn] Schmerzmittel für Kinder
just [dʒʌst] gerade; einfach; wirklich
just a moment [dʒʌst‿ə 'məʊmənt] nur einen Augenblick
just before [dʒʌst bɪ'fɔː] kurz vor
just like ['dʒʌst laɪk] genauso wie
I'm just looking. [aɪm ˌdʒʌst 'lʊkɪŋ] Ich sehe mich nur um.

K

kangaroo [ˌkæŋgə'ruː] Känguru
keen on ['kiːn‿ɒn] begeistert (von)
to **keep*** [kiːp] behalten, halten; bleiben
to keep a check on [ˌkiːp‿ə 'tʃek‿ɒn] Kontrolle behalten über

to keep a diary [ˌkiːp ə ˈdaɪərɪ] ein Tagebuch führen
to keep away [ˌkiːp əˈweɪ] fernhalten
to keep doing s.th. [kiːp] etwas wiederholt tun
to keep on doing s.th. [kiːp ɒn ˈduɪŋ ˈsʌmθɪŋ] fortfahren, etwas zu tun
to keep order [kiːp ˈɔːdə] die Ordnung wahren
to keep out [kiːp ˈaʊt] draußen halten/bleiben, fern halten, nicht hereinlassen
to keep s.o. interested [ˌkiːp ˌsʌmwʌn ˈɪntrəstɪd] dafür sorgen, dass jd. interessiert bleibt
°to keep s.th. in mind [ˌkiːp ɪn ˈmaɪnd] an etwas denken
keeper [ˈkiːpə] Wächter, Hüter
kettle [ˈketl] (Wasser-) Kessel
to put on (a kettle) [pʊt ˈɒn] (den Wasserkessel) aufsetzen
key [kiː] Schlüssel
keyboard [ˈkiːbɔːd] Keyboard
⟨to get one's kicks from⟩ [ˈget wʌnz ˈkɪks frəm] seinen Spaß haben an
to kick [kɪk] treten, einen Ball schießen
⟨to get kicked in the pants⟩ [get ˈkɪkt ɪn ðə ˈpænts] einen Tritt in den Hintern bekommen (ugs.)
kid [kɪd] Kind, Jugendliche/r
to kill [kɪl] töten, umbringen
kilometre [ˈkɪləˌmiːtə] Kilometer
°kind [kaɪnd] Art
all kinds of [ɔːl ˈkaɪndz əv] alle möglichen Arten
some kind of [ˈsʌm ˈkaɪnd əv] irgendein, irgendeine Art von
that's kind of you [kaɪnd] das ist lieb/nett von dir/Ihnen
kind of [ˈkaɪnd əv] irgendwie, ziemlich
King [kɪŋ] König
kitchen [ˈkɪtʃɪn] Küche
soup kitchen [suːp ˈkɪtʃɪn] Suppenküche
kitten [ˈkɪtn] Kätzchen
knee [niː] Knie
knife [naɪf] Messer
there's a knock [ðɜːz ə ˈnɒk] es klopft
to knock [nɒk] klopfen
knot [nɒt] Knoten
to know* [nəʊ] wissen, kennen
knowledge [ˈnɒlɪdʒ] Wissen, Kenntnis
koala [kəʊˈɑːlə] Koalabär
Korean [kəˈrɪən] koreanisch, Koreaner/in

L

lab [læb] Labor
label [ˈleɪbl] Etikett, Preisschild
°to label [ˈleɪbl] beschriften

laboratory [ləˈbɒrətrɪ] Labor
°labour [ˈleɪbə] Arbeit
⟨rope ladder⟩ [ˈrəʊp ˌlædə] Strickleiter
lady [ˈleɪdɪ] Dame
⟨to be laid down⟩ [leɪd ˈdaʊn] entstehen
lake [leɪk] (Binnen-) See
fishing lake [ˈfɪʃɪŋ ˌleɪk] Angelsee, Fischteich
lamp [læmp] Lampe
land [lænd] Land
to land [lænd] landen
landing [ˈlændɪŋ] Treppenabsatz, Flur
⟨landowner⟩ [ˈlændˌəʊnə] Landbesitzer/in, -eigentümer/in
lane [leɪn] Weg
language [ˈlæŋgwɪdʒ] Sprache
laptop [ˈlæptɒp] Laptop (tragbarer Computer)
large [lɑːdʒ] groß
lasagna [ləˈzænjə] Lasagne
⟨lash⟩ [læʃ] Peitsche
to last [lɑːst] dauern, andauern
at last [æt ˈlɑːst] endlich, schließlich
last year [lɑːst ˈjɪə] letztes Jahr
late [leɪt] spät, zu spät
to be late [bɪ ˈleɪt] spät dran sein
lateness [ˈleɪtnɪs] Zuspätkommen, Verspätung
later [ˈleɪtə] später
latest [ˈleɪtɪst] neueste/r/s
Latin America [ˌlætɪn əˈmerɪkə] Lateinamerika
latkes [ˈlætkɪs] Latkes (jüd. Pfannkuchen)
to laugh [lɑːf] lachen
to laugh at [ˈlɑːf ət] lachen über
launch [lɔːntʃ] Abschuss, Start
to launch [lɔːntʃ] abschießen, starten
law [lɔː] Gesetz
⟨martial law⟩ [ˌmɑːʃl ˈlɔː] Kriegsrecht
to lay* [leɪ] legen
⟨to lay a trap⟩ [ˌleɪ ə ˈtræp] eine Falle stellen
ozone layer [ˈəʊzəʊn ˌleə] Ozonschicht
lazy [ˈleɪzɪ] faul, träge
to lead* [liːd] führen
leader [ˈliːdə] Anführer/in; Leiter/in; Vorsitzende/r
⟨Leader of the Opposition⟩ [ˌliːdər əv ði ˌɒpəˈzɪʃn] Oppositionsführer/in
leaf, leaves (pl) [liːf, liːvz] Blatt, Blätter
leaflet [ˈliːflɪt] Informationsblatt, Faltblatt
⟨to leak⟩ [liːk] tropfen, Wasser verlieren
leap year [ˈliːp ˌjɪə] Schaltjahr
⟨to leap*⟩ [liːp] springen
to learn* [lɜːn] lernen
°to learn s.th. by heart [ˌlɜːn baɪ ˈhɑːt] etwas auswendig lernen

Learning Support [ˌlɜːnɪŋ səˈpɔːt] Lernunterstützung, Förderunterricht
°least [liːst] am wenigsten
at least [ət ˈliːst] zumindest, wenigstens
to leave* [liːv] verlassen; lassen; liegen lassen
Leave it to me! [ˈliːv ɪt tə ˈmiː] Überlass es mir! Lass mich nur machen!
Leave me alone! [ˌliːv mɪ əˈləʊn] Lass mich in Ruhe!
to leave (on one's own) [liːv] (allein) lassen
to leave enough time for [ˌliːv ɪˌnʌf ˈtaɪm fə] genug Zeit lassen für
°to leave out [ˌliːv ˈaʊt] auslassen
ledge [ledʒ] vorstehender Rand, Sims
left [left] links
left [left] übrig
leg [leg] Bein
legend [ˈledʒənd] Legende, Sage
legendary [ˈledʒndərɪ] legendär
leggings [ˈlegɪŋz] Leggings
lemon [ˈlemən] Zitrone
lemonade [ˌleməˈneɪd] Limonade
to lend* [lend] leihen, verleihen
⟨lender⟩ [ˈlendə] (Geld-) Verleiher/in
length [leŋθ] Länge
less [les] weniger, geringer
lesson [ˈlesn] Unterrichtsstunde
to let [let] lassen
let's (= let us) [lets] lass/lasst uns
°let's check [lets ˈtʃek] Lasst uns überprüfen (was wir können).
°Let's start [lets ˈstɑːt] Fangen wir an!
°to let s.o. do s.th. [let ˌsʌmwʌn ˈduː ˌsʌmθɪŋ] jdn. etwas tun/machen lassen
to let s.o. in [let ˌsʌmwʌn ˈɪn] jdn. hereinlassen
letter [ˈletə] Brief; Buchstabe
letter-box [ˈletəbɒks] Briefkasten
liar [ˈlaɪə] Lügner/in
liberty [ˈlɪbətɪ] Freiheit
library [ˈlaɪbrərɪ] Bibliothek, Bücherei
licence [ˈlaɪsəns] Lizenz; Fernsehgebühr
to lick [lɪk] lecken
lie [laɪ] Lüge
to lie* [laɪ] liegen
to lie [laɪ] lügen
life [laɪf] Leben
lifestyle [ˈlaɪfˌstaɪl] Lebensstil, Lebensweise
lift [lɪft] Aufzug, Lift
lift-off [ˈlɪftˌɒf] Start, Abheben
to lift [lɪft] heben, ab-, hochheben
to lift off [lɪft ˈɒf] abheben
light [laɪt] Licht
(to get) light [laɪt] hell (werden)
first light [ˈfɜːst ˈlaɪt] Morgengrauen, Tagesanbruch

to **light*** [laɪt] anzünden
light [laɪt] leicht
to **like** [laɪk] mögen, gern haben
I'd like [aɪd 'laɪk] Ich möchte .../
hätte gern ...
would like [wʊd 'laɪk] möchten,
würde gerne
like [laɪk] wie
just like ['dʒʌst laɪk] genauso wie
like this or like that [laɪk 'ðɪs ɔ: laɪk
'ðæt] so oder so
likeable ['laɪkəbl] sympathisch,
liebenswert
⟨**likely**⟩ ['laɪklɪ] wahrscheinlich
⟨the **likes** of⟩ ['laɪks_əv] so jemand
wie (ugs.)
°to **limit** ['lɪmɪt] begrenzen,
beschränken; einschränken
line [laɪn] Linie; Zeile
telephone line ['telɪfəʊn ˌlaɪn]
Telefonleitung
liner ['laɪnə] Passagierschiff
link [lɪŋk] Verbindung
to **link** [lɪŋk] verbinden
to link up with [lɪŋk_'ʌp wɪð]
zusammenhängen
lip [lɪp] Lippe
⟨'the **Lip**'⟩ [ðə 'lɪp] "die Lippe"
(Anspielung auf das Habsburger
Kinn)
lipstick ['lɪpstɪk] Lippenstift
list [lɪst] Liste
°to **list** [lɪst] auflisten
to **listen** (to) ['lɪsn tʊ] anhören,
zuhören
listener ['lɪsnə] Zuhörer/in, Hörer/in
listing ['lɪstɪŋ] Position
little ['lɪtl] klein
to **live** [lɪv] wohnen, leben
⟨**live**⟩ [laɪv] live, Live-
living room ['lɪvɪŋrʊm]
Wohnzimmer
⟨**lizard**⟩ ['lɪzəd] Eidechse
local ['ləʊkl] örtlich, am Ort, hiesig
°**location** [ləʊ'keɪʃn] Ort
⟨to **lock** oneself away⟩ [ˌlɒk ...
ə'weɪ] sich selbst einsperren
to be **locked** [bɪ 'lɒkt] abgeschlossen
sein
locker ['lɒkə] Schließfach
⟨**lode**⟩ [ləʊd] Ader (im Bergbau)
to **log on** [lɒg_'ɒn] einloggen,
anmelden, sich einklinken
°**logical** ['lɒdʒɪkl] logisch
⟨**loneliness**⟩ ['ləʊnlɪnəs] Einsamkeit
lonely ['ləʊnlɪ] einsam
long [lɒŋ] lang
before long [bɪˌfɔ: 'lɒŋ] bald
⟨to flush the **loo**⟩ [ˌflʌʃ ðə 'lu:] das
Klo spülen
look [lʊk] Blick
look [lʊk] Blick
to have a look [ˌhæv_ə 'lʊk] sich
etwas anschauen
to take a look at [ˌteɪk_ə 'lʊk_ət]
anschauen, betrachten
to **look** [lʊk] aussehen; schauen,
ansehen

I'm just looking. [aɪm ˌdʒʌst 'lʊkɪŋ]
Ich sehe mich nur um.
to **look after** [lʊk_'ɑ:ftə] aufpassen
auf
to **look at** ['lʊk_ət] anschauen,
ansehen
to **look for** ['lʊk fə] suchen
to **look forward to** [lʊk 'fɔ:wəd tə]
sich freuen auf
to **look out** (for) [lʊk_'aʊt]
Ausschau halten (nach)
to **look** s.th. **up** [lʊk_'ʌp] etwas
nachschlagen
⟨**looks**⟩ [lʊks] Aussehen
Lord [lɔ:d] Herr (Anrede für Gott)
⟨Lord Protector⟩ [ˌlɔ:d prə'tektə]
Cromwells Titel
⟨The House of **Lords**⟩ [ˌhaʊs_əv
'lɔ:dz] Oberhaus (GB)
to **lose*** [lu:z] verlieren
to be **lost** [bɪ 'lɒst] sich verlaufen
haben
parking **lot** ['pɑ:kɪŋ lɒt] Parkplatz
(AE)
a **lot** (of) [ə 'lɒt_əv] viel(e)
⟨a lot of guts⟩ [ə ˌlɒt_əv 'gʌts]
Mumm, Mut (ugs.)
lots of ['lɒts_əv] viele
loud [laʊd] laut
°to read out loud [ˌri:d_aʊt 'laʊd]
laut vorlesen
in **love** with [ɪn 'lʌv wɪð] verliebt
(sein)
Love ... [lʌv] Liebe Grüße ...
to **love** [lʌv] lieben, gern haben
lovely ['lʌvlɪ] schön, herrlich
nature **lover** ['neɪtʃə ˌlʌvə]
Naturliebhaber/in
low [ləʊ] niedrig, tief, gering;
untere/r/s
to **lower** ['ləʊə] hinunter-/
herunterlassen
⟨**loyalty**⟩ ['lɔɪəltɪ] Loyalität, Treue
Ltd. ['lɪmɪtɪd] GmbH
luck [lʌk] Glück
worse luck! [wɜ:s 'lʌk] (so ein)
Pech! (ugs.)
You are **lucky!** [jʊ_ə 'lʌkɪ] Du hast
Glück! Du hast es gut!
luggage ['lʌgɪdʒ] Gepäck
⟨**lunar**⟩ ['lu:nə] Mond-
lunch [lʌntʃ] Mittagessen
lunch time ['lʌntʃtaɪm] Mittagszeit
packed lunch [pækt 'lʌntʃ]
Lunchpaket
to have lunch [hæv 'lʌntʃ] zu
Mittag essen
°**lyrics** ['lɪrɪks] Liedtext

M

machine [mə'ʃi:n] Automat;
Maschine
answering machine [ˌɑ:nsrɪŋ
mə'ʃi:n] Anrufbeantworter
washing machine ['wɒʃɪŋ mə,ʃi:n]
Waschmaschine

macho ['mætʃəʊ] machohaft
magazine [mægə'zi:n] Zeitschrift,
Magazin
magic ['mædʒɪk] Magie, Faszination,
Zauber
magical ['mædʒɪkl] magisch,
zauberhaft
mailbox ['meɪlbɒks] Briefkasten
(AE)
main [meɪn] Haupt-, größte/r/s
mainly [meɪnlɪ] hauptsächlich, in
erster Linie, vorwiegend
⟨to **maintain**⟩ [meɪn'teɪn]
aufrechterhalten, wahren
Cycling Proficiency & **Maintenance**
[ˌsaɪklɪŋ prə'fɪʃənsɪ ənd
'meɪntənəns] Radfahren und
Fahrradreparatur
majority [mə'dʒɒrətɪ] Mehrheit
⟨**make-up**⟩ ['meɪkʌp] Make-up,
Schminke
to **make*** [meɪk] °lassen; machen,
bilden, anfertigen
it makes a change from ...
[tʃeɪndʒ] das ist mal was anderes
als ...
⟨they made no attempt to
prevent⟩ [ˌmeɪd 'nəʊ_ə'tempt tə
prɪ'vent] sie versuchten nicht zu
verhindern
°to make a date [ˌmeɪk_ə 'deɪt]
einen Termin setzen
to make a face [meɪk_ə 'feɪs] das
Gesicht verziehen
to make a film [ˌmeɪk_ə 'fɪlm]
einen Film drehen
to make a telephone call [ˌmeɪk_ə
'telɪfəʊn 'kɔ:l] telefonieren, einen
Anruf tätigen
to make it ['meɪk_ɪt] etwas
schaffen/erreichen
to make s.o. do sth. ['meɪk_ˌsʌmwʌn
'du: sʌmθɪŋ] jdn. dazu bringen
oder veranlassen, etw. zu tun
to make sense [meɪk 'sens] Sinn
machen, sinnvoll sein
°to make sure [meɪk 'ʃɔ:] sicher
gehen
to make the first move [ˌmeɪk ðə
fɜ:st 'mu:v] den ersten Schritt tun
°to make up [meɪk_'ʌp] bilden,
ausmachen; sich ausdenken,
erfinden
⟨**male**⟩ [meɪl] männlich
mall [mɔ:l] Einkaufszentrum
⟨**mammy**⟩ ['mæmɪ] Mama, Mami
(irisch)
man [mæn] der Mensch, die
Menschheit; Mann
⟨fellow man⟩ [ˌfeləʊ 'mæn]
Mitmensch
to **manage** ['mænɪdʒ] managen;
zurechtkommen mit, etwas
schaffen
manager ['mænɪdʒə] Manager/in
manure [mə'njʊə] Mist
many ['menɪ] viele
how many [haʊ 'menɪ] wie viele

Many happy returns! [ˌmenɪ 'hæpɪ rɪ'tɜːnz] Glückwünsche zum Geburtstag!

map [mæp] Landkarte, Stadtplan

March [mɑːtʃ] März

marina [məˈriːnə] Jacht-/Yachthafen

⟨**mark**⟩ [mɑːk] Zeichen

to **mark** [mɑːk] °kennzeichnen; ⟨korrigieren, benoten⟩

market [ˈmɑːkɪt] Markt
market square [ˌmɑːkɪt ˈskweə] Marktplatz

marriage [ˈmærɪdʒ] Heirat, Hochzeit

to get **married** [get ˈmærɪd] heiraten

⟨to **marry**⟩ [ˈmærɪ] heiraten

Mars [mɑːz] *Name eines Planeten*

⟨**martial** law⟩ [ˌmɑːʃl ˈlɔː] Kriegsrecht

Martians [ˈmɑːʃənz] Marsmenschen

mascot [ˈmæskət] Maskottchen

⟨to be an absolute **mask**⟩ [ˌbɪ ənˌæbsəluːt ˈmɑːsk] absolut ausdruckslos, wie eine Maske sein

mass (murderer) [mæs (ˈmɜːdərə)] Masse, Menge; Massen(mörder)

massage [ˈmæsɑːʒ] Massage

match [mætʃ] (Fußball-/Tennis-) Spiel; Streichholz

to **match** [mætʃ] °zuordnen; °zusammenpassen, zusammenstellen
°to match up [mætʃˈˌʌp] das Passende zu etw. finden

mate [meɪt] Freund, Kumpel *(ugs.)*

material [məˈtɪərɪəl] Material, Stoff

Maths [mæθs] Mathematik

no **matter** how [nəʊ ˌmætə ˈhaʊ] egal wie
What's the matter? [ˌwɒts ðə ˈmætə] Was ist los? Was haben Sie? Wie fühlen Sie sich?

to **matter** *(to s.o)* [ˈmætə] etwas ausmachen, wichtig sein

May [meɪ] Mai

may [meɪ] dürfen
he may be [meɪ] vielleicht ist er

maybe [ˈmeɪbɪ] vielleicht

me [miː] mir/mich
Leave it to me! [ˌliːv ɪt tə ˈmiː] Überlass es mir! Lass mich nur machen!

meadow [ˈmedəʊ] Weide, Wiese

meal [miːl] Mahlzeit, Gericht

to **mean*** [miːn] bedeuten; meinen, beabsichtigen

meaning [ˈmiːnɪŋ] Bedeutung

means *(pl.)* [miːnz] Mittel

⟨in the **meantime**⟩ [ɪn ðə ˈmiːntaɪm] in der Zwischenzeit

⟨**measure**⟩ [ˈmeʒə] Maßnahme

meat [miːt] Fleisch
meat loaf [ˈmiːt ˌləʊf] Fleischkäse, "Falscher Hase"
meat-eater [ˈmiːtˌiːtə] jmd., der Fleisch isst

mechanical [mɪˈkænɪkl] mechanisch

medicine [ˈmedsɪn] Medizin, Medikament

°**medium** *(sg.)*; **media** *(pl.)* [ˈmiːdɪəm; ˈmiːdɪə] Medium, Medien

to **meet*** [miːt] (sich) treffen

meeting [ˈmiːtɪŋ] Treffen

mega [ˈmegə] mega-, höchst *(ugs.)*

member [ˈmembə] Mitglied
⟨Member of Parliament *(MP)*⟩ [ˌmembərˌəv ˈpɑːləmənt (ˌem ˈpiː)] Mitglied des britischen Unterhauses

membership [ˈmembəʃɪp] Mitgliedschaft

memory [ˈmemərɪ] °Gedächtnis; ⟨Gedenken, Erinnerung⟩

men *(pl)* [men] Männer

⟨to **menace**⟩ [ˈmenɪs] bedrohen

Menorah [meˈnɔːrə] Menora *(jüd. Leuchter)*

to **mention** [ˈmenʃn] erwähnen

menu [ˈmenjuː] Menü, Speisekarte

merry [ˈmerɪ] fröhlich, froh(e)

mess [mes] Durcheinander

message [ˈmesɪdʒ] Nachricht

⟨**messed** up⟩ [mestˌʌp] durcheinander, ruiniert, verpfuscht

metal [ˈmetəl] Metall; Rockmusik
heavy metal band [ˌhevɪ ˈmetəl bænd] Heavy Metal Band (Hardrock)

metre [ˈmiːtə] Meter

Mexican [ˈmeksɪkən] mexikanisch, Mexikaner/in

mice *(pl)* [maɪs] Mäuse

microphone [ˈmaɪkrəfəʊn] Mikrofon

middle [ˈmɪdl] Mitte

midnight [ˈmɪdnaɪt] Mitternacht

⟨**Midsummer's** Day⟩ [ˌmɪdsʌməz ˈdeɪ] Sommersonnenwende

It **might** help if ... [ɪt ˌmaɪt ˈhelp ɪf] Es könnte helfen, wenn ...

⟨**mighty**⟩ [ˈmaɪtɪ] mächtig, gewaltig

mile [maɪl] Meile

⟨**militia**⟩ [mɪˈlɪʃə] Miliz

milk [mɪlk] Milch

milkshake [ˈmɪlkʃeɪk] Milchshake

million [ˈmɪljən] Million

to **mime** [maɪm] pantomimisch darstellen

mince pie [ˌmɪns ˈpaɪ] Weihnachtstörtchen gefüllt mit Rosinen etc.

mind [maɪnd] Kopf, Sinn
⟨peace of mind⟩ [ˌpiːs əv ˈmaɪnd] innere Ruhe
to come to mind [kʌm tə ˈmaɪnd] in den Sinn kommen
°to keep s.th. in mind [ˌkiːpˌɪn ˈmaɪnd] an etwas denken

to **mind** [maɪnd] etwas dagegen haben
never mind [ˌnevə ˈmaɪnd] macht nichts

mind you [ˌmaɪnd ˈjʊ] allerdings

mine [maɪn] Mine, Bergwerk

of **mine** [əv ˈmaɪn] mein/e/r

miner [ˈmaɪnə] Bergmann

minigolf [ˈmɪnɪgɒlf] Minigolf

⟨**mining**⟩ [ˈmaɪnɪŋ] Bergbau

⟨**mint**⟩ [mɪnt] Pfefferminz

minus [ˈmaɪnəs] ohne, mit ... weniger

minute [ˈmɪnɪt] Minute

mirror [ˈmɪrə] Spiegel

miserable [ˈmɪzrəbl] elend, jämmerlich

to **miss** [mɪs] vermissen; verpassen

°to be **missing** [bɪ ˈmɪsɪŋ] fehlen

mistake [mɪˈsteɪk] Fehler

Mister (= **Mr**) [ˈmɪstə] Herr *(Anrede)*

⟨**misty**⟩ [ˈmɪstɪ] neblig, diesig

°**misunderstanding** [ˌmɪsʌndəˈstændɪŋ] Missverständnis

to **mix** [mɪks] (ver)mischen
to mix up [ˈmɪksˌʌp] durcheinanderbringen, verwechseln
to mix with [ˈmɪks wɪð] (sich) vermischen mit, mit jdm. Umgang haben

⟨**mobile**⟩ [ˈməʊbaɪl] beweglich, fahrbar
⟨mobile unit⟩ [ˌməʊbaɪl ˈjuːnɪt] Ü-Wagen, Übertragung am Ort

modal [ˈməʊdl] modales Hilfsverb

model [ˈmɒdl] Mannequin, Model; Modell
role model [ˈrəʊl ˌmɒdl] Vorbild

model [ˈmɒdl] vorbildlich, Muster-

modern [ˈmɒdn] modern
modern-day [ˈmɒdən deɪ] heutig/e/r/s

°**modernized** [ˈmɒdənaɪzd] modernisiert

module [ˈmɒdjuːl] Modul, Bauelement; Lerneinheit

mom [mɒm] Mama, Mutti *(AE) (ugs.)*

moment [ˈməʊmənt] Augenblick, Moment
at that moment [ət ðæt ˈməʊmənt] in diesem Moment
just a moment [ˌdʒʌstˌə ˈməʊmənt] nur einen Augenblick

⟨**monarch**⟩ [ˈmɒnək] Herrscher/in, König/in

⟨**monarchy**⟩ [ˈmɒnəkɪ] Monarchie

⟨**monastery**⟩ [ˈmɒnəstərɪ] Kloster

Monday [ˈmʌndɪ] Montag

money [ˈmʌnɪ] Geld
⟨dole money⟩ [ˌdəʊl ˈmʌnɪ] Arbeitslosengeld *(ugs.)*
pocket money [ˈpɒkɪt ˌmʌnɪ] Taschengeld
to spend *(money)* [spend] ausgeben

monkey [ˈmʌŋkɪ] Affe; Anfänger/in

monster [ˈmɒnstə] Monster

month [mʌnθ] Monat

monthly [ˈmʌnθlɪ] monatlich

mood [muːd] Laune, Stimmung

moon [muːn] Mond
⟨to be over the moon⟩ [biːˌəʊvə ðə ˈmuːn] überglücklich sein *(ugs.)*

moonlight ['mu:nlaɪt] Mondlicht/
-schein

more [mɔ:] mehr, weitere
more popular [mɔ: 'pɒpjʊlə]
beliebter
⟨**more and more**⟩ ['mɔ:r‿ənd 'mɔ:]
immer mehr

morning ['mɔ:nɪŋ] Morgen
Good morning [ˌgʊd 'mɔ:nɪŋ]
Guten Morgen
in the morning [ɪn ðə 'mɔ:nɪŋ] am
Morgen, vormittags

mosque [mɒsk] Moschee

most [məʊst] die meisten

mother ['mʌðə] Mutter
⟨**motion**⟩ ['məʊʃn] Bewegung
⟨time and motion clock⟩ [ˌtaɪm‿
ənd 'məʊʃn ˌklɒk] Uhr zur
Effizienzprüfung

motor ['məʊtə] Motor

motorbike ['məʊtəbaɪk] Motorrad

mountain ['maʊntɪn] Berg
mountain rescue ['maʊntɪn
'reskju:] Bergrettungsdienst,
Bergwacht

mouse [maʊs] Maus
⟨**moustache**⟩ [məˈstɑːʃ] Schnurrbart

mouth [maʊθ] Mund
⟨my heart was in my mouth⟩ [maɪ
'hɑːt wəz‿ɪn maɪ 'maʊθ] mir
schlug das Herz bis zum Hals
to make the first **move** [ˌmeɪk ðə 'fɜːst
'muːv] den ersten Schritt tun

to **move** [muːv] (sich) bewegen;
umziehen
to move around [ˌmuːv‿əˈraʊnd]
sich (umher)bewegen
to move on [ˌmuːv‿'ɒn]
weiterziehen
°to move s.th. on [ˌmuːv … 'ɒn]
etw. vorantreiben, voran/
weiterbringen

⟨**movement**⟩ ['muːvmənt] Bewegung

movie ['muːvɪ] Film (AE)
movie theater ['muːvɪ ˌθɪətə] Kino
(AE)

⟨**moving**⟩ ['muːvɪŋ] bewegend,
ergreifend

⟨to **mow**⟩ [məʊ] mähen

Mr ['mɪstə] Herr (Anrede)

Mrs ['mɪsɪz] Frau (Anrede)

much [mʌtʃ] viel
how much [haʊ 'mʌtʃ] wie viel

to get **mugged** [get 'mʌgd] auf
offener Straße überfallen und
ausgeraubt werden

multi-ethnic [ˌmʌltɪ 'eθnɪk]
multinational, -kulturell,
Vielvölker-

Mum [mʌm] Mama, Mutti

to **murder** ['mɜːdə] ermorden,
umbringen
mass (**murderer**) [mæs ('mɜːdərə)]
Massen(mörder)

museum [mjuːˈzɪəm] Museum

music ['mjuːzɪk] Musik
Chamber Music ['tʃeɪmbə
ˌmjuːzɪk] Kammermusik

music centre ['mjuːzɪk ˌsentə]
Stereo-, Hifi-Anlage

musical ['mjuːzɪkl] Musik-

Muslim ['mʊslɪm] Moslem,
mohammedanisch

must [mʌst] müssen

mustang ['mʌstæŋ] Mustang

my [maɪ] mein/meine

myself [maɪˈself] mich/mir selbst

mysterious [mɪˈstɪərɪəs] mysteriös

mystery ['mɪstərɪ] Geheimnis, Rätsel
°mystery place [ˌmɪstərɪ 'pleɪs]
geheimer Ort

N

nail [neɪl] (Finger-) Nagel

⟨**naked**⟩ ['neɪkɪd] nackt, bloß

name [neɪm] Name
to call sb. names [kɔːl ˌsʌmbədɪ
'neɪmz] jdn. beschimpfen

to **name** [neɪm] nennen, (be)nennen

namely ['neɪmlɪ] nämlich

⟨**nanny**⟩ ['nænɪ] Kinderfrau/
mädchen

°**narrator** [nəˈreɪtə] Erzähler/in

narrow ['nærəʊ] eng

nasty ['nɑːstɪ] scheußlich, widerlich,
ekelhaft

nation ['neɪʃn] Nation, Volk
United Nations Children's Fund
[juːˌnaɪtɪd 'neɪʃnz 'tʃɪldrənz 'fʌnd]
UN Kinderhilfsorganisation

national ['næʃənl] national

nationality [ˌnæʃˈnælɪtɪ]
Nationalität, Staatsangehörigkeit

⟨**nationwide**⟩ ['neɪʃnwaɪd]
landesweit

native ['neɪtɪv] Ureinwohner/in

natural ['nætʃrəl] natürlich
natural gas [ˌnætʃrəl 'gæs] Erdgas

nature ['neɪtʃə] Natur
nature lover ['neɪtʃə ˌlʌvə]
Naturliebhaber/in

navy ['neɪvɪ] Marine

near [nɪə] bei, in der Nähe von

nearly ['nɪəlɪ] beinahe, fast

neck [nek] Hals
pain in the neck [ˌpeɪn‿ɪn ðə 'nek]
Nervensäge (ugs.)

to **need** [niːd] brauchen
need not [niːd 'nɒt] nicht müssen

negative ['negətɪv] negativ

neighbour ['neɪbə] Nachbar/in
next-door neighbours [ˌneksdɔː
'neɪbəz] Nachbarn von nebenan

neighbourhood ['neɪbəhʊd]
Nachbarschaft, Gegend, Viertel,
Umgebung

⟨**neither** … nor⟩ ['naɪðə … ˌnɔː]
weder … noch

nerve [nɜːv] Nerv; Frechheit
to get on s.o.'s nerves [ˌget‿ɒn …
'nɜːvz] jdm. auf die Nerven gehen

nervous (about) ['nɜːvəs‿əˌbaʊt]
nervös (wegen)

nest [nest] Nest

never ['nevə] nie, niemals
never mind [ˌnevə 'maɪnd] macht
nichts
⟨never … at all⟩ ['nevər…ət‿'ɔːl]
gar nicht

new-comer ['njuːkʌmə]
Neuankömmling, Neuling

new [njuː] neu
New Year's Eve [njuː jɪəz 'iːv]
Silvester
What else is new? [wɒt‿'els‿ɪz
ˌnjuː] ironisch: Weiß ich schon!

news [njuːz] Nachrichten

newsagent ['njuːzˌeɪdʒnt]
Zeitungshändler/in

newsletter ['njuːzletə] Mitteilungs-
blatt, Nachbarschaftszeitung

newspaper ['njuːsˌpeɪpə] Zeitung

next [nekst] als Nächstes;
nächste/r/s
next door [nekst 'dɔː] nebenan
next to ['nekst tə] neben
next-door neighbours [ˌneksdɔː
'neɪbəz] Nachbarn von nebenan

nice [naɪs] hübsch, schön, nett

nick [nɪk] Kerbe, Ritze

to **nick** [nɪk] anritzen, einkerben

night [naɪt] Nacht, Abend
at night [ət 'naɪt] nachts, abends

nine [naɪn] neun

nineteen [ˌnaɪnˈtiːn] neunzehn

ninety ['naɪntɪ] neunzig

nite [naɪt] Abend, Nacht (AE; ugs.
Schreibweise)

no [nəʊ] kein/keine; nein
⟨no big deal⟩ [ˌnəʊ bɪg 'diːl] nichts
Besonderes (ugs.)
no idea [ˌnəʊ‿aɪˈdɪə] keine
Ahnung
no matter how [nəʊ ˌmætə 'haʊ]
egal wie
no one ['nəʊ wʌn] keiner

nobody ['nəʊbədɪ] niemand, keiner

to **nod** [nɒd] nicken

noise [nɔɪz] Lärm, Geräusch

noisy ['nɔɪzɪ] laut

non- [nɒn] nicht, ohne, -los
non-countable [ˌnɒn'kaʊntbl]
nicht zählbar
°non-defining relative clause
[ˌnɒndɪˈfaɪnɪŋ 'relətɪv ˌklɔːz] nicht-
notwendiger Relativsatz
⟨non-elected⟩ [ˌnɒnɪˈlektɪd] nicht-
gewählte/r/s
non-suit [ˌnɒn 'sjuːt] nicht passend
Non-Uniform Day [nɒn 'juːnɪfɔːm
ˌdeɪ] ein Tag ohne Schuluniform
non-violent ['nɒn ˌvaɪələnt]
gewaltlos

none [nʌn] keine/r/s

nonsense ['nɒnsəns] Quatsch,
Unsinn

⟨**noon**⟩ [nuːn] Mittag

⟨**nope**⟩ [nəʊp] ne(e) (ugs. für
"nein")

neither … **nor** ['naɪðə … ˌnɔː] weder
… noch

normal ['nɔːml] normal
⟨**Norman**⟩ ['nɔːmən] normannisch; Normanne, Normannin
North [nɔːθ] Norden
nose [nəʊz] Nase
not [nɒt] nicht
  ⟨**not at all**⟩ [ˌnɒt_ət_'ɔːl] überhaupt nicht, gar nicht
  not ... any ['enɪ] kein/keine
  not ... anybody ['enɪˌbɒdɪ] niemand
  not ... anywhere ['enɪweə] nirgendwo
  °not ... yet [nɒt 'jet] noch nicht
  ⟨to not be well⟩ ['nɒt bɪ ˌwel] sich nicht gut fühlen, nicht gut gehen
note [nəʊt] (Bank-) Note; Notiz, Anmerkung
  °to **note** [nəʊt] beachten, bemerken
  °to **note** down [nəʊt 'daʊn] notieren, aufschreiben
nothing ['nʌθɪŋ] nichts
notice ['nəʊtɪs] Schild
  notice board ['nəʊtɪs ˌbɔːd] Anschlagbrett, Schwarzes Brett
to **notice** ['nəʊtɪs] bemerken, feststellen
⟨**notified**⟩ ['nəʊtɪfaɪd] eingezeichnet
°**noun** [naʊn] Nomen, Substantiv
°**novel** ['nɒvl] Roman
⟨**novelist**⟩ ['nɒvəlɪst] Romanschriftsteller/in
November [nəʊ'vembə] November
now [naʊ] nun, jetzt
nowadays ['naʊədeɪz] heute, heutzutage
nowhere ['nəʊweə] nirgendwo, nirgends
nuclear ['njuːklɪə] Nuklear-, Atom-
⟨in the **nude**⟩ [ɪn ðə 'njuːd] nackt
number ['nʌmbə] Zahl, Nummer
⟨**nursing**⟩ ['nɜːsɪŋ] Krankenpflege
nut [nʌt] Nuss

O

°**object** ['ɒbdʒɪkt] Gegenstand; Objekt
°**objective**(ly) [əb'dʒektɪv(lɪ)] objektiv
to **observe** [əb'zɜːv] beobachten, wahrnehmen
⟨to **obtain**⟩ [əb'teɪn] erlangen
obvious ['ɒbvɪəs] offensichtlich, deutlich
⟨to **occupy**⟩ ['ɒkjəpaɪ] besetzen
⟨**ocean**⟩ ['əʊʃn] Ozean
Och! [ɒx] Ach!
o'clock [ə'klɒk] ... Uhr
October [ɒk'təʊbə] Oktober
°**octopoem** ['ɒktəˌpəʊɪm] *Gedicht mit acht Elementen*
of [ɒv] von
  an example of [ən_ɪg'zɑːmpl_əv] ein Beispiel für
  in favour of ['feɪvə] für (etwas)

in support of [sə'pɔːt] zur/als Unterstützung
of (Irish) descent [ɒv ... dɪ'sent] (irischer) Abstammung
of course [əv 'kɔːs] natürlich, selbstverständlich
of one's own choice [əv wʌnz_'əʊn tʃɔɪs] freiwillig, aus eigener Wahl
⟨of ... origin⟩ [ɒv ... 'ɒrɪdʒɪn] ... Ursprungs
out of ['aʊt_əv] aus (heraus)
to run s.o. out of [ˌrʌn ... 'aʊt_əv] (hinaus)jagen
to think of ['θɪŋk_əv] denken an; vorhaben, etwas zu tun
off [ɒf]
  ⟨off⟩ ['ɒf] vor der Küste
  ⟨off the beaten track⟩ ['ɒf ðə ˌbiːtn 'træk] abgelegen
  off the coast [ˌɒf ðə 'kəʊst] vor der Küste
  to be off [bɪ_'ɒf] weggehen
  to fall off [fɔːl_'ɒf] herunter-, hinunterfallen
  to get off the bus [get_'ɒf] aussteigen
  to go off with [gəʊ_'ɒf wɪð] weggehen mit
  to lift off [lɪft_'ɒf] abheben
  to set off [set_'ɒf] starten, anzünden, losgehen lassen
  to switch off [swɪtʃ_'ɒf] abstellen, abschalten
  to take off [teɪk_'ɒf] ausziehen; entfernen
offer ['ɒfə] Angebot
to **offer** ['ɒfə] anbieten
office ['ɒfɪs] Büro
  ⟨tourist office⟩ ['tʊərɪst_ˌɒfɪs] Fremdenverkehrsamt
official [ə'fɪʃl] Angestellte/r in einer öffentlichen Institution, Beamter/in
official [ə'fɪʃl] offiziell; Amts-
often ['ɒfn] oft
oil [ɔɪl] Öl
OK [əʊ'keɪ] OK, in Ordnung
old [əʊld] alt
on [ɒn] an, auf
  keen on ['kiːn_ɒn] begeistert (von)
  on board [ɒn 'bɔːd] an Bord
  ⟨on demand⟩ [ɒn dɪ'mɑːnd] auf Verlangen
  on foot [ɒn 'fʊt] zu Fuß
  on holiday [ɒn 'hɒlɪdeɪ] im Urlaub
  on horse-back [ɒn 'hɔːsbæk] zu Pferd
  on one's own [ɒn wʌnz_'əʊn] allein
  on Saturday [ɒn 'sætədɪ] am Samstag
  on Saturdays (pl) [ɒn 'sætədɪz] samstags, jeden Samstag
  ⟨on the air⟩ [eə] auf Sendung
  on the other hand [ɒn ðɪ_'ʌðə ˌhænd] andererseits
  on the right [ˌɒn ðə 'raɪt] rechts
  on the run [ɒn ðə 'rʌn] auf der Flucht

on time [ɒn 'taɪm] pünktlich
on top of [ɒn 'tɒp_əv] oben(drauf); zusätzlich, außerdem
on TV [ɒn ˌtiː 'viː] im Fernsehen
on vacation [ɒn və'keɪʃn] in Urlaub, in den Ferien *(AE)*
s.th. is going on [ɪz ˌgəʊɪŋ_'ɒn] etwas ist los, passiert
to call on ['kɔːl_ɒn] aufrufen
°to concentrate (on) ['kɒnsəntreɪt_ɒn] sich konzentrieren (auf)
to depend (on) [dɪ'pend_ɒn] abhängig sein von; sich verlassen auf
to get on the bus [get_'ɒn] einsteigen
to go on [gəʊ_'ɒn] weiterreden
to hold on [həʊld_'ɒn] warten
to keep on doing s.th. [kiːp_ɒn 'duːɪŋ ˌsʌmθɪŋ] fortfahren, etwas zu tun
to log on [lɒg_'ɒn] einloggen, anmelden, sich einklinken
°to move s.th. on [ˌmuːv ... 'ɒn] etw. vorantreiben, voran/weiterbringen
to pick on s.o. ['pɪk_ɒn] jdn. ärgern, auf jdm. herumhacken
to put on (a kettle) [pʊt_'ɒn] (den Wasserkessel) aufsetzen
to turn on the radio [ˌtɜːn_ɒn ðə 'reɪdɪəʊ] das Radio einschalten
What's on? [ˌwɒts_'ɒn] was gibt es/was kommt/was läuft?
to go **on-line** [gəʊ 'ɒnlaɪn] online gehen, sich ins Computernetz einschalten
once [wʌns] einmal; früher einmal
  at once [ət 'wʌns] sofort
one [wʌn] eins
  °one of them ['wʌn_əv ˌðəm] eine/r von ihnen
  one Sunday [wʌn 'sʌndɪ] eines Sonntags, an einem Sonntag
  the first one [ðə 'fɜːst wʌn] der/die/das Erste
one [wʌn] man
  no one ['nəʊ wʌn] keiner
  the one who [ðə 'wʌn huː] der/diejenige, der/die
on **one's** own [ɒn wʌnz_'əʊn] allein
  of one's own choice [əv wʌnz_'əʊn tʃɔɪs] freiwillig, aus eigener Wahl
  to put up one's hand [ˌpʊt ʌp wʌnz 'hænd] die Hand heben
oneself [wʌn'self] sich
  to blame oneself (for) ['bleɪm wʌnˌself fə] sich Vorwürfe machen
  ⟨to declare oneself⟩ [dɪ'kleə] sich erklären/ernennen zu
  ⟨to hold oneself⟩ [həʊld] sich würdevoll verhalten
  to introduce oneself [ˌɪntrə'djuːs] sich (jdm.) vorstellen/bekannt machen
only ['əʊnlɪ] einzig; nur
onto ['ɒntuː] auf (etwas)

open-air [ˌəʊpnˈeə] Freiluft-; im Freien
to **open** [ˈəʊpn] öffnen
open [ˈəʊpn] geöffnet, offen
    to fall **open** [fɔːlˈəʊpn] plötzlich aufgehen, offen stehen
opening [ˈəʊpnɪŋ] Öffnung; Anfang; Eröffnung
    opening hours (*pl*) [ˈəʊpnɪŋ ˌaʊəz] Öffnungszeiten
opera [ˈɒprə] Oper
    soap **opera** [səʊpˈɒprə] Seifenoper
⟨within the range of **operations**⟩ [wɪˌðɪn ðə ˈreɪndʒ ˌəv ˌɒpəˈreɪʃnz] im Aktionskreis/in Reichweite der (militärischen) Operationen
operator [ˈɒpəreɪtə] Vermittlung
opinion [əˈpɪnjən] Meinung
    in my **opinion** [ɪn ˈmaɪ əˌpɪnjən] meiner Meinung nach
    to be of the **opinion** that [ˈbiː əv ðɪ ˌəˌpɪnjən ˈðæt] der Meinung sein, dass
opportunity [ˌɒpəˈtjuːnətɪ] Gelegenheit, Möglichkeit
opposite [ˈɒpəzɪt] Gegensatz
opposite [ˈɒpəzɪt] gegenüber
⟨Leader of the **Opposition**⟩ [ˌliːdər əv ðiː ˌɒpəˈzɪʃn] Oppositionsführer/in
optimism [ˈɒptɪmɪzm] Optimismus
or [ɔː] oder
    or else [ɔːrˈels] oder, sonst, andernfalls
orange [ˈɒrɪndʒ] orange
orchestra [ˈɔːkɪstrə] Orchester
order [ˈɔːdə] Befehl, Order; Reihenfolge
    °following **order** [ˈfɒləʊɪŋ ˌɔːdə] folgende Anordnung
    in **order** to [ɪnˈɔːdə tə] um ... zu
    to give **orders** [gɪvˈɔːdəz] Befehle erteilen, Anweisungen geben
    to keep **order** [kiːpˈɔːdə] die Ordnung wahren
    to take **orders** [teɪkˈɔːdəz] Befehle ausführen
    °to **order** [ˈɔːdə] bestellen
ordinary [ˈɔːdɪnərɪ] normal, gewöhnlich
organization [ˌɔːgənaɪˈzeɪʃn] Organisation
    human rights **organization** [ˌhjuːmən ˈraɪts ˌɔːgənaɪˈzeɪʃn] Organisation für Menschenrechte
to **organize** [ˈɔːgənaɪz] organisieren, ordnen
°**organizer** [ˈɔːgənaɪzə] Organisator/in
⟨of ... **origin**⟩ [ɒv ... ˈɒrɪdʒɪn] ... Ursprungs
original(*ly*) [əˈrɪdʒənəl(ɪ)] ursprünglich
an **Oscar** [ˈɒskə] *amerikanischer Filmpreis*
other [ˈʌðə] andere
    the **other** day [ðɪ ˌʌðə ˈdeɪ] neulich
otherwise [ˈʌðəwaɪz] sonst, andernfalls, ansonsten

ought to [ˈɔːt tə] sollen
our [ˈaʊə] unser/unsere
ours [ˈaʊəz] unsere
ourselves [aʊəˈselvz] uns selbst
out
    day **out** [deɪˈaʊt] Tagesausflug
    out (*of*) [ˈaʊt əv] aus (heraus)
    out of tune [aʊt əv ˈtjuːn] schief, unmelodisch, verstimmt
    to break **out** [breɪkˈaʊt] ausbrechen
    °to carry **out** [ˌkærɪˈaʊt] durchführen
    to check **out** [tʃekˈaʊt] überprüfen
    °to copy **out** [ˌkɒpɪˈaʊt] abschreiben, herausschreiben
    °to cross **out** [krɒsˈaʊt] durchstreichen
    to drop **out** [drɒpˈaʊt] (die Schule) abbrechen; aussteigen
    to eat **out** [iːtˈaʊt] aus(-wärts) essen gehen, zum Essen ausgehen
    to find **out** [faɪndˈaʊt] herausfinden
    to get **out** (of a car) [getˈaʊt] aussteigen
    to go **out** of the door [gəʊˈaʊt əv ðə ˈdɔː] das Haus verlassen
    to hand **out** [hændˈaʊt] austeilen, verteilen
    to hang **out** [hæŋˈaʊt] sich aufhalten/herumtreiben (*ugs.*)
    to keep **out** [kiːpˈaʊt] draußen halten/bleiben, fern halten, nicht hereinlassen
    to look **out** (*for*) [lʊkˈaʊt] Ausschau halten (nach)
    °to pick (*out*) [pɪk] aussuchen, heraussuchen
    to run **out** [rʌnˈaʊt] ausgehen, zu Ende gehen
    to run s.o. **out** of [ˌrʌn ... ˈaʊt əv] (hinaus)jagen
    to take **out** [teɪkˈaʊt] ausführen, herausnehmen
    to throw **out** [θrəʊˈaʊt] wegwerfen
    to try **out** for [traɪˈaʊt fə] sich versuchen bei/an/mit (*AE*)
    to walk **out** of [ˌwɔːkˈaʊt əv] etwas mitten drin verlassen
    to watch **out** (*for*) [wɒtʃˈaʊt] Ausschau halten, aufpassen, Acht geben (auf)
    °to work **out** [wɜːkˈaʊt] herausfinden
the '**outback**' [ðiː ˌˈaʊtbæk] das australische Hinterland
⟨**outcrop**⟩ [ˈaʊtkrɒp] Felsnase
outlaw [ˈaʊtlɔː] Geächteter/ Geächtete
°**outline** [ˈaʊtlaɪn] Skizze, Entwurf
⟨**outright**⟩ [ˈaʊtraɪt] geradeheraus, unumwunden
outside [aʊtˈsaɪd] draußen
to **outvote** [ˌaʊtˈvəʊt] überstimmen
oven [ˈʌvn] Ofen, Backofen

over [ˈəʊvə] über
    over there [əʊvə ˈðeə] dort drüben
    to blow **over** [bləʊˈəʊvə] umwerfen
    to fall **over** [fɔːlˈəʊvə] hinfallen
    to run **over** [rʌnˈəʊvə] hinüberlaufen
    to take **over** [teɪkˈəʊvə] übernehmen
    to talk s.th. **over** [ˌtɔːk ... ˈəʊvə] etwas bereden, besprechen
overcast [ˌəʊvəˈkɑːst] bedeckt
⟨**overhang**⟩ [ˈəʊvəhæŋ] Überhang
overload [ˈəʊvələʊd] Überbelastung, -gewicht
to **overlook** [ˌəʊvəˈlʊk] überblicken, einen Blick haben auf
overnight [ˌəʊvəˈnaɪt] über Nacht
to work **overtime** [wɜːkˈəʊvətaɪm] Überstunden machen
to **own** [əʊn] besitzen, haben
own [əʊn] eigen, eigene/r/s
    of one's **own** choice [əv wʌnzˈəʊn ˈtʃɔɪs] freiwillig, aus eigener Wahl
    on one's **own** [ɒn wʌnzˈəʊn] allein
    to leave (*on one's own*) [liːv] (allein) lassen
    °your **own** ideas [jɔːrˈəʊn aɪˌdɪəz] deine eigenen Ideen
owner [ˈəʊnə] Besitzer/in
Oz [ɒz] *Name für Australien (ugs.)*
ozone layer [ˈəʊzəʊn ˌleə] Ozonschicht

P

pack [pæk] Rudel, Meute; Paket
to **pack** [pæk] packen
packed lunch [pækt ˈlʌntʃ] Lunchpaket
packet [ˈpækɪt] Packung, Schachtel
page [peɪdʒ] Seite
    °front **page** [frʌnt ˈpeɪdʒ] erste Seite, Titelseite
pain [peɪn] Schmerz
    pain in the neck [ˌpeɪn ɪn ðə ˈnek] Nervensäge (*ugs.*)
painful [ˈpeɪnfəl] schmerzhaft, qualvoll
to **paint** [peɪnt] malen
painting [ˈpeɪntɪŋ] Bild, Gemälde
pair [peə] Paar
Pakistani [ˌpɑːkɪˈstɑːnɪ] pakistanisch, Pakistaner/in
to **pal** up with (*s.o.*) [pælˈʌp wɪð] sich anfreunden/zusammentun mit
palace [ˈpælɪs] Palast
pan [pæn] Pfanne
⟨to **pan** for⟩ [pæn] (Gold) waschen
pancake [ˈpænkeɪk] Pfannkuchen
solar **panel** [ˌsəʊlə ˈpænl] Sonnenkollektor
panic [ˈpænɪk] Panik
to **panic** [ˈpænɪk] in Panik geraten
⟨to get kicked in the **pants**⟩ [get ˈkɪkt ɪn ðə ˈpænts] einen Tritt in den Hintern bekommen (*ugs.*)

paper ['peɪpə] Papier; Zeitung
exam paper [ɪg'zæm ˌpeɪpə]
Prüfungsaufgaben,
Aufgabenstellung
paper shop ['peɪpə ʃɒp]
Zeitungskiosk
°piece of paper ['piːs ˌəv 'peɪpə]
Stück Papier
to do a paper round ['peɪpə raʊnd]
Zeitungen austragen
writing paper ['raɪtɪŋ ˌpeɪpə]
Briefpapier
paragraph ['pærəgrɑːf] Absatz,
Abschnitt
to **paraphrase** ['pærəfreɪz]
umschreiben
parents (pl) ['peərənts] Eltern
park [pɑːk] Park
ball park ['bɔːl pɑːk] Baseballpark
car park ['kɑː pɑːk] Parkplatz,
Parkhaus
park ranger ['pɑːk ˌreɪndʒə]
Aufseher im Nationalpark
theme park ['θiːm pɑːk]
Freizeitpark, Vergnügungspark
to **park** [pɑːk] parken
parking lot ['pɑːkɪŋ lɒt] Parkplatz
(AE)
⟨**parliament**⟩ ['pɑːləmənt]
Parlament
⟨Member of Parliament (MP)⟩
[ˌmembər ˌəv 'pɑːləmənt (ˌem 'piː)]
Mitglied des britischen
Unterhauses
⟨The Houses of Parliament⟩
[ˌhaʊzɪz ˌəv 'pɑːləmənt] das
Parlament(-sgebäude) (GB)
part [pɑːt] Rolle, Part; Teil
to take part [teɪk 'pɑːt] teilnehmen
⟨to **part**⟩ [pɑːt] sich trennen,
auseinander gehen
participle ['pɑːtɪsɪpl] Partizip
°past participle [pɑːst 'pɑːtɪsɪpl]
Partizip Perfekt
particular [pə'tɪkjʊlə] besondere/r/s,
bestimmt/e/r/s
partly ['pɑːtlɪ] zum Teil
partner ['pɑːtnə] Partner/in
party ['pɑːtɪ] Party, Fest
search party ['sɜːtʃ ˌpɑːtɪ]
Suchtrupp, -mannschaft
⟨a **pass** issued by the authorities⟩
[ə 'pɑːs ˌɪʃuːd baɪ ðiːˌɔː'θɒrɪtɪz]
ein behördlich ausgestellter
Passierschein
to **pass** [pɑːs] reichen, weitergeben;
vergehen
to pass (an exam) [pɑːs] bestehen
⟨to pass away⟩ [pɑːs ˌə'weɪ] sterben
to pass by [pɑːs 'baɪ] vorbeigehen
to pass on [pɑːs ˌ'ɒn] weitergeben,
weitersagen
passenger ['pæsɪndʒə] Passagier,
Reisender, Fahrgast
°**passive** ['pæsɪv] Passiv
past [pɑːst] Vergangenheit
°past participle [pɑːst 'pɑːtɪsɪpl]
Partizip Perfekt

°past progressive [pɑːst prə'gresɪv]
Verlaufsform der Vergangenheit
past [pɑːst] nach (Uhrzeit); vorbei
half past nine [hɑːf pɑːst 'naɪn]
halb zehn
quarter past one [ˌkwɔːtə pɑːst
'wʌn] Viertel nach eins
⟨to squeeze past⟩ [ˌskwiːz 'pɑːst]
vorbeizwängen, -quetschen
path [pɑːθ] Weg, Pfad
patient ['peɪʃnt] Patient
patient ['peɪʃnt] geduldig
St. **Patrick's** Day [snt 'pætrɪks ˌdeɪ]
Tag des Schutzheiligen Irlands
°**pattern** ['pætən] Muster
°**patterns** of behaviour ['pætənz ˌɒv
bɪ'heɪvjə] Verhaltensmuster
pause [pɔːz] Pause
to **pause** [pɔːz] Pause machen
⟨**pay**⟩ [peɪ] Lohn, Gehalt,
Bezahlung
°Pay TV ['peɪ tiːˌviː] Pay TV
to **pay*** [peɪ] bezahlen
to pay for ['peɪ fə] (be)zahlen
⟨to pay one's respects⟩ [ˌpeɪ wʌnz
rɪ'spekts] jdm. seine Aufwartung
machen
PE [piː 'iː] Sport (-unterricht)
peace [piːs] Frieden, Friede
⟨peace of mind⟩ [ˌpiːs ˌəv 'maɪnd]
innere Ruhe
peaceful(ly) ['piːsfəl(ɪ)] friedlich
⟨to **peal**⟩ [piːl] schlagen
⟨to **peck**⟩ [pek] picken
⟨**pellet**⟩ ['pelɪt] Kügelchen, Pellet
pen [pen] Füller, Kugelschreiber
pen pal ['pen ˌpæl] Brieffreund/in
pence [pens] Pence (englische
Münze)
pencil ['pensl] Bleistift
pencil case ['pensl ˌkeɪs]
Federmäppchen
pencil sharpener ['pensl ˌʃɑːpnə]
Bleistiftspitzer
⟨**pensioner**⟩ ['penʃənə] Rentner,
Pensionär
people (pl) ['piːpl] Leute, Menschen
per cent [pə'sent] Prozent
⟨**perception**⟩ [pə'sepʃn] Bild,
Wahrnehmung, Auffassung von
perfect ['pɜːfɪkt] perfekt,
vollkommen, genau
°conditional perfect [kən.dɪʃnl
'pɜːfɪkt] Konditional der
Vergangenheit
present perfect [ˌpreznt 'pɜːfɪkt]
Perfekt
perfume ['pɜːfjuːm] Parfüm
perhaps [pə'hæps] vielleicht
period ['pɪərɪəd] Schulstunde;
Zeitraum
period (of time) ['pɪərɪəd]
Zeitraum
⟨**permanently**⟩ ['pɜːmənəntlɪ] auf
Dauer, fest
⟨**permission**⟩ [pə'mɪʃn] Erlaubnis
permit ['pɜːmɪt] Erlaubnis,
Genehmigung

persecution [ˌpɜːsɪ'kjuːʃn]
Verfolgung
person ['pɜːsn] Person
in person [ɪn 'pɜːsn] persönlich
personal ['pɜːsnl] persönlich
⟨**perspective**⟩ [pə'spektɪv]
Blickwinkel, Sichtweise
°to **persuade** [pə'sweɪd] überreden,
überzeugen
pest [pest] Plage; Nervensäge
pet [pet] Haustier
⟨**petrol**⟩ ['petrl] Benzin
Philosophy [fɪ'lɒsəfɪ] Philosophie
phone [fəʊn] Telefon
phone-in ['fəʊn ˌɪn] Sendung, in
der sich Hörer/innen per Telefon
beteiligen können
to **phone** [fəʊn] anrufen
phonecard ['fəʊnkɑːd] Telefonkarte
photo ['fəʊtəʊ] Foto
to take a photo [ˌteɪk ə 'fəʊtəʊ]
ein Foto machen
⟨to **photograph**⟩ ['fəʊtəgrɑːf]
fotografieren
photographer [fə'tɒgrəfə] Fotograf/
in
phrase [freɪz] Ausdruck, Wendung
⟨**physical**⟩ ['fɪzɪkl] körperlich,
physisch
Physics ['fɪzɪks] Physik
piano [pɪ'ænəʊ] Klavier
to **pick** [pɪk] aussuchen; pflücken
°to pick (out) [pɪk] aussuchen,
heraussuchen
to pick on s.o. ['pɪk ˌɒn] jdn.
ärgern, auf jdm. herumhacken
to pick s.o. up ['pɪk ˌsʌmwʌnˌ'ʌp]
jdn. abholen
to pick up [pɪkˌ'ʌp] aufheben
picnic ['pɪknɪk] Picknick
picture ['pɪktʃə] Bild
piece [piːs] Stück, Teil
to fall to **pieces** [ˌfɔːl tə 'piːsɪz]
kaputtgehen, sich in seine
Bestandteile auflösen
pilgrim ['pɪlgrɪm] Pilger/in
pillow ['pɪləʊ] (Kopf-) Kissen
pilot ['paɪlət] Pilot
pin [pɪn] (Steck-) Nadel
pink [pɪŋk] pink, rosa
pint [paɪnt] britische Maßeinheit
pipe [paɪp] Pfeife
⟨pipe-line⟩ ['paɪplaɪn]
Rohrleitung, Pipeline
Piping and Drumming [ˌpaɪpɪŋ ˌənd
'drʌmɪŋ] Dudelsackspielen und
Trommeln
⟨**pirate**⟩ ['paɪrət] Pirat
⟨**pistol**⟩ ['pɪstl] Pistole
pit [pɪt] Grube
pizza ['piːtsə] Pizza
place [pleɪs] Ort, Platz, Stelle
⟨hiding place⟩ ['haɪdɪŋ ˌpleɪs]
Versteck
°to take place [ˌteɪk 'pleɪs]
stattfinden
⟨to **place**⟩ [pleɪs] stellen
plain [pleɪn] Ebene

plan [plæn] Plan
  to draw (plans) [drɔ:] (Pläne)
  schmieden, aushecken
to **plan** [plæn] planen, vorhaben
plane [pleɪn] Flugzeug
planet ['plænɪt] Planet
plant [plɑ:nt] Pflanze
to **plant** [plɑ:nt] pflanzen
  to plant bombs [plɑ:nt 'bɒmz]
  Bomben legen
plantation [plæn'teɪʃn] Plantage
plastic ['plæstɪk] Plastik, Kunststoff
  plastic bag [,plæstɪk 'bæg] Plastiktüte
plate [pleɪt] Teller
platform ['plætfɔ:m] Plattform;
  Bohrinsel
play [pleɪ] Schauspiel, Spiel
  Junior Play ['dʒu:nɪə 'pleɪ]
  (Unterstufen-) Theatergruppe
  role play ['rəʊl pleɪ] Rollenspiel
to **play** [pleɪ] spielen
  to play a joke [,pleɪ ə 'dʒəʊk]
  einen Streich spielen
  to play tricks [pleɪ 'trɪks] Streiche
  spielen
player ['pleɪə] Spieler/in
  tennis player ['tenɪs ,pleɪə]
  Tennisspieler/in
playground ['pleɪgraʊnd] Schulhof;
  Spielplatz
pleasant ['pleznt] angenehm,
  erfreulich, nett
⟨to be **pleased**⟩ [pli:zd] sich freuen
please [pli:z] bitte
plenty ['plentɪ] viel/e/es, eine
  Menge; genug
⟨**plot** of earth⟩ [,plɒt əv 'ɜ:θ]
  Grabstätte
°**plural** ['plʊərəl] Plural, Mehrzahl
⟨**plus**⟩ [plʌs] plus
p.m. (= **pm**) [,pi:'em] 12.00 – 24.00
  Uhr
pocket ['pɒkɪt] Tasche
  pocket money ['pɒkɪt ,mʌnɪ]
  Taschengeld
poem ['pəʊɪm] Gedicht
⟨**poet**⟩ ['pəʊɪt] Dichter/in
point [pɔɪnt] (inhaltlicher) Punkt
  ⟨boiling point⟩ ['bɔɪlɪŋ pɔɪnt]
  Siedepunkt
  point of view [,pɔɪnt ə 'vju:]
  Standpunkt, Sichtweise
  to take s.o.'s point [teɪk] jdm.
  zustimmen
  °turning point ['tɜ:nɪŋ pɔɪnt]
  Wendepunkt
to **point** (at) ['pɔɪnt] zeigen (auf)
  to point (to) ['pɔɪnt tʊ] zeigen,
  deuten (auf); hinweisen
poison ['pɔɪzn] Gift
⟨**pole**⟩ [pəʊl] Stock
police [pə'li:s] Polizei
  Chief of Police [,tʃi:f əv pə'li:s]
  Polizeichef
policeman [pə'li:smən] Polizist
Polish ['pəʊlɪʃ] polnisch
polite [pə'laɪt] höflich
political [pə'lɪtɪkl] politisch

politics ['pɒlətɪks] Politik
poll [pəʊl] Meinungsumfrage
⟨**pollutant**⟩ [pə'lu:tənt] Schadstoff
to **pollute** [pə'lu:t] verschmutzen
pollution [pə'lu:ʃn] (Umwelt-)
  Verschmutzung
Poms [pɒmz] australischer Name
  für Engländer bzw. Briten (ugs.)
pond [pɒnd] Teich
pool [pu:l] Poolbillard (AE)
⟨the **pools**⟩ [ðə 'pu:lz] (Fußball-)
  Toto (GB)
poor [pɔ:] arm
  the **poor** [ðə 'pɔ:] die Armen
pop star [pɒp 'stɑ:] Popstar
  pop music ['pɒp ,mju:zɪk]
  Popmusik
popcorn ['pɒpkɔ:n] Popcorn
⟨**pope**⟩ [pəʊp] Papst
popular ['pɒpjʊlə] beliebt
populated ['pɒpjʊleɪtɪd] bevölkert,
  bewohnt
population [,pɒpjʊ'leɪʃn]
  Einwohner/in, Bevölkerung
porch [pɔ:tʃ] Veranda (AE)
⟨**port** of exit⟩ [,pɔ:t əv 'eksɪt] Ort
  der Ausreise
⟨**porter**⟩ ['pɔ:tə] Träger
⟨**Portuguese**⟩ [,pɔ:tʃə'gi:z]
  portugiesisch; Portugiese/
  Portugiesin
position [pə'zɪʃn] Stellung, Position
positive ['pɒzətɪv] positiv
possible ['pɒsɪbl] möglich
post office ['pəʊst ,ɒfɪs] Postamt
⟨to **post**⟩ [pəʊst] (per Post) schicken
⟨**post** production⟩ [,pəʊst prə'dʌkʃn]
  Nachproduktion
postcard ['pəʊstkɑ:d] Postkarte
poster ['pəʊstə] Poster, Plakat
postman ['pəʊstmən] Briefträger
potato [pə'teɪtəʊ] Kartoffel
°**potential** [pə'tenʃl] möglich,
  potentiell
pottery ['pɒtərɪ] Töpferei
pound (= **£**) [paʊnd] Pfund
  (englische Währung)
  pound (= lb) [paʊnd] Pfund
  (Gewicht)
poverty ['pɒvətɪ] Armut
power ['paʊə] Energie; Macht, Kraft
  solar power [,səʊlə 'paʊə]
  Sonnen-, Solarenergie
⟨**powerful**⟩ ['paʊəfəl] leistungsstark;
  ⟨mächtig⟩
practically ['præktɪklɪ] praktisch; so
  gut wie
practice ['præktɪs] Übung; Training
to **practise** ['præktɪs] üben
prairie ['preərɪ] Prärie
°to **praise** [preɪz] loben
to **pray** [preɪ] beten; sehr auf etwas
  hoffen
prayer ['preə] Gebet
to **predict** [prɪ'dɪkt] vorher-/
  voraussagen
prediction [prɪ'dɪkʃn] Vorhersage,
  Prognose

to **prefer** (to) [prɪ'fɜ:] lieber mögen,
  vorziehen
°**prefix** ['pri:fɪks] Vorsilbe, Präfix
pregnant ['pregnənt] schwanger
⟨**prehistoric**⟩ [,pri:hɪ'stɒrɪk]
  prähistorisch, frühgeschichtlich
⟨**preparation**⟩ [,prepə'reɪʃn]
  Vorbereitung
to **prepare** [prɪ'peə] vorbereiten
°**preposition** [,prepə'zɪʃn]
  Präposition
⟨to **prescribe**⟩ [prɪ'skraɪb]
  vorschreiben
prescription [prɪ'skrɪpʃn] Rezept
present ['preznt] Geschenk;
  Gegenwart
  present perfect [,preznt 'pɜ:fɪkt]
  Perfekt
  present progressive [,preznt
  prə'gresɪv] Verlaufsform der
  Gegenwart
  present simple [,preznt 'sɪmpl]
  einfaches Präsens
to **present** [prɪ'zent] moderieren;
  °präsentieren, vorstellen, zeigen
presentation [,prezn'teɪʃn]
  Präsentation, Referat, Vortrag
presenter [prɪ'zentə] Moderator/in
°**president** ['prezɪdənt] Vorsitzen-
  de/r, Präsident/in
⟨the **press**⟩ [ðə 'pres] die Presse
pressure ['preʃə] Druck
  pressure group ['preʃə ,gru:p]
  Interessenverband, der z.B. auf
  die Regierung Druck auszuüben
  sucht
to **pretend** [prɪ'tend] so tun, als ob,
  vortäuschen/vorgeben
pretty ['prɪtɪ] hübsch
⟨they made no attempt to **prevent**⟩
  [,meɪd 'nəʊ ə'tempt tə prɪ'vent] sie
  versuchten nicht zu verhindern
⟨**previously**⟩ ['pri:vɪəslɪ] vorher,
  zuvor
bird of **prey** [,bɜ:d əv 'preɪ] Raubvogel
price [praɪs] Preis
⟨**pride**⟩ [praɪd] Stolz
⟨**primary** school⟩ ['praɪmərɪ ,sku:l]
  Grundschule
Prime Minister [,praɪ 'mɪnɪstə]
  Premierminister
to **print** [prɪnt] drucken
printer ['prɪntə] Drucker
prison ['prɪzn] Gefängnis
prisoner ['prɪznə] Gefangener/
  Gefangene
⟨**privacy**⟩ ['prɪvəsɪ] Privatleben,
  Privatsphäre
°**private** ['praɪvɪt] privat
prize [praɪz] Preis, Gewinn
probably ['prɒbəblɪ] wahrscheinlich
problem ['prɒbləm] Problem
⟨to **proceed**⟩ [prə'si:d] sich begeben
⟨to **proclaim**⟩ [prə'kleɪm]
  verkünden
to **produce** [prə'dju:s] produzieren,
  erzeugen, herstellen,
  hervorbringen

°**product** ['prɒdʌkt] Produkt, Erzeugnis
⟨post **production**⟩ [,pəʊst prə'dʌkʃn] Nachproduktion
professional [prə'feʃənl] professionell, Berufs-
professor [prə'fesə] Professor/in
Cycling **Proficiency** & Maintenance [,saɪklɪŋ prə'fɪʃənsɪ ənd 'meɪntənəns] Radfahren und Fahrradreparatur
⟨**profitable**⟩ ['prɒfɪtəbl] gewinnbringend
program ['prəʊgræm] Programm *(AE)*
to **program** ['prəʊgræm] programmieren
programme ['prəʊgræm] Sendung; Programm
computer **programmer** [kəm'pjuːtə ,prəʊgræmə] Programmierer/in
progress ['prəʊgres] Fortschritt(e)
in progress [ɪn 'prəʊgres] im Gange
°**past progressive** [pɑːst prə'gresɪv] Verlaufsform der Vergangenheit
⟨to **prohibit**⟩ [prə'hɪbɪt] verbieten
project ['prɒdʒekt] Projekt
⟨**promise**⟩ ['prɒmɪs] Versprechen
to **promise** ['prɒmɪs] versprechen
⟨to **promote**⟩ [prə'məʊt] werben für, Werbung machen für
pronoun ['prəʊnaʊn]
°reflexive pronoun [rɪ'fleksɪv 'prəʊnaʊn] Reflexivpronomen
°relative pronoun ['relətɪv 'prəʊnaʊn] Relativpronomen
to **pronounce** [prə'naʊns] aussprechen
°**pronunciation** [prə'nʌnsɪ'eɪʃn] Aussprache
proper ['prɒpə] richtig/e/r/s
°**proper**(*ly*) ['prɒpə(lɪ)] ordentlich, richtig
props [prɒps] Requisiten
°**pros and cons** [,prəʊz ənd 'kɒnz] Vorteile und Nachteile
prospect ['prɒspekt] Aussicht(en), Zukunft
⟨**prostitute**⟩ ['prɒstɪtjuːt] Prostituierte
⟨**prostitution**⟩ [,prɒstɪ'tjuːʃn] Prostitution
to **protect** [prə'tekt] (be)schützen, aufpassen auf
⟨Lord **Protector**⟩ [,lɔːd prə'tektə] *Cromwells Titel*
protest ['prəʊtest] Protest
to **protest** (*about*) [prə'test] (gegen etwas) protestieren
Protestant ['prɒtɪstənt] Protestant/in, evangelisch
protester [prəʊ'testə] Protestierende/r, Demonstrant/in
proud (*of*) [praʊd] stolz (auf)
⟨to **provoke**⟩ [prə'vəʊk] hervorrufen, provozieren
psycho thriller ['saɪkəʊ ,θrɪlə] Psychothriller

pub [pʌb] Kneipe
public ['pʌblɪk] öffentlich
public toilet [,pʌblɪk 'tɔɪlɪt] öffentliche Toilette
public transport [,pʌblɪk 'trænspɔːt] öffentliche Verkehrsmittel
⟨to **publish**⟩ ['pʌblɪʃ] veröffentlichen
pudding-bowl haircut ['pʊdɪŋbəʊl 'heəkʌt] "Pilzkopf"-Frisur
pudgy ['pʌdʒɪ] pummelig
to **pull** [pʊl] ziehen
to pull down [pʊl 'daʊn] abreißen
⟨to pull up⟩ [pʊl 'ʌp] hochziehen
pullover ['pʊl,əʊvə] Pullover
puma ['pjuːmə] Puma
pump [pʌmp] Pumpe
⟨to **pump**⟩ [pʌmp] in Schwung bringen
punctual ['pʌŋktʃʊəl] pünktlich
⟨**punctuation**⟩ [,pʌŋktʃʊ'eɪʃn] Zeichensetzung
pupil ['pjuːpl] Schüler/in
purple ['pɜːpl] lila, violett
⟨**purpose**⟩ ['pɜːpəs] Sinn, Zweck
to **purr** [pɜː] schnurren
purse [pɜːs] Portmonee
to **push** [pʊʃ] drängen; drücken
to push around [,pʊʃ ə'raʊnd] herumstoßen
to push s.o. away [pʊʃ ə'weɪ] jdn. wegstoßen
pussy cat ['pʊsɪ kæt] Kätzchen
to **put*** [pʊt] setzen, stellen, legen, stecken, bringen
°to put forward [pʊt 'fɔːwəd] vorbringen, vorschlagen
to put in [pʊt 'ɪn] hineintun
to put on [pʊt 'ɒn] anziehen
to put on (a kettle) [pʊt 'ɒn] (den Wasserkessel) aufsetzen
to put s.th. right [pʊt 'raɪt] etwas in Ordnung bringen
to put up one's hand [,pʊt ʌp wʌnz 'hænd] die Hand heben
to put up s.th. [pʊt 'ʌp] aufhängen, aufbauen
to put up with s.o. [pʊt 'ʌp wɪð] jdn. ertragen, dulden
puzzle ['pʌzl] Puzzle, Rätsel
pyjamas (*pl.*) [pə'dʒɑːməz] Pyjama, Schlafanzug

Q

quad bike trek [,kwɒd baɪk 'trek] Quad bike-Trek
qualification [,kwɒlɪfɪ'keɪʃn] Qualifikation (*meist pl.*)
quality ['kwɒlɪtɪ] Qualität, Eigenschaft
°**quantity** ['kwɒntətɪ] Mengenangabe
to **quarrel** ['kwɒrəl] sich streiten
quarter ['kwɔːtə] Viertel
quarter past ['kwɔːtə ,pɑːst] Viertel nach *(Uhrzeit)*

quarter to ['kwɔːtə ,tə] Viertel vor *(Uhrzeit)*
Queen [kwiːn] Königin
question ['kwestʃn] Frage
question tag ['kwestʃn ,tæg] Bestätigungsfrage
to ask a question [ɑːsk ə 'kwestʃn] eine Frage stellen
queue [kjuː] Schlange, Reihe
to **queue** [kjuː] Schlange stehen
quick [kwɪk] schnell
quiet ['kwaɪət] ruhig
⟨**quintessence**⟩ [kwɪn'tesəns] Quintessenz, das Wesentliche
quite [kwaɪt] ziemlich, ganz
quiz [kwɪz] Quiz

R

rabbit ['ræbɪt] Kaninchen
race [reɪs] Wettrennen
to **race** [reɪs] rasen, rennen, fahren
radiator ['reɪdɪeɪtə] Heizkörper
radio ['reɪdɪəʊ] Radio
(*radio*) collar ['kɒlə] Kragen; Halsband *(mit Peilsender)*
(*radio*) station ['reɪdɪəʊ ,steɪʃn] Rundfunksender
on the radio [ɒn ðə 'reɪdɪəʊ] im Radio
to turn on the radio [,tɜːn ɒn ðə 'reɪdɪəʊ] das Radio einschalten
⟨**radiotherapy**⟩ [,reɪdɪəʊ'θerəpɪ] Strahlentherapie
raffle ['ræfl] Tombola, Verlosung
rail track ['reɪl træk] Eisenbahnstrecke, -gleise
railroad ['reɪlrəʊd] Eisenbahn *(AE)*
rain [reɪn] Regen
to **rain** [reɪn] regnen
rainforest ['reɪn,fɒrɪst] (tropischer) Regenwald
rainy ['reɪnɪ] regnerisch
to **raise** [reɪz] (Geld) sammeln, auftreiben; aufwerfen, vorbringen
Ramadan ['ræmədæn] Ramadan *(muslim. Fastenmonat)*
ranch [rɑːnʃ] Ranch, Viehfarm *(AE)*
rancher ['rɑːntʃə] Rancher, Viehzüchter/in
ranchhouse ['rɑːntʃhaʊs] Farmhaus
⟨within the **range** of operations⟩ [wɪ,ðɪn ðə 'reɪndʒ əv ˌɒpə'reɪʃnz] im Aktionskreis/in Reichweite der (militärischen) Operationen
park **ranger** ['pɑːk ,reɪndʒə] Aufseher/in im Nationalpark
ranger station ['reɪndʒə ,steɪʃn] Parkaufseherhütte
rap [ræp] Rap
rat [ræt] Ratte
rather ['rɑːðə] ziemlich
rathole ['ræthəʊl] Rattenloch
rattle ['rætl] Rassel
rattlesnake ['rætlsneɪk] Klapperschlange

UV **rays** [ˌjuː ˈviː reɪz] UV-Strahlen
°to **re**-phrase [riːˈfreɪz] umformulieren
°to **re**-distribute [ˌriːdɪˈstrɪbjuːt] neu verteilen
°**re**-united [ˌriːjuːˈnaɪtɪd] wieder vereint
to **reach** [riːtʃ] erreichen, ankommen an
to **react** [rɪˈækt] reagieren
reaction [rɪˈækʃn] Reaktion
to **read*** [riːd] lesen
°to **read** out loud [ˌriːd ˌaʊt ˈlaʊd] laut vorlesen
reader [ˈriːdə] Leser/in
⟨**ready**-made⟩ [ˌredɪˈmeɪd] Fertig-
to get **ready** [get ˈredɪ] sich bereitmachen, sich vorbereiten
real [rɪəl] echt
a **real** shaker [ˌrɪəl ˈʃeɪkə] ein richtiger Schock, etwas richtig Schockierendes (ugs.)
real(ly) [ˈrɪəlɪ] wirklich
realistic [rɪəˈlɪstɪk] realistisch
virtual **reality** [ˌvɜːtʃʊəl rɪˈælɪtɪ] virtuelle Realität
to **realize** [ˈrɪəlaɪz] feststellen, erkennen, klar werden
reason [ˈriːzn] Grund
to **receive** [rɪˈsiːv] bekommen, erhalten
receiver [rɪˈsiːvə] (Telefon-)Hörer
⟨**recent**⟩ [ˈriːsnt] jüngste/r/s, neueste/r/s
°**receptionist** [rɪˈsepʃənɪst] Sprechstundenhilfe
recipe [ˈresɪpɪ] (Koch-)Rezept
⟨beyond … **recognition**⟩ [bɪˌɒnd … ˌrekəɡˈnɪʃn] bis zur … Unkenntlichkeit
to **recognize** [ˈrekəɡnaɪz] erkennen
record [ˈrekɔːd] Schallplatte; Aufnahme
to **record** [rɪˈkɔːd] aufnehmen
(video) **recorder** [rɪˈkɔːdə] Videorekorder
recording [rɪˈkɔːdɪŋ] Aufnahme
⟨to **recover**⟩ [rɪˈkʌvə] bergen; zurückbekommen
to **recycle** [ˌriːˈsaɪkl] wieder verwerten, recyceln
recycling centre [ˌriːˈsaɪklɪŋ ˌsentə] Wertstoffsammelstelle
red [red] rot
⟨**redback** (spider)⟩ [ˈredbæk (ˌspaɪdə)] australische Spinnenart
⟨**referendum**, referenda⟩ [ˌrefəˈrendəm, ˌrefəˈrendə] Volksentscheid(e), Referendum (Referenden/-a)
°**reflexive** pronoun [rɪˈfleksɪv ˈprəʊnaʊn] Reflexivpronomen
⟨**reform**⟩ [rɪˈfɔːm] Reform, (Ver-)Besserung
⟨to **refrain** from⟩ [rɪˈfreɪn frəm] unterlassen, sich von etw. zurückhalten

refrigerator [rɪˈfrɪdʒəreɪtə] Kühlschrank
to **refuse** [rɪˈfjuːz] verweigern, ablehnen
reggae [ˈreɡeɪ] Reggae
regime [reɪˈʒiːm] Regime
registration [ˌredʒɪˈstreɪʃn] Anwesenheitskontrolle
to **regret** [rɪˈɡret] etwas bedauern, Leid tun
regular [ˈreɡjʊlə] regelmäßig
rehearsal [rɪˈhɜːsl] Probe
to **rehearse** [rɪˈhɜːs] proben, einüben
⟨**reign**⟩ [reɪn] Regierungszeit, Herrschaft
°**reindeer** [ˈreɪndɪə] Rentier
⟨**relation**⟩ [rɪˈleɪʃn] Verwandte/r
°**relationship** [rɪˈleɪʃnʃɪp] Beziehung
°**relative** [ˈrelətɪv] Verwandter
°**relative** clause [ˈrelətɪv ˌklɔːz] Relativsatz
°non-defining **relative** clause [ˌnɒndɪˈfaɪnɪŋ ˈrelətɪv ˌklɔːz] nicht-notwendiger Relativsatz
°**relative** pronoun [ˌrelətɪv ˈprəʊnaʊn] Relativpronomen
°**relative**(ly) [ˈrelətɪv(lɪ)] relativ
religion [rɪˈlɪdʒən] Religion
religious [rɪˈlɪdʒəs] religiös, gläubig, fromm
Religious Education [rɪˌlɪdʒəs ˌedʒʊˈkeɪʃn] Religion
⟨**reluctant**⟩ [rɪˈlʌktənt] unwillig, widerwillig
to **remain** [rɪˈmeɪn] (übrig) bleiben
to **remember** [rɪˈmembə] sich merken, sich erinnern, behalten
to **remind** s.o. about s.th. [rɪˈmaɪnd] jdn. an etwas erinnern
⟨in **remission**⟩ [ɪn rɪˈmɪʃn] Remission, (vorübergehender Krankheitsstillstand)
⟨**remix**⟩ [ˈriːmɪks] Remix
remote [rɪˈməʊt] entlegen, abgelegen
removal man [rɪˈmuːvl ˌmæn] Möbelpacker
to **rent** [rent] mieten, leihen, Sendezeit kaufen
°to **reorganize** [riːˈɔːɡənaɪz] neu strukturieren, reorganisieren
to **repair** [rɪˈpeə] reparieren
to **repeat** [rɪˈpiːt] wiederholen
°**repetition** [ˌrepɪˈtɪʃn] Wiederholung
to **replace** [rɪˈpleɪs] ersetzen
to **reply** [rɪˈplaɪ] antworten, erwidern
report [rɪˈpɔːt] Bericht
to **report** [rɪˈpɔːt] berichten, melden
reporter [rɪˈpɔːtə] Reporter/in
to **represent** [ˌreprɪˈzent] repräsentieren, vertreten, stehen für
representation [ˌreprɪzenˈteɪʃn] Vertretung
republic [rɪˈpʌblɪk] Republik
⟨a banana **republic**⟩ [bəˈnɑːnə rɪˈpʌblɪk] eine Bananenrepublik

⟨to **request**⟩ [rɪˈkwest] bitten, ersuchen
°to **reread*** [riːˈriːd] wieder/noch einmal lesen
rescue team [ˈreskjuːˌtiːm] Rettungsmannschaft
mountain rescue [ˈmaʊntən ˈreskjuː] Bergrettungsdienst, Bergwacht
to **rescue** [ˈreskjuː] retten, erretten
research [rɪˈsɜːtʃ] Forschung
reservation [ˌrezəˈveɪʃn] Reservierung; Reservat
⟨**reservoir**⟩ [ˈrezəvwɑː] Reservoir, Wasserspeicher
°**resolution** [ˌrezəˈluːʃn] Vorsatz, Entschluss
ski **resort** [ˈskiː rɪˈzɔːt] Skiort
to **respect** [rɪˈspekt] achten, respektieren, anerkennen
⟨to pay one's **respects**⟩ [ˌpeɪ wʌnz rɪˈspekts] jdm. seine Aufwartung machen
to **respond** [rɪˈspɒnd] reagieren, antworten
responsible [rɪˈspɒnsəbl] verantwortungsvoll; zuständig
rest [rest] Rest; Pause
to **rest** [rest] ruhen, (sich) ausruhen
restaurant [ˈrestərɔːŋ] Restaurant
⟨**restricted**⟩ [rɪˈstrɪktɪd] begrenzt, beschränkt
⟨**restroom**⟩ [ˈrestˌrʊm] (öffentliche) Toilette (AE)
result [rɪˈzʌlt] Resultat, Ergebnis
to **return** [rɪˈtɜːn] zurückkehren
°to **revise** [rɪˈvaɪz] wiederholen
revision [rɪˈvɪʒn] Wiederholung (von Lernstoff)
revolution [ˌrevəˈluːʃn] Revolution
⟨The Glorious Revolution⟩ [ˌɡlɔːrɪəs ˌrevəˈluːʃn] Die Glorreiche Revolution
reward [rɪˈwɔːd] Belohnung
rewarding [rɪˈwɔːdɪŋ] lohnend (sein), sich lohnen
to **rewrite*** [riːˈraɪt] neu, nochmal schreiben
rhyme [raɪm] Reim
°to **rhyme** [raɪm] sich reimen
rhythm [ˈrɪðm] Rhythmus
⟨**ribbon**⟩ [ˈrɪbən] Band
rich [rɪtʃ] reich
°to get **rid** of s.o./s.th. [get ˈrɪd_əv] jdn./etwas loswerden
ride [raɪd] Fahrt; Vergnügungsfahrt
to **ride*** [raɪd] Rad fahren; reiten
rider [ˈraɪdə] Reiter/in
ridiculous [rɪˈdɪkjʊləs] dumm, lächerlich
Small-bore **Rifle** Shooting [ˌsmɔːl bɔːˌraɪfl ˌʃuːtɪŋ] Kleinkalibergewehrschießen
right [raɪt] Recht
right [raɪt] rechts; richtig
on the **right** [ˌɒn ðə ˈraɪt] rechts
Right! [raɪt] Also, gut!
right away [ˌraɪt_əˈweɪ] sofort

human **rights** organization [ˌhjuːmən ˈraɪts ˌɔːgənaɪˈzeɪʃn] Organisation für Menschenrechte
⟨The Bill of Rights⟩ [bɪl ˌəv ˈraɪts] Bürgerrechte (*hist.*)
to **ring*** [rɪŋ] klingeln, läuten
to **rise*** [raɪz] (an-/auf-)steigen
risk [rɪsk] Risiko
to take risks [ˌteɪk ˈrɪsks] Risiken eingehen
river [ˈrɪvə] Fluss
road [rəʊd] Straße
to **rob** [rɒb] berauben, bestehlen
robber [ˈrɒbə] Räuber/in
robbery [ˈrɒbərɪ] Raub
robot [ˈrəʊbɒt] Roboter
rock [rɒk] Fels, (Ge-)Stein; Rock
to **rock** [rɒk] wiegen, schaukeln
rocket [ˈrɒkɪt] Rakete
rocky [ˈrɒkɪ] felsig
rodeo [ˈrəʊdɪəʊ] Rodeo
role [rəʊl] Rolle
role model [ˈrəʊl ˌmɒdl] Vorbild
role play [ˈrəʊl pleɪ] Rollenspiel
roll [rəʊl] Brötchen
to **roll** [rəʊl] rollen
roller-blading [ˈrəʊləˌbleɪdɪŋ] In-Line-Skating
rollerskates [ˈrəʊləskeɪts] Rollschuhe
CD-**ROM** [ˌsiː diː ˈrɒm] CD-ROM
Roman [ˈrəʊmən] römisch; Römer/in
romance [rəʊˈmæns] Romanze, Liebesgeschichte
roof [ruːf] Dach
to hit the roof [hɪt ðə ˈruːf] an die Decke gehen
room [ruːm] Platz; Zimmer
to have room for [həv ˈruːm fɔː] Platz haben für
root [ruːt] Wurzel, Ursprung
⟨**rope**⟩ [rəʊp] Seil, Strick
⟨rope ladder⟩ [ˈrəʊp ˌlædə] Strickleiter
to **rot** (*away*) [rɒt ˌəˈweɪ] verrotten, verfaulen
rotten [ˈrɒtn] schlecht, kaputt, faul
round [raʊnd] rund, um, herum
round and round [ˌraʊnd ˌən ˈraʊnd] im Kreis herum
the wrong way round [ˌrɒŋ weɪ ˈraʊnd] falsch herum
to come round [kʌm ˈraʊnd] vorbeikommen, besuchen
to turn round [tɜːn ˈraʊnd] sich umdrehen
route [ruːt] Route, Strecke
cycle route [ˈsaɪkl ruːt] Fahrradweg
routine [ruːˈtiːn] Routine-, routinemäßig; normal
⟨**row**⟩ [rəʊ] Reihe
⟨**row**⟩ [raʊ] Streit
⟨**royal**⟩ [ˈrɔɪəl] königlich
to **rub** [rʌb] reiben
rubber [ˈrʌbə] Radiergummi
rubbish [ˈrʌbɪʃ] Abfall; Blödsinn
rucksack [ˈrʌksæk] Rucksack

rude [ruːd] unanständig, rau, grob
rugby [ˈrʌgbɪ] Rugby
⟨**ruin**⟩ [ˈruːɪn] Ruine
⟨heap of **ruins**⟩ [ˌhiːp ˌəv ˈruːɪnz] ein Haufen Trümmer/Überreste
to **ruin** [ˈruːɪn] ruinieren, zerstören
rule [ruːl] Regel
⟨to **rule**⟩ [ruːl] regieren
ruler [ˈruːlə] Lineal; ⟨Herrscher/in⟩
⟨**rum**⟩ [rʌm] Rum
⟨**run**⟩ [rʌn] (Weide-) Land
on the **run** [ɒn ðə ˈrʌn] auf der Flucht
⟨to take s.o. for a run⟩ [ˌteɪk sʌmwʌn. fɔːr ə ˈrʌn] mit jdm. eine Spritztour machen
to **run*** [rʌn] laufen, rennen; leiten, führen
to run around [rʌn əˈraʊnd] herumlaufen
to run away [rʌn əˈweɪ] weglaufen; ausreißen
to run into [rʌn ˈɪntə] zusammenstoßen mit
to run out [rʌn ˈaʊt] ausgehen, zu Ende gehen
to run over [rʌn ˈəʊvə] hinüberlaufen
to run s.o. out of [ˌrʌn … ˈaʊt ˌəv] (hinaus)jagen
Run for it! [ˈrʌn fər ˌɪt] Laufe/Renne, so schnell du kannst!
runaway [ˈrʌnəweɪ] Ausreißer/in
runner [ˈrʌnə] Läufer/in
⟨**runway**⟩ [ˈrʌnweɪ] Start- und Landebahn, Runway
gold **rush** [ˈgəʊld rʌʃ] Goldrausch
rush hour [ˈrʌʃ aʊə] Hauptverkehrszeit
to **rush** [rʌʃ] schnell laufen, sich beeilen
⟨to rush out⟩ [rʌʃ ˈaʊt] hinaus-, losstürzen
Russian [ˈrʌʃən] Russe/Russin, russisch, Russisch

S

sad [sæd] traurig
safe [seɪf] sicher
is **said*** to be [ˈsed tə biː] soll angeblich/ist, so sagt man
to **sail** [seɪl] segeln
sailing [ˈseɪlɪŋ] Segeln
⟨**sailor**⟩ [ˈseɪlə] Seefahrer
⟨For Christ's **sake**!⟩ [fə ˌkraɪsts ˈseɪk] Um Himmels Willen! (*ugs.*)
salad [ˈsæləd] Salat (*kein Kopfsalat!*)
sale [seɪl] Verkauf, Schlussverkauf
bring-and-buy sale [ˈbrɪŋ ˌən ˈbaɪ seɪl] Basar, Flohmarkt
for sale [fə ˈseɪl] zu verkaufen
salt [sɔːlt] Salz
the **same** [ðə ˈseɪm] der/die/das Gleiche
sanctuary [ˈsæŋktʃʊərɪ] Schutzgebiet, Zuflucht

sand [sænd] Sand
sandwich [ˈsænwɪdʒ] *belegtes Brot*
⟨**sane**⟩ [seɪn] normal, geistig gesund, vernünftig
⟨**sanitation**⟩ [ˌsænɪˈteɪʃn] sanitäre Anlagen
Santa Claus [ˈsæntə ˌklɔːz] Weihnachtsmann
satellite [ˈsætelaɪt] Satellit
Saturday [ˈsætədɪ] Samstag, Sonnabend
sausage [ˈsɒsɪdʒ] Wurst
⟨**savage**⟩ [ˈsævɪdʒ] Wilde(r)
to **save** [seɪv] sparen; retten
⟨**savings** bond⟩ [ˈseɪvɪŋz ˌbɒnd] Schatzbrief
⟨**saw**⟩ [sɔː] Säge
⟨**Saxons**⟩ [ˈsæksnz] Sachsen (*hist.*)
to **say*** [seɪ] sprechen, sagen
it doesn't say [ɪt ˌdʌznt ˈseɪ] es steht hier nicht
°**saying** [ˈseɪɪŋ] Redensart, Sprichwort, Redewendung
°to **scan** [skæn] überfliegend/absuchend lesen
to **scare** s.o. [skeə] jdm. Angst machen, jdn. erschrecken
to be **scared** [skeəd] Angst haben, sich ängstigen
scarf [skɑːf] Schal, Halstuch
scary [ˈskeərɪ] Angst einflößend, unheimlich, gruselig
scene [siːn] Szene
schedule [ˈʃedjuːl] Zeitplan, Stundenplan (AE)
school [skuːl] Schule
⟨(*school*) governor⟩ [(ˌskuːl) ˈgʌvənə] Mitglied des Schulbeirats
at school [ət ˈskuːl] in/an der Schule
boarding school [ˈbɔːdɪŋ ˌskuːl] Internat
comprehensive school [ˌkɒmprɪˈhensɪv ˌskuːl] Gesamtschule
Middle School [ˈmɪdl ˌskuːl] *Schulart (der Mittelstufe)*
⟨primary school⟩ [ˈpraɪmərɪ ˌskuːl] Grundschule
Science [ˈsaɪəns] Naturwissenschaften
°**science** fiction [ˌsaɪəns ˈfɪkʃn] Sciencefiction
science fiction film [ˌsaɪəns ˈfɪkʃn fɪlm] Sciencefictionfilm
scientist [ˈsaɪəntɪst] (Natur-) Wissenschaftler/in
scissors (*pl.*) [ˈsɪsəz] Schere
⟨**Scot**⟩ [skɒt] Schotte, Schottin
⟨**Scottish**⟩ [ˈskɒtɪʃ] schottisch
⟨Scottish Gaelic⟩ [ˌskɒtɪʃ ˈgeɪlɪk] *die schottische Form des Gälisch*
°**scout** [skaʊt] Pfadfinder
Scouts [skaʊts] *Pfadfinderorganisation für Jungen*
scrapbook [ˈskræpbʊk] Sammelalbum

⟨to **scratch**⟩ [skrætʃ] kratzen; scharren
scream [skri:m] Schrei
to **scream** [skri:m] schreien
screen [skri:n] Bildschirm; Leinwand
°**script** [skrɪpt] Skript, Drehbuch
to **scrub** [skrʌb] schrubben
sea [si:] Meer, die See
sea level ['si: ˌlevl] Meeresspiegel
seal [si:l] Dichtung
search party ['sɜ:tʃ ˌpa:tɪ] Suchtrupp, -mannschaft
to **search** ['sɜ:tʃ] suchen; ⟨durchsuchen⟩
at the **seaside** ['si:saɪd] am Meer
seat [si:t] Sitz, Autositz
⟨aisle seat⟩ ['aɪl ˌsi:t] Sitzplatz am Gang
seat-belt ['si:t belt] Sicherheitsgurt, Sitzgurt
second ['sekənd] Sekunde
second ['sekənd] zweite/r/s
secret ['si:krɪt] Geheimnis
⟨Foreign **Secretary**⟩ [ˌfɒrən 'sekrətrɪ] Außenminister/in
section ['sekʃn] Sektion, Gebiet; °Teil, Abschnitt
⟨**sediment**⟩ ['sedɪmənt] Sediment, Ablagerung
to **see*** [si:] sehen
See you soon! [ˌsi: jə 'su:n] Bis bald!
to see through [si: 'θru:] etw./jdn. durchschauen (*fig.*)
you see, ... [jʊ 'si:] wisst ihr, ...
to **seek*** [si:k, sɔ:t, sɔ:t] suchen
to **seem** [si:m] scheinen
°to **select** [sɪ'lekt] auswählen
selfish ['selfɪʃ] egoistisch, selbstsüchtig
to **sell*** [sel] verkaufen
to **send*** [send] schicken
senior ['si:njə] Oberstufen-schüler/in
sense [sens] Sinn; Verstand
there's no sense in [ˌðeəz ˌnəʊ 'sens ɪn] es macht keinen Sinn, dass
to have a sense of humour [sens ˌəv 'hjʊmə] (einen Sinn für) Humor besitzen
to make sense [meɪk 'sens] Sinn machen, sinnvoll sein
sensible ['sensəbl] vernünftig
⟨**sensitive**⟩ ['sensɪtɪv] empfindlich, sensitiv
sentence ['sentəns] Satz
full sentence [fʊl 'sentəns] ganzer Satz
°one sentence at a time [wʌn ˌsentəns ˌət ə 'taɪm] Satz für Satz
sentimental [ˌsentɪ'mentl] sentimental, gefühlsbetont
separate(*ly*) ['seprətlɪ] separat, getrennt
September [sep'tembə] September
Serbian ['sɜ:bjən] Serbe/Serbin, serbisch, Serbisch

series ['sɪəri:z] Serie(n)
serious ['sɪərɪəs] ernst, ernsthaft
to **serve** [sɜ:v] bedienen, servieren, (Essen) auftragen
Serves him right! [ˌsɜ:vz hɪm 'raɪt] Geschieht ihm recht!
service ['sɜ:vɪs] Dienst(-leistung), Service; Gottesdienst
Social Service [ˌsəʊʃl 'sɜ:vɪs] Sozialwesen, Sozialdienst
session ['seʃn] Phase
brainstorming session ['breɪnstɔ:mɪŋ ˌseʃn] Phase der Ideensammlung
TV **set** [ti:'vi: ˌset] Fernseher, Fernsehgerät
to **set*** [set] setzen, stellen
to be set (*in*) [bi: 'set] spielen (*literarisch*)
⟨to set (*an exam*)⟩ [set] (eine Prüfung, Prüfungsaufgaben) stellen
to set off [set 'ɒf] starten, anzünden, losgehen lassen
to set up [set 'ʌp] einrichten, arrangieren
to set up camp [set ʌp 'kæmp] zelten, kampieren
to **settle** [setl] ansiedeln, sich niederlassen
to settle down [ˌsetl 'daʊn] zur Ruhe kommen, ein geregeltes Leben führen
settlement ['setlmənt] Siedlung
settler ['setlə] Siedler/in
seven ['sevn] sieben
seventeen [ˌsevn'ti:n] siebzehn
seventy ['sevntɪ] siebzig
several ['sevrəl] einige, mehrere
severe [sɪ'vɪə] ernst; schwer, schlimm
⟨**sexual**⟩ ['sekʃʊəl] sexuell
shadow ['ʃædəʊ] Schatten
to **shake*** [ʃeɪk] schütteln
to shake in one's shoes [ʃeɪk ɪn wʌnz 'ʃu:z] schlotternde Knie haben
a real **shaker** [ˌrɪəl 'ʃeɪkə] ein richtiger Schock, etwas richtig Schockierendes (*ugs.*)
shall [ʃæl] soll, sollen
shalwaar kameeze ['ʃælwa: kə'mi:z] *pakistan. Kleidungsstück*
shape [ʃeɪp] Gestalt
to **share** [ʃeə] teilen, gemeinsam etwas tun
shark [ʃa:k] Haifisch
to **sharpen** ['ʃa:pn] (an)spitzen; wetzen, schärfen
sharp ['ʃa:p] scharf
she [ʃi:] sie
shed [ʃed] Schuppen
sheep [ʃi:p] Schaf, Schafe
shelf, shelves (*pl*) [ʃelf, ʃelvz] Regal, Regale
shelter ['ʃeltə] Obdachlosenunterkunft; Zuflucht, Schutz

to **shelter** ['ʃeltə] in Sicherheit bringen, sich unterstellen
sheriff ['ʃerɪf] Sheriff
to **shine*** [ʃaɪn] scheinen
ship [ʃɪp] Schiff
tall **ships** ['tɔ:l ʃɪps] Segelschiffe (*Klipper, Großsegler*)
⟨**shipyard**⟩ ['ʃɪpja:d] Schiffswerft
shirt [ʃɜ:t] Hemd
⟨to **shiver**⟩ ['ʃɪvə] zittern
shock [ʃɒk] Schock
to **shock** [ʃɒk] schockieren
shoe [ʃu:] Schuh
to shake in one's **shoes** [ʃeɪk ɪn wʌnz 'ʃu:z] sehr nervös sein, schlotternde Knie haben
⟨**shoot**⟩ [ʃu:t] Drehen, Drehtag
to **shoot*** [ʃu:t] (er)schießen
to get shot at [get 'ʃɒt ˌæt] beschossen werden
Small-bore Rifle **Shooting** [ˌsmɔ:l bɔ: ˌraɪfl ˌʃu:tɪŋ] Kleinkalibergewehrschießen
shop [ʃɒp] Geschäft, Laden
bookshop ['bʊkʃɒp] Buchhandlung
coffee shop ['kɒfɪ ʃɒp] Café
⟨corner shop⟩ ['kɔ:nə ˌʃɒp] Laden an der Ecke
paper shop ['peɪpə ˌʃɒp] Zeitungskiosk
shop assistant ['ʃɒp əˌsɪstənt] Verkäufer/in
shopping
shopping centre ['ʃɒpɪŋ ˌsentə] Einkaufszentrum
⟨shopping spree⟩ ['ʃɒpɪŋ ˌspri:] Großeinkauf
shopping street ['ʃɒpɪŋ stri:t] Einkaufsstraße
to do the shopping [du: ðə 'ʃɒpɪŋ] einkaufen gehen, die Einkäufe erledigen
to go shopping [gəʊ 'ʃɒpɪŋ] einkaufen gehen
shore [ʃɔ:] Küste, Strand
short [ʃɔ:t] kurz
short for ['ʃɔ:t fə] die Abkürzung für
to **shorten** ['ʃɔ:tn] (ver)kürzen, kürzer machen
shorts [ʃɔ:ts] Shorts
shotgun ['ʃɒtgʌn] Schrotflinte
should [ʃʊd] sollte, sollten
⟨**shout**⟩ [ʃaʊt] Ruf, Schrei
to **shout** [ʃaʊt] rufen, schreien
show [ʃəʊ] Show, Sendung
to **show*** [ʃəʊ] zeigen
to show up (*for*) [ʃəʊ ʌp fə] auftauchen, erscheinen bei/in, sich blicken lassen bei/in
shower ['ʃaʊə] Dusche
to **shrink*** ['ʃrɪŋk] schrumpfen
to **shut*** up [ʃʌt ʌp] den Mund/die Klappe halten (*ugs.*)
shut [ʃʌt] geschlossen, zu
shy [ʃaɪ] schüchtern
Siamese cat [saɪəˌmi:z 'kæt] Siamkatze

to feel **sick** [fi:l 'sɪk] sich krank/
schlecht fühlen, übel sein
side [saɪd] Seite
⟨**sigh**⟩ [saɪ] Seufzer, Seufzen
sight [saɪt] Anblick;
Sehenswürdigkeit
sightseeing tour ['saɪt,si:ɪŋ ,tʊə]
Stadtrundfahrt
sign [saɪn] Schild; Zeichen
to **sign** [saɪn] unterschreiben
signal ['sɪgnəl] Signal, Zeichen
silent ['saɪlənt] still, ruhig,
geräuschlos
silk [sɪlk] Seide
Silly! ['sɪlɪ] Dummkopf!
silly ['sɪlɪ] dumm, albern
silver ['sɪlvə] Silber
similar ['sɪmɪlə] ähnlich
°**similarity** [,sɪmɪ'lærɪtɪ] Ähnlichkeit
simple ['sɪmpl] einfach
present simple [,preznt 'sɪmpl]
einfaches Präsens
simply ['sɪmplɪ] einfach
since [sɪns] seit (einem Zeitpunkt);
da
to **sing*** [sɪŋ] singen
⟨**singed**⟩ ['sɪndʒd] versengt,
angesengt
singer ['sɪŋə] Sänger/in
single ['sɪŋgl] Single (Musik)
single ['sɪŋgl] einzelne/r/s;
einzige/r/s
to **sink*** (down) [sɪŋk]
(hinab)sinken
Sinny ['sɪnɪ] Sydney (austral.)
sister ['sɪstə] Schwester
to **sit*** [sɪt] sitzen; setzen
to sit down [sɪt 'daʊn] sich
(hin)setzen
site [saɪt] Ort, Platz, Stätte
situation [,sɪtjʊ'eɪʃn] Situation,
Lage
six [sɪks] sechs
sixteen [,sɪks'ti:n] sechzehn
(sixteen-)year-old ['jɪər_,əʊld]
(sechzehn-)jährige/r
sixty ['sɪkstɪ] sechzig
size [saɪz] Größe
to **sizzle** ['sɪzl] brutzeln
⟨**sizzler**⟩ ['sɪzlə] Ereignis, welches
zu explodieren droht
skate [skeɪt] Schlittschuh
skate hire ['skeɪt ,haɪə]
Schlittschuhverleih
ice-skating ['aɪs,skeɪtɪŋ]
Schlittschuhlaufen
to ice-skate ['aɪsskeɪt]
Schlittschuh laufen
ski resort ['ski: rɪ'zɔ:t] Skiort
°**skill** [skɪl] Fähigkeit, Fertigkeit,
Geschick
⟨to **skim**⟩ [skɪm] überfliegen,
schnell lesen
skin [skɪn] Haut
to **skip** [skɪp] auslassen,
überspringen
skirt [skɜ:t] Rock
sky [skaɪ] Himmel

skyline ['skaɪlaɪn] Skyline,
Silhouette
skyscraper ['skaɪ,skreɪpə]
Wolkenkratzer
skyway ['skaɪweɪ] "Himmelsstraße"
⟨**slam**⟩ [slæm] Knall, Stoß
⟨**slaughterhouse**⟩ ['slɔ:təhaʊs]
Schlachthof
slave [sleɪv] Sklave, Sklavin
⟨**sleep**⟩ [sli:p] Schlaf
°to go to sleep [,gəʊ tə 'sli:p]
einschlafen
to **sleep*** [sli:p] schlafen
sleepy ['sli:pɪ] verschlafen, schläfrig
°**slightly** adapted [,slaɪtlɪ ə'dæptɪd]
leicht geändert
to **slip** [slɪp] ausrutschen
⟨to slip away⟩ [slɪp_ə'weɪ] sich
davonstehlen, davonschleichen
°**slogan** ['sləʊgən] Slogan, Spruch
slot [slɒt] Schlitz
to **slow** s.th. down [sləʊ … 'daʊn]
verlangsamen
slow [sləʊ] langsam
to **slurp** [slɜ:p] schlürfen
small [smɔ:l] klein
Small-bore Rifle Shooting [,smɔ:l
bɔ:_'raɪfl ,ʃu:tɪŋ]
Kleinkalibergewehrschießen
°**smart** [smɑ:t] schick, fein, smart
smell [smel] Geruch, Gestank
to **smell*** [smel] riechen
smelly ['smelɪ] riechend, duftend
to **smile** [smaɪl] lächeln
⟨**smoke**⟩ [sməʊk] Rauch
to **smoke** [sməʊk] rauchen
to **smuggle** ['smʌgl] schmuggeln
snack [snæk] Imbiss
snack bar ['snæk bɑ:] Imbissstube
snake [sneɪk] Schlange
⟨to **snap**⟩ [snæp] brechen
⟨**snappy**⟩ ['snæpɪ] flott, eingängig
(ugs.)
⟨**snatched**⟩ [snætʃt] geschnappt (ugs.)
snob [snɒb] Snob, arroganter
Mensch
snow [snəʊ] Schnee
snowmobile ['snəʊməbi:l]
Schneemobil (AE)
snowy ['snəʊɪ] schneereich;
verschneit
so [səʊ] so
so-called ['səʊkɔ:ld] so genannte/r/s
so did … ['səʊ dɪd] (das) tat auch
so far [səʊ 'fɑ:] bis jetzt
So long! [sə 'lɒŋ] Tschüs!, Bis
bald!
soaked ['səʊkt] durchnässt
soap [səʊp] Seife; Seifenoper
soap opera [səʊp_'ɒprə]
Seifenoper
soccer ['sɒkə] Fußball (AE)
Social Service [,səʊʃl 'sɜ:vɪs]
Sozialwesen, Sozialdienst
°**society** [sə'saɪətɪ] Gesellschaft
⟨**sociology**⟩ [,səʊsɪ'ɒlədʒɪ]
Soziologie
socks [sɒks] Socken

sofa ['səʊfə] Sofa, Couch
soft(ly) [sɒft(lɪ)] leise; weich; nicht
streng; ⟨sanft, leicht⟩
soil[sɔɪl] Erde, Boden
solar ['səʊlə] Sonnen-, Solar-
solar panel [,səʊlə 'pænl]
Sonnenkollektor
solar power [,səʊlə 'paʊə]
Sonnen-, Solarenergie
soldier ['səʊldʒə] Soldat/in
solution [sə'lu:ʃn] Lösung, Ergebnis
some day ['sʌm deɪ] eines Tages
some [sʌm] einige; irgendein
⟨Some hopes!⟩ ['sʌm 'həʊps]
Schön wär's! (ugs.)
some kind of ['sʌm ,kaɪnd_əv]
irgendein, irgendeine Art von
somebody ['sʌmbədɪ] jemand
⟨**somehow**⟩ ['sʌmhaʊ] irgendwie
someone ['sʌmwʌn] jemand
someplace ['sʌmpleɪs] irgendwo
(irisch/AE)
something ['sʌmθɪŋ] etwas
sometimes ['sʌmtaɪmz] manchmal
somewhere ['sʌmweə] irgendwo
son [sʌn] Sohn
song [sɒŋ] Lied
soon [su:n] bald
as **soon** as [æz 'su:n_æz] sobald, als
the **sooner** the better [ðə 'su:nə ðə
,betə] je eher, desto besser
sorry ['sɒrɪ] Entschuldigung, tut mir
Leid
I'm sorry about … [,sɒrɪ ə'baʊt] Es
tut mir Leid wegen/um …
they feel sorry [ðeɪ fi:l 'sɒrɪ] es tut
ihnen Leid
to be sorry [bi: 'sɒrɪ] etwas
bedauern, Leid tun
sort [sɔ:t] Sorte, Art
to **sort** [sɔ:t] sortieren, einordnen
to sort s.th. out [sɔ:t_'aʊt] etwas
hinkriegen
soul [səʊl] Seele
sound [saʊnd] Laut, Ton, Geräusch
°sound track ['saʊnd træk] Tonspur
to **sound** [saʊnd] klingen; sich
anhören
soup [su:p] Suppe
soup kitchen [su:p 'kɪtʃɪn]
Suppenküche
source [sɔ:s] Ursache, Ursprung;
Quelle
south [saʊθ] Süden; südlich
southeast [saʊθ'i:st] Südosten;
südöstlich
southwest [,saʊθ'west] Südwesten;
südwestlich
souvenir [,su:v'nɪə] Andenken,
Souvenir
space [speɪs] (Welt-)Raum, Weltall
space shuttle ['speɪs ,ʃʌtl]
Spaceshuttle, Raumfähre
spaghetti [spə'getɪ] Spaghetti
Spanish ['spænɪʃ] Spanisch
⟨**spar**⟩ [spɑ:] Holzpfosten
⟨**spark**⟩ [spɑ:k] Funke
to **speak*** [spi:k] sprechen

speaker ['spiːkə] Sprecher/in, Redner/in
speaking ['spiːkɪŋ] am Apparat
⟨**spec** = expect⟩ [spek] (ich) erwarte
special ['speʃl] besondere/r/s
⟨special effects⟩ [ˌspeʃl_ɪ'fekts] Spezialeffekte
today's special [təˌdeɪz 'speʃl] Tagesgericht
speciality [ˌspeʃɪ'æləti] Spezialität
°**to speculate** (about) ['spekjʊleɪt] spekulieren/Vermutungen anstellen (über)
°**speculation** [ˌspekjə'leɪʃn] Spekulation, Vermutung
Speech [spiːtʃ] *Schulfach Sprechkunde*
ᵛindirect speech [ˌɪndɪrekt 'spiːtʃ] indirekte Rede
speech bubble ['spiːtʃ ˌbʌbl] Sprechblase
to spell* [spel] buchstabieren
spelling ['spelɪŋ] Schreibweise, Rechtschreibung
°spelling game ['spelɪŋ ˌgeɪm] Buchstabierspiel
to spend* [spend] verbringen
to spend (money) [spend] ausgeben
spice [spaɪs] Gewürz
spider ['spaɪdə] Spinne
⟨redback (spider)⟩ ['redbæk (ˌspaɪdə)] *australische Spinnenart*
⟨oil **spill**⟩ ['ɔɪl spɪl] Ölteppich
⟨**spiral** staircase⟩ [ˌspaɪrəl 'steəkeɪs] Wendeltreppe
spirit ['spɪrɪt] Geist, Atmosphäre, Stimmung
to split* (up) [splɪt(_'ʌp)] aufteilen; sich aufteilen
to spoil* [spɔɪl] verderben; verwöhnen
sponge [spʌndʒ] Schwamm
sponsor ['spɒnsə] Sponsor, Geldgeber
spoon [spuːn] Löffel
sport [spɔːt] Sport
sports centre ['spɔːts ˌsentə] Sportzentrum
sports ground ['spɔːts graʊnd] Sportplatz/-gelände
sportsbag ['spɔːtsbæg] Sporttasche
spot [spɒt] Ort, Stelle; Fleck
to spot [spɒt] sehen
spray [spreɪ] geworfene Ration
⟨**to spread*** ⟩ [spred] sich ausbreiten
⟨shopping **spree**⟩ ['ʃɒpɪŋ ˌspriː] Großeinkauf
spring [sprɪŋ] Frühling; Quelle
to spy [spaɪ] spionieren, sehen, erspähen
market **square** [ˌmɑːkɪt 'skweə] Marktplatz
square [skweə] viereckig
Squash [skwɒʃ] Squash

⟨**to squeeze**⟩ [skwiːz] drücken; (aus-) pressen
⟨to squeeze past⟩ [ˌskwiːz 'pɑːst] vorbeizwängen, -quetschen
⟨**squirt**⟩ [skwɜːt] Spritzer
St. Patrick's Day [snt 'pætrɪks ˌdeɪ] Tag des Schutzheiligen Irlands
ice-**stadium** ['aɪs ˌsteɪdjəm] Eisstadion
⟨**stage**⟩ [steɪdʒ] Stadium, Phase
stair [steə] Treppe
⟨spiral **staircase**⟩ [ˌspaɪrəl 'steəkeɪs] Wendeltreppe
stall [stɔːl] Stand
stamp [stæmp] Briefmarke
to stand* [stænd] ertragen, aushalten
to stand* (up) [stænd_'ʌp] (auf)stehen
⟨to stand upright⟩ [stænd_'ʌpraɪt] aufrecht/gerade stehen
stands [stændz] Tribüne
star [stɑː] Stern; Star
pop star [pɒp stɑː] Popstar
to star [stɑːr_ɪn] die Hauptrolle spielen in
to stare (at) [steə] (an)starren
start [stɑːt] Anfang
to start [stɑːt] anfangen, beginnen
to start an argument [stɑːt_ən_'ɑːgjʊmənt] einen Streit anfangen
starvation [stɑː'veɪʃn] Hunger
to starve [stɑːv] verhungern
state [steɪt] Staat; °Zustand
⟨state border⟩ [steɪt 'bɔːdə] Staatsgrenze
statement ['steɪtmənt] Aussage, Beitrag, Meinungsäußerung
station ['steɪʃn] Bahnhof; Station, Hütte
(radio) station ['reɪdɪəʊ ˌsteɪʃn] Rundfunksender
°**statistic** [stə'tɪstɪk] Statistik
°**stative** ['steɪtɪv] Zustands-
statue ['stætʃuː] Statue, Denkmal
to stay [steɪ] bleiben, übernachten
to stay fit [steɪ 'fɪt] fit/in Form/gesund bleiben
to stay stupid [steɪ 'stjuːpɪd] dumm bleiben
⟨**steadily**⟩ ['stedɪli] ständig
steak [steɪk] Steak
to steal* [stiːl] stehlen
⟨**steam** engine⟩ ['stiːm_ˌendʒɪn] Dampfmaschine
steel [stiːl] Stahl
°**step** [step] Step, Schritt
to step onto s.th. [step_'ɒntə] etwas betreten, auf etwas steigen
stick [stɪk] Stock
to stick* [stɪk] kleben; stecken
⟨to stick up for s.o.⟩ [stɪk_'ʌp] für jdn. eintreten
sticker ['stɪkə] Aufkleber
still [stɪl] dennoch; immer noch
to stink* [stɪŋk] stinken
stocking ['stɒkɪŋ] Strumpf

stomach-ache ['stʌməkeɪk] Magenschmerzen
⟨**stone**⟩ [stəʊn] Stein
to stop [stɒp] anhalten; aufhören, stoppen
°department **store** [dɪ'pɑːtmənt ˌstɔː] großes Geschäft, Kaufhaus, Warenhaus
to store [stɔː] lagern, aufbewahren; speichern
⟨**storm**⟩ [stɔːm] Sturm
story ['stɔːri] Geschichte
tall story [tɔːl 'stɔːri] Fantasiegeschichte
°**storyline** ['stɔːrilaɪn] Handlung, Handlungsverlauf
straight [streɪt] gerade; glatt; direkt
straight on [streɪt_'ɒn] geradeaus
to go straight to [gəʊ 'streɪt] direkt gehen zu/in
strange [streɪndʒ] merkwürdig
⟨**to strangle**⟩ ['stræŋgl] erwürgen
⟨**strategic**⟩ [strə'tiːdʒɪk] strategisch
°**strategy** ['strætɪdʒi] Strategie
street [striːt] Straße
back street ['bæk ˌstriːt] Seitenstraße
shopping street ['ʃɒpɪŋ ˌstriːt] Einkaufsstraße
stress [stres] Betonung
°**to stress** [stres] betonen
strict [strɪkt] streng
⟨**strike**⟩ [straɪk] Streik
⟨**to strike***⟩ [straɪk] treffen
strong [strɒŋ] stark
structure ['strʌktʃə] Konstruktion, Struktur
°**to be stuck*** [biː 'stʌk] nicht weiter wissen, können
to get stuck [get 'stʌk] stecken bleiben
student ['stjuːdnt] Schüler/in *(AE)*
°**studio** ['stjuːdɪəʊ] Studio
study ['stʌdi] Arbeitszimmer
⟨**to study**⟩ ['stʌdi] studieren
to stumble ['stʌmbl] stolpern
stupid ['stjuːpɪd] blöd, dumm
to stay stupid [steɪ 'stjuːpɪd] dumm bleiben
style [staɪl] Stil
hair style ['heə ˌstaɪl] Frisur
subject ['sʌbdʒɪkt] Schulfach; Subjekt, Satzgegenstand
suburbs ['sʌbɜːbz] Vororte, am Stadtrand
subway ['sʌbweɪ] U-Bahn *(AE)*
success [sək'ses] Erfolg
⟨**successful**⟩ [sək'sesfəl] erfolgreich
such as ['sʌtʃ_əz] wie, zum Beispiel
such a terrible thing [sʌtʃ_ə] so etwas Schreckliches
sudden ['sʌdn] plötzlich, unerwartet, jäh
suddenly ['sʌdnli] plötzlich
to suffer ['sʌfə] (er)leiden, ertragen
°**suffix** ['sʌfɪks] Nachsilbe, Suffix
⟨universal **suffrage**⟩ [ˌjuːnɪ'vɜːsl 'sʌfrɪdʒ] allgemeines Wahlrecht

sugar ['ʃʊgə] Zucker
to **suggest** [sə'dʒest] vorschlagen;
andeuten, suggerieren
suggestion [sə'dʒestʃn] Vorschlag,
Anregung
suitable ['sju:təbl] passend, geeignet
to **sum** up [sʌm ˌ'ʌp]
zusammenfassen
°to **summarize** ['sʌməraɪz]
zusammenfassen
°**summary** ['sʌmərɪ]
Zusammenfassung
summer ['sʌmə] Sommer
summer camp ['sʌmə ˌkæmp]
(Sommer-) Ferienlager
sun [sʌn] Sonne
to **sunbathe** ['sʌnbeɪð] sonnen
baden
suncream ['sʌnkri:m] Sonnencreme
Sunday ['sʌndɪ] Sonntag
sunglasses (pl.) ['sʌngla:sɪz]
Sonnenbrille(n)
sunny ['sʌnɪ] sonnig
sunrise ['sʌnraɪz] Sonnenaufgang
superhighway ['su:pəˌhaɪweɪ]
Superhighway (Autobahn)
superlative [su:'pɜ:lətɪv] Superlativ
supermarket ['su:pəˌma:kɪt]
Supermarkt
supermodel ['su:pəˌmɒdl] Super-/
Topmodel
supper ['sʌpə] Abendessen,
Abendbrot
supply [sə'plaɪ] Versorgung; Vorrat
support [sə'pɔ:t] Unterstützung
in support of [sə'pɔ:t] zur/als
Unterstützung
Learning Support [ˌlɜ:nɪŋ sə'pɔ:t]
Lernunterstützung,
Förderunterricht
to **support** [sə'pɔ:t] stützen,
unterstützen
to **suppose** [sə'pəʊz] denken,
annehmen, meinen, sich
vorstellen
is **supposed** to be [ɪz sə'pəʊzd
tə ˌbi:] ist angeblich/soll
sure [ʃɔ:] sicher
That's for sure! [ðæts fə: 'ʃɔ:] Das
ist sicher!
°to **make sure** [meɪk 'ʃɔ:] sicher
gehen
Sure, … [ʃʊə] natürlich, doch
(irisch)
surely ['ʃʊəlɪ] sicherlich, doch,
bestimmt
to **surf** [sɜ:f] surfen
surface ['sɜ:fɪs] Oberfläche
surfer ['sɜ:fə] Surfer/in
surfie ['sɜ:fɪ] Surfer/in (austral.)
surgery ['sɜ:dʒərɪ] Praxis,
Sprechzimmer, -stunde
surprise [sə'praɪz] Überraschung
to **surprise** [sə'praɪz] überraschen
surprising [sə'praɪzɪŋ] überraschend
⟨to **surrender**⟩ [sə'rendə] abgeben
to **surround** [sə'raʊnd] umgeben
survey ['sɜ:veɪ] Umfrage

survival [sə'vaɪvl] Überleben,
Überlebens-
to **survive** [sə'vaɪv] überleben
survivor [sə'vaɪvə] Überlebende/r
Swahili [swa:'hi:lɪ] Swahili
to **swallow** up [ˌswɒləʊ 'ʌp]
verschlucken
to **swap** [swɒp] tauschen
to **swear*** [sweə] schwören
swearing ['sweərɪŋ] Fluchen
⟨to **sweat**⟩ [swet] schwitzen; sich
Sorgen machen über
sweatshirt ['swetʃɜ:t] Sweatshirt
⟨**sweep**⟩ [swi:p] Überblick
sweet [swi:t] Nachtisch
sweet [swi:t] süß
⟨**sweetheart**⟩ ['swi:tha:t] Schatz,
Liebste(r)
sweets (pl.) [swi:ts] Süßigkeiten,
Bonbons
to **swim*** [swɪm] schwimmen
swimmer ['swɪmə] Schwimmer/in
swimming ['swɪmɪŋ] Schwimmen
swimming pool ['swɪmɪŋ pu:l]
Schwimmbad
to **switch** off [swɪtʃ ˌ'ɒf] abstellen,
abschalten
to switch on [swɪtʃ ˌ'ɒn]
anschalten, einschalten
sword [sɔ:d] Schwert
°**symbol** ['sɪmbl] Symbol; Zeichen
°**symbolic** [sɪm'bɒlɪk] symbolisch
⟨to **sympathize**⟩ ['sɪmpəθaɪz]
Mitleid/Verständnis haben für
sympathy ['sɪmpəθɪ] Mitleid,
Mitgefühl
synagogue ['sɪnəgɒg] Synagoge
synonym ['sɪnənɪm] Synonym
system ['sɪstəm] System

T

T-shirt ['ti:ʃɜ:t] T-shirt
table ['teɪbl] Tisch
table of contents [ˌteɪbl əv
'kɒntents] Inhaltsverzeichnis
tablet ['tæblɪt] Tablette
tacos (pl.) ['tækəʊz] Tacos (mexikan.
Gericht)
tactless(ly) ['tæktləs(lɪ)] taktlos;
gedankenlos
tail [teɪl] Schwanz
take-away ['teɪkəˌweɪ] Imbissstube/
Restaurant für Außer-Haus-
Verkauf
to **take*** [teɪk] dauern; nehmen
Take my advice. [teɪk maɪ əd'vaɪs]
Höre auf mich.
to take a look at [ˌteɪk ə 'lʊk ət]
anschauen, betrachten
to take a photo [ˌteɪk ə 'fəʊtəʊ]
ein Foto machen
to take a test [ˌteɪk ə 'test] einen
Test schreiben/eine Prüfung
ablegen
to take a vote on [ˌteɪk ə 'vəʊt ɒn]
abstimmen über

to take action [teɪk 'ækʃn] etwas/
Schritte unternehmen
⟨to take after⟩ [teɪk 'a:ftə]
ähneln, ähnlich sein
⟨to take an interest in⟩ [ˌteɪk ən
'ɪntrəst ɪn] sich für etw.
interessieren
to take for a walk [ˌteɪk fər ə
'wɔ:k] spazieren führen
to take off [teɪk ˌ'ɒf] ausziehen;
entfernen
to take orders [teɪk 'ɔ:dəz] Befehle
ausführen
to take out [teɪk 'aʊt] ausführen,
herausnehmen
to take over [teɪk ˌ'əʊvə]
übernehmen
to take part [teɪk 'pa:t] teilnehmen
°to take place [ˌteɪk 'pleɪs]
stattfinden
to take risks [ˌteɪk 'rɪsks] Risiken
eingehen
⟨to take s.o. for a run⟩ [ˌteɪk
sʌmwʌn fɔ:r ə 'rʌn] mit jdm. eine
Spritztour machen
to take s.o.'s point [teɪk] jdm.
zustimmen
to take to ['teɪk tə] bringen zu/
nach; ⟨sich erheben⟩
talent ['tælənt] Talent
talented ['tæləntɪd] talentiert
°to give a **talk** [gɪv ə 'tɔ:k] einen
Vortrag/eine Rede halten
to **talk** (to) [tɔ:k] sprechen, reden
(mit)
to talk back [tɔ:k 'bæk] frech
antworten
°to talk about ['tɔ:k ə ˌbaʊt]
sprechen über
to talk s.th. over [ˌtɔ:k … 'əʊvə]
etwas bereden, besprechen
°**talking** ['tɔ:kɪŋ] Sprechen
tall [tɔ:l] groß, lang
tall ships ['tɔ:l ʃɪps] Segelschiffe
(Klipper, Großsegler)
tall story [tɔ:l 'stɔ:rɪ]
Fantasiegeschichte
tandoori chicken [tænˌdʊərɪ 'tʃɪkɪn]
indisches Gericht
tank [tæŋk] Tank
tap [tæp] Wasserhahn
°**tape** [teɪp] Kassette
°demo tape ['deməʊ teɪp] Demo-
Aufnahme
°**task** [ta:sk] Aufgabe
⟨**taste**⟩ [teɪst] Geschmack
to **taste** [teɪst] schmecken
tasty ['teɪstɪ] schmackhaft
⟨**tax**⟩ [tæks] Steuer
taxi ['tæksɪ] Taxi
taxi driver ['tæksɪ ˌdraɪvə]
Taxifahrer/in
tea [ti:] Tee; Abendessen
tea room ['ti: ˌru:m] Teestube
to **teach*** [ti:tʃ] unterrichten,
lehren, beibringen
teacher ['ti:tʃə] Lehrer/in
teachings (pl.) ['ti:tʃɪŋz] Lehre(n)

team [ti:m] Team, Mannschaft
　rescue team ['reskju:ˌti:m]
　Rettungsmannschaft
tear [tɪə] Träne
to **tease** ['ti:z] necken, aufziehen
°**technique** [tek'ni:k] Technik,
　Methode
Technology [tek'nɒlədʒɪ]
　Technologie/techn. Werken
　Design technology [dɪ'zaɪn
　tek'nɒlədʒɪ] Designtechnologie
⟨**teddy bear**⟩ ['tedɪ beə] Teddybär
teen [ti:n] Teenager, *Jugendlicher*
　zwischen dreizehn und neunzehn
　Jahren
teenage ['ti:neɪdʒ] im Teenager-Alter
teenager ['ti:nˌeɪdʒə] Teenager
tooth, **teeth** [tu:θ, ti:θ] Zahn, Zähne
　to brush one's teeth [ˌbrʌʃ wʌnz
　'ti:θ] sich die Zähne putzen
telephone ['telɪfəʊn] Telefon
　°telephone call ['telɪfəʊn kɔ:l]
　Telefongespräch
　telephone line ['telɪfəʊn ˌlaɪn]
　Telefonleitung
　to make a telephone call [ˌmeɪk ə
　'telɪfəʊn 'kɔ:l] telefonieren, einen
　Anruf tätigen
to **telephone** ['telɪfəʊn] anrufen
to **tell*** [tel] erzählen, berichten,
　sagen
teller ['telə] Erzähler/in
temperature ['temprɪtʃə] Fieber;
　Temperatur
temple ['templ] Tempel
ten [ten] zehn
tennis ['tenɪs] Tennis
　tennis player ['tenɪs ˌpleɪə]
　Tennisspieler/in
tense [tens] Zeit(form)
tent [tent] Zelt
term [tɜ:m] Schultrimester
　(-halbjahr)
terrible ['terəbl] schrecklich
terrified ['terɪfaɪd] schreckliche
　Angst haben
⟨**territory**⟩ ['terətrɪ] (Staats-)
　Gebiet, Territorium
test [test] Test
　to take a test [ˌteɪk ə 'test] einen
　Test schreiben/eine Prüfung
　ablegen
to **test** [test] testen, (über)prüfen
text [tekst] Text
7th grade [ˌsevnθ 'greɪd] 7. Klasse *(in*
　amerik. Schulen) (AE)
　8th grader [ˌeɪtθ 'greɪdə] Acht-
　klässler *(in amerik. Schulen) (AE)*
than [ðæn] als
thank you ['θæŋk ju] Danke schön
thanks a lot [ˌθæŋks ə 'lɒt] vielen
　Dank
　thanks to ['θæŋks tə] wegen
Thanksgiving ['θæŋksˌgɪvɪŋ] (Ernte-)
　Dankfest
that [ðæt] so; das; der/die/das … da
　it says that … ['sez ðət] es steht
　hier, dass …

That'll be … ['ðætl bi:] Das
　macht …
That's for sure! [ðæts fɔ: 'ʃɔ:] Das
　ist sicher!
That's … for you [ˌðæts … 'fə ju:]
　So ist (nun mal) … *(ugs.)*
the [ðə] der/die/das
　the best [ðə 'best] der/die/das
　Beste
　the homeless ['həʊmlɪs] Heimat-/
　Obdachlose
　⟨the likes of⟩ ['laɪks ˌəv] so
　jemand wie *(ugs.)*
　the most [ðə 'məʊst] der/die/das
　meiste
　the most exciting [ðə ˌməʊst
　ɪk'saɪtɪŋ] der/die/das
　Aufregendste
　the one who [ðə 'wʌn hu:] der/
　diejenige, der/die
　the other day [ðɪ ˌʌðə 'deɪ] neulich
　°the same [ðə 'seɪm] der/die/das
　Gleiche
movie **theater** ['mu:vɪ ˌθɪətə] Kino
　(AE)
theatre ['θɪətə] Theater
their [ðeə] ihr/ihre
them [ðem] ihnen/sie
theme park ['θi:m pɑ:k]
　Freizeitpark, Vergnügungspark
themselves [ðəm'selvz] sich selbst
then [ðen] dann
there [ðeə] da, dort
　there are [ðeərˌ'ɑ:] es gibt, da sind
　there is [ðeərˌ'ɪz] es gibt, da ist
　there's a knock [ðɜ:zˌə 'nɒk] es
　klopft
　there's no sense in [ðeəz ˌnəʊ
　'sensˌɪn] es macht keinen Sinn,
　dass
　up there [ˌʌp 'ðeə] dort/da oben
thermometer [θə'mɒmɪtə]
　Thermometer
these [ði:z] diese (hier)
they [ðeɪ] sie
thin [θɪn] dünn
thing [θɪŋ] Ding, Gegenstand
all **things** considered [ˌɔ:l θɪŋz
　kən'sɪdəd] wenn man alles in
　Betracht zieht
　things like that [ˌθɪŋz laɪk 'ðæt]
　solche Sachen
to **think*** [θɪŋk] denken, glauben,
　meinen
　to think about ['θɪŋkˌəˌbaʊt]
　nachdenken über
　to think of ['θɪŋkˌəv] denken an;
　vorhaben, etwas zu tun
third [θɜ:d] dritte/r/s
thirsty ['θɜ:stɪ] durstig
thirteen [ˌθɜ:'ti:n] dreizehn
thirty ['θɜ:tɪ] dreißig
this [ðɪs] diese/r/s
those [ðəʊz] diese (da), jene
though [ðəʊ] jedoch, allerdings
　⟨even though⟩ [ˌɪvn 'ðəʊ] obwohl
thought [θɔ:t] Gedanke, Denken
thousand ['θaʊznd] tausend

three [θri:] drei
thriller ['θrɪlə] Thriller
⟨**throne**⟩ [θrəʊn] Thron
through [θru:] durch
　to cut through [kʌt 'θru:]
　durchkommen, fahren; führen
　⟨we've been through this⟩ [wi:v
　bɪn 'θru: ˌðɪs] wir haben dies
　besprochen
°**throughout** [θru:'aʊt] überall (in),
　… hindurch; im Laufe von
to **throw*** [θrəʊ] werfen
　to throw out [θrəʊ 'aʊt]
　wegwerfen
throwaway ['θrəʊəweɪ] *obdachlose*
　Kinder und Jugendliche, deren
　Eltern sie rausgeworfen haben
Thursday ['θɜ:zdɪ] Donnerstag
⟨**to tick away**⟩ [tɪk ə'weɪ]
　weiterticken
ticket ['tɪkɪt] Eintrittskarte,
　Fahrkarte
to **tidy** ['taɪdɪ] aufräumen
tidy ['taɪdɪ] ordentlich, aufgeräumt
tie [taɪ] Krawatte
to **tie** [taɪ] knüpfen, binden,
　befestigen
　to tie up [taɪ 'ʌp] fesseln
till [tɪl] bis
time [taɪm] Uhrzeit; Zeit
　at the time [ət ðə 'taɪm] damals, zu
　der Zeit
　at times [ət 'taɪmz] manchmal,
　beizeiten
　⟨by the time⟩ [baɪ ðə 'taɪm] bis
　every time [ˌevrɪ 'taɪm] jedes Mal
　free time [ˌfri: 'taɪm] Freizeit
　on time [ɒn 'taɪm] pünktlich
　period (of time) ['pɪərɪəd]
　Zeitraum
　⟨time and motion clock⟩ [ˌtaɪm
　ənd 'məʊʃn ˌklɒk] Uhr zur
　Effizienzprüfung
　time phrases ['taɪm ˌfreɪzɪz]
　Zeitangaben
　°time scale ['taɪm skeɪl]
　Zeitschiene
　°to go back in time [gəʊ ˌbæk ɪn
　'taɪm] in der Zeit zurückgehen
　to leave enough time for [ˌli:vˌɪˌnʌf
　'taɪm fə] genug Zeit lassen für
　What time is it? [wɒt 'taɪmˌɪzˌɪt]
　Wie spät ist es?
　°What time …? [wɒt 'taɪm] Wann
　…? Um wie viel Uhr …?
times [taɪmz] mal
timetable ['taɪmˌteɪbl] Stundenplan
tip [tɪp] Hinweis, Rat
to **tiptoe** ['tɪptəʊ] auf Zehenspitzen
　gehen
to be **tired** [bɪ 'taɪəd] müde sein
°**title** ['taɪtl] Titel, Überschrift
to [tʊ] vor *(Uhrzeit)*; bis; zu/zur/
　zum
　is said to be ['sed tə bi:] soll
　angeblich/ist, so sagt man
　is supposed to be [ɪz sə'pəʊzd təˌ
　bi:] ist angeblich/soll

it's up to you [ɪtsˌʌp tə 'juː] es ist deine/Ihre Entscheidung
to get to ['get tə] erreichen, gelangen zu
to get used to [get 'juːst tʊ] sich gewöhnen an
to give in to s.o. [gɪvˌ'ɪn tə] nachgeben
to go to ['gəʊ tə] gehen zu, gehen nach
to point to ['pɔɪnt tə] zeigen, deuten auf; hinweisen
toast [təʊst] Toast
⟨tobacco⟩ [ˌtə'bækəʊ] Tabak
today [tə'deɪ] heute
   today's special [təˌdeɪz 'speʃl] Tagesgericht
together [tə'geðə] zusammen
   °to get together [get tə'geðə] zusammenkommen
   °to join together [dʒɔɪn tə'geðə] verbinden
toilet ['tɔɪlɪt] Toilette
   public toilet [ˌpʌblɪk 'tɔɪlɪt] öffentliche Toilette
⟨tolerance⟩ ['tɒlərəns] Toleranz
to tolerate ['tɒləreɪt] tolerieren, ertragen, dulden
tomato, tomatoes (pl) [tə'mɑːtəʊ, tə'mɑːtəʊz] Tomate, Tomaten
⟨tombstone⟩ ['tuːmstəʊn] Grabstein
tomorrow [tə'mɒrəʊ] morgen
tone [təʊn] Ton
°tongue twister ['tʌŋ ˌtwɪstə] Zungenbrecher
tonight [tə'naɪt] heute Abend
too [tuː] auch
   too late [tʊ 'leɪt] zu spät
tooth, teeth [tuːθ, tiːθ] Zahn, Zähne
toothache ['tuːθeɪk] Zahnschmerzen
toothless ['tuːθləs] zahnlos
top [tɒp] Gipfel, Spitze
   °at the top [tɒp] oben
topic ['tɒpɪk] Thema, Themenbereich
torch [tɔːtʃ] Taschenlampe
tornado [tɔː'neɪdəʊ] Tornado, Wirbelsturm
⟨to toss away⟩ [tɒsˌə'weɪ] wegwerfen
to touch [tʌtʃ] berühren
⟨tough⟩ [tʌf] hart
tour [tʊə] Rundgang
   sightseeing tour ['saɪtˌsiːɪŋ ˌtʊə] Stadtrundfahrt
tourist ['tʊərɪst] Tourist/in
   ⟨tourist office⟩ ['tʊərɪstˌɒfɪs] Fremdenverkehrsamt
towards [tə'wɔːdz] auf … zu
town [taʊn] Stadt
   ⟨town council⟩ [ˌtaʊn 'kaʊnsl] Stadtrat
toy [tɔɪ] Spielzeug
track [træk] Fährte, Spur, Fahrspur
   ⟨off the beaten track⟩ ['ɒf ðə ˌbiːtn 'træk] abgelegen
⟨trade⟩ [treɪd] Handel

tradition [trə'dɪʃn] Tradition
traditional(ly) [trə'dɪʃnl(ɪ)] traditionell, Volks-; üblich(erweise)
traffic ['træfɪk] Verkehr
   traffic jam ['træfɪk ˌdʒæm] Verkehrsstau
⟨tragic(ally)⟩ ['trædʒɪk(əlɪ)] tragisch(erweise)
trail [treɪl] Weg, Pfad
train [treɪn] Zug
to train [treɪn] trainieren
trainers ['treɪnəz] Turnschuhe
training ['treɪnɪŋ] Training
transcontinental [trænzˌkɒntɪ'nentl] transkontinental
°transcript ['trænskrɪpt] Transkript
to translate [træns'leɪt] übersetzen
translation [træns'leɪʃn] Übersetzung
⟨transmission⟩ [trænz'mɪʃn] Übertragung
⟨transplant⟩ ['trænsplɑːnt] Transplantation
transport ['trænspɔːt] Transport, Beförderung
   public transport [ˌpʌblɪk 'trænspɔːt] öffentliche Verkehrsmittel
⟨to lay a trap⟩ [ˌleɪˌə 'træp] eine Falle stellen
to trap [træp] (mit einer Falle) fangen
trapper ['træpə] Trapper, Fallensteller/in
travel ['trævl] Reise, Fahrt
to travel ['trævl] reisen, fahren
traveller ['trævlə] Reisende/r
⟨treachery⟩ ['tretʃərɪ] Verrat
⟨treadmill⟩ ['tredmɪl] Tretmühle
⟨treat⟩ [triːt] Geschenk, Überraschung
to treat [triːt] behandeln
   ⟨to treat s.o.⟩ [triːt] jdn. einladen, jdm. etw. spendieren
⟨treatment⟩ ['triːtmənt] Behandlung
treaty ['triːtɪ] Vertrag (zwischen Ländern)
tree [triː] Baum
   °family tree [ˌfæməlɪ 'triː] Stammbaum
   gum tree ['gʌm triː] Eukalyptusbaum (ugs.)
⟨treehouse⟩ ['triːhaʊs] Baumhaus
trekking ['trekɪŋ] Trekking
trendy ['trendɪ] modern, schick, 'in'
trial ['traɪəl] Auswahlspiel
⟨tribe⟩ [traɪb] Stamm
trick [trɪk] Trick, Kunststück
   to play tricks [pleɪ 'trɪks] Streiche spielen
to trick [trɪk] hereinlegen
trip [trɪp] Ausflug, Tour
to trip [trɪp] stolpern
⟨trooper⟩ ['truːpə] Polizist (AE)
tropical ['trɒpɪkl] tropisch
trouble ['trʌbl] Schwierigkeiten, Ärger

to be in trouble [bɪˌɪn 'trʌbl] in Schwierigkeiten sein, stecken
trousers ['traʊzəz] Hose
⟨flag of truce⟩ [ˌflægˌəv 'truːs] (weiße) Flagge als Friedensangebot
truck [trʌk] Truck, Last(kraft)wagen (AE)
true [truː] wahr
to try* [traɪ] versuchen, probieren
   to try out for [traɪˌ'aʊt fɔ] sich versuchen bei/an/mit (AE)
tube [tjuːb] "Röhre" (Spitzname für die Londoner U-Bahn)
Tuesday ['tjuːzdɪ] Dienstag
out of tune [aʊtˌəv 'tjuːn] schief, unmelodisch, verstimmt
tunnel ['tʌnl] Tunnel
turban ['tɜːbən] Turban
turbine ['tɜːbaɪn] Turbine
turkey ['tɜːkɪ] Truthahn, Puter
Turkish ['tɜːkɪʃ] türkisch; Türkisch
°in turn [ɪn 'tɜːn] der Reihe nach
   my turn ['maɪ tɜːn] ich bin an der Reihe
°in turns [ɪn 'tɜːnz] abwechselnd
to turn [tɜːn] abbiegen, einbiegen
   to turn off [tɜːnˌ'ɒf] ausschalten, ausmachen
   to turn on the radio [ˌtɜːnˌɒn ðə 'reɪdɪəʊ] das Radio einschalten
   °to turn over [tɜːnˌ'əʊvə] umdrehen
   to turn round [tɜːn 'raʊnd] sich umdrehen
   to turn s.th. into s.th. [ˌtɜːn … 'ɪntə …] etwas in etwas ver-/umwandeln
   °to turn the page [tɜːn ðə 'peɪdʒ] umblättern
   °to turn the sound down [tɜːn ðə 'saʊnd ˌdaʊn] leiser stellen
°turning point ['tɜːnɪŋ pɔɪnt] Wendepunkt
tutor ['tjuːtə]
   tutor group ['tjuːtə ˌgruːp] Schulklasse (mit Klassenlehrer/in)
Tutorial [tjuː'tɔːrɪəl] Tutorium, Kolloquium
TV [ˌtiː'viː] Fernsehapparat
   Commercial TV [kə'mɜːʃl tiː'viː] Privatsender
   °Pay TV ['peɪ tiːˌviː] Pay TV
   to be on TV [ɒn ˌtiː 'viː] im Fernsehen sein
   to watch TV [wɒtʃ ˌtiː'viː] fernsehen
   TV company [tiːˌviː 'kʌmpənɪ] Fernsehanstalt
   °TV guide ['tiːviː ˌgaɪd] Fernsehzeitschrift, Fernsehprogramm
   TV set [tiːˌviː ˌset] Fernseher, Fernsehgerät
twelve [twelv] zwölf
twenty ['twentɪ] zwanzig
twice (a week) [twaɪs] zweimal (in der Woche, pro Woche)

⟨**twin**⟩ [twɪn] Zwilling(sschwester/-bruder)
to **twist** [twɪst] drehen
two [tuː] zwei
tycoon [taɪˈkuːn] Tycoon, Magnat
type [taɪp] Typ, Art, Sorte
to **type** [taɪp] tippen, mit der Maschine schreiben
typical [ˈtɪpɪkl] typisch
⟨flat **tyre**⟩ [flæt ˈtaɪə] platter Reifen, Platten

U

un- [ʌn] *negative Vorsilbe*
⟨(un)**bothered**⟩ [(ʌn)ˈbɒðəd] (un)bekümmert
uncle [ˈʌŋkl] Onkel
unclean [ʌnˈkliːn] unsauber, dreckig, verschmutzt
uncomfortable [ʌnˈkʌmftəbl] unbequem
uncommon [ʌnˈkɒmən] selten
under [ˈʌndə] unter
 down under [ˌdaʊn ˈʌndə] (in) Australien, Neuseeland *(ugs.)*
⟨to **undergo***⟩ [ˌʌndəˈgəʊ] sich unterziehen, durchmachen
underground [ˈʌndəgraʊnd] Untergrund (Bahn)
to **underline** [ˌʌndəˈlaɪn] unterstreichen
⟨**underneath**⟩ [ˌʌndəˈniːθ] unterhalb, nach unten
to **understand*** [ˌʌndəˈstænd] verstehen
⟨**understandable**⟩ [ˌʌndəˈstændəbl] verständlich, nachvollziehbar
understanding [ˌʌndəˈstændɪŋ] Verständnis, Verstehen
⟨**undoubtedly**⟩ [ʌnˈdaʊtədlɪ] ohne Zweifel, zweifellos
unemployed [ˈʌnɪmˌplɔɪd] arbeitslos
unfinished [ʌnˈfɪnɪʃt] unvollendet, noch nicht fertig
unfortunate(*ly*) [ʌnˈfɔːtʃənət(lɪ)] leider; unglücklich(erweise)
unfriendly [ʌnˈfrendlɪ] unfreundlich
unhappy [ʌnˈhæpɪ] unglücklich
uniform [ˈjuːnɪfɔːm] Uniform
 Non-Uniform Day [nɒn ˈjuːnɪfɔːm ˌdeɪ] *ein Tag ohne Schuluniform*
unimaginable [ˌʌnɪˈmædʒɪnəbl] unvorstellbar
uninvited [ˌʌnɪnˈvaɪtəd] nicht eingeladen
°**unit** [ˈjuːnɪt] Einheit, Lektion
 ⟨mobile **unit**⟩ [ˌməʊbaɪl ˈjuːnɪt] Ü-Wagen, Übertragung am Ort
to **unite** [juːˈnaɪt] vereinen
United Nations Children's Fund [juːˌnaɪtɪd ˈneɪʃnz ˈtʃɪldrənz ˈfʌnd] UN Kinderhilfsorganisation
⟨**universal** suffrage⟩ [ˌjuːnɪˈvɜːsl ˈsʌfrɪdʒ] allgemeines Wahlrecht
⟨**universe**⟩ [ˈjuːnɪvɜːs] Universum
university [ˌjuːnɪˈvɜːsətɪ] Universität
°**unknown** [ʌnˈnəʊn] unbekannt

to **unleash** [ʌnˈliːʃ] frei lassen; auslösen
unless [ʌnˈles] wenn nicht, es sei denn
unpopular [ʌnˈpɒpjʊlə] unbeliebt
unrest [ʌnˈrest] Unruhen
unsure [ˌʌnˈʃɔː] unsicher
until [ʌnˈtɪl] bis
untouched [ʌnˈtʌtʃt] unberührt
unused [ʌnˈjuːzd] unbenutzt
unwanted [ʌnˈwɒntɪd] ungewollt
⟨**up**-to-date⟩ [ˌʌp tə ˈdeɪt] auf dem neuesten Stand, aktuell
up [ʌp] oben, auch oben
 it's up to you [ɪts ˌʌp tə ˈjuː] es ist deine/Ihre Entscheidung
 °to build up [bɪld ˈʌp] aufbauen; zusammenstellen
 to catch up (*with*) [ˌkætʃ ˈʌp (wɪð)] einholen
 to clean up [kliːn ˈʌp] sauber machen; aufräumen
 to eat up [iːt ˈʌp] aufessen
 to end up [end ˈʌp] enden, landen *(ugs.)*
 to finish up doing s.th. [ˌfɪnɪʃ ˈʌp] mit etwas fertig werden/etwas beenden
 to get up [get ˈʌp] stärker werden
 ⟨to get upset⟩ [get ʌpˈset] die Fassung verlieren, bestürzt sein über
 to give up [gɪv ˈʌp] aufgeben
 to grow up [grəʊ ˈʌp] erwachsen werden
 °to hold up [həʊld ˈʌp] hochhalten
 to hurry up [hʌrɪ ˈʌp] beeilen
 to jump up [dʒʌmp ˈʌp] aufspringen
 to link up with [lɪŋk ˈʌp wɪð] zusammenhängen
 to look s.th. up [lʊk ˈʌp] etwas nachschlagen
 °to make up [meɪk ˈʌp] bilden, ausmachen
 °to match up [mætʃ ˈʌp] das Passende zu etw. finden
 to mix up [ˈmɪks ʌp] durcheinanderbringen, verwechseln
 to pick up [pɪk ˈʌp] aufheben
 to put up one's hand [ˌpʊt ʌp wʌnz ˈhænd] die Hand heben
 to put up with s.o. [pʊt ˈʌp wɪð] jdn. ertragen, dulden
 to set up [set ˈʌp] einrichten, arrangieren
 to set up camp [set ʌp ˈkæmp] zelten, kampieren
 to show up (*for*) [ʃəʊ ˈʌp (ˌfɒ)] auftauchen, erscheinen bei/in, sich blicken lassen bei/in
 to stand up [stænd ˈʌp] aufstehen
 to sum up [sʌm ˈʌp] zusammenfassen
 to swallow up [swɒləʊ ˈʌp] verschlucken

to wake up [weɪk ˈʌp] aufwachen; wecken
 to walk up to s.o. [wɔːk ˈʌp tə ˌsʌmwʌn] auf jdn. zugehen
 to warm up [wɔːm ˈʌp] aufwärmen
 up there [ˌʌp ˈðeə] dort/da oben
°to **update** [ʌpˈdeɪt] aktualisieren, auf den neuesten Stand bringen
upright [ˈʌpraɪt] aufrecht, vertikal
upset [ʌpˈset] bestürzt, betrübt
upside down [ˌʌpsaɪd ˈdaʊn] verkehrt (herum)
upstairs [ʌpˈsteəz] oben (im Haus)
 to go upstairs [gəʊ ʌpˈsteəz] die Treppe hinaufgehen
upwards [ˈʌpwədz] von ... an, und darüber
Urdu [ˈʊəduː] Urdu
us [ʌs] uns
⟨**usage**⟩ [ˈʌpsɪdʒ] Gebrauch
use [juːs] Gebrauch, Verwendung; Verwendungszweck
 it's no use [ɪts ˌnəʊ ˈjuːs] es hat keinen Zweck
to **use** [juːz] benutzen
 to get used to [get ˈjuːst tʊ] sich gewöhnen an
used to [ˈjuːst tə] früher etwas (regelmäßig) getan haben; zu tun gepflegt haben
useful [ˈjuːsfʊl] nützlich
useless [ˈjuːsləs] nutzlos
usual(*ly*) [ˈjuːʒə(lɪ)] normalerweise, gewöhnlich
UV rays [juː ˈviː reɪz] UV-Strahlen

V

vacation [vəˈkeɪʃn] Urlaub, Ferien *(AE)*
 on vacation [ɒn vəˈkeɪʃn] in Urlaub, in den Ferien *(AE)*
vacuum cleaner [ˈvækjʊəm ˌkliːnə] Staubsauger
to **vacuum** [ˈvækjʊəm] Staub saugen
Valentine's Day [ˈvæləntaɪnz ˌdeɪ] Valentinstag
valley [ˈvælɪ] Tal
van [væn] Lieferwagen
 ice cream van [ˈaɪskriːm ˌvæn] Eiswagen
vanilla [vəˈnɪlə] Vanille
°**various** [ˈveərɪəs] verschieden
⟨to **vary**⟩ [ˈveərɪ] sich unterscheiden
vase [vɑːz] Vase
vegetable [ˈvedʒtəbl] Gemüse
vegetarian [ˌvedʒɪˈteərɪən] vegetarisch; Vegetarier/in
⟨**vehemently**⟩ [ˈviːəməntlɪ] vehement, bestimmt
verb [vɜːb] Verb, Tätigkeitswort
°**verse** [vɜːs] Strophe
version [ˈvɜːʃn] Version
versus [ˈvɜːsəs] gegen
very [ˈverɪ] sehr
vet [vet] Tierarzt
veteran [ˈvetərən] Veteran/in

via ['vaɪə] über, via

victim ['vɪktɪm] Opfer

⟨**Victorian**⟩ [vɪk'tɔːrɪən] viktorianisch

video ['vɪdɪəʊ] Video
video recorder ['vɪdɪəʊ rɪˌkɔːdə] Videorekorder

Vietnamese [ˌvjetnə'miːz] vietnamesisch, Vietnamese/Vietnamesin

point of **view** [ˌpɔɪnt_ə_'vjuː] Standpunkt, Sichtweise

°**View** on Demand [ˌvjuː_ ɒn dɪ'mɑːnd] *View on Demand*

to **view** [vjuː] besichtigen; betrachten; fernsehen

°**viewing** habits ['vjuːɪŋ ˌhæbɪts] Sehgewohnheiten

village ['vɪlɪdʒ] Dorf

⟨**villager**⟩ ['vɪlɪdʒə] Dorfbewohner/in

vinegar ['vɪnɪgə] Essig

⟨**violation**⟩ [ˌvaɪə'leɪʃn] Verletzung, Übertretung, Verstoß (gegen)

violence ['vaɪələns] Gewalt

violent ['vaɪələnt] gewalttätig

virtual reality [ˌvɜːtʃʊəl rɪ'ælɪtɪ] virtuelle Realität

visit ['vɪzɪt] Besuch

to **visit** ['vɪzɪt] besuchen

visitor ['vɪzɪtə] Besucher/in

vocabulary [vəʊ'kæbjʊlərɪ] Vokabular

voice [vɔɪs] Stimme

volcanic [vɒl'kænɪk] vulkanisch

volunteer [ˌvɒlən'tɪə] Freiwillige/r

vote [vəʊt] Abstimmung, Wahl; ⟨Wahlrecht⟩
to take a vote on [ˌteɪk_ə 'vəʊt_ɒn] abstimmen über

to **vote** [vəʊt] wählen, abstimmen

⟨**voyage**⟩ ['vɔːɪdʒ] Reise, Seereise

W

wage [weɪdʒ] Lohn

wagon ['wægən] Wagen, Planwagen

to **wait** [weɪt] warten
I can't wait! [aɪ 'kɑːnt ˌweɪt] Ich kann's kaum erwarten!
to wait for ['weɪt fə] warten auf

waiter ['weɪtə] Kellner

waitress ['weɪtrɪs] Kellnerin

to **wake up*** [weɪk_'ʌp] aufwachen; wecken

walk [wɔːk] Spaziergang
to take for a walk ['teɪk fər_ə 'wɔːk] spazieren führen
walk-a-thon ['wɔːk_əˌθɒn] Geh-Marathon

to **walk** [wɔːk] (zu Fuß) gehen
to walk in [wɔːk_'ɪn] hineinspazieren
to walk on [wɔːk_'ɒn] weitergehen
to walk out of [ˌwɔːk_'aʊt_əv] etwas mitten drin verlassen
to walk up to s.o. [wɔːk_'ʌp tə ˌsʌmwʌn] auf jdn. zugehen

walkman ['wɔːkmən] Walkman

wall [wɔːl] Wand, Mauer

wallet ['wɒlɪt] Brieftasche, Geldbeutel

⟨to **waltz**⟩ [wɒls] Walzer tanzen

⟨**wanna**⟩ ['wɒnə] *umgangssprachl. für* want to

to **want** [wɒnt] wollen, wünschen

wanted ['wɒntɪd] gesucht

war [wɔː] Krieg

wardrobe ['wɔːdrəʊb] Kleiderschrank

to **warm up** [wɔːm_'ʌp] aufwärmen

warm [wɔːm] warm

global **warming** [ˌgləʊbl 'wɔːmɪŋ] globale (Erd-) Erwärmung, Erwärmung der Erdatmosphäre

warning ['wɔːnɪŋ] Warnung

to **wash** [wɒʃ] waschen

washing machine ['wɒʃɪŋ məˌʃiːn] Waschmaschine

waste [weɪst] Abfall, Müll
waste paper basket ['weɪst ˌpeɪpə ˌbɑːskɪt] Papierkorb

to **waste** [weɪst] verschwenden, vergeuden

watch [wɒtʃ] Armbanduhr

to **watch** [wɒtʃ] zuschauen, beobachten, schauen
to watch out (*for*) [wɒtʃ_'aʊt] Ausschau halten, aufpassen, Acht geben (auf)
to watch TV [wɒtʃ ˌtiː'viː] fernsehen
Watch out! [ˌwɒtʃ_'aʊt] Pass auf! Gib Acht!

water ['wɔːtə] Wasser

waterfall ['wɔːtəfɔːl] Wasserfall

waterproofs ['wɔːtəpruːfs] Regenjacke, -hose, -mantel, wasserfeste Jacke

wave [weɪv] Welle
brain **waves** ['breɪn ˌweɪvz] Gehirnwellen, -ströme

way [weɪ] °Art, Weise; Richtung; Weg, Strecke
by the way [ˌbaɪ ðə 'weɪ] übrigens
the wrong way round [ˌrɒŋ weɪ 'raʊnd] falsch herum

⟨**way** up⟩ ['weɪ_ˌʌp] weit oben

we [wiː] wir

weak [wiːk] schwach

⟨**wealthy**⟩ ['welθɪ] wohlhabend

to **wear*** [weə] tragen
to wear s.th. down [ˌweə ˌsʌmθɪŋ 'daʊn] abnutzen, abtragen

weather ['weðə] Wetter

⟨funnel **web** (spider)⟩ ['fʌnl web (ˌspaɪdə)] *australische Spinnenart*

Wednesday ['wenzdɪ] Mittwoch

week [wiːk] Woche

weekday ['wiːkdeɪ] Wochentag

weekend [wiːk'end] Wochenende
at the weekend [ət ðə 'wiːkˌend] am Wochenende

to **welcome** ['welkəm] begrüßen, herzlich willkommen heißen

⟨**well**⟩ [wel] Brunnen; (Öl)Quelle

well [wel] gut
to do well [du: 'wel] gut abschneiden, gut machen
⟨to not be well⟩ ['nɒt bi: ˌwel] sich nicht gut fühlen, nicht gut gehen
well-built [wel 'bɪlt] "gut gebaut", stämmig, kräftig
well-known [ˌwel'nəʊn] bekannt

as **well** [əs_'wel] auch, ebenfalls

well [wel] also; nun ja

Welsh [welʃ] Walisisch, Waliser/in

west [west] Westen, westlich

West Indian [ˌwest_'ɪndɪən] westindisch, Westinder/in

western ['westən] Western

wet [wet] nass

wetland ['wetlənd] Sumpfgebiet

whale [weɪl] Wal

what [wɒt] was
What about ...? ['wɒt_əˌbaʊt] Was hältst du von ...?, Was ist mit ...?
What colour is ...? [wɒt 'kʌlər_ɪz] Welche Farbe hat ...?
What else is new? [wɒt 'els_ɪz ˌnjuː] *ironisch* Weiß ich schon!
°What else? [wɒt 'els] Was sonst?
What time is it? [wɒt 'taɪm_ɪz_ɪt] Wie spät ist es?
°What time ...? [wɒt 'taɪm] Wann ...? Um wie viel Uhr ...?
What's on? [ˌwɒts_'ɒn] was gibt es/was kommt/was läuft?
What's the matter? [ˌwɒts ðə 'mætə] Was ist los? Was haben Sie? Wie fühlen Sie sich?
What's wrong? [wɒts 'rɒŋ] Was ist los?

wheel [wiːl] Rad

wheelchair [ˌwiːl'tʃeə] Rollstuhl

when [wen] als; wenn; wann

where [weə] wo, woher, wohin

°**wherever** [weə'revə] wo auch immer, egal wo

whether ['weðə] ob

which [wɪtʃ] welche/r/s

for a **while** [fər_ə 'waɪl] für eine Weile, eine Zeit lang

while [waɪl] während, solange

whiskers ['wɪskəz] Schnurrbarthaare

to **whisper** ['wɪspə] flüstern

whistle ['wɪsl] (Triller-) Pfeife

to **whistle** ['wɪsl] pfeifen

white [waɪt] weiß
white elephant stall [waɪt_'elɪfənt stɔːl] Gemischtwarenstand
white-water rafting ['waɪt ˌwɔːtə 'rɑːftɪŋ] Wildwasser-Rafting (*mit dem Floß fahren*)

who [huː] wer
the one who [ðə 'wʌn huː] der/diejenige, der/die

whole [həʊl] ganz/e/r/s

why [waɪ] warum

wide [waɪd] breit; weit

to **widen** ['waɪdn] erweitern, ausweiten

⟨**widespread**⟩ ['waɪdspred] weit verbreitet

wife [waɪf] Ehefrau
wild [waɪld] wild
wildlife ['waɪldlaɪf] Tier- und
  Pflanzenwelt
will* [wɪl] werden
  to be **willing** to do [ˌwɪlɪŋ tə 'duː]
  bereit sein, etwas zu tun
wimp [wɪmp] Schwächling,
  "Waschlappen" (*ugs.*)
⟨**win**⟩ [wɪn] Gewinn
to **win*** [wɪn] gewinnen
wind [wɪnd] Wind
⟨**windfall**⟩ ['wɪndfɔːl] unverhoffter
  Glücksfall/Geldsegen
window ['wɪndəʊ] Fenster
⟨**wine**⟩ ['waɪn] Wein(anbaugebiet)
⟨**wing**⟩ [wɪŋ] Flügel
°**winner** ['wɪnə] Gewinner/in,
  Sieger/in
winter ['wɪntə] Winter
⟨barbed **wire**⟩ [ˌbɑːbd 'waɪ]
  Stacheldraht
  ⟨**wire-netting**⟩ [ˌwaɪə'netɪŋ]
  Maschendraht
⟨**wise**⟩ [waɪz] klug, vernünftig
to **wish** [wɪʃ] (sich) wünschen
best **wishes** [best 'wɪʃɪz] alles Gute
with [wɪð] mit
  to agree (*with*) [ə'griː wɪð]
  übereinstimmen
  to get along with s.o. [get̬ ə'lɒŋ
  wɪð] mit jdm. auskommen/
  zurechtkommen
  to go with ['gəʊ wɪð]
  zusammenpassen
  to link up with [lɪŋk̬ 'ʌp wɪð]
  zusammenhängen
⟨**within** the range of operations⟩
  [wɪˌðɪn ðə 'reɪndʒ əv̬ ˌɒpə'reɪʃnz]
  im Aktionskreis/in Reichweite der
  (militärischen) Operationen
without [wɪ'ðaʊt] ohne
to **wobble** ['wɒbl] wackeln,
  schwanken
wolf, wolves [wʊlf, wʊlvz] Wolf, Wölfe
woman ['wʊmən] Frau
women (*pl*) ['wɪmɪn] Frauen
to **wonder** ['wʌndə] sich fragen
wonderful ['wʌndəfʊl] wunderbar
won't (= **will not**) [wəʊnt] nicht
  werden
⟨**woods**⟩ [wʊdz] Wald
⟨to crawl out of the **woodwork**⟩
  ['wʊdwɜːk] von allen Seiten
  angekrochen kommen
wool [wʊl] Wolle
word [wɜːd] Wort
  I want a word with … [aɪ ˌwɒnt̬ ə
  'wɜːd wɪð] Mit … habe ich noch
  ein Wörtchen zu reden.
work [wɜːk] Arbeit
  at work [ət 'wɜːk] bei der Arbeit
to **work** [wɜːk] arbeiten;
  funktionieren
  °to work out [wɜːk̬ 'aʊt]
  herausfinden
  to work overtime [wɜːk 'əʊvətaɪm]
  Überstunden machen

workbook ['wɜːkbʊk] Arbeitsheft
worker ['wɜːkə] Arbeiter/in
⟨**workshop**⟩ ['wɜːkʃɒp] Werkstatt
world ['wɜːld] Welt
  °the Third World [ðə ˌθɜːd 'wɜːld]
  die Dritte Welt
⟨**worm**⟩ [wɜːm] Wurm
to **worry** ['wʌrɪ] sich sorgen,
  Sorgen/Gedanken machen
worse [wɜːs] schlimmer
  worse luck! [wɜːs 'lʌk] (so ein)
  Pech! (*ugs.*)
to **worship** ['wɜːʃɪp] anbeten,
  Gottesdienst feiern
the **worst** thing [ðə 'wɜːst ˌθɪŋ]
  der/die/das Schlimmste
to be **worth** [bɪ 'wɜːθ] sich lohnen,
  wert sein
would [wʊd] würde
  would-be ['wʊdbiː] Möchtegern-
  would like [wʊd 'laɪk] möchten,
  würden gerne
wound [wuːnd] Wunde
Wow! [waʊ] "Wow!" (*Ausruf der
  Bewunderung/des Erstaunens*)
to **wrap** [ræp] einpacken
⟨to **wring***⟩ [rɪŋ] auswringen;
  (Hals) umdrehen
to **write*** [raɪt] schreiben
  °to write about ['raɪt̬ əˌbaʊt]
  schreiben über
  °to write down [raɪt 'daʊn]
  aufschreiben
writer ['raɪtə] Schriftsteller/in
writing ['raɪtɪŋ] Schreiben, Schrift,
  Handschrift
  °creative writing [krɪ'eɪtɪv ˌraɪtɪŋ]
  kreatives Schreiben
  writing paper ['raɪtɪŋ ˌpeɪpə]
  Briefpapier
wrong [rɒŋ] Unrecht
wrong [rɒŋ] falsch
  the wrong way round [ˌrɒŋ weɪ
  'raʊnd] falsch herum
  to go wrong [gəʊ 'rɒŋ] schief
  gehen

Y

yacht [jɒt] Jacht, Yacht
⟨**yard**⟩ [jɑːd] *Maßeinheit*:
  1 Yard = 0,91m
yardwork ['jɑːdwɜːk] Gartenarbeit
  (*AE*)
year [jɪə] Jahr
yearbook ['jɪəbʊk] Jahrbuch (*AE*)
⟨to **yell**⟩ [jel] schreien
yellow ['jeləʊ] gelb
yes [jes] ja
yesterday ['jestədɪ] gestern
yet [jet] schon; jedoch, aber
  not … yet [nɒt 'jet] noch nicht
⟨**Yippee**⟩ [jɪ'piː] juchhu, hurra
you [juː] du/ihr/Sie; dir/euch/
  Ihnen; dich/euch/Sie
  ⟨you've had it⟩ [juːv 'hæd̬ ɪt] du
  bist erledigt (*ugs.*)

young [jʌŋ] jung
your [jɔː] dein/deine; euer/eure;
  Ihr/Ihre
Yours faithfully [jɔːz 'feɪθfəlɪ]
  Hochachtungsvoll, Mit
  freundlichen Grüßen
yourself [jɔː'self] dich/dir selbst, ihr/
  euch selbst
youth club ['juːθ klʌb] Jugendklub
  Youth Activity Centre [juːθ̬
  æk'tɪvɪtɪ ˌsentə] Jugendzentrum
  youth advice centre [ˌjuːθ̬ əd'vaɪs
  ˌsentə] *Beratungsstelle für
  Jugendliche*
Yuk! [jʌk] Igitt!, Pfui!

Z

zoo [zuː] Zoo

Boys' names

⟨**Ainsley**⟩ ['eɪnzlɪ]
Alan ['ælən]
Andy ['ændɪ]
Asim [ʌ'siːm]
Ben [ben]
Bertie ['bɜːtɪ]
Bill [bɪl]
Bob [bɒb]
Brad [bræd]
Charlie ['tʃɑːlɪ]
Chiong [tʃɒŋ]
Chris [krɪs]
⟨**Clancy**⟩ ['klænsɪ]
Colin ['kɒlɪn]
Dan [dæn]
Daniel ['dænjəl]
Dave [deɪv]
David ['deɪvɪd]
Eddie ['edɪ]
Ellis ['elɪs]
⟨**Ethan**⟩ ['iːθən]
Frank [fræŋk]
Fred [fred]
Freddie ['fredɪ]
Gavin ['gævɪn]
Greg [greg]
Hank [hæŋk]
Harry ['hærɪ]
Henry ['henrɪ]
Ian ['ɪən]
Imran ['ɪmrɑːn]
Jamar [dʒə'mɑː]
James [dʒeɪmz]
Jason ['dʒeɪsn]
Jeremy ['dʒerɪmɪ]
Jesus ['dʒiːzəs]
Joe [dʒəʊ]
John [dʒɒn]
⟨**Josh**⟩ [dʒɒʃ]
Jun [jʊn]
Kevin ['kevɪn]
Lee [liː]
Liam ['lɪəm]
Luke [luːk]

⟨**Macon**⟩ ['meɪkən]
Mark [mɑːk]
Matthew ['mæθjuː]
Michael ['maɪkl]
⟨**Mick**⟩ [mɪk]
Mike [maɪk]
Nick [nɪk]
Olly ['ɒlɪ]
Patrick ['pætrɪk]
Paul [pɔːl]
Peter ['piːtə]
⟨**Philip**⟩ ['fɪlɪp]
Pip [pɪp]
⟨**Pluto**⟩ ['pluːtəʊ]
Rajiv [rɑːˈdʒɪv]
Ramon [rəˈmɒn]
Rangilal ['ræŋgɪˌlɑːl]
Robert ['rɒbət]
Salvador ['sælvədɔː]
Sam [sæm]
Simon ['saɪmən]
Steven ['stiːvn]
Terry ['terɪ]
Tim [tɪm]
Tobias [təˈbaɪəs]
Toby ['təʊbɪ]
Tom [tɒm]
Tommy ['tɒmɪ]
Tony ['təʊnɪ]
⟨**Vince**⟩ [vɪns]
Wayne [weɪn]

Girls' names

Aisha ['aɪʃə]
Alice ['ælɪs]
Alison ['ælɪsn]
Amy ['eɪmɪ]
Ann [æn]
Anna ['ænə]
⟨**Aurora**⟩ [ɔːˈrɔːrə]
Barbara ['bɑːbərə]
Becky ['bekɪ]
Bronwyn ['brɒnwɪn]
Caroline ['kærəlaɪn]
Catherine ['kæθrɪn]
⟨**Charlotte**⟩ ['ʃɑːlət]
⟨**Christabel**⟩ ['krɪstəbel]
Cindy-Lou [ˌsɪndɪ ˈluː]
Claire [kleə]
Clare [kleə]
Debby ['debɪ]
⟨**Elizabeth**⟩ [ɪˈlɪzəbəθ]
Emily ['emɪlɪ]
Fiona [fɪˈəʊnə]
Frannie ['frænɪ]
Hannah ['hænə]
Helen ['helen]
Holly ['hɒlɪ]
Jane [dʒeɪn]
Janet ['dʒænɪt]
Jassim ['dʒɑːsɪm]
Jennifer ['dʒenɪfə]
Jenny ['dʒenɪ]
Jessica ['dʒesɪkə]
Jill [dʒɪl]
Jo-Ann [dʒəʊˈæn]

Judith ['dʒuːdɪθ]
⟨**Juna**⟩ ['djuːnə]
Karen ['kærən]
⟨**Kate**⟩ [keɪt]
Kathleen ['kæθliːn]
Kelly ['kelɪ]
Laura ['lɔːrə]
Lesley ['lezlɪ]
Lila ['laɪlə]
Linda ['lɪndə]
Lisa ['liːsə]
Liz [lɪz]
Louise [luːˈiːz]
Lucy ['luːsɪ]
Mabel ['meɪbl]
Mandy ['mændɪ]
Marcia ['mɑːsjə]
Mary ['meərɪ]
⟨**Matilda**⟩ [məˈtɪldə]
Mel [mel]
Melanie ['melənɪ]
Miguela [mɪˈgelæ]
Nicola ['nɪkələ]
Pamela ['pæmələ]
Pat [pæt]
Pauline ['pɔːliːn]
Penny ['penɪ]
Rachel ['reɪtʃəl]
Rebecca [rɪˈbekə]
Rita ['riːtə]
Sabina [səˈbiːnə]
Sally ['sælɪ]
⟨**Samantha**⟩ [səˈmænθə]
Sammia ['sɑːmɪɑː]
Sandra ['sændrə]
Sarah ['seərə]
Scarlet ['skɑːlət]
Scott [skɒt]
Sharon ['ʃærən]
Shirin [ʃɪˈriːn]
Sophie ['səʊfɪ]
Steffi ['stefɪ]
Sue [suː]
Sukhi ['suːkɪ]
Susan ['suːzn]
⟨**Sylvia**⟩ ['sɪlvɪə]
⟨**Teresa**⟩ [təˈriːzə]
Tina ['tiːnə]
Tracy ['treɪsɪ]
Tricia ['trɪʃə]
Vasuda [vəˈsuːdə]
Victoria [vɪkˈtɔːrɪə]
Wendy ['wendɪ]
Yasmin [jæsˈmiːn]
Zoe ['zəʊɪ]

Surnames

⟨**Allen**⟩ ['ælən]
Anwar ['ænwɑːr]
Baker ['beɪkə]
Barber ['bɑːbə]
Bennett ['benɪt]
Bradley ['brædlɪ]
Burton ['bɜːtn]
Cassidy ['kæsɪdɪ]
Chowdury ['tʃaʊdrɪ]

Collins ['kɒlɪnz]
Conan Doyle [ˌkəʊnən ˈdɔɪl]
Costner ['kɒstnə]
Croft [krɒft]
⟨**Cushen**⟩ ['kʊʃn]
Dane [deɪn]
Davis ['deɪvɪs]
Denning ['denɪŋ]
Dixon ['dɪksn]
Doe [dəʊ]
Edmonds ['edməndz]
Evans ['evənz]
Fearless ['fɪəlɪs]
Ferraro [fəˈrɑːrəʊ]
⟨**Fossington-Gore**⟩ [ˌfɒsɪŋtən ˈgɔː]
Foster ['fɒstə]
Greenwood ['griːnwʊd]
Griffiths ['grɪfɪθs]
⟨**Indelkoffer**⟩ ['ɪndlˌkɒfə]
Jones [dʒəʊnz]
Katzoff ['kætsɒf]
Kellerman ['keləmən]
Landsberg ['lænsbɜːg]
Lee [liː]
Levine [ləˈviːn]
Martin ['mɑːtɪn]
McNeill [məkˈniːl]
Moloney [məˈləʊnɪ]
Narayan [nɑːˈraɪən]
O'Brien [əʊˈbraɪən]
⟨**O'Connor**⟩ [əʊˈkɒnə]
Ortiz [ɔːˈtiːz]
Owen ['əʊɪn]
Palmer ['pɑːmə]
Patel [pəˈtel]
Penrose ['penrəʊz]
Primrose ['prɪmrəʊz]
Scott [skɒt]
Sherwen ['ʃɜːwən]
Singh [sɪŋ]
Sitaram ['sɪtərəm]
Smith [smɪθ]
Spice [spaɪs]
Staunton ['stɔːntən]
⟨**Strong**⟩ [strɒŋ]
Taylor ['teɪlə]
Tran [træn]
Wang [wɒŋ]
Watson ['wɒtsn]
⟨**Wilmott**⟩ ['wɪlmət]
Ziegler ['ziːglə]

Geographical names

Africa ['æfrɪkə]
Alabama [ˌæləˈbæmə]
Alaska [əˈlæskə]
America [əˈmerɪkə]
Antarctica [ænˈtɑːktɪkə]
Arizona [ˌærɪˈzəʊnə]
Asia ['eɪʒə]
Atlanta [ətˈlæntə]
Atlantic Ocean [ətˌlæntɪk ˈəʊʃn]
Australia [ɒˈstreɪljə]
Austria ['ɒstrɪə]
Ayer's Rock [ˌeəz ˈrɒk]
the **Balkans** [ðə ˈbɔːlkənz]

Ballyconneely [ˌbælɪkəˈniːlɪ]
Ballynahinch [ˌbælɪnəˈhɪnʃ]
Barna [ˈbɑːnə]
⟨Barry⟩ [ˈbærɪ]
Belfast [ˌbelˈfaːst]
Berlin [bɜːˈlɪn]
Beverly Hills [ˈbevəlɪ ˈhɪlz]
Big Ben [bɪg ˈben]
Birmingham [ˈbɜːmɪŋəm]
Bismarck [ˈbɪzmɑːk]
Blackpool [ˈblækpuːl]
Bradford [ˈbrædfəd]
Brazil [brəˈzɪl]
Brighton [ˈbraɪtn]
Brighton Beach [ˌbraɪtn ˈbiːtʃ]
Bristol [ˈbrɪstl]
Britain [ˈbrɪtn]
°British Isles [brɪtɪʃˌˈaɪlz]
Bromley [ˈbrɒmlɪ]
the Bronx [ðə ˌbrɒŋks]
Brooklyn [ˈbrʊklɪn]
Buckingham Palace [ˈbʌkɪŋəm ˈpælɪs]
⟨Burt's Creek⟩ [ˌbɜːts ˈkriːk]
California [ˌkælɪˈfɔːnjə]
Camden Market [ˈkæmdən ˈmɑːkɪt]
Canada [ˈkænədə]
Canary Wharf [kəˈneərɪ wɔːf]
the Caribbean [ðə ˌkærɪˈbiːən]
Carna [ˈkɑːnə]
Central Australia [ˌsentrəl ɒsˈtreɪlɪə]
Chicago [ʃɪˈkɑːgəʊ]
China [ˈtʃaɪnə]
Clonakilty [ˌklɒnəˈkɪltɪ]
Cody [ˈkəʊdɪ]
Colchester [ˈkəʊltʃestə]
⟨Cologne⟩ [kəˈləʊn]
Colorado [ˌkɒləˈrɑːdəʊ]
Commonwealth [ˈkɒmənwelθ]
Coney Island [ˌkəʊnɪ ˈaɪlənd]
Connemara [ˌkɒnɪˈmɑːrə]
Coronado [ˌkɒrəˈnɑːdəʊ]
Cork [kɔːk]
Covent Garden [ˈkɒvənt ˈgɑːdn]
Croatia [krəʊˈeɪʃɪə]
Cuba [ˈkjuːbə]
Cumbria [ˈkʌmbrɪə]
Dallas [ˈdæləs]
⟨Delhi⟩ [ˈdelɪ]
Derry [ˈderɪ]
Detroit City [dɪˈtrɔɪt ˌsɪtɪ]
⟨Downing Street⟩ [ˈdaʊnɪŋ ˌstriːt]
Dun Laoghaire [dʌn ˈlɪərɪ]
Durango [dʊˈræŋgəʊ]
Eastern Europe [ˌiːstən ˈjʊərəp]
Eire [ˈeərə]
Empire State Building [ˈempaɪə ˈsteɪt ˈbɪldɪŋ]
England [ˈɪŋglənd]
Europe [ˈjʊərəp]
Exeter [ˈeksətə]
Florida [ˈflɒrɪdə]
⟨Forest of Dean⟩ [ˌfɒrɪst ˌəv ˈdiːn]
Forgan [ˈfɔːgən]
France [frɑːns]
Frankfurt [ˈfræŋkfət]
Fresno [ˈfresnəʊ]
Galway [ˈgɔːlweɪ]

Garrettstown [ˈgærətstaʊn]
Georgia [ˈdʒɔːdʒə]
Germany [ˈdʒɜːmənɪ]
Gibraltar [dʒɪˈbrɔːltə]
Glasgow [ˈglɑːzgəʊ]
Grand Mesa [grænd ˈmesə]
Great Britain [greɪt ˈbrɪtn]
Greece [griːs]
Grove City [ˌgrəʊv ˈsɪtɪ]
Hall of the Kings [ˌhɔːl ˌɒv ðə ˈkɪŋz]
Hamburg [ˈhæmbɜːg]
Havana [həˈvænə]
Hawaii [həˈwaɪiː]
Hill of the Kings [ˌhɪl ˌɒv ðə ˈkɪŋz]
⟨Himalayas⟩ [ˌhɪməˈleɪəz]
Hollywood [ˈhɒlɪwʊd]
Hong Kong [ˌhɒŋ ˈkɒŋ]
⟨The Horn of Africa⟩ [ˌhɔːn ˌəv ˈæfrɪkə]
Huntsville [ˈhʌntsvɪl]
Hyde Park [haɪd ˈpɑːk]
India [ˈɪndjə]
Ireland [ˈaɪələnd]
Isle of Dogs [aɪl ˌəv ˈdɒgz]
Italy [ˈɪtəlɪ]
Jamaica [dʒəˈmeɪkə]
⟨Jamesburg⟩ [ˈdʒeɪmzbɜːg]
Japan [dʒəˈpæn]
Jerusalem [dʒəˈruːsələm]
Kansas City [ˈkænzəs ˈsɪtɪ]
Karachi [kəˈrɑːtʃɪ]
Kinsale [kɪnˈseɪl]
Kilbrittain [kɪlˈbrɪtn]
⟨Kumunijayi⟩ [ˌkʊmʊnɪˈdʒɑːiː]
L.A. (Los Angeles) [elˈeɪ]
Lake Eyre [leɪk ˈeə]
The Lake District [ˈleɪk ˌdɪstrɪkt]
Leeds [liːdz]
Leicester Square [ˌlestə ˈskweə]
⟨Leicestershire⟩ [ˈlestəʃə]
Little Havana [ˌlɪtl həˈvænə]
Little Odessa [ˌlɪtl əˈdesə]
London [ˈlʌndən]
Los Angeles [lɒs ˈænʒɪliːz]
Madrid [məˈdrɪd]
Malibu [ˈmælɪbuː]
⟨Manchester⟩ [ˈmæntʃɪstə]
Manhattan [mænˈhætn]
Marina del Rey [məˈriːnə del reɪ]
Mc Gucken Park [məˌgʊkən ˈpɑːk]
⟨Mercer⟩ [ˈmɜːsə]
Mesa Verde [ˌmesə ˈvɜːdɪ]
Mexico [ˈmeksɪkəʊ]
Miami [maɪˈæmɪ]
⟨Middlesex⟩ [ˈmɪdlseks]
Midwest [mɪdˈwest]
Milan [mɪˈlæn]
New Jersey [ˌnjuː ˈdʒɜːzɪ]
New Orleans [ˌnjuː ˈɔːlɪənz]
New South Wales [ˈnjuː ˌsaʊθ ˈweɪlz]
New York [ˌnjuː ˈjɔːk]
New York City [ˌnjuːjɔːk ˈsɪtɪ]
New York State [ˌnjuːjɔːk ˈsteɪt]
New Zealand [ˌnjuː ˈziːlənd]
Newcastle [ˈnjuːˌkɑːsl]
⟨Norfolk⟩ [ˈnɔːfək]
North Carolina [ˌnɔːθ ˌkærəˈlaɪnə]
North Dakota [ˌnɔːθ dəˈkəʊtə]

Northern Ireland [ˌnɔːðn ˈaɪələnd]
the North of England [nɔːθ ˌəv ˈɪŋglənd]
Norwood [ˈnɔːwʊd]
Nottingham [ˈnɒtɪŋəm]
Nuremberg [ˈnjʊərəmbɜːg]
Ocean Front Walk [ˈəʊʃn frʌnt wɔːk]
⟨Oileán islands⟩ [ˈɪlɔːnˌˈaɪləndz]
Oklahoma [ˌəʊkləˈhəʊmə]
Old Man of Coniston [əʊld mænˌəv ˈkɒnɪstn]
Oughterard [ˈɒxtərɑːd]
Oxford Street [ˈɒksfəd striːt]
PA (Pennsylvania) [piːˈeɪ]
Pacific Avenue [pəˈsɪfɪk ˈævənjuː]
Pacific Ocean [pəˈsɪfɪk ˈəʊʃn]
Pakistan [ˌpɑːkɪˈstɑːn]
Paris [ˈpærɪs]
Parkway City Mall [ˈpɑːkweɪ ˈsɪtɪ mɔːl]
Peking [piːˈkɪŋ]
Pennsylvania [ˌpensɪlˈveɪnɪə]
Phoenix [ˈfiːnɪks]
Pittsburgh [ˈpɪtsbɜːg]
Poland [ˈpəʊlənd]
Princeton [ˈprɪnstən]
Purgatory [ˈpɜːgətɒrɪ]
Queens [kwiːnz]
Queensland [ˈkwiːnzlənd]
⟨Rhine⟩ [raɪn]
Rochester [ˈrɒtʃɪstə]
Rocky Mountains [ˌrɒkɪ ˈmaʊntɪnz]
Russia [ˈrʌʃə]
⟨Salisbury⟩ [ˈsɔːlzbərɪ]
Salzburg [ˈsæltsbɜːg]
San Francisco [ˌsæn frnˈsɪskəʊ]
San Diego [sæn dɪˈeɪgəʊ]
⟨Sandwell⟩ [ˈsændwel]
Scotland [ˈskɒtlənd]
Screebe [skriːb]
Seattle [sɪˈætl]
Serbia [ˈsɜːbjə]
Sherwood [ˈʃɜːwʊd]
Sherwood Forest [ˌʃɜːwʊd ˈfɒrɪst]
Silverton [ˈsɪlvətən]
⟨South Africa⟩ [saʊθˌˈæfrɪkə]
South America [saʊθ əˈmerɪkə]
South Australia [ˌsaʊθ ɒsˈtreɪlɪə]
South Central [saʊθ ˈsentrəl]
South Dakota [saʊθ dəˈkəʊtə]
South Parade [saʊθ pəˈreɪd]
Space and Rocket Center [speɪs ˌənd ˈrɒkɪt ˈsentə]
Spain [speɪn]
⟨Stonehenge⟩ [stəʊnˈhendʒ]
Surfrider Beach [ˌsɜːfraɪdə ˌbiːtʃ]
Swansea [ˈswɒnzɪ]
Sydney [ˈsɪdnɪ]
Sydney Cove [ˈsɪdnɪ ˈkəʊv]
Tara [ˈtɑːrə]
Thames [temz]
Timoleague [ˌtɪməʊˈliːg]
⟨Tokyo⟩ [ˈtəʊkɪəʊ]
Tower Bridge [ˈtaʊə brɪdʒ]
Trafalgar Square [trəˈfælgə skweə]
⟨Trenton⟩ [ˈtrentən]
⟨Troon⟩ [truːn]
Truro [ˈtrʊərəʊ]
Turkey [ˈtɜːkɪ]

Uganda [juːˈgændə]
U.K. [ˌjuːˈkeɪ]
Ulster [ˈʌlstə]
Uluru [ʊləˈruː]
United Kingdom [juːˌnaɪtɪd ˈkɪŋdəm]
United States [juːˌnaɪtɪd ˈsteɪts]
USA [ˌjuːesˈeɪ]
Venice [ˈvenɪs]
Victoria [vɪkˈtɔːrɪə]
Vienna [vɪˈenə]
Virginia [vəˈdʒɪnjə]
Wales [weɪlz]
⟨Walsall⟩ [ˈwɔːlsɔːl]
⟨Wanga Hill⟩ [ˌwæŋgə ˈhɪl]
Washington D. C. [ˌwɒʃɪŋtən diː ˈsiː]
West Africa [westˈæfrɪkə]
⟨Winchester⟩ [ˈwɪntʃɪstə]
Wind River Mountains [wɪnd ˌrɪvə ˈmaʊntɪnz]
⟨Windsor⟩ [ˈwɪnzə]
Woolwich [ˈwʊlɪtʃ]
World Trade Center [wɜːld treɪd ˈsentə]
⟨Wyndham⟩ [ˈwɪndəm]
Wyoming [waɪˈəʊmɪŋ]
Yellowstone National Park [ˌjeləʊstəʊn ˌnæʃənl ˈpɑːk]
York [jɔːk]
Yorkshire [ˈjɔːkʃə]
Yorkshire Moors [jɔːkʃə ˈmɔːz]

Other names

Adrian Mole [ˌeɪdrɪən ˈməʊl]
⟨Alan Shepard High School⟩ [ˌælən ˈʃepəd ˈhaɪ skuːl]
⟨Albert Namatjira⟩ [ˌælbət næməˈtʃɪərə]
Amnesty International [ˈæmnɪstɪ ˌɪntəˈnæʃnl]
⟨Angela Smythe⟩ [ˌændʒələ ˈsmaɪð]
⟨Anne Boleyn⟩ [ˌæn bəˈlɪn]
⟨Anne Tyler⟩ [ˌæn ˈtaɪlə]
⟨The Armada⟩ [ɑːˈmɑːdə]
⟨Artist & Repertoire⟩ [ˈɑːtɪstˌənd ˈrepətwɑː]
⟨Australia Day⟩ [ɒsˈtreɪlɪə deɪ]
⟨Australian Pacific Tours⟩ [ɒsˌtreɪlɪən pəˌsɪfɪk ˈtʊəz]
⟨B. Watterson⟩ [ˌbiː ˈwɒtəsən]
⟨Barry Kent⟩ [ˌbærɪ ˈkent]
BBC [ˌbiː biː ˈsiː]
The BBC World Service [ðə ˌbiːbiːˈsiː ˌwɜːld ˈsɜːvɪs]
⟨Bernie Taupin⟩ [ˌbɜːnɪ ˈtɔːpɪn]
The Brent Spar [ðə ˈbrent ˈspɑː]
British Telecom (BT) [ˌbrɪtɪʃ ˈtelɪkɒm]
⟨The British Empire⟩ [ˌbrɪtɪʃˈempaɪə]
⟨Bruce Woodley⟩ [ˌbruːs ˈwʊdlɪ]
⟨Calvin and Hobbes⟩ [ˌkælvɪnˌənd ˈhɒbz]
Cape Canaveral [ˌkeɪp kəˈnævərəl]
⟨Capt. Arthur Phillip⟩ [ˌkæptɪn ˌɑːθə ˈfɪlɪp]
⟨Captain Cook⟩ [ˌkæptɪn ˈkʊk]

⟨Carl Phillips⟩ [ˌkɑːl ˈfɪlɪps]
⟨Catherine Sefton⟩ [ˌkæθrɪn ˈseftən]
⟨The Channel Tunnel⟩ [ˌtʃænl ˈtʌnl]
⟨Charles I⟩ [ˌtʃɑːlz ðə ˈfɜːst]
⟨The Charlie McCarthy Show⟩ [ðə ˌtʃɑːlɪ məˈkɑːθɪ ˌʃəʊ]
⟨Chris Colón⟩ [ˌkrɪs kɒˈlɒn]
CIA (= Central Intelligence Agency) [ˌsiːˌaɪˈeɪ]
⟨Classic FM⟩ [ˈklæsɪkˈefˈem]
4-H club [ˌfɔːˈeɪtʃ klʌb]
⟨Columbia Broadcasting System (CBS)⟩ [kəˌlʌmbɪə ˈbrɔːdkɑːstɪŋ ˌsɪstəm (siː biː ˈes)]
⟨Columbus⟩ [kəˈlʌmbəs]
⟨Coronation Street⟩ [ˌkɒrəˈneɪʃn ˌstriːt]
⟨Corporation of Public Broadcasting⟩ [ˌkɔːpəˈreɪʃnˌəv ˈpʌblɪk ˈbrɔːdkɑːstɪŋ]
The Daily Mail [ðə ˌdeɪlɪ ˈmeɪl]
⟨The Declaration of Independence⟩ [ˌdekləˈreɪʃnˌ əvˌɪndɪˈpendəns]
⟨Dobe Newton⟩ [ˌdəʊb ˈnjuːtn]
⟨(Francis) Drake⟩ [(ˌfrɑːnsɪs) ˈdreɪk]
⟨East Enders⟩ [ˌiːstˈendəz]
⟨Elton John⟩ [ˌeltən ˈdʒɒn]
⟨Emma Doyle⟩ [ˈemə ˌdɔɪl]
⟨Emmeline Pankhurst⟩ [ˌemɪliːn ˈpæŋkhɜːst]
⟨Environment Agency⟩ [ɪnˈvaɪrənmənt ˌeɪdʒənsɪ]
F.A. (Football Association) [efˈeɪ]
Fidel Castro [frˈdel ˈkæstrəʊ]
⟨Francis Drake⟩ [ˌfrɑːnsɪs ˈdreɪk]
Friar Tuck [fraɪə ˈtʌk]
Friends of the Earth [ˌfrendz əv ðɪˈɜːθ]
⟨Gareth Owen⟩ [ˌgærəθˈəʊɪn]
⟨Genesis⟩ [ˈdʒenəsɪs]
Gestapo [gəˈstɑːpəʊ]
⟨The Glasgow Herald⟩ [ðə ˌglɑːzgəʊ ˈherəld]
⟨Goanna Gorge⟩ [gəʊˌænə ˈgɔːdʒ]
Greenpeace [ˈgriːnpiːs]
⟨Grover's Mill⟩ [ˌgrəʊvəz ˈmɪl]
⟨Hadrian's Wall⟩ [ˌheɪdrɪənz ˈwɔːl]
⟨Henry the Eighth⟩ [ˌhenrɪ ðiːˌ ˈeɪtθ]
⟨H.G. Wells⟩ [ˈeɪtʃ dʒiː ˈwelz]
⟨Holton School⟩ [ˌhəʊltn ˈskuːl]
⟨The Industrial Revolution⟩ [ɪnˌdʌstrɪəl ˌrevəˈluːʃn]
Intercity [ˌɪntəˈsɪtɪ]
⟨Intercontinental Radio News⟩ [ˌɪntəˌkɒntɪˈnentl ˈreɪdɪəʊ ˌnjuːz]
IRA (= Irish Republican Army) [ˌaɪɑːrˈeɪ]
Italia Conti [ɪˌtɑːlɪə ˈkɒntɪ]
⟨ITV⟩ [ˌaɪ tiːˈviː]
⟨Ivan Southall⟩ [ˌaɪvən ˈsaʊθɔːl]
⟨Jackie Kay⟩ [ˌdʒækɪ ˈkeɪ]
⟨Jimi Hendrix⟩ [ˌdʒɪmɪ ˈhendrɪks]
⟨John Ciardi⟩ [ˌdʒɒn ˈtʃɑːdɪ]
John F. Kennedy Space Center [ˌdʒɒn ef ˌkenɪdɪ ˈspeɪs sentə]
⟨John Owen⟩ [ˌdʒɒnˈəʊɪn]
⟨Johnny Depp⟩ [ˌdʒɒnɪ ˈdep]

⟨Julia Francis⟩ [ˌdʒuːlɪə ˈfrɑːnsɪs]
⟨Julian Colbeck⟩ [ˌdʒuːljən ˈkəʊlbek]
⟨King Philip⟩ [ˌkɪŋ ˈfɪlɪp]
⟨Klondiker⟩ [ˈklɒndaɪkə]
⟨London Weather Centre⟩ [ˈlʌndən ˈweðə ˌsentə]
The London Dungeon [ðə ˌlʌndən ˈdʌndʒən]
The London Underground [ðə ˌlʌndən ˈʌndəgraʊnd]
⟨Madonna⟩ [məˈdɒnə]
⟨The Magna Carta⟩ [ˌmægnə ˈkɑːtə]
Maid Marian [meɪd ˈmeərɪən]
Malcolm X [ˌmælkəmˈeks]
⟨Manchester Airport⟩ [ˌmæntʃɪstərˈeəpɔːt]
⟨Marilyn Monroe⟩ [ˌmærɪlɪn mənˈrəʊ]
Martin Luther King [ˌmɑːtɪn lʊðə ˈkɪŋ]
Mayflower [ˈmeɪflaʊə]
⟨Megacorpse⟩ [ˈmegəkɔːps]
⟨Melissa Turner⟩ [məˌlɪsə ˈtɜːnə]
⟨Mercury Theatre Of The Air⟩ [ˈmɜːkjʊrɪ ˈθɪətəˌəv ðiˌ ˈeə]
⟨Michael Sharp⟩ [ˌmaɪkl ˈʃɑːp]
⟨The Midas Project⟩ [ˈmaɪdəs ˌprɒdʒekt]
⟨Miss Quinlan⟩ [ˌmɪs ˈkwɪnlən]
Mohaph [ˈməʊhɑːf]
⟨Montgomery Smith⟩ [məntˌgʌmərɪ ˈsmɪθ]
NASA (The National Aeronautics and Space Administration) [ˈnæsə, ðə ˌnæʃənl eərəˌnɔːtɪks ənd ˈspeɪs ədmɪnɪˌstreɪʃn]
National Socialism [ˌnæʃənl ˈsəʊʃəlɪzm]
The National Trust [ðə ˌnæʃənl ˈtrʌst]
The Natural History Museum [ðə ˌnætʃrl ˈhɪstərɪ mjuːˈzɪəm]
⟨Ned Kelly⟩ [ˌned ˈkelɪ]
Newcastle United [ˌnjuːkɑːsl juːˈnaɪtɪd]
⟨No-name⟩ [ˈnəʊneɪm]
⟨Norma Jean⟩ [ˌnɔːmə ˈdʒiːn]
⟨Oliver Cromwell⟩ [ˌɒlɪvə ˈkrɒmwəl]
⟨Orson Welles⟩ [ˌɔːsn ˈwelz]
⟨Pam Ayres⟩ [ˌpæm ˈeəz]
⟨Pandora⟩ [pænˈdɔːrə]
⟨Pat Lowe⟩ [ˌpæt ˈləʊ]
⟨Paula Danziger⟩ [ˌpɔːlə ˈdæntsɪgə]
Peanuts [ˈpiːnʌts]
⟨Phil Collins⟩ [ˌfɪl ˈkɒlɪnz]
Plymouth [ˈplɪməθ]
President Reagan [ˌprezɪdnt ˈreɪgən]
⟨Prince William of Orange⟩ [ˌprɪns ˈwɪljəmˌəvˌˈɒrɪndʒ]
⟨Professor Pearson⟩ [prəˌfesə ˈpɪəsn]
⟨Queen Elizabeth II⟩ [ˌkwiːnˌ ɪˈlɪzəbəθ ðə ˈsekənd]
⟨Radio Licensing Agency⟩ [ˈreɪdɪəʊ ˈlaɪsnsɪŋ ˌeɪdʒənsɪ]
Radio Nightlife [ˌreɪdɪəʊ ˈnaɪtlaɪf]
⟨Radio Times⟩ [ˌreɪdɪəʊ ˈtaɪmz]
⟨Red Dwarf⟩ [red ˈdwɔːf]
⟨Richard Hill⟩ [ˌrɪtʃəd ˈhɪl]
⟨Ricky Benson⟩ [ˌrɪkɪ ˈbensn]

⟨**Robert Treborlang**⟩ [ˌrɒbət ˈtrebərlæŋ]
Robin Hood [ˌrɒbɪn ˈhʊd]
⟨**Roger McGough**⟩ [ˌrɒdʒə məˈgɒf]
⟨**Ron Atkins**⟩ [ˌrɒn ˈætkɪnz]
Royal Mail [ˌrɔɪl ˈmeɪl]
Salvation Army [sælˈveɪʃn ˈɑːmɪ]
⟨**Sara Dunlop**⟩ [ˌseərə ˈdʌnlɒp]
Sarasota-Bradenton Airport
   [ˌsærəˌsəʊtə ˌbrədentən ˈeapɔːt]
Second World War [ˌsekənd ˌwɜːld ˈwɔː]
Shell [ʃel]
Sherlock Holmes [ˌʃɜːlɒk ˈhəʊmz]
⟨**Sister Attracta**⟩ [ˌsɪstər əˈtræktə]
Snoopy [ˈsnuːpɪ]
Statue of Liberty [ˌstætʃuː ˌəv ˈlɪbətɪ]
⟨**Steven Morris**⟩ [ˌstiːvn ˈmɒrɪs]
⟨**Sue Townsend**⟩ [ˌsuː ˈtaʊnzend]
Superman [ˈsuːpəmæn]

Sweet Valley High [swiːt ˌvælɪ ˈhaɪ]
Sydney International Airport [ˈsɪdnɪ ɪntəˌnæʃnl ˈeəpɔːt]
⟨**Talk Radio**⟩ [ˈtɔːk ˌreɪdɪəʊ]
⟨The **Technological Revolution**⟩
   [ˌteknəˈlɒdʒɪkl ˌrevəˈluːʃn]
the **Challenger** [ˈtʃælɪndʒə]
The **Times** [ðə ˈtaɪmz]
Tourist Information Centre [ˈtʊərɪst ɪnfəˈmeɪʃn sentə]
⟨The **Tower of London**⟩ [ðə ˌtaʊər ˌəv ˈlʌndən]
⟨"**Triangular Trade**"⟩ [traɪˌæŋgjʊlə ˈtreɪd]
⟨**TV Times**⟩ [ˌtiː viː ˈtaɪmz]
⟨**Two's Company**⟩ [ˌtuːz ˈkʌmpənɪ]
Universal Studios [ˌjuːnɪˈvɜːsl ˈstjuːdɪəʊz]
⟨The **University of Westminster**⟩ [ðə ˌjuːnɪˈvɜːsɪtɪ ˌəv ˈwestmɪnstə]

UVF (= *Ulster Volunteer Force*)
   [ˌjuːviːˈef]
⟨**Vici McCarthy**⟩ [ˌvɪkɪ məˈkɑːθɪ]
⟨**War of the Worlds**⟩ [ˌwɔːr ˌəv ðə ˈwɜːldz]
⟨**Water Services Association**⟩
   [ˈwɔːtə ˌsɜːvɪsɪz əˌsəʊsɪˈeɪʃn]
⟨**Waterwise**⟩ [ˈwɔːtəwaɪz]
⟨The **Weekly**⟩ [ðə ˈwiːklɪ]
⟨**Westminster**⟩ [ˈwestmɪnstə]
⟨**William Leahy**⟩ [ˌwɪljəm ˈliːhɪ]
William Shakespeare [ˌwɪljəm ˈʃeɪkspɪə]
William the Conqueror [ˌwɪljəm ðə ˈkɒŋkərə]
Witness Security Program [ˌwɪtnɪs sɪˌkjʊərɪtɪ ˈprəʊgræm]
⟨The **World's Greatest Mistakes**⟩
   [ðə ˈwɜːldz ˌgreɪtɪst mɪˈsteɪks]
⟨**Ziontree camp**⟩ [ˌzaɪəntriː ˈkæmp]

List of irregular verbs

Die Liste umfasst alle unregelmäßigen Verben, die in *Password Green 1, 2, 3, 4* und *5* vorkommen.

infinitive	past tense	past participle	German
awake [eɪ]	awoke [əʊ]	awoken [əʊ]	erwachen
be [i:]	was, were [ɒ, ɜ:]	been [i:]	sein
bear [eə]	bore [ɔ:]	borne	gebären, tragen, ertragen
beat [i:]	beat [i:]	beaten [i:]	schlagen
become [ʌ]	became [eɪ]	become [ʌ]	werden
begin [ɪ]	began [æ]	begun [ʌ]	anfangen, beginnen
bend [e]	bent [e]	bent	biegen, beugen
bet [e]	bet	bet	wetten
bite [aɪ]	bit [ɪ]	bitten [ɪ]	beißen
bleed [i:]	bled [e]	bled	bluten
blow [əʊ]	blew [u:]	blown [əʊ]	blasen
break [eɪ]	broke [əʊ]	broken [əʊ]	(zer)brechen
bring [ɪ]	brought [ɔ:]	brought	(her)bringen
broadcast [ɑ:]	broadcast	broadcast	senden *(Rundfunk)*
build [ɪ]	built [ɪ]	built	(er)bauen
burn [ɜ:]	burnt, burned [ɜ:]	burnt, burned	ver(brennen)
buy [aɪ]	bought [ɔ:]	bought	kaufen
catch [æ]	caught [ɔ:]	caught	fangen
choose [u:]	chose [əʊ]	chosen [əʊ]	wählen
come [ʌ]	came [eɪ]	come [ʌ]	kommen
cost [ɒ]	cost	cost	kosten
cut [ʌ]	cut	cut	schneiden
dig [ɪ]	dug [ʌ]	dug	graben
do [u:]	did [ɪ]	done [ʌ]	machen, tun
draw [ɔ:]	drew [u:]	drawn [ɔ:]	zeichnen
dream [i:]	dreamt, dreamed [e, i:]	dreamt, dreamed	träumen
drink [ɪ]	drank [æ]	drunk [ʌ]	trinken
drive [aɪ]	drove [əʊ]	driven [ɪ]	fahren
dwell [e]	dwelt [e]	dwelt	wohnen, weilen
eat [i:]	ate [eɪ]	eaten [i:]	essen
fall [ɔ:]	fell [e]	fallen [ɔ:]	fallen
feed [i:]	fed [e]	fed	füttern
feel [i:]	felt [e]	felt	fühlen
fight [aɪ]	fought [ɔ:]	fought	(be)kämpfen
find [aɪ]	found [aʊ]	found	finden
flee [i:]	fled [e]	fled	fliehen
fling [ɪ]	flung [ʌ]	flung	schleudern
fly [aɪ]	flew [u:]	flown [əʊ]	fliegen (lassen)
forget [e]	forgot [ɒ]	forgotten [ɒ]	vergessen
freeze [i:]	froze [əʊ]	frozen [əʊ]	frieren
get [e]	got [ɒ]	got	bekommen; gelangen; werden; verstehen; holen
give [ɪ]	gave [eɪ]	given [ɪ]	geben
go [əʊ]	went [e]	gone [ɒ]	gehen, fahren
grow [əʊ]	grew [u:]	grown [əʊ]	wachsen
hang [æ]	hung [ʌ]	hung	hängen
have [æ]	had [æ]	had	haben
hear [ɪə]	heard [ɜ:]	heard	hören
hide [aɪ]	hid [ɪ]	hidden [ɪ]	(sich) verstecken
hit [ɪ]	hit	hit	schlagen, treffen
hold [əʊ]	held [e]	held	halten
hurt [ɜ:]	hurt	hurt	schmerzen
keep [i:]	kept [e]	kept	(be)halten
know [əʊ]	knew [u:]	known [əʊ]	kennen, wissen
lay [eɪ]	laid [eɪ]	laid	legen
lead [i:]	led [e]	led	führen
lean [i:]	leant, leaned [e, i:]	leant, leaned	sich lehnen
leap [i:]	leapt, leaped [e, i:]	leapt, leaped	springen
learn [ɜ:]	learnt, learned [ɜ:]	learnt, learned	lernen
leave [i:]	left [e]	left	(ver)lassen

infinitive	past tense	past participle	German
lend [e]	lent [e]	lent	leihen, verleihen
let [e]	let	let	lassen
lie [aɪ]	lay [eɪ]	lain [eɪ]	liegen
light [aɪ]	lit [ɪ]	lit	anzünden
lose [uː]	lost [ɒ]	lost	verlieren
make [eɪ]	made [eɪ]	made	machen
mean [iː]	meant [e]	meant	bedeuten, meinen
meet [iː]	met [e]	met	(sich) treffen
pay [eɪ]	paid [eɪ]	paid	bezahlen
put [ʊ]	put	put	setzen, stellen, legen
quit [ɪ]	quit, quitted [ɪ]	quit, quitted	aufgeben, aufhören
read [iː]	read [e]	read	lesen
rewind [aɪ]	rewound [aʊ]	rewound	wieder aufziehen
ride [aɪ]	rode [əʊ]	ridden [ɪ]	reiten; fahren
ring [ɪ]	rang [æ]	rung [ʌ]	klingeln, läuten
rise [aɪ]	rose [əʊ]	risen [ɪ]	(an/auf)steigen
run [ʌ]	ran [æ]	run [ʌ]	laufen, rennen
say [eɪ]	said [e]	said	sagen
see [iː]	saw [ɔː]	seen [iː]	sehen
seek [iː]	sought [ɔː]	sought	suchen
sell [e]	sold [əʊ]	sold	verkaufen
send [e]	sent [e]	sent	schicken, senden
set [e]	set	set	setzen, stellen
shake [eɪ]	shook [ʊ]	shaken [eɪ]	schütteln
shine [aɪ]	shone [ɒ]	shone	scheinen, leuchten
shoot [uː]	shot [ɒ]	shot	(er)schießen
show [əʊ]	showed [əʊ]	shown [əʊ]	zeigen
shrink [ɪ]	shrank [æ]	shrunk [ʌ]	schrumpfen
shut [ʌ]	shut	shut	schließen
sing [ɪ]	sang [æ]	sung [ʌ]	singen
sink [ɪ]	sank [æ]	sunk [ʌ]	sinken
sit [ɪ]	sat [æ]	sat	sitzen
sleep [iː]	slept [e]	slept	schlafen
sling [ɪ]	slung [ʌ]	slung	schleudern, werfen
smell [e]	smelt [e]	smelt	riechen
speak [iː]	spoke [əʊ]	spoken [əʊ]	sprechen
speed [iː]	sped, speeded [e, iː]	sped, speeded	beschleunigen
spell [e]	spelt, spelled [e]	spelt, spelled	buchstabieren
spend [e]	spent [e]	spent	verbringen
spin [ɪ]	span [æ]	spun [ʌ]	erzählen
spoil [ɔɪ]	spoilt, spoiled [ɔɪ]	spoilt, spoiled	verderben; verwöhnen
spring [ɪ]	sprang [æ]	sprung [ʌ]	springen
stand [æ]	stood [ʊ]	stood	stehen
steal [iː]	stole [əʊ]	stolen [əʊ]	stehlen
stick [ɪ]	stuck [ʌ]	stuck	steckenbleiben
stink [ɪ]	stank [æ]	stunk [ʌ]	stinken
strike [aɪ]	struck [ʌ]	struck	treffen
swear [eə]	swore [ɔː]	sworn [ɔː]	schwören
swim [ɪ]	swam [æ]	swum [ʌ]	schwimmen
swing [ɪ]	swung [ʌ]	swung	schwingen
take [eɪ]	took [ʊ]	taken [eɪ]	nehmen; dauern
teach [iː]	taught [ɔː]	taught	beibringen, unterrichten, lehren
tell [e]	told [əʊ]	told	erzählen, sagen
think [ɪ]	thought [ɔː]	thought	denken, meinen
throw [əʊ]	threw [uː]	thrown [əʊ]	werfen
understand [æ]	understood [ʊ]	understood	verstehen
wake(up) [eɪ]	woke [əʊ]	woken [əʊ]	aufwachen, aufwecken
wear [eə]	wore [ɔː]	worn	tragen (Kleidung)
win [ɪ]	won [ʌ]	won	gewinnen
wring [ɪ]	wrang [æ]	wrung [ʌ]	auswringen
write [aɪ]	wrote [əʊ]	written [ɪ]	schreiben

Bildquellen

Umschlag: Michael K. Daly/Stock Market, Düsseldorf.

S. 10/11: Großfoto, Musik + Show, Hamburg. S. 10: u., Carsten Rehder/dpa. S. 11: li. o., 'Smash Hits' Umschlag, © Smash Hits magazine, re. mi., dpa. S. 12: li. o. dpa. S. 12/13: © 1993 Nick Sharratt in, 'Tell Madonna I'm at Lunch, © Vici McCarthy /Penguin Books, London. S. 14: li. o. VCL/Bavaria, re. o. Bavaria, li. u. Topham, re. u. Dr. D.J. Müller/Mauritius. S. 15: cartoon by B. Watterson. S. 16: Ronald Grant Archive. S. 23: li. Paul Buller/IPC Magazines 1995, re. BBC Worldwide Ltd. 1998. S. 24/25: © Italia Conti School, London. S. 25: o. und m. A Shot in the Dark, Nottingham, u. KNA Bild. S. 26: © Richard Greenhill. S. 28: Shout Magazine, 1. Oct. 1994. S. 31: © 1984 Caroline Holden. S. 32: Italia Conti School, London. S. 38: li. Klett-Archiv, Stuttgart, re. A Shot in the Dark, Nottingham. S. 39: The Independent, © Newsteam Int. Ltd., Birmingham. S. 40/41: Großfoto: Alice und Werner Beile, Iserlohn. S. 40: mi. VCL/Bavaria, li. u. Hulton Deutsch, re. u. J. Allan Cash. S. 41: mi. © Sally & Richard Greenhill/Richard Greenhill. S. 42: Shout Magazine, D.C. Thomson & Co. Ltd. S. 43: Bilderberg/Hans Madej. S. 46/47: IFA. S. 46: o. Tony Stone/World Perspectives, u. Tony Stone/Kevin Kelley. S. 47: o. IFA/Photam, u. Tony Stone/John Lund. S. 48: dpa/Foesterling. S. 50: 1. Mauritius, 2. Mauritius/ Superstock, 3. Tony Stone, 4. Mauritius/Sammy, 5. Mauritius/Ace, 6. Tony Stone. S. 52: von li. nach re. Sally Greenhill (rothaariges Mädchen), J. Allan Cash (Rentnerin), J. Allan Cash (Taxi Fahrer), A Shot in the Dark (Junge), J. Allan Cash (junges Punk Paar, Bildhauer). S. 54: Animal Aid. S. 55: o. Animal Aid, u. VCL/Bavaria. S. 57: o. © Water Services Association, u. 1. B. Bramaz/Bavaria, 2. TCL/Bavaria, 3. M. Barth/Bavaria, 4. Color Stock/Bavaria, 5. Hubert Manfred/Bavaria. S. 58/59: Mauritius/O'Brien. S. 59: Mauritius/Lacz. S. 60: Topham/Picturepoint. S. 64: © PONS. S. 65: Großfoto: Mauritius, kleines Foto: Tony Stone/Mark Lewis. S. 66/67: Großfoto: The Slide File. S. 66/67: l. J. Allan Cash, 2.–6. The Slide File. S. 67: re. o. J. Allan Cash. S. 72: Hintergrund: Papunya Tula Artists Pty. Ltd. Aboriginal Artists Agency Ltd., National Library, Australia, 1. Mauritius/Kerscher, 2. Richard McBride, London, 3. Mauritius/SST, 4. Mauritius/Vidler. S. 73: 1. Mauritius/ACE, 2. J. Carnemol/ZEFA-AL, 3. Fritz/Mauritius, 4. ZEFA/Schäfer, 5. ZEFA/APC. S. 74: © Australia Post. S. 75: © Vivienne Goodmann 1994. S. 76: Fritz/Mauritius. S. 77: Mit freundlicher Genehmigung von Quantas Airways Ltd. S. 78: Mark Knight/Major Mitchell Press. S. 79: Kanus/Geopress, München. S. 80: o. dpa, u. Kinoarchiv Peter Engelmeier, Hamburg. S. 81: o. dpa Fotoreport, u. dpa/Nestor Bachmann. S. 85: © The Daily Mail. S. 86: J. Allan Cash. S. 87: © B. Watterson. S. 88: D. Walker/Gamma Liaison. S. 89: © Puffin Books 1974, August Robertson, 1971. S. 90: Photodisc. S. 91: "PA" News Photo Library, London. S. 92: © The Sunday Times. S. 93: Robert Weight/Ecoscene, Corbis. S. 94: action press. S. 95: Mna sa b Pobal, Muintearas, Republic of Ireland. S. 97: Florian Wagner/Bilderberg. S. 98: a) The Bridgeman Art Library, London, b) Vidler/Mauritius, c) The Bridgeman Art Library, London, d) Photodisc, u. li. The Bridgeman Art Library, London. S. 99: e) J. Allan Cash, f) Mary Evans Picture Library, g) Vidler/Mauritius, h) Mary Evans Picture Library. S. 101: 1. Pigneter/Mauritius, 2. dpa/Sanden, 3. Geoffrey Shakerley/Camera Press, London, 4. MSI, London. S. 108: Donegan/Punch, 4 September 1985. S. 111: Punch, 15 September 1989. S. 122: Punch, 15 January, 1991. S. 128: Greg Evans/United Feature Syndicate. S. 135: Tony Husband/Private Eye. S. 141: Ken Pyne/Punch, 17 August, 1990. S. 145: Private Eye, 17 April, 1998. S. 150: Punch, 19 February, 1988.

Textquellen

S. 12/13: from 'Tell Madonna I'm at Lunch' by Vici McCarthy, Penguin Books, London © Vici McCarthy 1993. S. 14: The Daily Mail, 8 October 1997. S. 15: 'Infobox' Source: Corporation of Public Broadcasting (USA); Radio Licensing Agency (GB). S. 20: from 'The Penguin Dictionary of Jokes' © Fred Metcalf 1993/Penguin Books Ltd., London. S. 22: PONS Schülerwörterbuch Englisch-Deutsch/Deutsch-Englisch © Ernst Klett Verlag. S. 28: 'I've no one to go round with' © D. C. Thomson & Co. Ltd. S. 29: 'A model pupil betrayed', The Daily Mail, 28 März 1996. S. 30: from 'The Growing Pains of Adrian Mole' by Sue Townsend 1984, Methuen. S. 31: 'The leader' by Roger McGough, from 'The Kingfisher Book of Comic Verse', selected by Roger McGough, Kingfisher Books 1986, London. S. 42: 'My Sister is a Runaway', Shout Magazine, 20 December 1996. S. 43: 'Runaways & Throwaways: Life on the Streets', Youth, May/June 1987. S. 44: 'Home comforts', Glasgow Herald, 28 December 1996. S. 45: 'No Son of Mine' by Phil Collins and Genesis © 1991 Anthony Banks Ltd./Philip Collins Ltd./Michael Rutherford Ltd./Hit and Run Music (Publishing) Ltd. S. 46/47: from 'This Place has no Atmosphere' by Paula Danziger, Heineman 1987, Piper Edition Pan Books. S. 49: o. Boys/Girls, The Times, London, 30 December 1996. S. 49: u. Poem by John Ciardi, from 'The Walker Book of Poetry for Children', selected by Jack Prelutsky, Random House 1983/Walker Books 1985, GB. S. 55: 'The Battery Hen' by Pam Ayres, from 'All Pam's Poems' by Pam Ayres, Hutchinson & Co. (Publishers) Ltd., London. S. 57: 'Water Aid', from: Waterwise, Water Services Association, London. S. 64: PONS Schülerwörterbuch Englisch-Deutsch/Deutsch-Englisch © Ernst Klett Verlag. S. 68/69: from 'Starry Night' by Cathrine Sefton © Hamish Hamilton 1986, London. S. 71: 'The Connemara Trail' by William Leahy, Galway, Eire. S. 74: 'I am Australian' by Bruce Woodley and Dobe Newton. From 'Pocket Full of Tunes' by Bruce Woodley and Dobe Newton © In Tune Music/Warner Chappell Music Publishing, Australia. S. 75/76: from 'The girl with no name' by Pat Lowe, Puffin Books Australia Ltd. © Pat Lowe 1994. S. 78: from 'How to be normal in Australia' by Robert Treborlang © Major Mitchell Press 1987. S. 80: 'Candle in the wind' sung by Elton John, written by Bernie Taupin © Copyright 1973 for the world by Dick James Music Limited, 47 British Grove, London W4. S. 81: The Times Magazine 1015. S. 82: from 'War of the Worlds' by H. G. Wells, adapted by Orson Welles (1938 Radio Broadcast) © 1940 Howard Koch © Renewed 1967, Heritage Media Ltd., Durham (GB). S. 83: 'Death of a Film Star' by Richard Hill, from 'Strictly Private' ed. by Roger McGough © Kestrel 1981/Puffin Books 1982, London. S. 84: 'Dear Examiner' by Gareth Owen. © Gareth Owen. S. 85: 'Classroom cruelty in black and white' by Steven Morris, The Daily Mail, 30 July 1996. S. 86: 'A mother's love', The Independent Magazine, December 1996. S. 87: from 'Two's Company' by Jackie Kay, Puffin Books 1992, London. S. 88: from 'The Accidental Tourist" by Anne Tyler © 1985 by Anne Tyler Modarressi/Alfred A. Knopf Inc., New York. S. 89: from 'Josh' by Ivan Southall © Puffin Books 1974/August Robertson 1971. S. 90: 'Earth and Sun and Moon', by James Moginie © Sony ATV Music Publishing (Germany GmbH), Frankfurt. S. 92: 'Gold in Britain' by Simon Barr/British Geological Survey, The Sunday Times, 11 August 1996. S. 93: 'Trekking Permit', Department of Immigration, Pokhara, Nepal. S. 94: '1999' by Tommy Sands © 1992 'HAMMER' Musik GmbH für Europa ex. Großbritannien und Irland. S. 96/97: from 'Stories from the Waterfront' by John Morrison, Penguin Best Australian Short Stories 1991.